£3

Perenials

From fence.

Thymus Serpyl

Dianthus Deltoides (5).

Sagina Subulata (5).

Sedum Kamtschaticum (5).

Iberis Sempervirens (5).

Ferns for shade.

Must have moisture retentive soil.

Driopteris 5'
Hardy maidenhair 2'
Heart's tongue.

PERCY THROWER'S
ENCYCLOPAEDIA OF GARDENING

Percy Thrower's

ENCYCLOPAEDIA

OF

GARDENING

COLLINGRIDGE BOOKS
LONDON · NEW YORK · SYDNEY · TORONTO

Published for
Collingridge Books by
The Hamlyn Publishing Group Ltd.,
Hamlyn House, 42 The Centre,
Feltham, Middlesex
Filmset in Great Britain by
Photoprint Plates Ltd., Basildon, Essex
Printed and bound
in Great Britain by
Redwood Burn Limited
Trowbridge & Esher
First published in 1962
© *The Hamlyn Publishing Group Ltd. 1962*
Twelfth impression 1974

ISBN 0 600 44226 8

PREFACE

It could be said 'Why another encyclopaedia'? Yet despite the number that already exist I am confident there is a place for a reasonably priced volume which includes everything that the average amateur is likely to need, and is lavishly illustrated. On every gardener's bookshelf there should be such a straightforward reference book to which he can turn to find the name of a plant, the details of its cultivation, the way to do the ordinary garden operations or to use the ordinary garden chemicals which seem to get more numerous every year. Such a book must be written in everyday language free of jargon. It must be easy of reference and easy to understand. Above all it must be well illustrated for so often it is by the picture only that the ordinary gardener can recognise the plant he wants, or learn how to do the operation which he has never seen performed. That is the kind of book I have tried to prepare.

Propagation is, I find, one of the most fascinating of all garden operations. How exciting it is to be able to grow any plant one desires from a seed, a cutting, a leaf, a piece of root, perhaps even just a bud. A plant we have grown from the outset ourselves has a personal interest which no purchased plant can ever quite equal. It is for this reason that I have included methods of propagation for every plant named and have tried to explain as clearly as possible how these various methods are carried out.

One of the secrets of good gardening is to do the right thing at the right time. One cannot follow the calendar slavishly, for every season differs, yet one cannot afford to stray too far from the calendar. Seeds must be sown, plants must be moved, cuttings taken, pruning seen to within a span of time which varies with the work in question. Sometimes, as with the planting of roses or shrubs, there may be a period of several months during which it can be done. For other things, such as the planting of spring cabbages, the correct season is confined within a few weeks.

Hardly a day passes without my getting a flower, perhaps only a few leaves or a fruit to identify. One of the greatest pleasures in gardening is that there is so much to know that one has never finished learning. Pictures can help a lot here and so I have tried, wherever possible, to include at least one picture of every genus of plants described in this encyclopaedia.

Pests and diseases have to be identified, too, unwelcome though they are. Even the best of gardeners can never entirely escape them though modern methods of control are making it far easier to keep many of these foes under control. But one must know what to do when trouble does occur and often one must be ready to act promptly before the pest or disease gets too firm a hold to be readily dislodged.

Side by side with the advance in chemical warfare against foes has gone another kind of chemical warfare against weeds. It is much easier today than it was in the days of my apprenticeship to gardening to maintain a weed-free lawn thanks to the introduction of weedkillers that are selective in their action, killing the unwanted weeds and moss but sparing the grass. But here again there are pitfalls for the unwary.

The feeding of plants has been the subject of much intensive study. Nowadays highly soluble foods are available which will show a result almost in hours, certainly in a few days. Other foods can be applied to the soil to build up its fertility over a long period and the gardener must know how to use each kind to best advantage and without injury to his plants.

There are no fruits or vegetables so fresh or so sweet as those gathered from one's own garden. Perhaps this is a side of gardening which gets less attention in times of peace than in time of war but that seems to me to be a pity. I hope that one result of this encyclopaedia will be to encourage more people to grow and enjoy the produce of their own gardens.

The greenhouse, once a luxury, has now become almost an essential piece of garden equipment. Here, too, science and mechanics between them have made it possible for the gardener to enjoy facilities once undreamed of; automatically controlled heating and ventilation, electrical soil warming, standardised composts for seeds and plants, even, for those who like such things, automatic watering and automatic pest control. But the basic skills remain the same and the greenhouse owner must learn, by study and observation, to know at once when a plant is beginning to get out of condition and equally to know how to bring it back into full health again. That is why such vital operations as potting, watering, damping down, ventilation and fumigation are described in some detail.

I hope this encyclopaedia, which has given such pleasure in the preparation, will give comparable pleasure to many thousands of gardeners and help them to garden more easily, more successfully and with even greater profit to themselves.

PERCY THROWER

ENCYCLOPAEDIA

AARON'S BEARD, *see* Hypericum.

ABELIA *abb-**ee**-lee-a.* Graceful deciduous and ever-green flowering shrubs of medium size with numerous small pink or white flowers in summer or early autumn. Most are a little too tender for outdoor planting except in sheltered seaside gardens. *A. chinensis* has white, pink tinted flowers, *A. triflora* pure white flowers, and both are scented. *A. schumannii* is a soft lilac-rose, *A. grandiflora* a little paler in colour and evergreen in a mild winter. *A. floribunda*, with rose-coloured flowers, is evergreen and one of the most beautiful but needs greenhouse protection.
Culture: Plant in autumn or spring in ordinary well-drained soil and a sunny, sheltered position. No regular pruning is required.
Propagation: By cuttings of firm young shoots in summer in sandy soil in a propagating frame.

ABIES a-*bees* (Fir). Evergreen cone-bearing trees most of which are too large for the garden. *A. nordmanniana*, the Norway Fir, and *A. pinsapo*, the Spanish Fir, are handsome, quick-growing trees which will reach a height of 100 ft. or more. By contrast *A. balsamea nana* is a dwarf, flat-topped plant only a foot or so high and suitable for the rock garden.
Culture: Plant from October to April in ordinary soil and open, sunny position.
Propagation: By seed sown in a frame or outdoors in March. Special garden forms by grafting in spring on to seedlings of the related species.

ABUTILON *abb-**u**-til-on* (Chinese Bell Flower, Flowering Maple, Indian Mallow). Greenhouse and half-hardy evergreen shrubs bearing red or yellow funnel or chalice-shaped flowers and often with handsome foliage. *A. vitifolium*, with blue flowers in summer, may be grown outdoors in sheltered places and *A. megapotamicum* will succeed against a wall in southern England. The bell-shaped flowers are red and yellow and they appear during the spring and summer. Other good kinds are *A. striatum thompsonii* which has orange flowers and yellow variegated leaves and *A. × milleri* with pale yellow flowers.
Culture: The greenhouse kinds should be grown in John Innes compost; *A. vitifolium* and *A. megapotamicum* will succeed in any reasonably well-drained soil. All delight in sunny positions. Plant *A. vitifolium* and *A. megapotamicum* in October or April; pot other kinds in March. Regular pruning is not essential, but overgrown plants can be cut back in March. Temperature of greenhouse kinds: March to September, 55° to 65°; September to March, 45° to 50°. All kinds, but particularly *A. striatum thompsonii*, may be used for summer bedding from June till September.
Propagation: The species are increased by seed sown in spring in a temperature of 60° to 65°. Hybrids and garden varieties are increased by cuttings in spring or early summer, rooted in a close frame.

ACACIA a-**kay**-*she-a* (Mimosa, Wattle). Evergreen greenhouse flowering shrubs or trees with yellow flowers. Most of the species come from Australia,

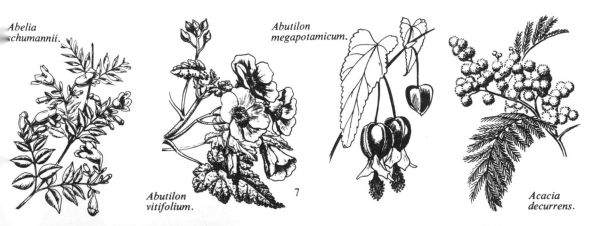

Abelia schumannii.

Abutilon megapotamicum.

Abutilon vitifolium.

Acacia decurrens.

7

and in their natural home many make tall trees. The Silver Wattle (*A. dealbata*) makes a tree up to 100 ft. tall. It can be grown outside against a sheltered wall in mild districts but elsewhere plants are best kept in a frost-proof greenhouse for the winter. The clusters of scented yellow flowers appear in late winter or early spring. The Green Wattle, *A. decurrens*, differs mainly in that it does not have the silvery foliage of *A. dealbata*. The Sidney Golden Wattle, *A. longifolia*, is another good kind with long narrow leaves and attractive yellow flowers.

Culture: Acacias may be grown in John Innes compost in large pots, tubs, or planted in the greenhouse border in loamy soil. Pot or plant in March. Overgrown plants can be pruned immediately after flowering, all thin or straggling shoots being shortened considerably. Temperature: March to September, 55° to 65°; September to March, 45° to 50°. Water freely while plants are in growth; moderately at other times.

Propagation: Seeds may be sown in spring in a temperature of 60° or cuttings prepared from half-ripened shoots may be rooted during early summer in a close frame with gentle bottom heat.

ACALYPHA *ak-al-if-a*. Although not often seen these are fine shrubby plants for a warm greenhouse. Some, such as *A. godseffiana*, have attractive green and white foliage but *A. hispida* is perhaps the most striking with its long, red, tassel-like flowers, 12 in. to 18 in. long.

Culture: To grow them well a minimum temperature of 55° is needed but in the summer temperatures of 70° to 80° can be maintained, provided the atmosphere is kept moist by regular syringeing and damping. Shade from the sun should also be given in the summer. Re-pot when necessary in spring.

Propagation: Cuttings of young shoots can be taken in the spring and they will make roots within a few weeks in a warm, moist atmosphere.

ACANTHUS *ak-an-thus* (Bear's Breech, Bear's Foot). Hardy herbaceous perennials with handsome, broadly thistle-like foliage and stiff spikes of chocolate-brown and white flowers in summer. *A. mollis* is the species

commonly grown. *A. spinosus* has more deeply cut foliage which is also spiny.

Culture: Any ordinary soil will suit acanthus, and they can be planted in full sun or partial shade, but the foliage will not be fully developed on poor, stony ground. Liberal watering in summer and a spring mulch of rotted manure or compost will improve the quality of the leaves. Plant in spring or early autumn. Disturbance of established plants should be avoided as far as possible.

Propagation: By careful division or removal of rooted suckers at planting time, or by root cuttings in spring.

ACER *a-ser* (Maple, Sycamore, Box Elder). Deciduous trees, many of which are unsuitable for small gardens, but a few, notably *A. japonicum*, and *A. palmatum*, the Japanese Maples and, *A. negundo*, the Box Elder, and their varieties may be planted even in quite restricted areas. Many maples have handsomely cut or scalloped leaves, some give magnificent autumn colour and a few such as *A. pensylvanicum*, the Snake-Bark Maple, and *A. griseum*, the Paperbark Maple, have attractive striped or peeling bark.

Culture: All species will thrive in ordinary garden soil. Most are not particular regarding position, but *A. japonicum*, *A. palmatum*, and their varieties are a little liable to be cut by spring frosts and should be planted in a reasonably sheltered place, and in well-drained soil. Planting time is from November till February. Regular pruning is not necessary, but overgrown trees can be reduced in February.

Propagation: True species can be increased by seeds sown in autumn or spring either outdoors or in an unheated frame. Varieties are propagated by budding or grafting on to seedlings of their own species.

ACHILLEA *ak-il-ee-a* (Milfoil, Yarrow). Hardy herbaceous perennials, some suitable for border planting, and others for rock gardens or dry walls. *A. filipendulina* has flat heads of yellow flowers on 4 ft. stems in summer. *A. ptarmica*, has clusters of small white flowers on 2 ft. stems in summer, its variety The Pearl, has double white flowers. *A. tomentosa* is prostrate, woolly-leaved and yellow-flowered. *A. tay-*

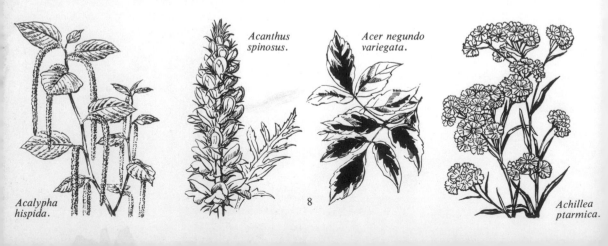

Acanthus spinosus.

Acer negundo variegata.

Acalypha hispida.

8

Achillea ptarmica.

getea is like a smaller, lemon-yellow *A. filipendulina* and also in the same style, but golden yellow and very continuous flowering is *A.* Coronation Gold. *A. millefolium* is 2 ft. high, has ferny foliage and white, pink or carmine flowers in summer.

Culture: All will thrive in ordinary soils and open positions but some, such as *A. taygetea*, resent excess moisture in winter.

Propagation: By division at planting time.

ACHIMENES *ak-ee-mee-nees* (Hot-water Plant). Greenhouse perennials with small, scaly, tuberous roots, which rest in winter. Growth begins in the spring and the plants produce their showy, tubular, purple, red or white flowers in the summer. It is sometimes called the Hot-water Plant because of the erroneous belief that hot water should be used for watering.

Culture: Pot tubers in February to April, 1 in. apart, and 2 in. deep, in pots, pans or baskets in John Innes compost. Place in a sunny greenhouse, temperature 55° to 60°. Water moderately at first, freely when in growth. After flowering gradually withhold water and, when foliage dies, leave the tubers in their pots and store them in a dry, frost-proof place until they are required for re-potting.

Propagation: By seeds sown in a temperature of 65° to 70° in March; by removal of scales from tubers in February or by cuttings in spring in a close frame.

ACID. A term implying sourness or sharp, biting flavour. In chemistry an acid is a substance which, in combination with some bases, will form salts, hydrogen being liberated as a result of the combination.

When this term is applied to soil it generally means that the latter is other than calcareous. All soils contain acids in a greater or lesser degree, but some, such as peat or other vegetable moulds, are often too abundantly charged with acids for certain plants. Old garden soils which have been persistently manured and over-charged with decomposed vegetable matter develop acidity. The usual corrective measure is to apply lime, ground limestone or chalk in some form and to improve defective drainage. Hydrated lime is usually applied at about 3 oz. to 4 oz. per square yard, ground limestone or chalk at 6 oz. to 8 oz. per square yard.

Plants which like rather acid soils are rhododendrons, azaleas, heathers and lupins. Too much lime or chalk may kill these and other acid-loving (or lime-hating) plants. Another effect of soil acidity is that it causes the flowers of coloured varieties of hydrangeas to come blue or purple. By contrast in alkaline soils the same varieties will produce red or pink flowers.

ACIDANTHERA *ass-id-an-the-ra* Bulbous-rooted perennials, the most popular species being *A. bicolor* which is similar in habit to a gladiolus. The drooping flowers, produced in summer, are white with a purple

Achimenes hybrida.

Abies nordmanniana.

Applying lime before planting lime-loving plants.

9

blotch in the centre and they are pleasantly scented.
Culture: In mild districts plants can be grown outside, but elsewhere it is best to grow them in pots in a
cool greenhouse. The corms can be planted in March
and in a good summer flowers should appear in July.
Withhold water in the winter and keep the corms in a
warm, frost-proof place.

Propagation: Offsets, removed from the old corms
after the foliage has died down, can be grown-on the
following season to increase the stock, or plants can
be raised from seed, which is best sown under glass
in the spring.

ACONITE, *see* Aconitum.

ACONITUM *ak-o-***ni***-tum* (Monkshood; Wolfsbane;
Aconite). Hardy herbaceous perennials suitable for
partially shaded borders. The prevailing colours are
blue and purple in varying tones but there are also
white and bicoloured varieties and one, *A. lycoctonum*,
with yellow flowers. Plants grow erect, from 2½ ft. to
5 ft. and have hooded flowers in long spikes. Among
the best are *A. napellus*, deep violet, *A. cammarum
bicolor*, white edged blue, and *A. fischeri*, medium blue.
Culture: Plant October to March in ordinary soil
in an open or partly shaded place. Division and replanting is desirable about every fourth year. By
planting various species a flowering season may be
had from July to October.

Propagation: By seeds sown ½ in. deep in a sheltered
position outdoors in April, or in boxes of light soil
in a cold frame in March or by division of roots in
autumn or spring.

ADAM'S NEEDLE, *see* Yucca.

ADIANTUM *ad-ee-***an***-tum* (Maidenhair Fern).
Greenhouse and hardy ferns, with very elegant fronds,
some evergreen, some deciduous.
Culture: Pot in early spring. Compost: 2 parts peat,
1 part loam and 1 part silver sand. Water moderately, September to March, freely afterwards. Position:
shady at all times. The more tender kinds such as *A.
cuneatum*, *A. decorum*, *A. tenerum*, and *A. williamsii*

need an average temperature of 60° to 65°, but such
kinds as *A. capillus-veneris*, *A. pedatum*, and *A. venustum* can be grown in an unheated house. Atmosphere
should be humid, but foliage should not be syringed
or otherwise wetted. By potting-on gradually, plants
may be developed into large specimens.

  A. cuneatum and *A. decorum* may be maintained
in good condition for reasonable periods in cool,
well-lighted rooms, but plants should not stand where
direct sunshine reaches them. Coal or gas fires cause
injury by drying the atmosphere, this being a common
cause of deterioration of the fragile fronds. *A. capillus
veneris*, the British Maidenhair, is only found on the
western seaboard. It thrives best in shaded frames in
summer and cool greenhouses in winter. *A. pedatum*
and *A. venustum* are hardier and may be planted in
sheltered nooks in rock gardens in a mixture of fibrous
loam and peat.

Propagation: By spores sown on fine peat and brickdust kept moist and shaded under a glass jar. It is wise
to sterilise the compost before sowing by scalding it
with boiling water. An easier method of propagation
is by carefully dividing plants between April and June.

AECHMEA eek-*me-a*. Like most bromeliads the
members of this large genus have tough, often spiny
leaves, arranged in large rosettes and bizarre, colourful
flower heads. Though best grown in a humid greenhouse, and needing plenty of warmth to produce
flowers, they are very good house plants, and a plant
bought in flower will remain attractive for a long time.
Relatively few are in commerce, however. *A. fulgens*
with scarlet and purple flowers above recurving green
leaves, and *A. fasciata* (often called *Billbergia rhodocyanea*) with broad grey, silver-mottled leaves and large
rose-pink flower heads, are often available.
Culture: Pot in March in a mixture of equal parts
peat, oak or birch leaf-mould and coarse sand. Water
freely and maintain water in the cup-like centre of the
plant. Temperature: March to September, 70° or more;
September to March, 60° to 65°.
Propagation: By taking off the suckers which form
after flowering and rooting them in moist, warm
conditions in a temperature of 80° if possible.

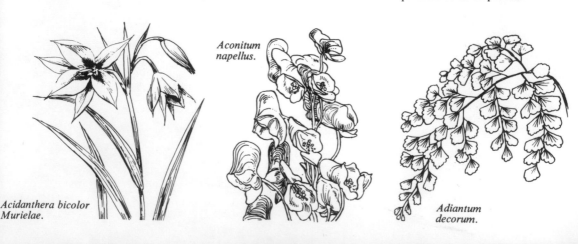

Aconitum
napellus.

Acidanthera bicolor
Murielae.

Adiantum
decorum.

Aechmea fasciata.

Using an aerosol.

Aerating a lawn.

Lawns that have received heavy wear may become too closely packed and be poorly aerated in consequence. Then pricking with a fork or with a spiked roller will improve their condition. This can be done at any time of the year but autumn is a usual time for routine lawn aeration.

AEROSOL. A solution, usually an insecticide or fungicide, released under pressure to form a mist from which the liquid carrier soon evaporates, leaving the active ingredient suspended as fine particles in the air. The aerosol must not be directed at the plant or damage will result. As a means of fumigating greenhouses aerosols are usually preferable to smokes.

AERATION. The maintenance of an adequate amount of air in the soil to keep it in sweet and healthy condition. Soils that are too closely packed or are waterlogged become sour. As a result the roots of plants die and the plants themselves suffer or actually die. Aeration is obtained by cultivation, e.g. digging, forking and hoeing, and also by incorporating bulky organic material with the soil such as animal manure, straw, compost, and seaweed which help to keep it open. Some chemicals such as lime and sodium alginate coarsen the texture of very fine soils and so prevent them from binding and improve their aeration.

AETHIONEMA *eeth-ee-o-**nee**-ma* (Stone Cress; Lebanon Candytuft). Hardy evergreen perennials or small shrubs for sunny, well-drained rock gardens and dry walls. The heads of small pink flowers appear in May and June. Among the best kinds are *A. grandiflorum*, *A. pulchellum*, and *A. warleyense*.

Culture: Plant October to March in light soil in crevices or on ledges, in dry walls and other well-drained places.

Propagation: By cuttings inserted in sandy soil in a frame in July or by seeds scattered where they may remain and later thinned out where crowded. Choice kinds by seeds sown in pots of sandy soil in a green-house or frame in spring.

AFRICAN CORN LILY, *see* Ixia.

AFRICAN LILY, *see* Agapanthus.

AFRICAN MARIGOLD, *see* Tagetes.

AFRICAN VIOLET, *see* Saintpaulia.

AGAPANTHUS *agg-a-***pan**-*thus* (African Lily). Evergreen herbaceous plants suitable for cool green-house or well-drained borders in sunny situations. *A. orientalis* (also called *A. mooreanus*) a blue flowered

species, and its white variety are the best for outdoor culture. *A. umbellatus* is a larger plant, also with blue flowers. The leaves are strap-shaped and the flowers carried in heads in summer, on 2 ft. to 3 ft. high stems. This makes a good tub plant to flower outdoors in summer and pass the winter in a cool greenhouse.
Culture: Pot in March in John Innes potting com-post. Water freely March to September, moderately afterwards. Temperature: September to March, 32° to 40°. Outdoors the African Lily will succeed in any reasonably good soil and is best planted in March or April.
Propagation: The simplest way is to divide large clumps in early spring but new plants can be raised from seed. It usually takes 5 to 6 years before plants reach flowering size.

AGAPETES *agg-a-***pee**-*tees*. *A. macrantha* is a lovely but rarely seen evergreen shrub for a warm greenhouse. The hanging, bell-shaped flowers appear in clusters in January and they are white in colour with delicate red veining.
Culture: It belongs to the heather family which means it must have lime-free soil containing plenty of coarse sand and moist peat. It can be grown in large pots or in a border of soil in the greenhouse. A tem-perature of 50° in winter rising naturally in summer is adequate. Water freely in spring and summer, moder-ately at other times. No regular pruning is required. To see the flowers to their best advantage the shoots should be trained under the greenhouse roof.
Propagation: Cuttings made from firm, young shoots can be rooted in pots of sandy soil in a propagating box with a temperature of 60° to 65°.

AGAVE **agg**-*a-vee* (American Aloe; Century Plant; Mexican Soap Plant). A family of tender succulent plants noted chiefly for their handsome, fleshy leaves. Although they do flower it is only after 7 or 8 years at the earliest and in fact they are commonly called Century Plants from the mistaken idea that they only flower when one hundred years old! The most popular one in cultivation is *A. americana* and particularly the variegated form, *marginata*, with creamy-coloured margins to the ultimately 3 ft. leaves.
Culture: Grown in large pots of rich, open compost this species will thrive in ordinary greenhouse tempera-tures provided it is not exposed to frost, although in summer it may be stood outside, where it can be a very striking feature. It needs plenty of water in sum-mer and only enough to keep it going in winter.
Propagation: Either by seeds sown in heat in spring or by offsets taken off at any time and potted up in warmth.

AGERATUM *adj-er-***a**-*tum* (Bastard Agrimony; Floss Flower). Half-hardy annuals with close heads of blue or white flowers in summer. *A. houstonianum*, also known as *A. mexicanum*, is the species grown and

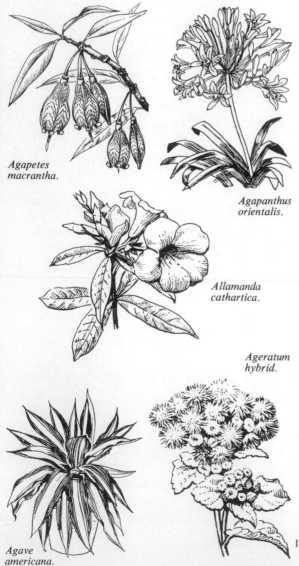

Agapetes macrantha.

Agapanthus orientalis.

Allamanda cathartica.

Ageratum hybrid.

Agave americana.

Cutting a stem for air layering.

Enclosing the layer in moss and polythene.

there are several improved garden varieties of it.

Culture: Sow in light soil in a temperature of 60° to 65° in March. Prick off 2 in. apart each way into boxes of John Innes potting compost and harden off for planting out 6 in. to 8 in. apart in ordinary soil in sunny beds or borders in late May or early June.

AIR LAYERING. Also known as pot-layering, circumposition and Chinese layering. A means of rooting branches or shoots which are still attached to the parent plant but which are too high or stiff to be layered in the normal way. The stem is first wounded immediately beneath a joint, either by making an inch-long, upward slanting cut which is kept open by a tiny wedge, or by removing a narrow strip of bark round the stem. The wound may be dusted with hormone rooting powder and is then surrounded with damp sphagnum moss held in place by a few turns of thread. This is enveloped in a sheet of polythene film, which must be well overlapped and tied securely top and bottom. When roots are seen through the moss the stem is cut below the moss ball, and the plant carefully potted up. Before polythene film was available air layering was practised by carefully splitting a flower pot in half and then placing it around the wounded stem, binding the two halves together and filling with peat, soil or sphagnum moss which had to be kept constantly moist.

Apart from propagation air layering is sometimes used to shorten the stems of leggy plants by rooting the upper portion in the way described, after which it is potted up and the lower portion is discarded.

AJUGA *a-ju-ga.* The most widely grown of the ajugas is the perennial *Ajuga reptans.* This is an effective ground cover plant with deep blue flower spikes appearing in May and June. Varieties include

the purple-foliaged *atropurpurea*, the bronze and red foliaged *multicolor* and the cream-variegated *variegata*.

Culture: The ajugas will grow well in poor soil and semi-shade, but their readiness to spread makes it necessary to exercise caution in their use.

Propagation: By division in spring or autumn.

ALKALINE. The opposite of acid. Soils which contain a lot of lime or chalk are usually alkaline and for that reason not suitable for the cultivation of rhododendrons, azaleas, many heathers, and other acid-soil plants. Hydrangeas with coloured flowers turn red or pink in alkaline soils. Some essential plant foods including iron and magnesium tend to get locked up in alkaline soils so that plants cannot use them and fall into ill-health as a result. To some extent this can be overcome by feeding the plants with special forms of iron known as chelated iron or iron sequestrols or by counteracting the alkalinity of the soil with heavy dressings of acid peat or dung. Alum is also used to increase the acidity (or reduce the alkalinity) of soil and so turn the flowers of coloured hydrangeas blue or purple.

ALKANET, *see* Anchusa.

ALLAMANDA *al-a-man-da.* These are evergreen climbers for the greenhouse. The large, tubular-shaped flowers of *A. cathartica grandiflora* are pale yellow in colour and *A. c. hendersonii* has orange-yellow flowers which appear in June.

Culture: Grow in large pots in John Innes potting compost or plant in a border of good soil. Maintain a minimum temperature of 55° rising with sun heat. Water freely in summer, moderately at other times. Some annual pruning is usually needed and side shoots can be cut back to within 1 or 2 buds of their base in January or February.

Propagation: The tips of the shoots that are removed when pruning can be used as cuttings. They should be placed in pots of moist peat and coarse sand, in a temperature of 65° to 70°.

ALLIUM al-*e-um*. Hardy, bulbous-rooted perennials. Some species, such as *A. moly*, *A. ostrowskianum*, and *A. neapolitanum*, are of purely decorative value, with white, yellow or pink flowers, but others are important kitchen garden vegetables. This latter group includes the onion (*A. cepa*), leek (*À. porrum*), shallot (*A. ascalonicum*), chives (*A. schoenoprasum*), and garlic (*A. sativum*), each described under its common name.

Culture of Ornamental Species: These can be grown in any ordinary garden soil and open, sunny position. Bulbs should be planted in the autumn and should not be disturbed annually as they will often continue to grow in one place for many years without any falling off in quality. *A. neapolitanum* is often grown in pots under glass. It stands forcing well if the pots are first plunged beneath 3 in. or 4 in. of ashes in a cool place outdoors for 8 to 10 weeks. Subsequently they can be transferred to a sunny greenhouse and a temperature of 55° to 60°. Water freely while in growth, but after flowering reduce water gradually to allow the bulbs to ripen off.

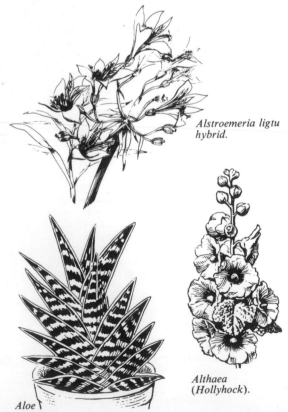

Alstroemeria ligtu hybrid.

Althaea (Hollyhock).

Aloe variegata.

Propagation of Ornamental Kinds: By seeds sown in a frame or cool greenhouse in spring, the seedlings being hardened off for planting out in a sunny bed in May, or by division of the bulb clusters at planting time.

ALMOND, *see* Prunus.

ALOCASIA al-o-**kas**-e-a. These belong to the arum family but they are grown primarily for their large, handsome foliage. *A. indica* produces leaves 12 in. to 14 in. long, and 6 in. to 7 in. wide on stalks roughly 2 ft. long. The leaf blades are plain green with prominent veins. There are also several forms of this species such as the variety *metallica* with purple leaves and *violacea* having pale violet leaves.

Culture: To grow well the plants need tropical conditions and a minimum temperature of 60°. They should be shaded from strong sunshine in the summer and given ample supplies of water. Potting is best done in early spring using a mixture of moist peat, loam fibre, sphagnum moss and some coarse sand. The root-stock should be raised on a mound of compost to ensure that drainage is good.

Propagation: Dividing the root-stock at potting time in the spring is the simplest means of increasing alocasia.

ALOE al-*o-ee*. The aloes are succulent plants but, unlike many succulents, will stand mixed greenhouse conditions as long as they have plenty of light. They are also good plants for a sunny windowsill, and one, *A. variegata*, has long been a popular indoor plant. The decorative white flecking on the tight-packed, triangular, dark-green leaves gives it the name Partridge-breasted Aloe. It sometimes sends up a spike of pink flowers. Most aloes make spreading rosettes of spiny leaves on a short woody trunk, like *A. arborescens*.

Culture: A thoroughly porous compost should be used with plenty of sand, a little powdered brick, and not too much peat or leaf-mould. Water fairly freely in summer, moderately in spring and autumn, sparingly in winter. Grow in a sunny greenhouse with a minimum temperature of 45° from October till May, but plants can be used for bedding outdoors if desired from June till September. Re-potting, when necessary, should be done in March. Good drainage is essential.

Propagation: By offsets removed from old plants when they are re-potted or by seed sown in a temperature of 70° in the spring.

ALPINE HOUSE. A greenhouse, usually unheated, designed for the growing of alpine or other rock plants which will not winter satisfactorily in the open, or are seen to better advantage when protected from wind and rain, alternating with frost. Maximum light and ventilation, both at the top and sides, are its

14

Alocasia metallica.   *Plants in an alpine house.*

main features as the aim is to simulate outdoor conditions as far as possible but without the excessive damp that prevails in our winters. Freedom from drip is therefore another important factor. In a properly constructed alpine house even severe cold is not likely to harm the plants, and if heat is used at all it should only be to dry the atmosphere on very foggy or damp days.

ALPINE WALLFLOWER, *see* Erysimum.

ALSTROEMERIA *al-stro-**meer**-e-a* (Peruvian Lily). Hardy and half-hardy, fleshy-rooted perennials with clusters of gaily coloured flowers in summer. The best species for cultivation outdoors are *A. aurantiaca*, orange, and *A. ligtu* hybrids, pink, salmon and flame.
Culture: These plants are sun-lovers and should be grown in warm, rather sheltered places. They delight in a deep, light, and well-drained soil, and in cold places should be given the protection of a south wall and a covering of straw or bracken in winter. October is the best month for planting the fleshy roots, which should be spread out thinly in trenches 5 in. deep. There may not be much growth the first season. Beds should be left undisturbed as long as possible.
Propagation: By division at planting time and also by seeds sown in March in a greenhouse.

ALTHAEA *al-thee-a* (Hollyhock). Hardy perennials often grown as biennials and some forms as annuals. There are forms with single flowers and others with double or semi-double blooms. All grow 6 ft. or more in height, and flower in summer.
Culture: These plants delight in a deep, rather rich well-drained soil. April is the best month for planting in permanent quarters. Strong stakes, 6 ft. in length, are necessary to support the long flower spikes. The hollyhock rust disease can be prevented by spraying the foliage with Bordeaux mixture in June and again in July.

Allium neapolitanum.

Propagation: By seed, for all ordinary purposes, sown in a frame or sheltered place outdoors in April or May. Seedlings are pricked out in a nursery bed in June or July. Annual forms are sown in a warm greenhouse in February or early March, pricked out into deep boxes and hardened off for planting out in May. Very choice varieties may be propagated by root cuttings in winter, placed in sandy soil in a frame and planted a few inches apart in a nursery bed in May, or as soon as they have made sufficient growth to be transplanted easily.

ALUM. The common name for aluminium sulphate, a chemical sometimes used to kill slugs and snails, sometimes to reduce the alkalinity of chalky or limy soils, and so turn the flowers of coloured hydrangeas from red or pink to purple or blue. As a slug killer 4 oz. of powdered alum is dissolved in each gallon of water and applied from a watering-can fitted with a fine rose to vacant ground, greenhouse paths and other places frequented by slugs. Alternatively a ring of powdered alum can be sprinkled around any plant liable to be attacked by slugs or snails. To increase the acidity (or reduce the alkalinity) of soil, alum is forked or raked in at rates of from 4 oz. to 16 oz. per square yard. It can be mixed with potting soil at rates varying from ½ lb. to 2½ lb. per hundredweight.

ALYSSUM al-*iss-um* (Madwort; Gold Dust). Hardy annuals and hardy herbaceous perennials. *A. maritimum*, popularly known as Sweet Alyssum, is a fragrant white-flowered annual frequently used for edging and carpet bedding in summer, while *A. saxatile*, a perennial with yellow flowers in spring, is a favourite rock garden and wall plant. There is a pale yellow form of this known as *citrinum* and also a variety with double flowers which is even more showy.
Culture: Alyssums will grow in any ordinary soil and open sunny position. The perennial kinds are inclined to die off in winter if drainage is bad, and all flower most profusely in soil that is rather poor. Seed of the annual alyssum is sown in April where the plants are to flower, the seedlings being thinned to 6 in. apart. Alternatively seed can be sown in a frame or greenhouse in March, seedlings being pricked off and hardened off for planting out in May or early June. The perennial varieties can be planted in spring or early autumn.
Propagation: Perennial kinds by seed sown in a cold frame in March or in a sheltered border during June. The double-flowered yellow alyssum and other special forms of the perennial species should be increased by cuttings of firm young growth inserted in sandy soil in a frame during July or early August.

AMARANTH FEATHERS, *see* Humea.

AMARANTHUS am-a-**ran**-*thus* (Love Lies Bleeding; Prince's Feather). Half-hardy annuals. *A. caudatus*, the well-known Love Lies Bleeding with long crimson racemes of flowers suggestive of plush tassels, is the species most frequently grown, but *A. tricolor*, with foliage as vividly coloured as a coleus, is strikingly effective in summer bedding schemes.
Culture: Sow in March in a temperature of 60° to 65°. Prick out seedlings as soon as they can be handled and harden them off for planting outdoors towards the end of May or early in June in ordinary soil and a warm sunny position.

AMARYLLIS am-a-**rill**-*is* (Belladonna Lily; Jersey Lily). Slightly tender bulbous plants with fragrant, pink, lily-like flowers in early autumn. The only species grown is *A. belladonna*, but there are several varieties, one with white flowers. (See also Hippeastrum.)
Outdoor Culture: Plant in a warm, sheltered place, preferably near the base of a wall with a south aspect. The soil should be deep and well-drained with plenty of sand and leaf-mould. The best time for planting is August, and in cold places the bulbs should be covered with 3 in. or 4 in. of soil. In mild districts it is better to plant with the 'noses' of the bulbs just peeping through the soil as in this way they get the full benefit of sun heat to ripen them in summer. Once established, they should be left undisturbed as long as possible. In cold districts a little dry straw can be spread over them in winter for additional protection.
Greenhouse Culture: Pot in August, one bulb in each 6 in. pot, using John Innes potting compost. Keep in a minimum temperature of 45°. Water moderately at first, but more freely as growth proceeds. Gradually discontinue watering in early summer as the leaves turn yellow and die down. Annual re-potting is not necessary.
Propagation: By offsets detached from the parent bulb at planting time or by seed sown in a warm greenhouse in spring, but seedlings may take seven years or more to flower.

AMAZON LILY, *see* Eucharis.

AMELANCHIER am-el-**an**-*che-er* (Snowy Mespilus; June Berry). Large deciduous shrubs or small

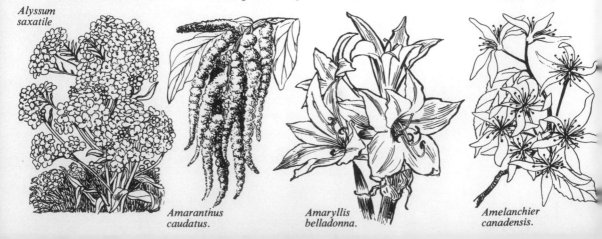

Alyssum saxatile

Amaranthus caudatus.

Amaryllis belladonna.

Amelanchier canadensis.

American Blight on apple.   *American Gooseberry Mildew.*

trees with abundant small white flowers in April. The foliage of some species colours well in autumn. The best for general planting is *A. canadensis*, 20 ft. to 25 ft. high. Other good kinds are *A. laevis*, 15 ft. to 20 ft.; *A. grandiflora*, 20 ft. to 25 ft.; and *A. oblongifolia*, 10 ft. to 15 ft.

Culture: Plant November to March in ordinary soil and open, sunny position. No regular pruning is necessary, but branches can be shortened or thinned in winter.

Propagation: By seed sown in a frame in spring or by rooted offsets removed in November from the base of the shrub.

AMERICAN ALOE, *see* Agave.

AMERICAN BELL-BIND, *see* Ipomoea.

AMERICAN BLIGHT. A pest belonging to the aphis family which frequently attacks apple trees. It feeds by sucking the sap, and collects in crevices in the bark, covering itself with a white woolly secretion, for which reason it is often known as Woolly Aphis. Growth buds may be killed and the attacked shoots develop a swollen, gouty appearance. Remedies consist in brushing petrol or methylated spirit into the woolly patches at any time, or spraying forcibly with lindane or malathion, or winter spraying with strong tar oil or DNC winter wash.

AMERICAN GOOSEBERRY MILDEW. This disease, caused by a fungus, is confined to gooseberries and attacks leaves, fruits and stems. In its early stages it has a cobwebby appearance, changing to a light and powdery condition. During the summer spores are developed freely and are easily conveyed to healthy

shoots by the agency of wind, insects, etc. Later still, the mildew changes from white to brown. The remedy is to spray twice with lime sulphur wash at summer strength just before the bushes come into flower and again as soon as the fruit is set. Lime sulphur may damage the varieties Careless, Golden Drop, Leveller and Early Sulphur, so for these a mixture of 1 lb. washing soda, 1 lb. soft soap, and 5 gal. of water should be used instead. Several further applications of this wash may be needed as it is readily removed by rain and so should be applied as far as possible in dry weather.

AMMONIA, *see* Sulphate of Ammonia.

AMPELOPSIS *am-pel-***op***-sis*. Most of the plants commonly known as ampelopsis in gardens are hardy climbers, correctly named vitis. One of them, *A. brevipedunculata elegans* (which may also be seen under the names *A. heterophylla*, *A. variegata* or *A. tricolor*) is offered as a pot plant. It has small, deeply lobed triangular leaves marbled in white and pink upon green.

Culture: Like its relations, the cissus, it should be kept cool, out of direct sun and away from hot stuffy air in winter, which may make the thin leaves wither and fall. It will thrive in John Innes Potting compost in pots or may be planted in a bed or border of good loamy soil. Watering should be moderate, allowing partial drying out in between waterings.

Propagation: Cuttings of tip growths root readily in close conditions in summer.

ANAGALLIS *an-a-***gal***-iss* (Pimpernel). Half-hardy annuals of trailing habit with small blue or scarlet flowers in summer, suitable for planting as an edging to beds and borders or as a groundwork beneath taller plants. The species commonly grown is *A. linifolia*, of which *monelli* is a good variety.

Culture: The pimpernels are sun-lovers and flower most freely in a rather light, well-drained soil. Seed is sown outdoors in April or early May where the plants are to flower. For early blooms seed should be sown in a frame during March, the seedlings being pricked out and hardened off for planting outdoors in May.

ANANAS *an-an-ass.* *A. comosus* is the pineapple, and its wide-spreading, narrow grey leaves in a rosette make it an attractive greenhouse or indoor plant. Some of its forms have cream, yellow and pink stripes and are very attractive, though they take up a lot of room. In a warm, humid greenhouse fruit may be produced, though not in a cool house or a room.

Culture: A suitable compost is 2 parts fibrous loam, 1 part leaf-mould or peat, and 1 part sand; it must be really porous. The plants need a winter temperature of 60°, rising to 75° or more in summer. No shade is required but the atmosphere should be kept moist in spring and summer. Water freely while in growth, moderately in winter and keep rather dry while fruit is ripening.

Propagation: Bought pineapples can sometimes be converted into plants by cutting off the spiky rosette at the top, removing all the flesh and placing it lightly on sand kept moist, in as high a temperature as possible—a propagating case at 75° is ideal. Suckers, seeds, and stem cuttings can also be used, all needing high temperatures around 75° to 80°.

ANBURY, *see* Club-root.

ANCHUSA *an-chew-sa* (Alkanet). Hardy herbaceous perennials and biennials. All have blue flowers in early autumn. The best of the perennials is *A. italica*, growing 3 ft. to 5 ft. high and flowering in June. *A. myosotidiflora* is a prostrate plant with small flowers like forget-me-nots. *A. caespitosa* is about 15 in. high and flowers in late spring and summer. The biennial species commonly grown is *A. capensis*, 18 in. high flowering in summer.

Culture of Perennials: Plant spring or early autumn in any ordinary garden soil and open sunny position. *A. italica* and its varieties are inclined to deteriorate, especially on heavy soil, and so it is advisable to raise new stock fairly frequently to replace old, worn-out clumps.

Culture of Biennials: Transplant seedlings sown in May in a frame or sheltered position outdoors, in September or spring to a sunny position in good, well-drained soil.

Propagation: Perennial species by seed sown outdoors in May or June. Selected garden varieties by root cuttings in a frame or greenhouse in the winter.

ANDROSACE *an-dros-a-see* (Rock Jasmine). Hardy perennial rock plants with pink or white flowers in spring. Some species come from very high altitudes and require careful treatment in the garden, but such popular kinds as *A. lanuginosa* and *A. sarmentosa* are quite easy to grow. All are prostrate, either trailing or cushion forming.

Culture: The easily grown androsaces, of which *A. sarmentosa* and *A. lanuginosa* are typical, can be grown in any well-drained soil containing stone chippings and leaf-mould or peat in an open and sunny position. *A. lanuginosa* succeeds at the top of a dry wall or ledge in the rock garden. The more difficult androsaces, such as *A. glacialis* and *A. arachnoidea*, need a compost of sharp sand and stone chippings, with just a little good loam, peat, and leaf-mould in a sunny moraine, or in pots or pans in an alpine house or frame.

Propagation: By seeds sown in a frame in spring, or by careful division of the roots at planting time.

ANEMONE *an-em-on-ee* (Windflower). An extensive and varied genus of hardy perennials, some tuberous rooted, some rhizomatous, and some fibrous rooted. Some are suitable for flower borders, for bedding, or for informal massing in woodlands, others are excellent rock garden plants. Several are early flowers of spring, others bloom in summer or autumn. Among the principal species of this very diverse family are *A. apennina* and *A. blanda*, both with

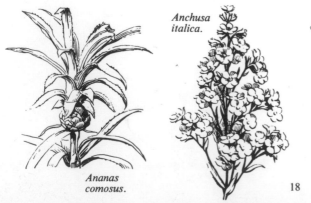

Anchusa italica.

Ananas comosus.

Androsace lanuginosa.

Annual Marigold.

blue flowers in early spring and making mats of ferny leaves; *A. nemorosa*, rather similar but with white or pink-tinted nodding flowers; *A, coronaria* and *A. fulgens* with flowers of many colours, often brilliant scarlet or purple and very popular as cut flowers (there are improved strains such as St. Brigid and De Caen); and *A. hybrida* (better, but erroneously, known as *A. japonica*) with white, pink or rose flowers on 3 ft. stems in late summer and autumn.

Culture: The various types require different treatment. Most of the fibrous-rooted species will thrive in ordinary garden soil. *A. apennina*, *A. blanda*, *A nemorosa*, and a few others, revel in the leafy soil and shade of woodland glades. Early autumn is the best season for planting these types, and it is wise to start with small, young plants.

Tuberous-rooted Species: *A. coronaria* and *A. fulgens* may be planted in October to November for spring flowering or at intervals from February to the end of April for successional flowering. In frames some may be had in bloom during winter provided the tubers have been left undisturbed after previous flowering. Outdoors it is usually advisable to lift the roots immediately the foliage dies down to allow a short rest (storing in trays) and replant in autumn or spring. Plant tubers 3 in. deep and about 6 in. apart; water liberally in dry weather.

Herbaceous Species: *A. hybrida* thrives in any ordinary soil and sunny or shady position but resents root disturbance and is sometimes slow to get started after being transplanted.

Propagation: By seeds, best sown as soon as ripe in a frame. Mix fluffy seeds with silver sand to facilitate even distribution. Cover lightly with sandy soil; water and keep close and shaded until germination takes place. Prick out seedlings when second leaf appears, providing a sheltered nursery bed. Plant in flowering quarters during the following season. Fibrous-rooted and herbaceous kinds can be propagated by division of roots in early autumn or early spring.

ANGELICA TREE, *see* Aralia.

ANGEL'S TRUMPET, *see* Datura.

ANNUAL. A plant that lives but one year, dying immediately after ripening its seed. The plants are of widely varying character and serve many purposes. Annual plants may be divided into sections under the headings 'hardy', embracing those that can spend their entire life in the open ground of a British garden; 'half-hardy', those which cannot endure frost but can be planted in the open when danger of frost is past; and 'tender', comprising those that are for greenhouse culture rather than for the open garden. All must be renewed annually from seed.

ANNUAL ASTER, *see* Callistephus.

Anemone nemerosa.

Anemone coronaria de Caen.

Anemone hybrida.

19

ANT. An insect sometimes tiresome in gardens. Although not generally recognised as an attacker of plants, it will develop the habit where food, and particularly moisture, prove to be scarce. Ants can be killed by sprinkling DDT or lindane where they are seen to congregate, or in or near their nests, or by spraying or dusting with malathion.

ANTHEMIS an-**thee**-miss (Chamomile).   Hardy perennials, one of which, A. nobilis, is used as a herb and is popularly known as the common chamomile. Varieties of A. tinctoria are good border plants, flowering all through the summer. The yellow, daisy-like flowers are excellent for cutting and the finely cut grey or green foliage on bushy plants 1½ ft. to 3 ft. high is also attractive.
Culture: Ordinary soil and a sunny position will suit these plants, but A. tinctoria is rather intolerant of bad drainage in winter. Plant in spring but on light well-drained soil it is possible to plant early autumn.
Propagation: Species can be raised by seeds sown in a frame in March, or outdoors in May. Selected varieties of A. tinctoria are best raised by cuttings of firm young growths inserted in sandy soil in an unheated frame during the summer. All flower heads should be cut from a few plants in June to encourage production of suitable side growths to supply cuttings.

ANTHERICUM an-**ther**-ee-cum (St. Bernard's Lily).   Hardy herbaceous perennials with white lily-like flowers on 2 ft. spikes in summer.
Culture: Deep, well-drained, but rather rich soil is most suitable. The position should be shaded from the sun during the hottest part of the day. Spring is the best time for planting, though anthericums can also be planted in early autumn on well-drained soil. Plants should be left undisturbed for several years.
Propagation: By careful division of the roots at planting time, or by seeds sown in an unheated frame in the spring. Seedlings do not bloom until 3 or 4 years old.

ANTHURIUM an-**thu**-ree-um (Flamingo Flower; Tail Flower).   Hothouse plants, some with orna-

mental flowers and others grown principally for their foliage. Those known as Flamingo Flowers are so-called because of their flamboyant, long-lasting flowers, consisting of a flattish, fleshy-pink, red, or orange spathe and an erect or twisted yellow spadix (they belong to the same family as the arum lily). The two most often grown for their spathes are A. andreanum, with heart-shaped leaves, and A. scherzerianum, with long narrow leaves. Among those grown for the beautifully veined and coloured leaves are A. veitchii, A. warocqueanum and A. crystallinum.
Culture: Young plants must have a minimum temperature of about 60° even in winter, but well-established plants will survive an occasional drop of a few degrees below that. On average 60° to 65° is the correct temperature from September to March rising to 70° or over from March to September. A suitable compost is equal parts of fibrous peat and chopped sphagnum moss, with a little sand and charcoal. When potting, the crown of each plant should be kept 2 in. above the rim of the pot by working the compost into a mound in the centre. Annual re-potting is essential, the best time being in summer immediately after the main flowering period. Kinds grown solely for their foliage can be potted in the spring. Water freely from March to November, but moderately during the winter.
Propagation: By careful division of the roots or removal of rooted suckers at potting time and also by seeds sown in March, in a temperature between 70° and 80°.

ANTIRRHINUM an-te-**ri**-num (Snapdragon). Hardy herbaceous perennials which nowadays are always treated as half-hardy annuals. There are several different classes, including Tom Thumb varieties, about 6 in. in height, intermediate forms from 15 in. to a couple of feet, and tall kinds up to 3 ft. There are also varieties with double flowers. Colours include, yellow, orange, apricot, pink, scarlet, crimson and white. All flower in summer.
Culture: Antirrhinums succeed best in well-drained soil, not too rich, but containing plenty of lime. Seed should be sown in January or February in a greenhouse at about 60°. The seedlings are pricked out into

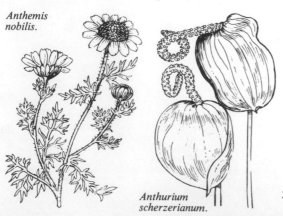

Anthemis nobilis.

Anthurium scherzerianum.

Antirrhinum (Snapdragon).

Aphelandra squarrosa louisiae.

Planting a bush apple.   *Cordon-trained apples.*

deeper boxes as soon as they can be handled, and are subsequently hardened off for planting outdoors in May. Plant the smaller varieties 9 in. to 12 in. apart, the larger varieties 12 in. to 18 in.

APHELANDRA *aff-ell-an-dra.* Several of these handsome plants have long been grown in warm greenhouses, notably the orange-flowered *A. aurantiaca*, scarlet *A. tetragona*, and orange-red *A. squarrosa*. One of them, *A. squarrosa louisiae*, has recently become extremely popular as an indoor plant. It has a cockade of brilliant yellow bracts above large dark green leaves heavily marked with white on the veins. It cannot be said to be a very tolerant plant indoors, for it is sensitive to dry, stuffy air and cold nights, but it is surprisingly tough considering its greenhouse origins.
Culture: All kinds prefer a winter temperature of 55° to 60° and plenty of humidity. They need a leafy soil and plenty of water at all times, while summer feeding will improve the capacity of *A. squarrosa louisiae* to stand the winter in a room. If it should lose many leaves in winter the stem is best cut back hard in spring, when new growths should spring from the base.
Propagation: Side-shoots taken with a heel root readily in heat.

APHIS (plural aphides) **a-*fiss*.** Many different species of plant louse, popularly known as greenfly, blackfly, dolphin, blight, etc. All are harmful, sucking the sap from leaves and stems, checking and distorting growth, causing leaf cockling and discolouration and often damaging fruits such as those of apple and pears. More seriously aphides frequently transfer virus diseases from infected to healthy plants, their way of feeding being an efficient method of inoculation.

In warm, equable weather aphides will breed at an appalling rate, producing mainly wingless offspring;

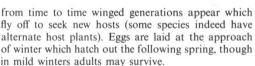

Summer pruning trained apples.

from time to time winged generations appear which fly off to seek new hosts (some species indeed have alternate host plants). Eggs are laid at the approach of winter which hatch out the following spring, though in mild winters adults may survive.

Insecticides which effectively control aphides are malathion, derris, BHC and, in warm conditions, nicotine. Systemic insecticides containing fluoracetamide or menazon are also used. Eggs on fruit trees are dealt with by tar oil or DNC sprays in winter.

APONOGETON, *see* Aquatic.

APPLE. Apples will grow in almost any reasonably good garden soil, although the best results are obtained in a rather deep loam with good drainage. On heavy waterlogged soil some varieties are apt to suffer from canker, while on poor sandy or gravelly soil the fruits are likely to be of small size and inferior quality. Well rotted manure or compost can be used freely in the preparation of the ground, which should be dug as deeply as possible. Apples can be trained in a great variety of different shapes. Standards and bushes are most serviceable where there is plenty of room and big crops of average quality are required. Against fences, walls, or horizontal training wires apple-trees can be trained as single or double-stemmed cordons, as horizontal trained trees, and in various other ways.

The best time for planting is in early November, but the work may be continued throughout the winter until March, provided soil conditions are favourable. Holes should be of adequate size to allow roots to be spread out to their full extent, and sufficiently deep to enable the uppermost roots to be covered with 2 in. or 3 in. of soil. All trees should be staked firmly to prevent root disturbance.

Pruning of trained trees should be done in both summer and winter. During July and the early part of August the new side shoots should be shortened to 3 or 4 leaves each, not counting the basal rosette of small leaves. Then in November these laterals can be still further shortened to within 2 or 3 dormant buds of the main stem to encourage production of fruiting spurs. At the same time the leading shoots should be shortened by about a third. It is not essential to carry out such restrictive pruning with well-established standard and bush apple-trees, which after a while can be left to go their own way, with little beyond thinning out of badly placed branches in November, to prevent overcrowing and the removal of any cankered or otherwise diseased branches or shoots. When trees are cropping freely it is necessary to reduce the number of fruits to not more than two at each spur or if exhibition fruits of culinary varieties are required, only one should be left at each spur. This thinning should be done when the fruits are about the size of marbles.

Propagation: By grafting in March or April, or by budding in July and August. As stocks, seedling crab apples are sometimes used, but selected stocks increased by layering are to be preferred as being more reliable. These are obtained in a number of forms known by number. For example, Malling II is a good average stock for bushes and small standard trees, Malling IX for cordon or dwarf bush, and Malling XVI for large standards. The Malling-Merton (M.M.) root-stocks are hybrids and they are resistant to woolly aphis.

APPLE SAWFLY. The small pale cream grubs of this fly injure the fruit of apples by boring into them. The damage caused is very similar to that of

Apple Sawfly grub and damage.

the codling moth caterpillar, but the main attack occurs earlier, in May or June rather than in July and August. All attacked fruits should be collected and burned without delay before the larvae have time to escape into the soil and pupate. Spray with BHC or malathion about 10 days after blossom fall, and keep soil under trees frequently cultivated to expose grubs or pupae to birds.

APPLE SCAB. One of the worst diseases of apples; a related fungus attacks pears. The first indication of an attack is the appearance of roundish black spots on the leaves. These spots rapidly increase in size and coalesce. Later the fungus spreads to the fruit, causing brown patches on these, and, in bad attacks, deep, dry-looking cracks.

Scab can be controlled by spraying with fungicides such as lime sulphur or captan. At least three applications should be given, the first, at full winter strength if lime sulphur is used, when the flower buds

Apply Scab disease.

burst out of their winter covering and can be seen as small green balls not as yet showing any trace of petal colour; the second at the same strength about a fortnight or three weeks later when the first trace of pink colouring can be seen in the expanding blossom buds; and the third at summer strength about 10 days after blossom can be shaken from the topmost branches. In very severe cases it may be necessary to give a fourth or even a fifth spraying at summer strength in June and July. Captan is used at the same strength throughout and more applications may be required as this fungicide is easily washed off by rain. All shoots with shrivelled bark should be cut off and burned in autumn, and diseased fruits and leaves should also be gathered and burned.

A few varieties of apples are liable to be scorched badly by lime sulphur, and for these captan or Bordeaux mixture should be used instead. The most notable kinds are Lane's Prince Albert, Beauty of Bath, Newton Wonder, Lord Derby, Rival, and Stirling Castle.

APRICOT. In many respects this stands midway between the plum and the peach as regards culture. Apricots can be grown in the open, but they rarely fruit satisfactorily unless given wall protection. A sunny position must be chosen and the trees trained as fans. The soil should be prepared as for peaches and nectarines, and planting done in November.

The apricot bears on spurs produced on the old wood as well as on shoots one year old. In consequence it is not necessary to disbud so drastically as with peaches. Instead, unwanted or badly placed shoots can be pinched in July or August and in November young growth made during the previous summer can be trained in at almost full length where there is room for it but to prevent overcrowding some of the new growths may have to be cut back to within two dormant buds of the main stems.

Propagation: By budding during the summer months on to plum root-stocks.

AQUATIC. A plant that lives in water. From a garden standpoint such plants may be considered in three groups: those that are wholly submerged except for their flowers, those that have floating leaves, and those whose leaves and flowers are above water though their roots are submerged. The first group is mainly of importance to the gardener because it contains plants such as the Canadian Pond weed (elodea) and Water Hyacinth (eichhornia) which give off oxygen into the water and so help to keep it sweet and healthy. Some of the loveliest water plants, including water lilies (nymphaea) and Water Hawthorn (*Aponogeton distachyus*) are in the floating group, with their roots anchored in the mud at the bottom of the pool. The third group is mainly composed of plants such as Arrowhead (sagittaria), Reed Mace (typha) and Water Iris which thrive in shallow water and so are useful to adorn the margins of pools or streams.

All aquatics are best planted in spring, usually during April and May. The submerged plants can be planted by the simple process of tying a small stone to the bottom of each and dropping it into the water. Floating aquatics and the marginal plants may be planted in baskets or boxes filled with soil, and sunk in position or the pool can be emptied, the plants put into the soil in the bottom and then the pool refilled. This is usually done a little at a time over a period of several weeks so that the leaves as they grow, are kept just floating on the surface, but this is not essential.

AQUILEGIA *ak-wil-ee-je-a* (Columbine). Hardy perennials suitable for sunny or partially shady borders and also, particularly the dwarfer species, for rock gardens. The long-spurred hybrid strains, flowering in early summer, include numerous colours and beautiful blendings of subtle shades.

Culture: Any good garden soil will grow the hybrid aquilegias, provided it is well-drained. Plant during August or September while the plants are still quite small. Large plants resent root disturbance. The smaller species such as *A. glandulosa* and *A. caerulea*

An oxygenating plant for a pool.

Planting a water lily.

Filling a newly planted pool.

23

Aquilegia hybrid.

Araucaria excelsa.

Aralia elata.

are best grown on the rock garden in rather gritty, well-drained soil and open sunny positions.

Propagation: Seeds sown in boxes of sandy soil in a cold frame in spring will produce sturdy plants by August. A sowing can also be made outdoors in April or May. The seedlings must be pricked out as soon as they have formed their first true leaves.

ARABIS *ar-***ab***-is* (Rock Cress). Hardy perennial trailing plants. The single and double flowered forms of *A. albida* are suitable for rock gardens, dry walls and as edgings or for carpeting beds and borders. All flower in spring. *A. albida* is white and the smaller, more tufted, *A. aubrietioides*, pink.

Culture: A sunny position is most suitable, but *A. albida* will grow almost anywhere in reasonably drained soil. *A. aubrietioides* requires a little more care but similar conditions. Plant in spring or autumn and cut back after flowering to encourage a more compact habit.

Propagation: By seeds sown in frame or greenhouse in April or by cuttings prepared from the young shoots and inserted in a shady border, or by division at planting time.

ARALIA *ar-***ray***-le-a* (Angelica Tree). The variegated forms of *A. elata* (syn. *A. chinensis*) all make striking foliage plants for the greenhouse or home, or even for a sheltered position outside.

Culture: Grow in large pots in John Innes compost and re-pot as necessary in spring. Water freely spring and summer, moderately at other times. To produce bushy plants up to about 4 ft. high the tips may be pinched out as required. During the summer the plants may stand outside, but in winter they need the protection of a frost-proof greenhouse. *A. elata* may also be planted outdoors in mild sheltered places and will eventually make a handsome tree 30 ft. or thereabouts in height. *Aralia sieboldii* is correctly known as *Fatsia japonica*.

Propagation: By suckers or root cuttings taken in March. The latter soon root in a warm propagating frame, after which they should be potted on as necessary in a mixture of 2 parts loam and 1 part peat, with enough coarse sand to keep the mixture open.

ARAUCARIA *a-raw-***care***-ee-a* (Monkey Puzzle; Norfolk Island Pine). Hardy and half-hardy evergreen trees. Only one species, *A. araucana*, the Monkey Puzzle, is hardy. It will eventually make a handsome and highly distinctive tree 50 ft. or more in height. Other species make pleasing pot plants in the young stages. *A. excelsa*, the Norfolk Island Pine, looks like a neat pale green artificial Christmas Tree, with its branches arranged in equally spaced horizontal tiers. It is ideal for a cool greenhouse and stands room conditions well, though hot stuffy air and draughts must be avoided.

Culture: The Monkey Puzzle is a tree for the milder

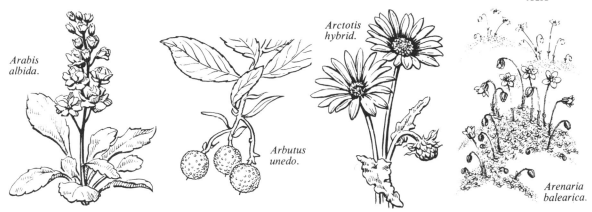

Arabis albida.

Arctotis hybrid.

Arbutus unedo.

Arenaria balearica.

parts of the country. Plant in deep, rich, loamy soil in September, April or early May. A winter temperature of 40° is quite sufficient for the greenhouse species, and plants can be potted in March in John Innes compost with a little extra sand. Water freely during the growing season.

Propagation: By seed sown in a warm greenhouse, but this is a slow process. A better method with the greenhouse kinds is to take cuttings about 6 in. long from the ends of young shoots and insert them in sandy loam in a temperature of 60° to 65°.

ARBOR-VITAE, *see* Thuja.

ARBUTUS *ar-bu-tus* (Strawberry Tree). Hardy evergreen trees of which *A. unedo* is by far the best known. Its late display of white flowers is accompanied by red, strawberry-like fruits which keep the tree bright through much of the winter.

Culture: *A. unedo* has a decided liking for lime, though it will also do quite well on peaty soils. Planting is best done in September or towards the end of April, and it is always advisable to start with young plants, as all species resent root disturbance. A fairly sheltered position should be chosen as the flowers do not appear until late autumn. Little or no pruning is required.

Propagation: By seeds sown in sandy peat in a cool greenhouse during February or March; by layering in May or June.

ARCTOTIS *ark-toe-tis*. Half-hardy South African annuals with daisy-like flowers in summer of graceful form, varied colouring and a glistening satiny-sheen. *A. stoechadifolia*, often known as *A. grandis*, is the most popular species. The flowers are white and pale blue.

Culture: Ordinary well-drained soil and a sunny position are best.

Propagation: Sow in temperature of 55° to 60° in February or March. Pot the seedlings singly, and harden off in a frame before planting out in May or early June.

ARENARIA *ar-en-air-ee-a* (Sandwort). Hardy perennials for carpeting the rock garden, or the more vigorous trailing kinds, such as *A. montana*, for clothing dry walls. Few of them exceed 6 in. in height; there are many as low as 2 in. to 3 in. and *A. balearica* hugs the soil and face of rocks like a film of fine green moss studded with tiny white stars in spring.

Culture: A moist position with partial shade is preferable but they are not particular about soil. Plant during October or March. *A. montana* will do well in an open, sunny site.

Propagation: By seeds sown in sandy soil in a cold frame in March. Most kinds may also be divided with the greatest ease. Small pieces pressed firmly into the soil in spring quickly take root and begin to spread.

ARISTOLOCHIA *ar-is-to-lo-ke-a* (Birth-wort; Dutchman's Pipe). Handsome climbing plants for the greenhouse, and a few hardy enough for the open garden in sheltered places. The different members of this genus are generally called the Dutchman's Pipe, but this common name applies particularly to the hardy species, *A. macrophylla*, often known as *A. sipho*, which has yellowish-green flowers curved like a meerschaum pipe. Those seen most generally in greenhouses are *A. elegans*, which has curious purple blooms marked with white lines, and *A. grandiflora sturtevantii*. It is usually called the Swan or Pelican Flower, the very large purple flower having an appendage, similar to the neck of a bird, up to 3 ft. long.

Culture: In any reasonably good and well-drained soil *A. macrophylla* grows luxuriantly and is a good climber for walls and arches. Plant in either autumn or spring. *A. elegans* and the other greenhouse kinds demand a rich soil and are best planted in a greenhouse border and trained to pillars and rafters. They need a temperature of 60° to 65° if they are to flower freely.

Propagation: By cuttings prepared from young shoots during the summer. Cuttings of *A. sipho* will root well in sandy soil in a temperature of 55° to 60°. Those of *A. elegans* require a higher temperature and are best rooted in a propagating box.

ARMERIA *ar-meer-ee-a* (Sea Pink; Thrift). Herbaceous plants useful as edgings or for carpeting sunny borders and rockeries. *A. maritima* is a native plant with pink or rose flowers on 6 in. stems in spring. *A. pseudoarmeria* is a taller plant, up to 2 ft., with large heads of flowers. One of the most attractive forms of this is Bees' Ruby, growing over 1 ft. high and bearing globular cerise-red flower heads in summer.

Culture: Plant in spring or autumn in any well-drained garden soil. *A. caespitosa*, a small tufted plant with pale pink stemless flowers, requires an even more open compost with plenty of stone chippings and a little leaf-mould or peat.

Propagation: By division in October or March; also by seeds sown in pans of sandy soil in March. The seeds can be germinated in a cold frame and should be lightly covered.

ARROWHEAD, *see* Aquatic.

ARROWROOT PLANT, *see* Maranta.

ARTEMISIA *ar-tem-is-ee-a* (Old Man; Wormwood; Tarragon; Southernwood). Hardy shrubs and herbaceous perennials. *A. abrotanum*, the Southernwood, is the best known of the shrubby species, and *A. dracunculus* is the herb tarragon. There are numerous kinds, such as *A. ludoviciana* and *A. stelleriana*, with white or grey stems and leaves. *A. lactiflora* is a stately herbaceous plant with loose sprays of cream flowers in late summer.

Culture: All the artemisias are intolerant of wet, sticky soils. They like open, sunny places but otherwise are not fussy. October and March are ideal planting times. *A. abrotanum* may be trimmed into shape in spring. Tarragon is best replanted annually in March or April. The foliage should be cut in

September and dried for use during the winter.
Propagation: Cuttings provide a simple means of increasing the shrubby kinds. Cuttings of tarragon are best inserted in boxes of sandy soil and root in a temperature of 55°. With the shrubby species, firm young shoots should be chosen and rooted during July or early August in a cold frame or in a sheltered shady border. Division in October or March is the simplest means of increasing the herbaceous species.

ARTICHOKE, GLOBE. A vegetable grown for the flower heads, which are cooked and the scale leaves eaten as a delicacy. Plants can be grown from seed sown in a frame in March or outdoors in April but a better method is to detach offsets in early April from plants known to produce good crops. These offsets are planted 3 ft. apart each way in fairly rich, well dug soil and an open position. Mulch with manure in May and remove all flower stems the first year. Best results are obtained in second and third years when flower heads should be gathered regularly as soon as they are plump and before they commence to expand. Remove dying leaves in autumn and protect crowns from frost with dry straw or bracken.

ARTICHOKE, JERUSALEM. A vegetable grown for its tuberous roots which are cooked and served in a similar manner to potatoes. Jerusalem artichokes are very hardy and easily grown in any ordinary soil and open position. Plant tubers in February, 6 in. deep and 15 in. apart, in rows 2½ ft. apart. Hoe occasionally drawing soil towards the rows. Lift as required for use in autumn and winter.

ARTILLERY PLANT, *see* Pilea.

ARUM LILY, *see* Zantedeschia.

ARUNCUS *a-run-kus* (Goat's Beard). *A. sylvester* is a vigorous hardy herbaceous perennial 4 ft. to 5 ft. high, with large plumes of creamy-white flowers in June. It has a less vigorous variety with finely cut leaves named *kneiffii*. These plants were formerly known as spiraea.

Armeria maritima.

Artemisia lactiflora.

26

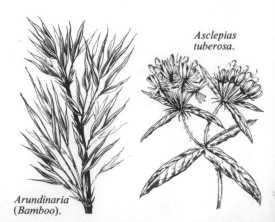

Arundinaria (Bamboo).

Asclepias tuberosa.

Aristolochia elegans.

Aruncus sylvester.

Culture: Plant October to April in good, preferably rather moist soil in full sun or partial shade. Do not disturb unnecessarily.

Propagation: By division in March; by seed in spring. Self-sown seedlings often appear around established plants.

ARUNDINARIA *ar-un-***din**-*air-ee-a* (Bamboo). One of the three genera of hardy bamboos, the other two being bambusa and phyllostachys. Useful to form a screen or background in damp places, around pools or under trees. Among the best species are *A. auricoma*, 4 ft. to 5 ft., green and yellow leaves; *A. fastuosa*, 20 ft. to 25 ft., very strong canes; *A. japonica*, 10 ft. to 12 ft., narrow green leaves; and *A. nitida*, 10 ft. to 15 ft., graceful habit, dark green leaves.

Culture: Plant in April in ordinary soil and sunny or shady places but for preference with some shelter from cold winds which may disfigure the foliage.

Propagation: By division at planting time.

ASCLEPIAS *ass-***klep**-*ee-ass* (Milkweed). There are two useful species of asclepias, the hardy border perennial *A. tuberosa*, with orange flowers, which will also thrive as a pot plant in a cold greenhouse, and the tender *A. curassavica*, with orange-red flowers, which enjoys warmer conditions and must be kept frost-free in winter. The curiously shaped flowers are in both cases carried in large terminal heads on stout stems and are excellent for cutting.

Culture of Hardy Kinds: Plant in spring in good but well-drained soil and a sunny sheltered position.

Culture of Tender Kinds: Pot in spring in John Innes No. 2 potting compost. Water moderately at first, more freely later. Maintain a temperature of 60° or more. When the flowering period, from July to September, is over, the plants should be kept on the dry side until early spring, when they may be either divided or used to provide cuttings.

Propagation: Cuttings of firm young shoots root readily in a propagating frame, and they should then be potted up into 3 in. pots of John Innes No. 2 potting compost or a rich, peaty mixture. Re-potting into 5 in. or 6 in. pots, using a similar compost, should be done before the plants become potbound. To produce bushy plants the stems should be pinched out at about 4 in. high.

ASPARAGUS *as-***par**-*a-gus*. This genus includes not only the edible asparagus, but also such popular climbing foliage plants as *A. sprengeri*, *A. plumosus*, and *A. asparagoides*, better known as smilax.

Culture of Edible Asparagus: Drainage is important, and except on light land it is advisable to raise beds a foot above the surrounding level. The ground should be deeply dug and given a good dressing of well-rotted manure. The planting season is April, and the plants should be placed 15 in. apart with 18 in. between the rows. Beds 4 ft. wide accommodating three rows are most convenient. One- or two-year-old plants are best, but no shoots must be cut the first year after planting. Ample supplies of water must be given during dry weather. After cutting down the growth, about the first week in November, an annual dressing of well-decayed manure should be applied. Cutting should never be continued beyond mid-June, and sufficient growth must also be allowed to remain to keep plants sturdy.

Culture of Greenhouse Species: Grow in John Innes compost in pots or baskets or in good loamy soil in beds on the floor of the house. *A. sprengeri* is seen to best advantage if grown in pots or baskets suspended from the roof. *A. plumosus* and *A. asparagoides* may be grown either in pots or in a border and trained to wires running up to the rafters of the house. Pot or plant in March, and syringe with water frequently in summer. A minimum temperature of 50° is sufficient.

Propagation: The edible asparagus is easily raised from seed sown in light soil in rows 1 in. deep in early April. Thin seedlings to a foot apart and plant in their permanent quarters the following April. Seed of greenhouse species should be sown in spring in pans of a light compost in a temperature of 65°. Pot the seedlings singly at a very early stage, and pot on by easy stages.

ASPIDISTRA *as-pid-***is**-*tra* (Parlour Palm). Few window or room plants are better equipped to withstand neglect or adverse conditions than this. The variegated forms are most effective.

Culture: Aspidistras will grow for several years without re-potting, and until it is obvious that further root room is required it is inadvisable to move them.

Asparagus sprengeri.

Astilbe hybrid.

Asplenium bulbiferum.

When re-potting is essential it is done in March, using John Innes compost. Plenty of water is required during the summer months, but excess must be avoided in winter. The leaves must be regularly cleansed, and, if spraying is impossible, should be sponged with tepid water at least once a fortnight. Green leaves which appear on the variegated types must be cut out.

Propagation: Division of the roots when re-potting is the only satisfactory method of increasing stock.

ASPLENIUM *as-***plee**-*nee-um* (Spleenwort). Greenhouse and hardy ferns. Amongst the best of the hardy species are *A. adiantum-nigrum*, the Black Maidenhair Spleenwort and *A. trichomanes*, the Maidenhair Spleenwort. *A. bulbiferum* is a popular greenhouse Spleenwort.

Culture of Hardy Kinds: Early autumn or April are the best periods for planting. A border in full or partial shade should be chosen. Peat, loam, leaf-mould and sand with a dash of old mortar rubble provide the ideal compost. In dry weather copious supplies of water are essential.

Culture of Greenhouse Kinds: A suitable compost is 6 parts peat and 1 part each of loam, charcoal and silver sand. Pot in March, and water freely during the summer months; winter temperature: 50° to 60°.

Propagation: By division of roots at planting or potting time or by spores, when fully ripe, on the surface of moist soil in a greenhouse. *A. bulbiferum* produces young plants on the surface of the older fronds. These may be detached and pricked out in shallow pans or small pots. Keep in a close frame until sufficiently established to be potted singly.

ASTER **as**-*ter* (Michaelmas Daisy). All the true asters are hardy perennials. The annual or China aster is botanically known as callistephus and is dealt with under that name. There are several types of the perennial asters, beginning in July and August, with the early flowering kinds such as *A. alpinus*, *A. thomsonii*, *A. acris* and *A. amellus*, following in September with the true Michaelmas Daisies, derived from the North American species *A. novi-belgii* and *A. novae angliae*, and finishing in October with the latest flowering species such as *A. ericoides* and *A. tradescantii*. Most highly developed of these in gardens is *A. novi-belgii* of which there are scores of varieties ranging in height from 9 in. to 6 ft. and in colour from white, through pink to carmine and through lavender to deep violet. Some varieties have single flowers, some semi-double, some fully double.

Culture: Plant in autumn or spring (*A. amellus* in spring only) in any good garden soil and open position. The stronger growing varieties should be divided and replanted every second year. For exhibition blooms it is essential to thin out each clump to only 3 or 4 stems in spring. The taller varieties require staking.

Propagation: Division at planting time is the simplest

Planting asparagus crowns.

Top-dressing an asparagus bed.

Cutting asparagus shoots.

Aster (Michaelmas Daisy).

method, but cuttings prepared in spring from firm young shoots 3 in. or 4 in. in length will yield even better results. They are easily rooted in sandy soil in a cold frame. Seeds may also be sown in a cold frame in March, but named varieties do not come true to type or colour.

ASTILBE *as-**til**-bee*. Herbaceous perennials commonly known as spiraeas. The *arendsii* hybrids provide many lovely plants for culture in the herbaceous border, beside ponds or streams, and also for forcing in pots. They have plumes of pink, red or white flowers and they make excellent pot plants in a greenhouse. Suitable varieties are Fanal, Peach Blossom and Rhineland.

Culture Outdoors: All astilbes like deep and reasonably moist soils and are never at home in dry, hot places. Planting may be carried out in either autumn or spring, and plants should not be disturbed unnecessarily.

Greenhouse Culture: Plants can be dug up from outside in the autumn and potted in 5 in. or 6 in. pots. They should be kept outside until the turn of the year and exposure to hard frost will not harm the plants— it will probably encourage earlier flowering when the plants are taken indoors. Little water is needed until growth commences after the plants are taken into the greenhouse. A temperature of 45° is adequate, but it can be raised gradually if very early flowers are required. Plants that have been grown under glass should not be forced again the following season as good results cannot be expected.

Propagation: By division in either autumn or spring, or by seed sown in a frame or cool greenhouse in spring, but seedlings may not flower for several years.

ASTRANTIA *as-**tran**-tee-a* (Masterwort). Hardy herbaceous perennials, suitable for shady borders or margins of woodlands. The foliage is pleasing and flowers uncommon in style. Stars of greenish white

29

Azalea Hi No Degiri.

Astrantia major.

Bark ringing an apple.

surround cushion centres of pale pink florets which last a long time in early summer. The most popular kinds are *A. major*, 2 ft., and *A. carniolica*, 1 ft.

Culture: Plant October or March in ordinary soil, or naturalise in grass that does not grow too strongly.

Propagation: By seeds sown in sandy loam in a cold frame in April; division of roots in October or March.

AUBRIETA correctly *aw-bree-ay-ta* but usually erroneously called *aw-bree-she-a* (Purple Rock-cress). Hardy evergreen trailing perennials useful for rock gardens, dry walls, banks, edgings or borders, and for spring bedding. Colours embrace many shades of mauve, purple, pink and red.

Culture: Plant in ordinary soil and sunny position in October or spring. Trim straggly plants fairly closely after flowering in spring.

Propagation: By cuttings prepared from young shoots in June inserted in sandy soil in a shady frame; by division in autumn or spring or by seed sown in a frame or greenhouse in spring, but seedlings may vary in colour.

AUCUBA **aw-***ku-ba* (Spotted Laurel; Variegated Laurel). Hardy evergreen shrubs with ornamental foliage. There are two sexes, the female bushes bearing red berries freely in winter if a male bush is planted close by, or if a branch of male blossom is placed on the female plant when in bloom. Useful also for pot culture in cool greenhouse or windows in winter.

Culture: Plant October, November, March, or April, in open or shady position and ordinary soil. Plants can be pruned to shape in May.

Propagation: By seeds sown ¼ in. deep in cold frame in spring or by cuttings inserted in sandy soil in sheltered border or cold frame in autumn.

AURICULA, *see* Primula.

AUSTRALIAN GUM, *see* Eucalyptus.

AUSTRALIAN HEATH, *see* Epacris.

AUTUMN CROCUS, *see* Colchicum.

AVENS, *see* Geum.

AZALEA *az-ay-lee-a*. Forced plants of *A. indica* (which is really a rhododendron correctly named *R. simsii*) are very popular at Christmas time and during the latter part of the winter. They are evergreen and usually have double flowers shaded pink, white and red. The Kurume azaleas, such as the varieties Hi No Mayo and Hi No Degiri, are forms of *R. obtusum*, which are normally grown out of doors but are also useful pot plants for greenhouse decoration in early spring. (See also Rhododendron.)

Culture: Plants that have been used for room decoration are best removed to a greenhouse after flowering as the dry atmosphere of a living room can cause the leaves to fall. During the summer the plants in their pots can be stood outside in a partially shaded spot and they appreciate light overhead sprays of water each day. Re-potting should be necessary only every other year and as azaleas resent lime an acid compost of 2 parts moist peat and 1 part coarse sand is adequate. Feeding at 10-day intervals with 2 teaspoonfuls of dried blood, and 1 teaspoonful of sulphate of potash will encourage good growth. From October to May plants should be placed either indoors or in a frost-proof greenhouse, but high temperatures are not desirable.

Propagation: New plants can be raised by removing

BAMBOO, *see* Arundinaria and Bambusa.

BAMBUSA *bam-***bu***-sa* (Bamboo). One of the three genera of hardy bamboos the other two being arundinaria and phyllostachys. Culture and propagation are as for arundinaria. Only one species is commonly grown, *B. metake*. It has rather broad leaves and will reach a height of about 12 ft. Botanists now classify this plant as *Pseudosasa japonica*.

BAPTISIA *bap-***tis***-ee-a* (False Indigo). Hardy herbaceous perennials flowering in summer. Flowers blue and pea-shaped, in spikes somewhat resembling small lupins. The kind usually grown is *B. australis*, 3 ft.
Culture: Plant October to April in ordinary soil in sunny, well-drained border. Allow room for the spreading, underground stems.
Propagation: By seeds sown $\frac{1}{8}$ in. deep in sandy soil in a cold frame in April, or in sunny borders outdoors in May; careful division in March.

BARBARY FIG, *see* Opuntia.

BARBERRY, *see* Berberis.

BARBERTON DAISY, *see* Gerbera.

BARK-RINGING. A method of checking excessive wood growth and so promoting bearing in fruit trees. It consists of cutting away, down to the wood, a ring of bark about $\frac{1}{4}$ in. wide right around the trunk or main branches of a tree, and is best done in May. Ringing is not recommended for plums, cherries and other stone fruits as it may cause gumming but is satisfactory with apples and pears.

BARRENWORT, *see* Epimedium.

BARTONIA, *see* Mentzelia.

BASIC SLAG. A phosphatic fertiliser obtained from the linings of blast furnaces. The composition varies considerably, but it always contains some 'free' lime as well as phosphates. It is very slow in action

moderately firm shoots during the summer. These will form roots if placed in pots of sand and peat which should be stood in a propagating box in a greenhouse.

AZOBENZENE *ay-zo-***ben***-zene*. A chemical used in glasshouses for the control of red spider mite. It can be used as a vapour spray but is more commonly applied as a smoke, special azobenzene smoke generators being available for this purpose. A second application is usually necessary a week to 10 days later to complete the kill. Azobenzene should not be used on plants with dry roots or in bright sunshine, and as it is injurious to certain plants the maker's warning in this respect should be carefully observed.

BACTERIAL CANKER, *see* Canker.

BALLOON FLOWER, *see* Platycodon.

BALSAM, *see* Impatiens.

Aubrieta hybrid.

Aucuba japonica variegata.

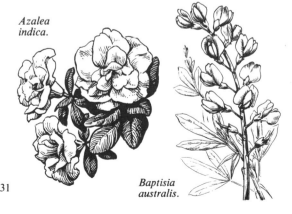

Azalea indica.

Baptisia australis.

and is usually applied in autumn as a dressing of from 6 oz. to 8 oz. per sq. yd. Specially useful on soils which are too acid.

BASTARD AGRIMONY, *see* Ageratum.

BAY-TREE, *see* Laurus.

BEANS, BROAD, *see* Broad Bean.

BEANS, RUNNER, *see* Runner Beans.

BEAR'S BREECHES, *see* Acanthus.

BEAR'S FOOT, *see* Acanthus.

BEE BALM, *see* Monarda.

BEETROOT. There are three principal types of beetroot: globe rooted, long rooted and tankard, which is intermediate between the other two. Globe beet is favoured for early crops, long and tankard for main crop and storing.

Seed should be sown in April, May and June in groups of two or three, 6 in. to 8 in. apart in drills 1 in. deep and 15 in. apart. Later, seedlings should be thinned to 6 in. to 8 in. apart. Well worked ground manured for a previous crop and dressed with a good compound fertiliser prior to sowing is best. Keep well hoed, lift roots from July to October when of the desired size for kitchen use, and store in sand or ashes in a shed or other sheltered place.

BEGONIA *be-go-nee-a*. An extensive and varied genus of plants, some of which are chiefly remarkable for the beauty of their flowers, others for their strikingly handsome foliage. The popular tuberous begonia, serviceable both for pot culture and summer bedding, is obtainable in both double- and single-flowered forms and widely varying colours. *B. semperflorens* is a dwarf fibrous-rooted plant with clusters of small single flowers in shades of pink, scarlet and crimson as well as pure white. It is useful for summer bedding and also for winter flowering under glass. Gloire de

Well-grown beetroot.

Lorraine, another single-flowered type with sprays of pink flowers ranks among the finest of winter flowering greenhouse plants, and the summer flowering pendulous begonias are ideal for hanging baskets in summer.

Among foliage plants, the varieties of *B. rex* must be considered as real gems, the colouring, veining, and shapes of their leaves being extremely rich and attractive. Many other kinds are available, some of low spreading habit, some tall and stalwart, and others of climbing or rambling growth.

Culture: The tuberous begonias can be started into growth in February, March or April, by pressing the tubers into shallow boxes of moist peat. They need a minimum temperature of 45° and when growth begins they are ready for potting into 3 in. pots of John Innes potting compost. As they develop, re-pot the plants into 5 in. or 6 in. pots. The small single flowers that form on either side of the double ones should be removed. Light shade from strong sunshine is needed in the summer and the compost must never be allowed to dry out. After flowering, when the leaves begin to wither, water should be withheld gradually until the compost is dry. The dormant tubers must be stored in a dry frost-proof place for the winter. Treatment of tubers intended for bedding is similar, except that after potting they are gradually hardened off in preparation for planting out in early June. Lifting in their case must take place during October or as soon as the first frost has tipped their flowers and leaves. They must not be completely dried off. Instead, during their period of rest after flowering, they should be given just sufficient water to keep the stems plump.

Plants of *B. rex* need a minimum winter temperature of 45° in a greenhouse and they enjoy a moist, shady position. They are often used for room decoration but they soon deteriorate in hot, dry conditions and they are best kept in a light place in a cool room. They must not, however, be stood in the direct rays of the sun.

The Lorraine begonias need a minimum tempera-

Begonia rex.

Begonia Gloire de Lorraine.

Starting begonia tubers.

Potting a young begonia.

ture of 55° and after flowering the old stems can be cut back to induce new young growths. These can be removed for cuttings which need to be placed in sandy soil in a warm propagating box. The first potting is in 3 in. pots and as the plants develop they should be moved on gradually to 5 in. or 6 in. pots. Shade from strong sunshine is needed in the summer when the temperature can rise to 70° to 75°. To produce shapely plants the delicate stems should be staked neatly with thin canes.

Propagation: The tuberous-rooted section can be raised from seed sown in January or February on the surface of well-drained pans of light sandy soil and kept in a temperature of 60° to 65°. Before the tiny plants have a chance to overcrowd they must be pricked off into pans, and they can later be potted singly.

The rex varieties are usually increased in spring by placing a fully developed leaf, with the midrib severed in a few places, on the surface of a pan of sandy soil in a warm greenhouse. The leaves can be held in position with small stones or with hairpin-like wires. When the tiny plants which form are large enough to handle they can be pricked out in pans of light compost.

Cuttings of the winter-flowering hybrids are taken in spring as already described.

B. semperflorens is raised from seed sown in a warm greenhouse in February or March, seedlings being pricked off 2 in. apart each way into boxes or potted singly and later hardened off for planting outdoors in early June.

BELLADONNA LILY, *see* Amaryllis.

BELL FLOWER, *see* Campanula.

BELOPERONE *bel-o-per-o-nee* (Shrimp Plant). The salmon-red bracts in drooping spikes which surround the flimsy white flowers of *B. guttata* give it

A large-flowered tuberous begonia.

Beloperone guttata

33

the apt name of Shrimp Plant. In a moderately warm greenhouse they are produced almost continuously, especially in the summer and autumn. As a room plant it tends to be difficult in winter, when its leaves fall off if conditions are too cold or too stuffy; but it should perform well during the summer in part shade.

Culture: Pot in spring in John Innes potting compost. Water fairly freely in spring and summer, moderately in autumn and winter. Grow in a temperature around 60° to 65° which may occasionally drop to 45° in winter. If the leaves do drop, cut the stem back hard to encourage new growth from the base in spring.

Propagation: Stem cuttings root in spring and summer with some bottom heat.

BERBERIS ber-*ber-is* (Barberry). Hardy evergreen and deciduous shrubs with ornamental leaves and berries which may be red, purple or blue-black. Favourite evergreen kinds are *B. darwinii* and *B. stenophylla*, the former with orange, the latter with deep yellow flowers in spring. Good deciduous barberries are *B. rubrostilla* and *B. wilsoniae*, both with coral-red berries in autumn. *B. thunbergii*, also deciduous, is grown mainly for its foliage which turns scarlet in autumn. It has a variety, *atropurpurea*, with purple leaves.

Culture: Plant in autumn or late winter in sun or shade in any ordinary soil. Small young plants are best, as big plants sometimes resent disturbance. Pruning required only when plants become unwieldy when some thinning out and cutting back can be done

Billbergia nutans.

Berberis darwinii.

Bitter Pit of apples.

Big Bud of blackcurrants.

in February or March for deciduous kinds immediately after flowering for evergreens. Some kinds, particularly *B. darwinii* and *B. stenophylla* make a good hedge and will tolerate necessary trimming after flowering.

Propagation: By seeds sown in a frame or greenhouse in spring or by cuttings of firm shoots in sandy soil in a propagating frame in July or August.

BERGAMOT, *see* Monarda.

BETONY, *see* Stachys.

BETULA bet-*u-la* (Birch). The common Silver Birch, *B. verrucosa*, is too well known to need description and is one of the few forest trees suitable for the garden. It will reach a height of 50 ft. to 60 ft. It has a cut-leaved variety, often known as the Swedish Birch and several weeping forms of which the best is named *youngii* or Young's Weeping Birch. Also worth planting is the Paper Birch, *B. papyrifera*, a stouter tree with very white bark.

Culture: Plant November to March in ordinary, well-drained soil. No pruning is desirable.

Propagation: Species by seed. Garden varieties by grafting in spring on to seedlings of common birch.

BHC. An abbreviation for benzene hexachloride, a synthetic insecticide available as a dust for direct application, as a dispersible powder to be mixed with water, as a liquid to be diluted with water and combined in a smoke generator for the fumigation of glasshouses. It is effective against most caterpillars, weevils, beetles, wireworms, cut-worms, chafer larvae, aphides, thrips, capsids, various flies including carrot fly and leaf miners. Crude BHC will taint some crops including potatoes, carrots, cucumbers, tomatoes, currants and gooseberries. A refined form of BHC known as gamma-BHC or lindane is far less liable to cause tainting. Under glass this insecticide is used chiefly as a fumigant. The maker's instructions as to plants liable to be injured or tainted by it must be carefully followed, and in houses where cucumbers or roses are growing it is best to use lindane.

BIENNIAL. A plant that takes 2 years to complete its life; growing up from seed the first year, it continues its development and flowers, sets seed and dies the following year. Examples are, Canterbury bells and foxgloves. The usual practise is to sow such plants annually during the late spring or early summer, transplant to a nursery bed in July and transfer to flowering quarters in autumn or spring.

BIG BUD. A pest of the blackcurrant, caused by a gall-mite, so named from the swollen appearance of affected buds. Big bud can be checked by spraying the bushes with lime sulphur at double the normal winter strength in the spring as soon as the most forward leaves attain the size of two-shilling pieces. In very

Merton Thornless blackberry.

(Left) Normal blackcurrant leaf. (Right) Leaf affected by Reversion.

severe cases it may be necessary to cut back all affected growth almost to ground level in winter and burn these prunings without delay, or even to dig up and burn bushes, replacing with clean stock. The mite that causes the trouble migrates from bud to bud and even from bush to bush in spring and may carry virus disease with it. This is a common method of distribution for the virus that causes blackcurrant reversion.

BIGNONIA, *see* Campsis.

BIG TREE, *see* Sequoia.

BILLBERGIA *bil-***ber**-*gee-a.* A large group of bromeliads of which only a few are generally available. *B. nutans,* with a rosette of long narrow, toothed leaves, is almost hardy, but needs a fairly warm greenhouse if it is to produce its curious drooping flowers in yellow, green, red and blue. A hybrid with this and *B. decora* is *B. windii,* which has more handsome, wider leaves and large bracts of bright pink above the flowers. *B. zebrina,* with an almost tubular rosette, is sometimes seen; it has greenish flowers and salmon-pink bracts. The plant called *B. rhodocyanea* is really *Aechmea fasciata.*
Culture: The billbergias need similar treatment to the aechmeas and like them make excellent indoor plants, resistant to dry air.
Propagation: By offsets removed in spring or early summer and rooted in sand and peat in a propagating frame, temperature: 65° to 75°.

BIRCH, *see* Betula.

BIRD CHERRY, *see* Prunus.

BIRD OF PARADISE FLOWER, *see* Strelitzia.

BIRTH-WORT, *see* Aristolchia.

BISHOP'S HAT, *see* Epimedium.

BITTER-PIT. A condition affecting apples, causing brown spots in the flesh of the fruit. It is held to be the outcome of an unbalanced soil condition, particularly great fluctuations in moisture content. Good drainage, good soil texture and well balanced feeding are the best remedies.

BITTERWORT, *see* Lewisia.

BLACKBERRY. There are improved varieties more suitable for garden cultivation than the wild blackberry. They include Bedford Giant, Himalaya, John Innes, Merton Thornless and Parsley-leaved.
Culture: Plant October to March, 6 ft. apart in good, loamy soil. Train shoots to fence, trellis or wires strained between posts. Prune annually as soon as crop has been gathered, cutting out all old canes that have borne fruit but retaining all new canes and training these in place of the old ones. Top-dress each February or March with rotted manure or compost.
Propagation: By fixing the tips of strong growths to the soil in May or June when they will form roots and new shoots. These layers can be severed from the parent plant in September and lifted and planted in October or November.

BLACKCURRANT, *see* Currant, Black.

BLACKCURRANT REVERSION. A virus disease of the blackcurrant characterised by a change in the form of the leaves which become small, narrow

Blackfly on carnation.

and nettle-like. All affected bushes should be removed and burned as soon as it is certain that they are really suffering from the disease. June and July are most favourable months for undertaking the diagnosis but really it is wise, even then, to seek expert advice if reversion is suspected as it is not an easy disease to recognise with certainty. Blackcurrants should only be propagated from bushes that are known to be entirely free from reversion and from big bud mite, a pest which spreads the disease.

BLACK-EYED SUSAN, *see* Rudbeckia.

BLACKFLY. A species of aphis distinguished from the familiar greenfly by its black colour. It is also known as bean aphis because it so frequently attacks the young growth of broad beans. Other popular names are dolphin fly and collier. Chrysanthemums are often attacked and so are runner beans, spinach, beetroot, turnips and rhubarb. The blackflies suck the sap from the plants crippling them and in severe cases killing them outright. Blackfly can be killed by spraying with BHC, malathion, derris or pyrethrum. Attacks on broad beans can often be prevented by pinching out the soft tips of the plants as soon as the first beans start to form.

BLANCHING. A process whereby certain plants (e.g. seakale, celery, leeks, endive and chicory) are prevented, by the exclusion of light, from developing their natural green pigment or chlorophyll. The object is to render such plants more pleasing in appearance, more tender, or more delicately flavoured. Blanching

is carried out by covering with pots (seakale), with saucers (endive), earthing up or surrounding with paper or cardboard collars (celery and leeks) or by tying the leaves together over the heart (some varieties of cos lettuce).

BLANKET FLOWER, *see* Gaillardia.

BLAZING·STAR, *see* Liatris.

BLEEDING HEART, *see* Dicentra.

BLEEDING (VINES). This trouble arises when grape vines are pruned too near the time of starting them into growth, with the result that the rising sap exudes from the cut ends of the shoots. It may be alleviated by dressing these ends with painters' knotting when pruning is being done, but the best thing is to prevent the trouble arising by pruning soon after leaf-fall and keeping the vines cool for a few weeks to rest them. A different form of bleeding occurs sometimes during the growing season, when drops of sap may appear on the young shoots of vigorous vines, but this is not harmful and may in fact be regarded as a natural means of getting rid of surplus sap.

BLIGHT, *see* Aphis.

BLINDS. These provide the best means of shading greenhouses as they are so adaptable to changes in the weather. They may be made of a light material such as scrim or hessian, or of narrow wooden slats, but both types should preferably be made to work on a roller system so that they can be readily let down or drawn up. They are usually fitted to the ridge of the greenhouse, where they may be rolled up into a box to protect them from the weather when not in use, and so protected they should last for years, a factor which does to some extent offset the initial relatively high cost.

BLOOD FLOWER, *see* Haemanthus.

BLOOD MANURE. A useful nitrogenous manure frequently used in compound fertilisers and valuable by itself as a stimulant for producing rapid growth. Blood can be used fresh, but as it has an extremely unpleasant smell it is much better to dry it. This is done by pouring the blood into a tank or vessel containing sufficient spongy soil to absorb the liquid; 1 lb. of slaked lime for every 2 gal. bucketful of blood should be spread thinly over the surface. The mixture is left until the moisture has dried out sufficiently to leave a crumbly compost, which may then be forked in at the rate of 4 oz. to 8 oz. per sq. yd. Proprietary dried blood must be used according to manufacturer's instructions.

BLOODROOT, *see* Sanguinaria.

BLOSSOM END ROT. This is a physiological disorder of tomatoes which becomes visible as a dark, flattish area at the apex of the fruit, although it is present on the inside of the fruit before then. It occurs chiefly on the first-formed fruits and is caused by insufficient water reaching them. Vigorous plants with large, soft foliage are the most liable to it, as on such plants the leaves tend to absorb moisture which should be going to the fruits. The best method of preventing the trouble is to aim at well-balanced growth with a good root system which can take up sufficient water for both leaves and fruit.

BLOTCHY RIPENING. This is the term given to a condition of tomatoes in which instead of the fruits ripening to an even red colour they become blotched with yellow or orange. It may be due to potash deficiency and then may often be corrected by 2 or 3 dressings of sulphate of potash, applied at up to 2 oz. per sq. yd. The best thing, however, is to make sure of a balanced fertiliser treatment before planting, and to aim at a good root system, together with adequate soil moisture, so that the plant can take up the necessary potash. Blotchy ripening may also occur when fruits are unduly exposed to the hot rays of the sun under glass.

BLUEBEARD, *see* Caryopteris.

BLUEBELL, *see* Scilla.

BLUE COWSLIP, *see* Pulmonaria.

BLUE CUPIDONE, *see* Catananche.

BLUE DAISY, *see* Felicia.

BLUE-EYED GRASS, *see* Sisyrinchium.

BLUE GUM, *see* Eucalyptus.

BLUE MARGUERITE, *see* Felicia.

BLUE MOONWORT, *see* Soldanella.

BLUE POPPY, *see* Meconopsis.

BLUE SPIRAEA, *see* Caryopteris.

BLUE SUCCORY, *see* Catananche.

BOG MOSS, *see* Sphagnum.

BONEMEAL. A valuable organic phosphatic fertiliser consisting of ground-up bones from which the fat has been removed. It normally contains about 22% of insoluble phosphoric acid and 4% nitrogen, and although usually regarded as a slow-acting fertiliser the rapidity of action depends to some extent on the fineness of grinding and on the soil in which it is used. It is most rapid on light sands and gravels and comparatively slow on heavy soils. Usual rates of application are 3 oz. to 4 oz. per sq. yd. or it may be mixed with potting soil at the rate of 4 oz. per bushel.

BORDEAUX MIXTURE. A useful fungicide which can be used as a preventive for many diseases of fungal origin. It can be purchased in powder or paste form, ready for mixing with water according to manufacturer's instructions, or, if preferred, it can be prepared by dissolving 5 oz. of hydrated lime in water and 7 oz. of copper sulphate in some more water in a separate vessel, preferably of wood or plastic, adding this slowly to the lime solution, stirring meanwhile, and making up to 5 gal. This mixture should be used immediately.

BORECOLE, *see* Brassica.

BORONIA *bor-o-ne-a.* The most popular species, possibly because it is fragrant, is *B. megastigma*. It is a shrubby plant needing a cool greenhouse and it comes from Australia. The flowers are brown and yellow in colour and they appear in the spring. During the summer plants can be stood outside in a sunny spot so that the growths become well ripened.
Culture: John Innes potting compost is suitable for potting and 5 in. or 6 in. pots are adequate for the final potting. Grow in a temperature of 45° to 50° in

Earthing up celery to blanch the stems.

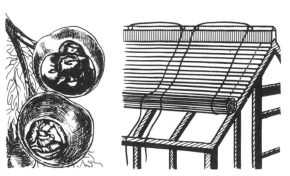

Blossom End Rot of tomatoes.   *Blinds for a greenhouse.*

winter. Water carefully at all times, maintain a rather dry atmosphere and let plants have plenty of sun. Re-pot annually after flowering.

Propagation: Partly matured shoots will root in the summer if they are placed in a propagating box in a greenhouse.

BOTRYTIS. A name given to a group of fungal diseases of which by far the most common and destructive is *B. cinerea*, the Grey Mould. This attacks such widely differing subjects as potatoes, vines, turnips, lettuces, tomatoes, lilies, peas, onions, strawberries and gooseberries, and is exceedingly difficult to control. Spraying the foliage with Bordeaux mixture or captan is sometimes effective, but in severe cases it may be necessary to destroy the plants. Botrytis is a disease associated with damp, cool conditions and is most severe in autumn. Under glass it can usually be kept at bay by maintaining a temperature of 55° or more with as much ventilation as possible to keep the air dry and in circulation. Avoid overcrowding the plants.

BOTTLE BRUSH, *see* Callistemon.

BOTTOM HEAT. Cuttings root best where the soil is warmer than the air, and although in the open this requirement may be met by making use of the natural summer warmth of the soil some artificial means of heating the rooting medium is usually necessary in greenhouses, particularly for the more tender or difficult plants. The simplest form of applying bottom heat is that produced by the time-honoured hotbed of freshly decaying manure but the modern method is by electric soil warming cables buried in the soil. These may either be low voltage, in which case they are usually bare wires supplied from a 12-volt transformer, or mains voltage, in which case they are specially insulated. Other methods of providing bottom heat are by hot-water pipes running beneath the propagating bed or on a small scale by a paraffin heater placed beneath the cuttings. To increase its efficiency it is usually advisable to enclose the area beneath the propagating bed so that as little heat as possible escapes into the open greenhouse.

BOUGAINVILLEA *boo-gain-**vil**-lee-a.* Tender climbing deciduous shrubs with showy bracts around their flowers in purple, red, shades of pink and orange in early summer. They are commonly seen in Mediterranean regions growing outside against walls but in this country they need the protection of a greenhouse. Plants can be grown in pots of John Innes potting compost or where there is plenty of space planting can be done in a greenhouse border. Full sunshine and plenty of water are the main requirements in the summer but in winter little water is needed. Weak and straggly growths can be pruned back in March just before growth recommences. Temperatures: February to May, 55° to 60°; May to September, 65° to 75°; September to February, 50° to 55°.

Propagation: By cuttings of young shoots removed with a heel of older wood and inserted in sandy soil in a propagating frame in a temperature of 70° in spring.

BOUVARDIA *boo-**var**-dee-a.* Evergreen greenhouse shrubs 2 ft. to 3 ft. high, with fragrant white, pink or scarlet flowers, double as well as single in autumn and early winter. This plant is rarely seen today but at the beginning of the century it was a popular winter flowering subject for a warm greenhouse. Although plants do not seem to be available in commerce, seed of *B. triphylla* can be purchased.

Culture: Pot in March in John Innes potting compost. Prune February, shortening shoots of previous year's growth to within 1 in. of their base. Water moderately February to May and August to November, freely March to August, little November to February. Temperatures: February to September, 55° to 75°; September to February, 55° to 60°. Place plants in a cold frame from June to September.

Propagation: Seed is best sown in the spring in a temperature of 65° but plants can be raised from cuttings. When old plants have been cut back in the spring the new shoots that develop can be removed when 2 in. to 3 in. long. They must be inserted in a propagating box with a temperature of 65° to 70° to encourage root formation.

BOW STRING HEMP, *see* Sansevieria.

Browallia speciosa major.

Boronia megastigma.

Bougainvillea glabra.

BOX ELDER, *see* Acer.

BOX TREE, *see* Buxus.

BRASSICA bras-*sik-a*. This is the largest of the vegetable families and includes borecole or kale, broccoli, brussels sprouts, cabbage (including colewort and savoy cabbage), kohl rabi, mustard and turnip.

Culture: There are many points which the brassicas share in common. First and foremost amongst them is a demand for a rich but well-firmed soil. In loose land they are never satisfactory. Every endeavour should therefore be made to have sites for them prepared some considerable time in advance of planting, or simply to rake down ground vacated by early short-season crops, in order that the soil may have a moderate degree of solidity. Given firm soil and a reasonable supply of plant food none of the cabbage tribe is difficult to grow, but as they take a good deal out of the ground it is advisable to make sure that they are crop-rotated, and by so doing danger of disease is lessened. This is important as a bad attack of clubroot, to which all brassicas are subject, will wipe out a crop. Regular liming serves as a deterrent to this disease, and all brassicas like limy soils.

BRIDAL WREATH, *see* Francoa; Spiraea.

BROAD BEAN. Sow early long-pod varieties in November, or February to April. Windsor varieties in March or April, in rich, well-manured soil in drills 3 in. deep and 2 ft. apart, seeds to be 4 in. to 6 in. apart in drills. Nip off points of plants when a reasonable number of pods have formed. Water late crops well in dry weather, especially to prevent attack by black-fly on light soils. The taller varieties may require support which can be provided by driving in stakes at each side of every row, and straining string between.

BROCCOLI. There is no real distinction between broccoli and cauliflower, both of which are grown for the close white heads (or the numerous purple or white shoots of the sprouting broccoli). However in gardens the term broccoli is usually applied to the hardy autumn and spring kinds and the term cauliflower reserved for the more delicate summer varieties. All are brassicas and have the same general requirements as other brassicas. There are numerous varieties of broccoli differing in the time at which they produce their heads or curds and in addition there are sprouting varieties which produce a succession of shoots in spring with white or purple flower buds in close clusters. These are cut as required and, when cooked, make very good eating.

Culture: Sow in March or April outdoors and transplant in May or June to good rich, well-worked but firm soil. Plant 3 ft. apart in rows 3 ft. apart. Feed during summer with small top-dressings of a com-

Bouvardia longifolia.

Botrytis on haricot bean.

pound vegetable fertiliser. Draw a little soil around the stems in autumn to provide better anchorage. Break some leaves over the curds as they form to protect them from frost. Cut curds as soon as they are well grown or gather shoots of sprouting kinds before the flower buds commence to open.

BROOM, *see* Cytisus; Genista.

BROWALLIA *brow*-**a**-*le-a*. Plants with blue flowers that are not difficult to grow in a frost-proof greenhouse. *B. demissa* (syn. *B. elata*) is a half-hardy annual that is easily raised from seed in the spring, and *B. speciosa major*, which can also be raised from seed, is a perennial.

Culture: To have plants for flowering in the winter seed can be sown in July. Young plants can be potted in 3 in. pots but as they develop they should be moved on into 5 in. pots of John Innes potting compost, or 3 plants of *B. demissa* can be grown together in a 6 in. pot to produce large specimen plants. It is wise to pinch out the tips of the shoots of *B. speciosa major* to encourage a bushy habit.

BROWN ROT. This disease attacks many fruits including apples, pears, plums, peaches and nectarines. At first there is a brownish discoloration of the skin followed by the emergence of greyish-brown tufts arranged in irregular circles. Fruit attacked by this fungus either decays, or remains in a dry, mummified condition, either lying on the ground or hanging on the trees throughout the winter. All infected fruit should be gathered and burned without delay, and any dead or withering shoots or spurs should be cut off and burned in the autumn. Spraying has little effect on this disease.

BROWN SCALE. A scaly insect which infests the stems of the black, red, and white currant, also gooseberry, raspberry, and peach. The scale-like coverings are merely shelters for the insects within. The female first lays a large number of very small eggs. In due course these eggs hatch into oval maggots. These settle down, insert their snouts firmly into the bark, and there remain permanently during their short lives. Winter spraying with a tar oil wash is the most efficient remedy for this pest. During spring and summer brown scale can be treated with a combined spray of nicotine, and white-oil emulsion.

BRUNFELSIA *brun-***fel**-*se-a.* Evergreen flowering shrubs needing a minimum winter temperature of 60°. *B. calycina* is the species most commonly seen and it has lavender-purple flowers during late winter and spring. It grows about 2 ft. tall and good specimens will succeed in 6 in. pots.
Culture: As soon as the flowers have faded plants can be potted in a mixture of lime-free loam, moist peat, and coarse sand. During the summer a warm and humid atmosphere should be maintained and ventilation can be given when the temperature rises to 80°.

Once the plants have filled their pots with roots, weekly feeds can be given with liquid manure.
Propagation: Cuttings of moderately firm shoots, 3 in. to 4 in. long, will root in the summer in a propagating box.

BRUSSELS SPROUTS. This popular vegetable belongs to the brassica family and has the same general requirements as other brassicas (*see* Brassica). Varieties are available to crop from about September until February or later according to season.
Culture: Sow in February in a frame or cool greenhouse or in March outdoors. Plant in April or May, 3 ft. apart each way in good rich, well-worked but firm soil. Feed occasionally in the summer with small dressings of a compound vegetable fertiliser and water freely in dry weather. Stake large plants individually. Gather sprouts a few at a time starting from the bottoms of the stems. Remove yellowing leaves at any time but do not cut off the tops of the plants until all sprouts have been gathered.

BUDDING. A method of propagation by inserting a growth bud or 'eye' of a choice variety of a tree or plant in the stem of a common species, technically called the stock. It is the usual method of increasing roses; some kinds of fruits, such as apples, pears, cherries, peaches, plums; some flowering shrubs, such as lilacs and thorns; and various other subjects. The bud is taken from a piece of wood of the current year's growth at a time when the wood is half-ripened. It must be cut in such a manner that a piece of the stem bark surrounds the eye, and the edges of this 'shield' or 'plate' of bark must be perfectly smooth and regular so that they will fit precisely on to the stem of the stock. With rose buds the small slice of wood which is cut away with the outer shell of bark must be carefully removed before inserting in the stock, but this is not always done with fruit tree buds. A T-shaped slit is made in the bark of the stock, the edges being prised open with the ivory end of a budding knife to enable the bud to be pushed under them. It is then bound in position with a strand of worsted or broad raffia. Budding is usually done in July and August. The

Brunfelsia calycina.

Buddleia alternifolia.

Buddleia davidii.

following winter or early spring the stock is cut off just above the bud, which should then grow and provide all the subsequent top-growth of the plant. The young shoot from the bud is best tied to a small cane until it gets sufficiently robust to stand on its own without danger of being blown out.

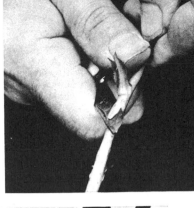

Cutting out a rose bud.

BUDDLEIA bud-*lee-a.* Hardy or slightly tender deciduous or partially evergreen flowering shrubs. The common name Orange-ball Tree is given to *B. globosa*, which has spherical, orange-coloured flowers. Most other buddleias have purple flowers the most popular being *B. davidii* with large pointed flower spikes in late summer. There are numerous varieties varying in colour from white and pale mauve to deep purple. *B. alternifolia* flowers early in summer and carries its small, soft purple flowers on slender arching stems with willow-like leaves.

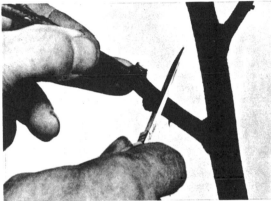

Making a T-shaped incision for budding a standard rose.

Culture: Plant October to March in ordinary well-drained soil and open sunny positions. Slightly tender species such as *B. colvillei* against west walls, or in pots in unheated greenhouses. Prune *B. davidii* and its varieties by cutting hard back before growth commences in spring. Thin out *B. globosa* and *B. alternifolia* as required to maintain shape and vigour.

Propagation: By cuttings of well-ripened shoots inserted in sandy soil outdoors or in a frame in October; cuttings of half-ripe shoots in a propagating frame July or August; seed in a frame or outdoors in spring.

BUD-DROPPING. This is a fairly common trouble with several plants, including sweet peas, runner beans, lupins and tuberous begonias. It may be caused by sudden changes of temperature, a too-dry soil or atmosphere, or poor growth due to faulty root action. Under glass the aim should be to maintain an even temperature with adequate humidity, and in the open mulching of the plants will often alleviate the trouble, particularly if the plants are also sprayed overhead with water in the evenings of hot days. There is less chance of bud dropping if the plants are allowed to become well developed before they are allowed to flower.

Inserting the bud in a side branch of the stock.

BUDS. On certain plants the main central flower bud at the tip of the stem is known as the 'crown bud', but on chrysanthemums the terminology applied to the buds is more complicated. Thus, on an unstopped chrysanthemum, i.e. one that has been allowed to grow naturally with no pinching of the growing shoots, the first bud to form is known as the 'break bud', as when it develops new shoots break from buds in the axils of the leaves beneath it. In practice, however, this bud is seldom allowed to form as earlier side-shoots or laterals are produced if the tip of the stem is pinched out before the break bud stage is reached. These laterals in turn produce flower buds, of which the main one on each stem is known as the 'first crown', and this may be retained to provide the bloom. On certain varieties, though, or where a greater num-

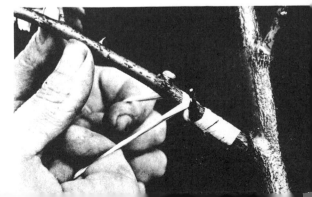

Tying in the bud for a standard rose.

ber of blooms per plant is required, these laterals may be stopped before the first crown bud is formed, so as to produce a greater number of stems, and the main buds which form on these secondary growths are known as 'second crown' buds. Both 'first' and 'second crown' buds may be surrounded by a number of smaller flower or growth buds which must be removed if large flowers are required (*see* also Disbudding).

BUGBANE, *see* Cimicifuga.

BUG-WORT, *see* Cimicifuga.

BULB. A bulb consists of a stem (the thickened 'plate' at its base), while the upper and main part is composed of scales, which are modified leaves or leaf bases. A naked or scaly bulb is one in which the scales are thick but usually narrow, as in a lily. A tunicated or coated bulb has thin papery scales as in the hyacinth and onion. Many plants have swollen structures of similar outward appearance, and are frequently termed bulbs on that account, whereas, correctly speaking, they are tubers or corms. One important difference is that these are solid, fleshy bodies without layers. All bulbs, corms and tubers act as storage organs which enable a plant to survive for a considerable time with little or no water. In their natural habitats bulbous or tuberous rooted plants frequently loose all their top growth during this dry period and are said to be at rest. In cultivation it is often important to provide a comparable resting period.

BULB FIBRE. Bulbs grown in bowls without drainage holes are planted in a compost of 6 parts by bulk peat, 2 parts crushed oyster shell and 1 part crushed charcoal, which must be moistened thoroughly before use. No fertilisers should be added. The charcoal enables the bulb fibre to remain sweet even though there is no outlet for surplus moisture. Bulbs planted in fibre need at least 8 weeks in a cool dark place, or they will fail to make roots. As bulb fibre contains no food material bulbs grown in it lose quality and are only fit for planting outside another year.

BULBILS OR BULBLETS. These are small bulbs produced above ground in the axils of the leaves of some plants, such as the tiger lily, and in the flower clusters of certain onions and leeks. They also occur underground on large bulbs, in all cases affording a means of increasing stock true to the individual characteristics of the parent bulb. In their juvenile stages the underground bulblets are sometimes known as spawn.

BUNCH BERRY, *see* Cornus.

BUSHEL. A measure of volume, equal to 8 gal. or 2,220 cubic in., widely used for the marketing of fruit and vegetables, for which purpose it may vary slightly according to the contents and locality. In the garden a bushel box, 22 in. by 10 in. by 10 in., although not strictly accurate, makes a very useful measure for the mixing of composts and so on. Alternatively, any gallon tin will contain ⅛ bushel or a 2 gal. bucket will contain ¼ bushel.

BUSH HONEYSUCKLE. *see* Weigela.

BUSH MUSK, *see* Mimulus.

BUSY LIZZIE, *see* Impatiens.

BUTCHER'S BROOM, *see* Ruscus.

BUTOMUS *bu-***tome**-*us* (Flowering Rush). *B. umbellatus* is a native water plant with long, narrow leaves and heads of pink flowers carried in August on rush-like stems 4 ft. high.
Culture: Plant April or May in good loamy soil at the margins of pools or slow-moving streams. The crowns of the plants should not be covered with more than 3 in. of water.
Propagation: By division at planting time.

BUTTERCUP, *see* Ranunculus.

BUTTERFLIES, *see* Cabbage Butterflies.

BUTTERFLY FLOWER, *see* Schizanthus.

BULBS OF VARIOUS KINDS

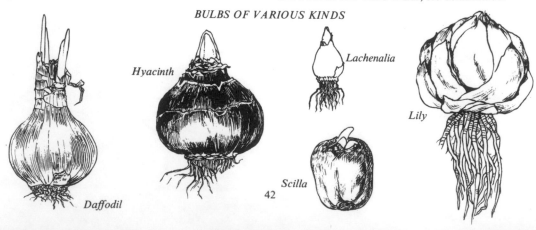

Hyacinth

Lachenalia

Lily

Scilla

Daffodil

Horse Chestnut buds.

Placing moist bulb fibre in a bowl.

Lily bulbils.

BUTTERFLY ORCHID, *see* Oncidium.

BUTTON SNAKE ROOT, *see* Liatris.

BUXUS. buks-*us* (Box Tree).   Hardy evergreen shrubs with green, golden, or silver variegated leaves. Suitable for hedges, topiary specimens and planting in open or shady shrubberies. The common box is *B. sempervirens* and its dwarf variety, *suffruticosa*, is used for edging beds and borders and for outlining geometrical designs in the garden.
Culture for Edgings: Plant divisions with roots attached in a trench 6 in. deep in October, November or March. Allow plants nearly to touch each other and to have their tips about 2 in. above soil. Press soil firmly. Trim plants April or August. A nursery yard of box will make 3 yd. of edging.
Box Hedges: Plant ordinary green box 15 in. apart in September or October in good soil. Trim annually in April or August. Specimen bushes are planted like other shrubs and are shaped by pruning and periodical clipping.
Propagation: By cuttings of young shoots 3 in. long inserted in a shady border in August or September; division of old plants in October or March; layering in September or October.

CABBAGE.   There are quick growing varieties of cabbage such as Primo, Velocity and Greyhound for summer use, slower growing kinds such as Rearguard and Winningstadt for autumn use, very late and hardy kinds such as January King which can be used in winter, yet others such as Ellams Early and Harbinger to be sown in summer and cut the following spring, and red cabbages grown specially for pickling. All are members of the brassica family and have the general requirements of other brassicas (*see* Brassica).

Velocity cabbage.

Culture: Sow the summer cabbages in a frame or greenhouse in February or outdoors in March and plant out in April or May. Sow the autumn cabbages outdoors in March, April or early May and plant out from May to early July. Sow the spring cabbages outdoors between mid-July and mid-August and plant out in September or October.

All require good, well-worked but firm soil. Most varieties should be spaced 18 in. apart in rows 2 ft. apart, but the big drumhead and pickling varieties need a little more room and the small spring varieties can have a little less. The summer, autumn and winter varieties should be fed occasionally in summer with small dressings of a compound vegetable fertiliser. Spring cabbage should not be fed in this way until danger of prolonged frost is over, say in April and May.

43

CABBAGE BUTTERFLIES. The bright green caterpillars of two kinds of butterfly, the cabbage large white and the cabbage small white, attack all kinds of brassicas in summer including cabbages, brussels sprouts, cauliflowers, broccoli and kale. In a severe attack they may reduce the leaves to skeletons in a few days so it is important to watch for the familiar creamy white butterflies in summer and, when they are seen, to spray brassicas occasionally with DDT.

CABBAGE MOTHS. The caterpillars of several moths feed upon the cabbage and its allies. The species known as the cabbage and turnip moth appears from June onwards, and, like most moths, flies only at night. It is fairly large, greyish in colour, with black markings on the forewings. The caterpillars are large and fat, greenish in colour, but somewhat variable in this respect. If disturbed, they roll themselves into a ring. They gnaw their way into the heart of cabbages and cauliflowers, fouling them with their green excreta. Remedies are hand picking and spraying with DDT.

CABBAGE ROOT FLY. The small white grubs of this fly attack the lower part of the stem or upper root of cabbages and allied crops, causing the plants to assume a leaden colour and eventually collapse. The fly, which is not unlike an ordinary housefly, appears from May onwards and the eggs are laid on the stems just below the surface of the ground.

Effective control can be obtained by forking or raking either aldrin or dieldrin into the soil immediately prior to planting.

CACTUS kak-*tus*. Although this is actually the name of one particular genus it is commonly used for the whole family of Cactaceae, which includes some 225 genera and more than 2,400 species. Most of these are natives of hot, dry regions, chiefly the warmer parts of America and the neighbouring islands, although some species have become naturalised elsewhere. Some species live on trees in humid jungles. Most of the family are succulents consisting of leaf-less, fleshy stems which vary considerably in shape; for instance, they may be flat, round, cylindrical or conical and either ribbed or tuberculate—this last term is applied to those with small, hard, somewhat wart-like growths. The main distinguishing feature of the cacti is the spiny 'areole' (sometimes also hairy or woolly) which appears on the ribs or tubercles, or in the case of opuntias, on the flat pads. This particular feature is believed to take the place of a branch and it is not found in any other family. Many plants to which the uninitiated apply the name 'cactus' are really succulent members of different genera and natural orders. The majority of cacti are injured by frost, but dislike high temperatures produced by artificial heat in winter. A few of the opuntias will survive average British winters in the open, but on the whole cacti are plants for greenhouses sited to receive maximum sunshine and with heating facilities adequate to keep out frost. Many will flourish on indoor window sills.

The flowers, generally short-lived, are often spectacular in formation and colouring; in some cases they are small and insignificant individually but are produced in great numbers. The epiphyllums rank among the most imposing and beautiful of the whole family, the blossoms being large, glistening like satin, and of intense colours.

Culture: The basic principle of cactus culture is to provide a very porous compost which will avoid stagnant moisture at the roots at any time. Four parts John Innes potting compost and 1 part extra coarse sand, pulverised brick or pot chips, is suitable for most. Manure and rich leaf-mould are unsafe materials, inducing decay of roots and bases of the fleshy stems except for the epiphytic cacti (zygocactus, epiphyllum, aporocactus, etc.). Plenty of water can be given in summer, with less in spring and autumn, dwindling down to almost nil in the winter, again excepting the epiphytes which need some winter watering and rather warmer conditions. Plenty of fresh air should be given except during frost or dense fog.

Propagation: Seeds germinate easily if sown on the surface of thoroughly well-drained pans of very porous compost. Watering should only be done by

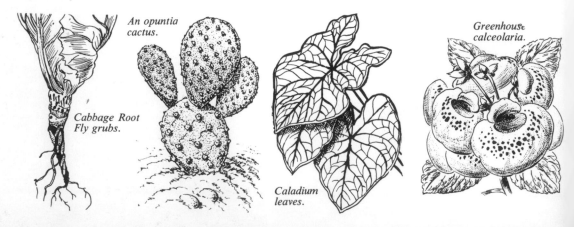

An opuntia cactus.

Cabbage Root Fly grubs.

Caladium leaves.

Greenhouse calceolaria.

immersion, allowing moisture to percolate upward toward, but not over the surface. Cover pans with sheets of glass until seedlings become visible. Germination will be hastened if gentle bottom heat can be given but in early summer the seeds may be sown in an unheated greenhouse. Seedlings should be pricked out 2 in. apart when they can be handled.

Pieces of stem from columnar cacti, and 'pads' of opuntias may be treated as cuttings and rooted in small pots of very sandy compost at any time between March and September. Allow cuttings to lie on a shelf for a week or two until the cut ends become dried before insertion.

Mammillarias, echinopsis, and other spherical cacti produce offsets around the base of older growths. These, if gently prised away from the parent plant, may be potted singly in small pots.

CAFFRE LILY, *see* Schizostylis.

CALADIUM *cal-a-dee-um.* Tender, herbaccous, tuberous-rooted perennials with ornamental foliage. Leaves green, white, crimson, red, rose, veined, netted, and margined with contrasting colours. All the garden caladiums are varieties of *C. bicolor* and make handsome foliage plants for warm greenhouses.
Culture: Grow in John Innes potting compost with a little extra peat in a warm greenhouse in the shade. Pot February or March moderately firm, in sizes just large enough to take tubers. Transfer to larger pots in April or May. Water moderately February to April and September to November; freely April to September; keep quite dry November to February. Temperatures: February to September, 70° to 80°; September to November, 65° to 70°; November to February, 55° to 65°.
Propagation: By dividing the tubers in February or March.

CALATHEA, *see* Maranta.

CALCAREOUS *kal-ka-ree-us.* Pertaining to chalk or limestone. May be applied to soil or to plants inhabiting chalky soils or limestone rocks. The leaves of certain plants (e.g. encrusted saxifrages) are sometimes described as calcareous owing to the chalk glands they contain.

CALCEOLARIA *kal-see-o-lair-ee-a* (Slipper Flower). A popular genus of outdoor and indoor flowering plants bearing gaily-coloured blooms shaped like pouches or inflated bags. The herbaceous calceolarias with large, gaudy pouched flowers are very popular for cool greenhouse cultivation. They are best treated as annuals by raising new plants from seed each year in June. The shrubby kinds are used as summer bedding plants, and there are also a few small species which make good rock garden plants in warm, sheltered places.

Cabbage White caterpillars and female butterfly.

Re-potting a cactus.
Taking cactus cuttings.

45

Calendula officinalis
(*Pot Marigold*).

Roots of brassica seedling dipped in calomel paste.

Callistephus chinensis
(*Annual Aster*).

Culture of Greenhouse Varieties: Sow seed in June in pots or pans in an unheated greenhouse or frame and as it is very fine, covering with a layer of sifted soil is not necessary. Within 10 days germination should have occurred and as soon as possible the seedlings must be pricked out into boxes. The young plants will be happy in a cold frame until early autumn. As growth develops pot them into 3 in. pots and by early October they should be ready for a move to 5 in. pots, and, if necessary, into 6 in. or 7 in. pots the following February or early March. Ventilate as freely as weather will permit and maintain a temperature of 45° to 55°. Water carefully at all times, keeping water off leaves and crowns of plants as much as possible. Calceolarias like a cool, equable atmosphere. Plants should flower from April to June.

Culture of Bedding Calceolarias: Plant in May in reasonably rich, and well-drained soil in a sunny or partially shaded position. Water liberally during dry spells. Pinch out the growing points of the main stems once or twice in the early stages to encourage a bushy habit of growth.

Propagation: Seed is the only practical method of raising stock of greenhouse varieties. Bedding varieties are best raised each year from cuttings prepared from the young shoots in September. These can be rooted in sandy soil in a cold frame. Keep the frame closed and shaded until the cuttings are rooted, but from that time on the young plants should be kept as hardy as possible by free ventilation on all favourable occasions. In the event of severe frost, protect the lights with mats or old sacking.

CALENDULA *kal*-**en**-*dul-a* (Pot Marigold). Hardy annuals, summer-flowering, in bright yellow and orange shades. Admirable for bedding or massing in borders.

Culture: Sow seeds ⅛ in. deep outdoors in March or April in ordinary soil in a sunny position where plants are to flower, or sow in August and September for early flowering next year. Thin out seedlings 9 in. to 12 in. apart. Once established, plants reproduce themselves freely from self-sown seed but such naturalised plants are likely to decline in the quality of the flowers.

CALICO BUSH, *see* Kalmia.

CALIFORNIAN BLUE-BELL, *see* Nemophila.

CALIFORNIAN LILAC, *see* Ceanothus.

CALIFORNIAN POPPY, *see* Eschscholtzia.

CALIFORNIAN TREE POPPY, *see* Romneya.

CALLISTEMON *kal-is-***tee**-*mon* (Bottle Brush). The main attraction of these Australian shrubs is the unusual flowers which have a mass of prominent

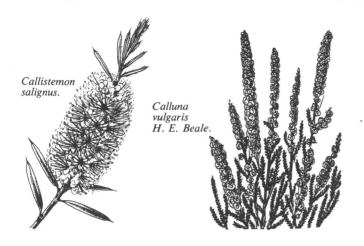

Callistemon salignus.

Calluna vulgaris H. E. Beale.

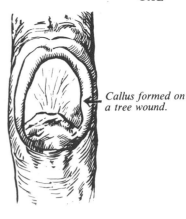

Callus formed on a tree wound.

stamens giving the appearance of a bottle brush. This has given rise to the popular name of bottle brush plant. *C. citrinus splendens* has brilliant red stamens and *C. salignus*, which is one of the hardiest species, has pale yellow stamens.

Culture: Plants will thrive outdoors in mild districts when grown against a warm, sunny wall, but elsewhere they should be given the protection of a frost-proof greenhouse in winter. It is convenient to grow the shrubs in large pots so that they can be stood outside in a sunny place in the summer.

Complete re-potting need be done only every other year and this should be done after flowering as new growth appears. A light trimming of long shoots can be undertaken after the flowers have faded.

Propagation: Cuttings of firm shoots will root in close, shaded conditions in a greenhouse during the summer.

CALLISTEPHUS *kal-is-**tee**-fuss* (China or Annual Aster). The well-known annual so largely grown for summer bedding and for the supply of cut flowers.

All forms of China aster have been evolved from *C. chinensis*. They include double- and single-flowered kinds, varying in height from 9 in. to 3 ft. and with considerable variety in flower forms and colours.

Culture: Sow seeds in March and germinate in a temperature of 55° to 60°. As soon as the first true leaves are formed prick out into boxes and later harden off for planting out, 1 ft. apart in May or early June in good, well-dug soil and a sunny or slightly shady place. Disbud for large flowers, water liberally during dry weather and give weak liquid feeds. Good results can also be obtained by sowing annual asters in mid-April out of doors where they are to bloom, later thinning the seedlings to 1 ft. apart each way.

CALLUNA *kal-**loo**-na* (Ling; Heather). Hardy evergreen flowering shrubs suitable for open beds and borders. *C. vulgaris* is the common purple-flowered ling of British moorlands, and there are varieties with white or pink flowers such as H. E. Beale and also with bronze and golden foliage.

Culture: Plant in autumn or spring in lime-free loam and peat. Peg down straggling shoots or occasionally thin out old branches. Trim annually after flowering.

Propagation: Division of plants in October or April is a rough-and-ready method, but best results are obtained by inserting small side shoots as cuttings in sharp sand in July in a propagating frame. Alternatively plants can be layered in May by making a small trench alongside a plant, pressing the longer stems down into this, covering with soil and making thoroughly firm. By the autumn roots should be formed and the rooted shoots can be severed from the parent plant.

CALLUS. When a stem or root is wounded a natural healing process starts, involving the growth of new, hard tissue over the surface. This can be most obviously seen where tree branches have been removed and the wood has healed, but in the garden the term callus is more often applied to the rather corky substance which forms at the base of cuttings before new roots are emitted. With some plants, such as certain conifers, this callus may in fact be so hard that it must be pared before the roots can emerge, but in general the formation of the callus is a good sign that roots will be produced.

CALOMEL. The popular name for mercurous chloride, a poisonous chemical used in gardens as a preventive of club-root disease and also to kill the maggots of the cabbage root fly and the onion fly. For these purposes it is manufactured as a dust containing 4% calomel. To kill fly larvae this dust can be sprinkled along the rows of onion seedlings in May and early June or around brassica plants after they have been planted out from the seed bed. As a club-root preventive about a teaspoonful of the dust is placed in each planting hole prepared for a brassica seedling or alternatively the dust can be mixed with water to a paint-like consistency and the roots of each brassica plant dipped in this prior to planting. As an additional precaution calomel dust can be sprinkled lightly over the brassica seed bed prior to sowing and be raked in.

CALTHA kal-*tha* (Marsh Marigold; King Cup). Hardy herbaceous perennials with golden yellow buttercup-like flowers in spring, suitable for damp borders or banks of ponds, streams or lakes. *C. palustris* is the species commonly grown and there is also a double-flowered variety which is very showy. *C. polypetala* has large individual flowers.

Culture: Plant October or March in rich soil, close to, but not actually submerged in, water.

Propagation: By division of roots in March or July.

CAMELLIA kam-ee-*le-a* (Tea Plant). Greenhouse and slightly tender evergreen flowering shrubs suitable for pots or tubs in a greenhouse, against walls or in sheltered shrubberies and thin woodlands outdoors. Apart from the exotic looking flowers the glossy green leaves are also attractive. There are several different species but the numerous varieties of *C. japonica* are the most popular. It eventually makes a big shrub and the white, pink, scarlet or crimson flowers, which may be single or double, are produced in winter and spring.

Culture under Glass: Pot March or April. Water moderately September to March, freely afterwards. Prune little except to retain balance and, when this is essential, in March. Temperatures: September to March, 45° to 50°. High temperatures can be responsible for the dropping of the buds in winter. When the temperature rises with sun heat cooler conditions can be maintained by damping down and shading. During the summer the plants can be stood outside until September in partial shade and the compost must never be allowed to dry out. Re-potting need be done only every 2 or 3 years, but to encourage healthy growth regular feeding with liquid manure in the summer is necessary. A suitable potting compost consists of 2 parts moist peat, 1 part lime-free loam and 1 part coarse sand.

Outdoor Culture: Plant in autumn in lime-free loam and leaf-mould or peat, in a sheltered position. Prune back straggly shoots only after flowering but usually little or no pruning is required.

Propagation: By seeds sown $\frac{1}{8}$ in. deep in sandy peat in 75° in March. Cuttings made from nearly ripe shoots in summer can be rooted in a greenhouse or leaf bud cuttings can be taken in spring. These consist of a piece of stem, about 1 in. long, to which is attached a leaf and a bud.

CAMPANULA kam-**pan**-*u-la* (Bell Flower; Canterbury Bell). Hardy herbaceous perennials, rock plants and hardy biennials.

This is a big genus of plants, and from the cultural stand-point must be split up into several distinct sections. First, there are the hardy herbaceous campanulas typified by such species as *C. persicifolia*, *C. lactiflora*, *C. latifolia* and *C. glomerata*. These are all plants for the herbaceous border or wild garden. Then there are the rock garden species, such as *C. garganica*, *C. portenschlagiana*, and *C. poscharskyana*. Some of these, and notably *C. pusilla* and *C. carpatica*, can also be used as edgings, while one species, *C. isophylla*, is not reliably hardy. Thirdly, there are the biennial campanuals, such as the Canterbury Bell (*C. medium*) and the Chimney Bellflower (*C. pyramidalis*), which must be renewed from seed annually if a constant supply of flowering plants is to be maintained. Two species are commonly grown under glass: *C. pyramidalis*, which may reach 4 ft. tall, and the trailing *C. isophylla*, which has starry flowers and makes a fine basket plant. Both are normally blue but have white forms, while *C. isophylla* also has a woolly variegated-leaved form called *mayi*.

Culture of Hardy Herbaceous Perennials: These are all easy to grow, and will succeed in any ordinary garden soil. Most kinds prefer an open, sunny position, but some species, notably *C. lactiflora* and *C. latifolia*, will succeed in partial shade and may be established in thin woodland. All may be planted with safety in spring or early autumn and can be most readily increased by careful division of the roots at planting time.

Culture of Rock Garden Species: Most of these can

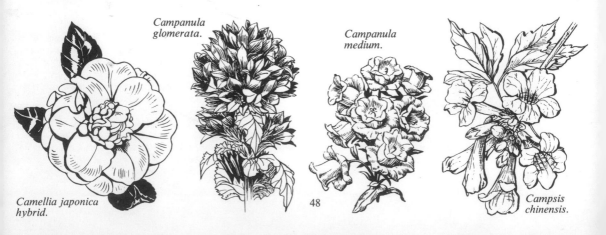

Campanula glomerata.

Campanula medium.

Camellia japonica hybrid.

48

Campsis chinensis.

Caltha palustris.

Campanula lactiflora (garden form).

be grown in an open, sunny rock garden and well-drained soil but a few of the high mountain species, such as *C. excisa* and *C. zoysii*, are more exacting and must be grown in a compost mainly of limestone chippings and sand, with just a sprinkling of leaf-mould, peat and loam. If possible they should be supplied with water from below during the summer months. *C. isophylla* may be grown in pots or hanging baskets in any unheated greenhouse or conservatory in John Innes potting compost. The best time for planting is spring, and propagation is by careful division or by seed sown in an unheated frame in March. *C. isophylla* is suitable as a room plant: it is often seen in cottage windows. Coolness and moist atmosphere are essential for success.

Culture of Biennial Campanulas: The Canterbury Bell thrives in rather rich soil, which should be well dug. Seed is sown either in an unheated frame or in a sheltered border in May or early June. The plants are transferred to a nursery bed in a sunny, sheltered place as soon as they make 3 or 4 leaves each and will be ready for removal to their flowering quarters in August or September. Seed of *C. pyramidalis* should be sown in a frame or cool greenhouse in March or April, the seedlings being pricked out as soon as they can be handled and hardened off for planting out in a sunny, sheltered place in June. This campanula is often grown in pots in the greenhouse in which case John Innes potting compost should be used. During the summer the pots can be stood out of doors if desired. Ventilation should be free at all times as cool conditions must be maintained throughout. Water must be given freely in summer but moderately in winter.

CAMPION, *see* Lychnis.

CAMPSIS kamp-*sis* (Trumpet Creeper). Slightly tender climber with orange, trumpet-shaped flowers in late summer. The hardiest kind is *C. radicans* but *C. chinensis* has larger flowers. Both are self-clinging by means of aerial roots but *C. radicans* is more strongly so than *C. chinensis*. There is a good hybrid between these species named *C. tagliabuana*.

Culture: Plant March or April in good, well-drained soil against sunny, sheltered walls. If plants have to be restricted they can be pruned in November or February when as many as necessary of the previous years growths can be cut back to within 1 in. or so of the main vines. (Sometimes listed under bignonia.)

CANADIAN POND WEED, *see* Aquatic.

CANARY CREEPER, *see* Tropaeolum.

CANDYTUFT, *see* Iberis.

CANKER. A term used for several quite distinct diseases which cause the bark of fruit trees, rose bushes, etc., to become cracked or destroyed. Apple canker is characterised by scars and gaping wounds on the bark, often exposing the wood, and surrounded by a rugged, malformed rind. Treatment consists of cutting away all cankered wood until clean tissue is reached and then painting this with Stockholm tar or a special wound dressing to prevent reinfection. Scab disease should also be controlled as canker often finds its way in through the small bark lesions caused by scab. Some varieties, such as Cox's Orange Pippin, are very prone to the disease, but Newton Wonder and Bramley's Seedling are resistant.

Rose canker is a somewhat similar disease attacking roses, causing swellings and gaping wounds, usually at the base of the stem and often at the graft union. Treatment consists of cutting out badly diseased shoots and spraying the roses in winter, when all leaves have fallen, with a fungicide made by dissolving 1 oz. of copper sulphate in a gallon of water.

Bacterial canker is a disease of stone fruits, principally cherries and plums, characterised by the sudden death of whole branches usually accompanied by considerable exudation of resinous gum. An early symptom is the appearance of small round holes in the leaves. There is no satisfactory cure. Some varieties are more susceptible than others. All affected branches should be cut out and wounds painted with Stockholm tar or a bituminous wound dressing.

CANNA kann-*a* (Indian Shot). Greenhouse or half-hardy herbaceous plants with handsome green or bronze foliage and gaily coloured flowers which may be red, yellow or orange and are produced all summer. May be grown in pots or outdoors in the summer.

Greenhouse Culture: The root-stocks must be stored in a dry frost-proof place in the winter and in the spring they can be started into growth in 6 in. or 8 in. pots of John Innes potting compost. They do not need much heat but prefer a warm, light position in the greenhouse. When in full growth water can be given freely with feeds of liquid manure. Apply weak liquid manure twice a week to plants in healthy growth. In early autumn, after flowering, gradually withhold water.
Outdoor Culture: Start in pots as for greenhouse but harden off in May and plant outdoors early in June in good, rich soil and a sunny position. Lift roots in September, place them in boxes filled with ordinary soil kept dry, and store in a frost-proof position till potting time.
Propagation: By seeds steeped for 24 hours in tepid water, then sown ½ in. deep in light soil in a temperature of 75° in February; or division of roots at potting

Canna indica.

Cantua buxifolia.

time. It will facilitate germination if a slight notch is filed in each seed before sowing.

CANTERBURY BELL, *see* Campanula.

CANTUA kan-*tew-a*. Attractive evergreen shrubs for a cool greenhouse. One of the best kinds is *C. buxifolia* which grows about 4 ft. tall and has 1½ in. yellow and scarlet tubular flowers in May.
Culture: Plants are not difficult to grow in a frost-proof greenhouse and they will succeed well in John Innes potting compost. Re-potting and pruning is best done after flowering. Winter temperature 45°.
Propagation: Cuttings of young shoots will root in sandy soil during the spring and summer.

CAPE COWSLIP, *see* Lachenalia.

CAPE FIGWORT, *see* Phygelius.

CAPE GOOSEBERRY, *see* Physalis.

CAPE JASMINE, *see* Gardenia.

CAPE LEADWORT, *see* Plumbago.

CAPE LILY, *see* Crinum.

CAPE PRIMROSE, *see* Streptocarpus.

CAPER SPURGE, *see* Euphorbia.

CAPSID BUGS. There are numerous different species some of which have a superficial resemblance to greenflies—but are much more active—with a similar habit of piercing leaves, stems or fruits and sucking out the sap. The parts around the puncture

Capsid Bug.

turn brown, die, and fall out leaving holes, or in apple fruits produce corky warts. Where chrysanthemums are grown the most troublesome is the tarnished plant bug, also known as the bishop bug on account of the 'bishop's mitre' pattern on its back. It is about ¼ in. long and pale green with brownish markings. It does most damage in late summer, when it feeds at the tips of the young shoots, causing blind buds, deformed flowers and spotted, distorted leaves. Control is by regular dustings with nicotine, BHC or DDT, good cultivation and removal of weeds.

CAPTAN kap-*tan*. A synthetic fungicide specially useful for the control of apple and pear scab, strawberry grey mould and rose black spot. It is not effective in the control of mildews. It has proved particularly valuable in orchards where lime sulphur cannot be used on account of some varieties being sulphur-shy. Captan can be obtained as a dust for direct application or as a wettable powder for mixing with water and application as a spray.

CARDINAL FLOWER, *see* Lobelia.

CARNATIONS. There are two quite distinct races of carnation, the border carnations which are hardy and flower outdoors in June or early July, and the perpetual flowering carnations, which are only half-hardy and flower in greenhouses, more or less throughout the year. Despite their different appearances and habit both have been developed from the same wild plant, *Dianthus caryophyllus.* The picotee is not a different plant but a particular form of border carnation in which there is a narrow band of a deeper or contrasting colour around each petal.

Culture of Border Carnations: Plant in September, October, March or April in good rich soil in an open sunny position. Space at least 18 in. apart. Stake and tie flower stems. Reduce flower buds to one per stem for the best flowers. As a rule plants need to be replaced by young stock at least every second year.

Culture of Perpetual Flowering Carnations: A high temperature is not necessary and 45° is adequate in winter, provided ventilation is given whenever possible to prevent damp, stuffy conditions. To obtain the best results it is wise to have one greenhouse solely for the carnations, or at least to reserve part of a greenhouse for the plants. Young rooted cuttings can be purchased in early spring ready for potting in 3 in. pots. As they develop they should be potted on to 5 in. and 8 in. pots or they can be planted direct into special beds in the greenhouse from the 3 in. pots. In a small greenhouse it is probably best to grow the carnations in pots so that they can be grown in a deep cold frame in the summer. This will allow other plants to be grown in the greenhouse during this period. To induce bushiness the shoots must be stopped. This is best done first thing in the morning when the stems a e brittle. It involves removing the tip from a young plant when it has made about 8 pairs of leaves. The side shoots that develop afterwards are usually stopped as well. The tips are removed to leave about 4 pairs of leaves. Apart from stopping, disbudding should also be carried out to produce good blooms.

Plants in good health will grow several feet tall and supports are required. Special wire stakes and rings are obtainable for plants in pots. As a rule plants need to be replaced by young stock every second or third year.

Propagation: Border carnations by layers prepared in July from non-flowering stems in which an incision has been made at a joint and which are then pegged to the soil around the parent plant. Layers should be

Gumming—a sign of Bacterial Canker.

Small, round holes, indicating bacterial canker, in cherry leaf.

Cankered apple stem.

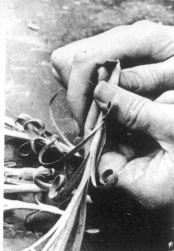

Left: *Taking a perpetual carnation cutting.* Centre: *Trimming the cutting below a joint.* Right: *Stopping a young perpetual flowering carnation.*

kept well watered and be severed from parent plants when well rooted, usually in September. A week or so later they can be lifted and planted or potted singly to be overwintered in a frame for spring planting.

Perpetual flowering carnations by cuttings prepared from November to March from short non-flowering side growths. Those appearing about mid-way up the flowering stems are best. Insert in pure sand or very sandy soil in a propagating frame, temperature 60°. Pot cuttings singly in John Innes potting compost in small pots as soon as well rooted and grow on in the greenhouse as for mature plants. Pot on to larger sizes as smaller pots become well filled with roots.

Both border and perpetual flowering carnations can also be raised from seed sown in a temperature of 60° in spring in a greenhouse. Seedlings vary in colour of flower, habit and other features and a proportion are likely to be worthless but some very beautiful forms can be obtained if seed is saved from good parent plants.

CARRION FLOWER, *see* Stapelia.

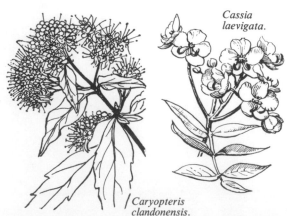
Cassia laevigata.
Caryopteris clandonensis.

CARROT. The four types of carrot in general cultivation are the shorthorn, stump-rooted, intermediate, and long-rooted. The first is used mostly for forcing in frames. The stump-rooted varieties are quick maturing and will supply roots in early summer, while the intermediate and long-rooted kinds are best for storing during the winter. There are numerous varieties of each type.

Culture: Light land suits carrots best and heavy soils should be improved by thorough cultivation. No fresh manure must be used, or the roots may fork badly. Deep digging in autumn or winter followed just before sowing by a dressing of a compound fertiliser with a high phosphatic content is all the preparation required. Apart from hoeing, the main point in the summer months is to keep the carrot fly at bay by raking or hoeing aldrin into the soil.

Main crop and intermediate varieties lifted in October can be stored in sand or ashes in a cool shed, or they may be put in clamps of the same types as used for storing potatoes.

March is soon enough to sow outdoors, starting with the shorthorn varieties. These are best sown in small successional batches. Maincrop sowings should be made in April; 12 in. must be allowed between the rows with long-rooted and intermediate varieties but 8 in. is enough for the shorthorn and stump-rooted kinds. Only a very light covering of soil is needed and thinning to 4 in. to 8 in. apart, must be undertaken as soon as the seedlings are large enough to handle. Pull small-rooted varieties as soon as large enough to use.

CARROT FLY. The small white maggots of this fly attack the roots of carrots. They are most troublesome in late April and throughout May and late-

Carrot Root Fly damage.

Catananche caerulea.

sown (June or July) carrots often escape damage. The maggots can be killed by dusting aldrin around the young carrots in spring and early summer and particularly after thinning when the soil has been disturbed and an attack is most likely to occur.

CARYOPTERIS *kar-ee-op-ter-is* (Moustache Plant; Blue Spiraea; Bluebeard). A hardy, deciduous shrub producing clusters of small blue flowers in autumn. The species cultivated is *C. mastacanthus* but there is an improved variety known as *clandonensis*.

Culture: Plant in early spring in well-drained soil and a rather warm, sunny position. If desired stems may be cut back quite severely each April to keep plants fairly compact and bushy.
Propagation: By cuttings of the young shoots in summer rooted in sandy soil in a frame.

CASSIA *kass-ee-a*. The species that are usually grown in this country are shrubs that succeed in a cool greenhouse. *C. corymbosa* and *C. laevigata* grow 5 ft. to 6 ft. tall and they both have clusters of yellow flowers in the summer.
Culture: Plants can be grown in large pots or tubs in John Innes potting compost, or they can be planted in a border of well-drained soil. A light, sunny part of the greenhouse should be chosen for the plants. Water freely in summer, moderately at other times. Minimum winter temperature 45°.
Propagation: By cuttings of moderately firm shoots which should be inserted in sandy soil in a warm, shady part of the greenhouse.

CASTOR OIL PLANT, *see* Ricinus.

CATALPA *kat-al-pa* (Indian Bean). Hardy deciduous ornamental-leaved trees, producing white and purple flowers in June and July followed by bean-like seed pods. The species grown is *C. bignonioides* but there is also a variety with golden leaves named *aurea*. Both will eventually make trees 40 ft. to 50 ft. high and as much in diameter.
Culture: Plant October to April in good soil and sunny, open positions. Branches may be pruned in late winter to any extent necessary to restrict size or spread. Hard pruning increases the size of the leaves.
Propagation: By cuttings of firm shoots inserted in sandy soil in a propagating frame in a temperature of 55° to 65° in summer. By seeds sown in a similar temperature in spring.

CATANANCHE *kat-an-an-che* (Blue Cupidone; Blue Succory). Hardy perennials of which the best is *C. caerulea*. The blue flowers may be cut when fully developed and dried for winter decoration. They are at their best in late summer and a plant grows 1½ ft. to 2 ft. tall.
Culture: Plant in spring in ordinary well-drained soil and sunny position. Old plants do not transplant well.
Propagation: By seeds sown in a temperature of 55° in March, transplanting seedlings outdoors in June; careful division in spring.

CATCHFLY, *see* Silene.

CATERPILLAR. A general term for the larvae of butterflies and moths. Many caterpillars are injurious to garden crops and plants but the advice often given, to destroy every butterfly and moth, is not sound since the larvae of many also do good service by devouring noxious weeds. Caterpillars can be destroyed by hand picking, by spraying with insecticides such as DDT, BHC, malathion, derris or pyrethrum; or, in the case of some species which attack fruit trees, the female moths can be trapped on grease-bands placed around the trunk or the main branches of each tree (*see* Grease Bands).

CATMINT, *see* Nepeta.

CATTLEYA kat-*lee-a***.** One of the most handsome genera of orchids, all tender plants for the warm greenhouse. The cattleyas have big flowers often in shades of purple or mauve with white or yellow. They last well when cut and are much used by florists for corsages, etc. There are a great many species and even more hybrids which are now principally grown in gardens. All are epiphytes, i.e. they get most of their nourishment from the air.
Culture: Pot in spring or early summer when growth starts. Use a compost of 3 parts chopped sphagnum moss and 2 parts osmunda fibre, with a good sprinkling of broken charcoal. Maintain a temperature of 65° to 70° in summer and a minimum temperature of 55° in winter. Water fairly freely in summer, sparingly for a month or so after flowering, moderately in spring. Maintain a fairly moist atmosphere at all times. Shade in summer from direct sunshine.
Propagation: By careful division of the clusters of pseudo-bulbs when re-potting.

CAULIFLOWER. There is no real difference between cauliflower and heading broccoli but in gardens the former name is usually applied exclusively to the more tender summer varieties.
Culture: Cauliflowers need to be grown quickly in good, rich, well-manured soil. First sowings can be made in February in a frame or greenhouse to be followed by a further frame sowing in March and an outdoor sowing in April. An outdoor sowing can also be made in early September, the seedlings being transplanted to a frame at the end of October. In this they will spend the winter and will be planted out the following April for an early crop. Plant at least 2 ft. apart in rows 2½ ft. apart, water freely in dry weather and feed occasionally with small dressings of a compound vegetable fertiliser with a high nitrogen

Celosia cristata pyramidalis.

Ceanothus Gloire de Versailles.

content. When curds commence to form break in some inner leaves over them to keep them white. Cut as soon as well grown.

CEANOTHUS *see-an-***o-***thus* (Californian Lilac). Hardy and half-hardy evergreen and deciduous flowering shrubs, including some excellent blue-flowered plants suitable for training against walls. Among the best evergreen kinds are *C. burkwoodii, C. dentatus, C. rigidus, C. veitchianus* and *C. thyrsiflorus.* All these are blue and flower in spring or early summer. Most of the deciduous varieties grown in gardens are hybrids. They flower in late summer and may be blue or pink.
Culture: Plant October to March in well-drained ordinary soil and sunny sheltered positions or against south or west walls or fences. Evergreen kinds may be pruned lightly after flowering to keep them in shape. Deciduous kinds can be cut back quite hard each March if desired to limit their size.
Propagation: By cuttings of firm shoots inserted in soil in a propagating frame in July or August. Seeds sown in a temperature of 60° in spring.

CEDAR, *see* Cedrus.

CEDAR WOOD. The wood of the Western Red Cedar (*Thuja plicata*) is widely used for outdoor woodwork such as greenhouses and frames and, also, as 'shingles' in the construction of roofs of summer houses, etc. Owing to its essential oils it is very weather and insect resisting and thus needs no painting, and although it is a soft, light wood it is extremely durable.

CEDRUS sed-*rus* (Cedar). Evergreen cone-bearing trees only suitable for large gardens. Three species are commonly grown, the Cedar of Lebanon, *C. libani,* distinguished by its very horizontal branching; the Deodar, *C. deodara,* the young shoots of which have a weeping habit; and the Atlas Cedar, *C. atlantica* most familiar in the variety *glauca* with blue-grey foliage.
Culture: Plant October to April in good, rich, loamy soil and open, sunny situation. No pruning desirable.
Propagation: By seeds sown in a greenhouse or frame in March. Selected garden varieties by grafting in spring on to seedlings of the related species.

CELERIAC. This vegetable is closely allied to celery, but it is the bulbous growth between the roots and the leaf stems that is the serviceable part of the plant. It is often used as a substitute for celery for flavouring soups and stews. Seeds and seedlings are treated in exactly the same way as those of celery. The soil must be well-dug and manured but no earthing up is necessary. Plants are placed outdoors early in May, 9 in. apart, in rows 1 ft. apart. Subsequently the only attention required is regular hoeing and liberal watering in dry weather.

Cattleya hybrid. *Celeriac.* *Self-blanching celery.*

CELERY. There are three principal types of celery, white, pink or red and self-blanching. All must be grown in deeply dug and well-manured soil. A common practice is to prepare trenches 18 in. to 2 ft. in width and as much in depth, throwing out the soil from these and then returning most of it mixing well-rotted farmyard or stable manure with it. The top 5 in. or 6 in. of the trench is not refilled and the surplus soil is built up into ridges on either side of each trench, to be used later in earthing up the stems. During the early summer months catch-crops of lettuce, radish, etc., can be grown on these ridges.

Seed is sown in a warm greenhouse in March, or for an early crop at the end of February. The seedlings are pricked off into deep boxes and are hardened off for planting outdoors 12 in. apart in May or early June.

During the growing season it is hardly possible to over-water celery. Once plants are established, feed regularly with very weak liquid manure.

Approximately 6 to 8 weeks is required for blanching. Paper is wrapped around each plant to prevent soil getting into the heart and then soil is drawn up around the plants at intervals of a week or so until only the final tuft of leaves is exposed.

During severe weather the tops of ridges may require some protection, with straw or bracken laid along them. Self-blanching celery is grown in a similar manner except that it is planted in blocks, the plants 9 in. apart each way, and no earthing up is required. It is suitable for summer and early autumn use. Next, the white celery should be used, the pink or red varieties being left until last as they are hardiest.

CELERY FLY. The maggot of this fly bores into the leaves of celery and feeds within them. In a bad attack the leaves may be so severely tunnelled that only the skin remains. The larvae are very small,

Bending cauliflower leaves to protect the curd.

legless, and white or green in colour, and the flies themselves are about ⅙ in. long, with brown bodies and transparent wings. Mild attacks can be controlled by picking off and burning affected leaves, but usually it is necessary to spray occasionally from May to August with DDT or BHC. Deep winter digging also helps.

CELOSIA *se-lo-see-a* (Cockscomb; Prince of Wales' Feathers). There are two types that are popular for greenhouse decoration in the summer. They are *C. cristata*, which is commonly called cockscomb, and *C. c. pyramidalis*. The former have crests of tightly packed red flowers and the plants grow 9 in. to 12 in. tall.

The other type has plumes of red or yellow flowers about 18 in. tall. They are treated as annuals by raising plants from seed each year.
Culture: Sow in well-drained pans of light soil in a temperature of 65° in March. Transplant seedlings 2 in.

apart when 1 in. high. Later transfer to well-drained pots of John Innes potting compost and keep in a temperature of 60° to 65°. Move again in June to 5 in. pots. Celosias need careful cultivation and, although they must never be allowed to become dry, watering must be done very carefully, particularly when they are young, as overmoist conditions can cause losses. Syringe foliage twice daily. Apply a liquid feed when flowers appear. May be used for summer bedding if planted out in sunny sheltered beds or borders in late May or early June.

CENTAUREA sen-**taw**-ree-a (Cornflower; Sweet Sultan). Hardy and half-hardy perennials and annuals. The blue cornflower, C. cyanea, is an annual too well known to need description. There are also pink and white varieties. The ordinary type grows 3 ft. tall but there is also a dwarf type 12 in. or less in height. Another good annual is C. moschata, the Sweet Sultan. This produces larger flowers in a variety of colours, the plants being about 2 ft. tall. Perennial species range from quite short plants such as C. montana to the massive species such as C. babylonica, 6 ft. high. The principal half-hardy kinds are C. gymnocarpa, C. cineraria and C. ragusina, all with silvery leaves which are decorative in summer flower beds.
Culture of Annual Species: Sow seeds in well-drained soil in a sunny position outdoors in April where plants are required to flower. Thin seedlings to 12 in. apart for the tall type, 6 in. or 8 in. for the dwarf type.
Culture of Perennial Species: Plant autumn or spring in ordinary well-drained soil in sunny borders.
Culture of Half-Hardy Species: Plant out in May or early June in ordinary soil and sunny positions. Lift in early October and keep in a frost-proof greenhouse during winter, or discard old plants and raise new stock annually from cuttings or seeds. In mild seaside districts plants may survive outdoors for many winters and make quite large bushes.
Propagation: Perennial kinds by seed sown outdoors in April; also by division of roots in autumn or spring. Half-hardy kinds by cuttings taken in spring or autumn and rooted in sandy soil in a frame or green-

house; also by seeds sown in March in a temperature of 60° to 65°.

CENTRANTHUS sen-**tran**-thus (Red Valerian). Hardy herbaceous perennial with red, pink or white flowers in early summer, suitable for dry walls, sunny rock gardens or borders, and for chalky soils. The species grown is C. ruber.
Culture: Plant in autumn or spring in ordinary well-drained soil and sunny position.
Propagation: By seeds sown in frame or greenhouse in March, or in sunny position outdoors in April, May or June; also by division in spring. Once established plants often spread by self-sown seed.

CENTURY PLANT, see Agave.

CERASTIUM ser-**ass**-tee-um (Snow in Summer). Low growing hardy perennials of spreading habit suitable for dry borders, rockeries, banks and as edgings for flower beds. White flowers are produced in early summer. The species commonly grown is C. tomentosum but C. biebersteinii is a less invasive plant.
Culture: Plant March or April in ordinary soil but not near small, choice plants which may easily be overrun.
Propagation: By division of plants in March or April.

CERATOSTIGMA ser-at-o-**stig**-ma (Leadwort). Low growing hardy perennial (C. plumbaginoides) and slightly tender dwarf shrub (C. willmottianum) both with blue flowers in late summer and autumn.
Culture: Plant in autumn or spring in well-drained ordinary soil on sunny rockery or at edges of borders sheltered from cold winds.
Propagation: By division in spring; C. willmottianum also by cuttings of firm growths in propagating frame in July or August.

CERCIS ser-sis (Judas-tree; Red-bud). Hardy deciduous flowering trees with purplish-red flowers in May and June, suitable for lawns or warm, sheltered shrubberies, or trained against a south wall in cold

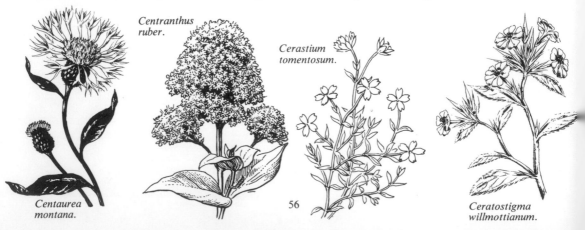

Centranthus ruber.

Cerastium tomentosum.

Centaurea montana.

Ceratostigma willmottianum.

parts of the country. The species grown is *C. sili-quastrum* and it will make a tree 20 ft. to 30 ft. high.

Culture: Plant October to March in rich, deep, well-drained soil. No regular pruning required.

Propagation: By seeds sown ¼ in. deep in light sandy soil in a temperature of 55° to 60° in March, transplanting seedlings outdoors when growing freely, or by layers of strong shoots in spring.

CEREUS *se-ree-us* (Torch Thistle; Night-flowering Cactus). Tender succulent plants of the cactus family with fleshy, spiny stems and no leaves. There are many species and varieties.

Culture: Pot every 3 or 4 years in March in well-drained pots using a John Innes potting compost with a little additional coarse sand and pounded brick. Grow in a sunny greenhouse or window. Water very sparingly September to April, more liberally in summer. Temperature: September to March, 50° to 55°; in summer natural temperatures are sufficient. Give full sunshine and free ventilation.

Propagation: By seeds sown ⅛ in. deep in well-drained pans of sandy soil in a temperature of 75° in March; cuttings of stems inserted in small pots of sandy soil kept barely moist in summer; grafting choice varieties on common kinds in April.

CEROPEGIA *scr-o-pee-gee-a* (Hearts Entangled). Most of the ceropegias are bizarre-looking succulents, but *C. woodii* makes an attractive trailing plant which does well in a cool greenhouse or room. It has small fleshy leaves with silver mottling, more or less heart-shaped, which give it the name Hearts Entangled; they are carried on thin stems which trail but will twist around each other or a support. In warm conditions the curiously-formed, tubular, silvery-purple flowers may be produced. The stems also carry round tubers which root readily if pushed into moist soil.

Culture: In a greenhouse the plant is perhaps best grown in a wide shallow pan, where the tubers may be pegged down and the chance of flowering is increased, but indoors it may be more convenient to grow it as a trailer in a pot. Grow in John Innes potting compost with a little extra sand or some pounded brick. Moder-

Cereus hybrid.

ate watering is needed, with little in winter.

Propagation: It can be increased from stem cuttings but the tubers are more convenient.

CESTRUM *ses-trum*. Attractive shrubs with red, yellow or greenish-white tubular flowers for growing in a frost-proof greenhouse. The most popular species is *C. newellii* which can be grown outside on a warm wall in South Devon and Cornwall. The red flowers are produced in clusters and each one is about 1 in. long. *C. aurantiacum* is another good kind with orange-coloured flowers.

Culture: Cestrums grow best when planted in a border of well-drained soil, but they can be grown in tubs or large pots. When planted in a border the stems should be tied to wires or trellis on a wall in the greenhouse.

Propagation: Cuttings of partly mature shoots root readily in sandy soil if they are placed in warm and close conditions.

CHAENOMELES *ky-nom-el-ees* (Japanese Quince; Japonica). These showy, early flowering shrubs, frequently trained against walls, are more familiar to most gardeners under their former name, cydonia. The most popular species is *C. speciosa* (formerly *Cydonia japonica*), up to 10 ft. high with scarlet

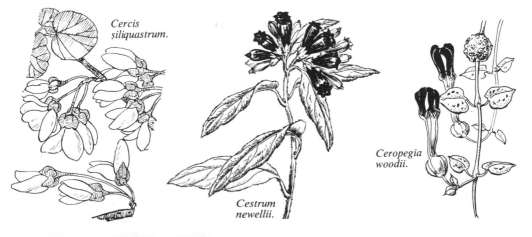

Cercis siliquastrum.

Cestrum newellii.

Ceropegia woodii.

flowers in March and April. There are also white and pink varieties. *C. japonica* (formerly known as *Cydonia maulei*) is a lower growing shrub, up to 3½ ft., wide-spreading and freely branched with red flowers in spring or crimson in the variety *simonii*.

Culture: Plant November to March in ordinary soil in a sunny or partially shady place. Pruning is not essential but when planted against walls it may be necessary to thin out branches and shorten side growths annually after flowering.

Propagation: By rooted suckers removed in November; layering in spring or early summer.

CHAFER BEETLES. Beetles of several kinds, those familiar in gardens being the cock-chafer and summer chafer. These, both as adults and larvae, are destructive to foliage and roots. The adult beetles are familiar by reason of the buzzing noise they make and their apparent aimless flight on warm summer evenings. The dirty creamy-white fat larvae live in the soil and, though they are usually found curled up and inactive, in fact do a great deal of damage to roots and crowns of plants. These larvae can be killed by forking or raking aldrin into the soil at any time of the year. Cultivation also exposes them to their natural enemies.

CHALK. Carbonate of lime, convertible into quick-lime by burning in kilns. Ground chalk is extremely useful in improving the texture of soils, rendering light land more retentive of moisture and opening up clay soils. Chalk also tends to correct soil acidity, or 'sourness', and to set free locked up stores of some plant foods. Having no caustic properties, it may be used with greater safety than quick lime on soils which are deficient in humus but it is less effective in breaking up stiff clay. The more finely chalk is ground the more rapidly will its effect be seen. An excess of chalk on garden soil is unfavourable to the growth of some plants, notably heathers, rhododendrons, azaleas and some lilies. There are, however, also chalk-loving plants, such as scabious, poppies and many species of dianthus and these should be given preference for planting in gardens on chalk downs

and cliffs. For potting composts chalk is the best material for providing the necessary lime.

CHAMAECYPARIS *kam-ee-sy-par-is* (False Cypress). Hardy evergreen trees grown for their ornamental foliage. The species are for the most part large trees growing to a height of 50 ft. and more, and with spreading branches, but there are many garden varieties, some of which are tall but narrow in habit, while others are dwarfs, never exceeding a few feet in height. Several species make excellent hedge shrubs, the best for this purpose being *C. lawsoniana* and some of its more erect forms such as *allumii* and *erecta viridis* (*see* also Cupressus).

Culture: The false cypresses are not particular as to soil, but they thrive best in a well-cultivated and rather rich loam. Choice large varieties should be planted in avenues or as single specimens with plenty of room for development, while the dwarf varieties are suitable for planting in the rock garden. For hedge making place the young shrubs from 2 ft. to 2½ ft. apart and allow them to grow upwards unchecked until they reach the desired height. Then remove the tops in May. The sides of the hedge may be trimmed occasionally in summer right from the start. Plant cypresses at any time from October until April when the weather is reasonably mild and the soil is in good working condition.

Propagation: Species by seeds sown in a cool greenhouse or frame in spring; garden varieties by grafting in spring onto seedlings of the type species. Some varieties also grow readily from cuttings taken from July to September and rooted in a propagating frame.

CHAMAEDOREA, *see* Neanthe.

CHAMAEROPS kam-*ee-rops* (Fan Palm; Hardy Palm). *C. humilis* is the only palm found wild in Europe. It is virtually hardy, at any rate in southern and western parts of Britain and also does well in a greenhouse or fairly cool room. It will eventually reach about 20 ft. with fan-shaped leaves 18 in. long, but the young specimens usually sold grow slowly enough and it may be years before they exceed 6 ft. or 8 ft.

Culture: Cool conditions suit it well: stuffy air and draughts will wither the leaf tips. Regular sponging of the leaves and moderate, but regular, watering will keep it happy. Under glass grow in large pots or tubs in John Innes potting compost and water freely in spring and summer, rather sparingly at other times. Minimum winter temperature: 45°. Outdoors plant in sunny sheltered places in good loamy soil.

Propagation: It is increased by rooting suckers in heat.

CHAMOMILE, *see* Anthemis.

CHAPLET FLOWER, *see* Stephanotis.

Cheiranthus cheiri (Wallflower).

Chamaerops humilis.

Chaenomeles speciosa moerloesii.   *Chamaecyparis lawsoniana erecta.*   *Tying a fan-trained Morello cherry.*

CHARCOAL. This may be roughly described as the impure carbon left as a solid when wood is partially burned. Although it has no value as a fertiliser and is completely insoluble in water, it is often used, either crushed or in small lumps, as an ingredient of potting composts, where it assists drainage and keeps the soil sweet by absorbing gases. For this reason it is always included in bulb fibre. It is particularly valuable for orchids and slow-growing plants.

CHEIRANTHUS *ki-**ran**-thus* (Wallflowers). Hardy perennials some of which, including the common wallflower, *C. cheiri* and the Siberian wallflower *C. allionii*, are commonly treated as biennials. All are spring-flowering, colours ranging from yellow to deep crimson. *C. cheiri* and its varieties are very fragrant.
Culture of Wallflowers: Sow seed in May outdoors in open situations. Transplant seedlings in June, 6 in. apart in rows 12 in. apart, in good soil and sunny situations. Pinch out tips to encourage branching. Transplant to flowering quarters August to October, the earlier the better.
Culture of Other Species: Plant October to March in ordinary well-drained soil and sunny beds, rock gardens or dry walls.
Propagation: By seed as for wallflowers also by cuttings of firm young shoots inserted in sandy soil in a frame in spring or early summer.

CHERRY. Varieties grown for their fruit must be considered in two groups—the sweet cherries, usually grown as standards and bearing their fruit mainly on spurs on the older wood, and the cooking or Morello cherries, often grown as fan-trained trees against walls and bearing their fruits mainly on young stems made the previous year.

Both sweet and Morello cherries thrive in fairly rich, loamy soils preferably well supplied with lime. Plant November to March, the sweet cherries in an open, sunny place, Morello cherries in sun or shade.

Sweet cherries make large trees and do not like much pruning so should be planted at least 25 ft. apart. Any thinning necessary to keep trees in shape is best done in April.

Morello cherries can be pruned much more drastically and may be planted 12 ft. to 15 ft. apart. During summer the new shoots appearing on the fruiting stems should be gradually reduced to 2 per stem, 1 at or near the tip, the other near its base. Then after the crop has been gathered, the fruiting stems can be cut back and the young growths near their bases trained in their place.

Cherries are increased by budding in summer on to seedlings of the gean or wild cherry.

CHERRY LAUREL, *see* Prunus.

CHERRY PIE, *see* Heliotropium.

CHESHUNT COMPOUND. The damping-off of seedlings can be largely prevented or controlled by use of this fungicide, which may be either bought ready-made or prepared by thoroughly mixing 2 parts of ammonium carbonate with 2 parts of copper sulphate (both materials in finely-powdered form). The mixture should be stored in an air-tight non-metallic container and allowed to stand for 24 hours before use, although if stored properly it will keep for a long time and may be used as required. For use: 1 oz. of the mixture should be dissolved in a little hot-

Storing chicory roots under sand.

Preparing chicory roots for forcing.

water which should then be made up to 2 gal. with cold water. The solution is harmless to seedlings and may be safely applied overhead, either as a preventive measure before damping-off appears or as a control where the trouble has already occurred. In the latter case any affected seedlings should be removed first, and in all circumstances further applications, at about fortnightly intervals, are advisable.

CHICORY. This vegetable is grown for the young growths, or 'chicons', which are blanched and either eaten cooked or raw. Seed is sown in early June in good, well-drained soil and drills ½ in. deep and 15 in. apart. Thin seedlings to 1 ft. apart. Remove flowering stems should any appear. Lift roots as required for forcing in autumn and winter. Cut off tops about 1 in. above crowns and place close together, right way up, in large pots or deep boxes with any fairly light soil such as old potting or seed soil. Forcing should be in complete darkness and in a temperature of 50° to 55°. Cellars, sheds or the space under staging in greenhouses may be used. Outdoors chicory can be blanched where it has grown by covering each root with an inverted flower pot or by drawing soil up in a ridge along the rows as when earthing celery. Whatever method is used the blanched growths are broken off close to the crowns when about 9 in. high.

CHILEAN BELLFLOWER, *see* Lapageria.

CHILEAN GLORY-FLOWER, *see* Eccremocarpus.

CHILEAN GUM BOX, *see* Escallonia.

CHIMNEY BELLFLOWER, *see* Campanula.

CHIMONANTHUS *ky-mon-an-thus* (Winter

Sweet). The only species, *C. praecox*, is a hardy deciduous shrub 10 ft. high with pale yellow and purple flowers in mid-winter. It is notable for its very sweet perfume.

Culture: Plant November to March in good, well-drained soil and sheltered position. Will do well against a wall facing south or west. No pruning is essential but when trained against a wall it may be desirable to carry out a little annual thinning and shortening of young stems which is best done immediately after flowering.

Propagation: By layering in spring or early summer.

CHINA ASTER, *see* Callistephus.

CHINCHERINCHEE, *see* Ornithogalum.

CHINESE BELLFLOWER, *see* Abutilon.

CHIONODOXA *ki-on-o-doks-a* (Glory of the Snow). Hardy bulbous plants with blue or blue and white flowers in spring. The two species commonly grown are *C. luciliae* and *C. sardensis*. Both are 6 in. to 8 in. high.

Outdoor Culture: Plant bulbs 3 in. apart and 1 in. deep in September in ordinary well-drained soil on sunny rock gardens or as edging to beds, borders or shrubberies. Lift and replant every 3 or 4 years.

Propagation: By offsets removed at planting time.

CHIVES. A relative of the onion, the leaves of which are used in salads and for flavouring. Any ordinary garden soil will serve for this plant which should be given a sunny position. Plant in March 6 in. apart in rows 6 in. apart. No subsequent attention beyond hoeing is required, and the plants can be left undisturbed for 3 or 4 years, after which they should be lifted, divided, and replanted.

Potting chicory roots for forcing.   Chicory forced in complete darkness.   Chives.

CHLOROPHYTUM *klor-o-fi-tum* (Spider Plant). There are two species of chlorophytum. *C. capense* (syn. *C. elatum*) and *C. comosum* grown as greenhouse or house foliage plants. They are very similar, and both are normally grown in their variegated forms, in which cream or ivory stripes run the length of the long, gracefully arching leaves in rosettes. The small, starry, white flowers which appear on the rather stiff flower stems are nothing much to look at, but do not cut the stems—when the flowers have faded small leaf rosettes appear on the stems and bend them down as they grow, giving a pretty 'waterfall' effect. The plant is sometimes called the Spider Plant on account of these adventitious rosettes.

Culture: The chlorophytums are among the most attractive of foliage plants for greenhouse or room, and also among the most tolerant, standing sun or some shade, cool or warm conditions. Their only real need is for plenty of water, though rich soil is appreciated. When pots become overcrowded with roots plants should be re-potted, preferably in spring.

Propagation: The rosettes on the old flower stems can be detached and potted separately or old plants can be divided in spring.

CHLOROSIS *klor-o-sis.* A condition caused by the failure of leaves to maintain their normal amount of green colouring matter or chlorophyll. As a result they become yellow and weak and may in severe cases fail. Chlorosis is a symptom of some diseases or may be brought about by lack of iron or magnesium. These deficiencies may, in turn be due to an excess of lime in the soil and chlorosis is particularly troublesome on chalk or limestone soils. Deficiency chlorosis can be remedied by the free use of animal manures, peat and leaf-mould to lower the pH of the soil, by good cultivation and by feeding or spraying with Epsom salts (sulphate of magnesium), sulphate of iron dissolved in water at 1 oz. per gal. or with specially prepared iron sequestrols (chelated iron), used according to manufacturer's directions.

CHOISYA choy-*see-a* (Mexican Orange-flower). Evergreen shrub with white fragrant flowers in May. Suitable for sheltered shrubberies, against south walls, etc. The species grown, *C. ternata*, makes a rounded shrub 6 ft. to 8 ft. high.

Culture: Plant October or March in ordinary soil and sunny position. No regular pruning required.

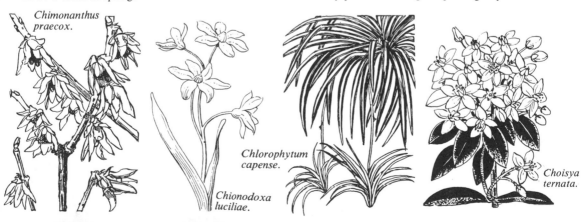

Chimonanthus praecox.

Chlorophytum capense.

Chionodoxa luciliae.

Choisya ternata.

Propagation: By cuttings of firm shoots inserted in sandy soil in a propagating frame in July or August; cuttings of ripe shoots in an unheated frame in autumn.

CHRISTMAS CACTUS, *see* Zygocactus.

CHRISTMAS CHERRY, *see* Solanum.

CHRISTMAS ROSE, *see* Helleborus.

CHRISTMAS TREE, *see* Picea.

CHRYSANTHEMUM *kri-***san**-*the-mum* (Ox-eye Daisy; Marguerite; Pyrethrum; Corn Marigold; Shasta Daisy). As is indicated by the list of common names the genus chrysanthemum includes not only the well-known greenhouse and border chrysanthemums, but numerous hardy perennial and annual species. The popular greenhouse and garden varieties are very numerous and are divided into many sections, according to shape and size of flower, time of flowering, etc. There are single-flowered, double-flowered, and anemone-flowered forms. Early flowering or border chrysanthemums are those which normally open their flowers outdoors before the end of September.

Most popular of the hardy perennial chrysanthemums are *C. leucanthemum*, the Ox-eye Daisy, and *C. maximum*, the Shasta Daisy flowering in summer. *C. uliginosum*, the Giant Ox-eye, flowers in early autumn. All have large white flowers.

The annual chrysanthemums, of which there are numerous varieties, are derived from *C. carinatum*, *C. coronarium* and *C. segetum*, and have variously-coloured flowers in summer.

The marguerite, a popular summer bedding plant with white or yellow flowers all summer, is *C. frutescens.*

Culture of Border Chrysanthemums: Root cuttings of firm young basal shoots in February or March in a greenhouse; temperature 60° to 65°. Pot singly in John Innes potting compost when well rooted and harden off for planting outdoors in early May in sunny situations in a good, rich, well-dug soil. Stake and tie securely and, if large flowers are required, restrict each plant to 6 or 8 stems and each stem to 1 flower bud. Lift some plants for stock in October, place in pots or boxes and overwinter in a frame or greenhouse. These plants will provide the cuttings from which new stock is grown after which the old plants should be discarded.

Culture of Greenhouse Chrysanthemums: Much the same as for border chrysanthemums. Cuttings may be taken from December to May and, if planted out in May, must be lifted and brought back into a greenhouse before the end of September. More usually they are grown in pots throughout, being moved on to larger sizes as they fill the smaller pots with roots. Eventually they may need pots 8½ in. to 9 in. in diameter and John Innes 2 or 3 compost plus regular summer feeding with a specially prepared chrysanthemum fertiliser of which there are several excellent proprietary brands which should be used according to manufacturer's instructions. From mid-May to late September pots are stood outdoors in a sunny but sheltered place. Plants in pots need watering very carefully, particularly in the summer when the compost is liable to dry out very rapidly, and the plants must be supported adequately to prevent them being blown about by wind. Stopping, which consists of removing the tips of the shoots, is necessary. Generally mid-season varieties are given one stop and the later ones are stopped twice. There are, however, exceptions to this rule. To obtain large flowers, side shooting and disbudding is also required. Plants are brought back into the greenhouse before there is danger of frost. From then on a temperature of 50° to 60° should be maintained with free ventilation whenever possible. After flowering some plants are cut down and kept for stock as for the border varieties the rest being discarded.

Culture of Hardy Perennial Chrysanthemums: Plant October to March in ordinary soil and sunny positions. Lift and divide roots every third or fourth year.

Culture of Annual Chrysanhemums: Sow thinly in March, April or September, in ordinary soil and sunny beds or borders where plants are to flower. Thin to 8 in. or 9 in. apart. Discard after flowering.

Culture of Marguerites: Root cuttings of firm young shoots in spring or late summer in sandy soil in a greenhouse in a temperature of about 60°. Pot in John Innes potting compost when rooted. Keep in a frost-proof greenhouse in winter but harden off for planting outdoors in May or early June in ordinary soil and sunny positions. Also suitable for hanging baskets or ornamental pots and urns.

CIMICIFUGA *sim-iss-ee-***fu**-*ga* (Snake-root; Bugbane; Bug-wort). Hardy herbaceous perennials with white flowers in narrow spikes in late summer. The species commonly grown are *C. japonica* and *C. simplex*, both about 3 ft. tall and *C. racemosa*, 5 ft. to 6 ft.

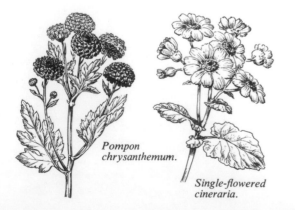

Pompon chrysanthemum.

Single-flowered cineraria.

Taking chrysanthemum cuttings.

Inserting the cuttings in a small pot of sandy soil.

The final potting of a chrysanthemum.

Spraying chrysanthemums against insects.

Disbudding a chrysanthemum.

CINERARIA *sin-er-**air**-ee-a*.   Tender perennials treated as annuals and grown as pot plants in the greenhouse. The botanical name of this plant is *Senecio cruentus*. Cinerarias are indispensable for a colourful display in late winter and spring in a cool greenhouse. There are several different types varying considerably in habit and apart from the compact forms with large single flowers there are the much taller 'stellata' types as well as intermediate kinds. The colour of the daisy-like flowers also varies. Blue, purple, pink and red are predominant, but there are various intermediate shades.

Culture: Sow seeds during April, May or June in an unheated greenhouse $\frac{1}{16}$ in. deep in well-drained pans or pots containing John Innes seed compost. Transplant seedlings when 3 leaves have formed, singly in small pots using John Innes potting compost. Transfer to a frame and keep shaded from strong sunshine. Shift into 5 in. pots in July, 6 in. or 7 in. size in August. Remove to light airy greenhouse in October with a temperature of 45° to 55°. Apply weak liquid feed weekly from September onwards.

Cinerarias are not difficult to grow provided it is remembered that they like cool conditions and in summer shade from strong sunshine. At this time they are best in a cold frame, but the plants should be removed to a frost-proof greenhouse in early autumn. Plants dislike cold, damp conditions in winter.

CINQUEFOIL, *see* Potentilla.

CISSUS sis-*us* (Kangaroo Vine). Apart from some peculiar succulents, the cissus are climbing plants of the vine family. Two of them are tough house plants. *C. antarctica,* the Kangaroo Vine; has large notched leaves, pale green, while *C. sicyoides* has glossy five-lobed leaves. *C. striata* is a much smaller, graceful version of *C. sicyoides,* but has not the same stamina and tends to lose its leaves in winter. In the really warm, moist greenhouse, the exotic-looking *C. discolor,* with velvety, silver-mottled leaves, red beneath, will thrive; it is sometimes sold as a house plant but will never last long in room conditions in winter. *C. adenopodus* is remarkable for the red hairs that cover the young growths and leaves and *C. gongylodes* for the bright red aerial roots and aerial tubers which it forms in a moist atmosphere. The tropical species, such as *C. discolor,* need much more warmth and moisture, a winter minimum of 60° rising to 70° or 80° in summer and more water at the roots particularly in summer.

Culture: *C. antarctica, C. sicyoides* and *C. striata* prefer cool conditions and shade from full sun, the Kangaroo Vine in particular tending to drop its leaves if it gets too hot. The soil should be allowed to dry out partly between waterings. If a lot of leaves fall, the stem should be cut back to encourage new shoots.
Propagation: All the cissus like rich but porous soil, and are easily increased by cuttings struck in a close, moderately warm propagator.

CISTUS sis-*tuss* (Rock Rose; Gum Cistus). Hardy and half-hardy evergreen shrubs. Suitable for cold greenhouses, sunny rock gardens and banks, shrubberies, etc. The flowers, produced in summer, resemble single roses in form. Among the best kinds for the garden are *C. cyprius,* white and purple, 4 ft. to 6 ft.; *C. ladaniferus,* white, 4 ft. to 5 ft.; *C. purpureus,* rose-purple and yellow, 3 ft. to 4 ft.; C. Silver Pink, pink, 2 ft. to 3 ft.
Culture: Plant from pots October to March in ordinary but well-drained soil and sheltered, sunny positions. Protect in severe weather. Prune any

Constructing clamp for storing potatoes.

damaged growths when winter has passed.
Propagation: By seed sown in sandy soil in a cold frame or unheated greenhouse in March, transplanting seedlings into small pots and planting outdoors when growing strongly; by cuttings of half-ripe shoots in July or August in a propagating frame.

CLAMP. A place in which various root crops such as potatoes, carrots and beetroots are stored in the open.

The roots are put in a ridge or cone-shaped heap on a good layer of straw and well covered with more straw or bracken, and finally with 6 in. or so of soil beaten smooth. Also known as Pie or Pit. Dahlia tubers are sometimes stored in clamps.

CLARKIA klar-*ke-a.* Hardy annuals with variously coloured flowers in summer, suitable for sunny or partially shaded beds or borders. May also be flowered early as pot plants in cool greenhouse.
Culture: Sow seeds $\frac{1}{8}$ in. deep in ordinary soil in March, April, May or September, where plants are to flower. Thin seedlings to 6 in. or 9 in. apart. For pot culture sow in early September. Pot seedlings in small pots in autumn; winter on a greenhouse shelf

Cistus purpureus.

Clarkia elegans.

Cissus sicyoides.

Clerodendrum thomsonae.

Clematis montana rubens.　　*Pruning clematis in February.*　　*Cleome spinosa.*

and shift into larger pots about February. Use only moderate heat. Ventilate freely.

CLARY, *see* Salvia.

CLEMATIS klem-*a-tis* (Old Man's Beard; Traveller's Joy; Virgin's Bower). Hardy and tender climbing plants and hardy herbaceous perennials. The best of the tender climbing species is *C. indivisa*, an evergreen with white flowers in spring. *C. armandii*, another evergreen species, can be cultivated outdoors in sheltered positions. Many of the popular hardy summer flowering clematis are hybrids. They are grouped into classes according to the species from which they are mainly derived, e.g. *Jackmanii, lanuginosa, patens, viticella, florida*. In each group there are numerous varieties and colours range from white, pale pink and mauve to deep purple and crimson. One of the most vigorous and popular species is *C. montana* with small white flowers in May. There is a pink form named rubens. The hardy herbaceous kinds are not so well known but are useful border plants. Typical of these are *C. heracleifolia* and its variety *davidiana* both with blue flowers in clusters in summer.

Culture: All the climbing species and hybrids like a cool root run and a sunny place in which to spread their foliage. The best times for planting are March and October. Plants should be purchased in pots so that they may be planted with the minimum root disturbance. Plant slightly deeper than in the pots, so that roots may form from the base of the stem. All summer and autumn flowering kinds should be pruned in February. Early flowering kinds such as *C. montana* may be pruned immediately after flowering, but only sufficiently to keep them within bounds and to get rid of diseased or worn-out growth. Hybrids of the *C. jackmanii* and *C. viticella* groups may be pruned fairly hard every year and this is the best method of obtaining large flowers. Shoots made the previous summer are shortened to within 9 in. of the main 'vines' from which they grow. With other groups of hybrid clematis, remove weak or over-crowded branches and train in sturdy one-year-old shoots at practically full length.

C. indivisa should be grown in a greenhouse with a minimum temperature of 45° and free ventilation in spring and summer. A loamy compost with some lime or chalk suits it well. Water freely during spring and summer, moderately at other times.

The hardy herbaceous clematis will thrive in any ordinary garden soil and open, sunny positions. They may be planted in spring or early summer.

Propagation: Nurserymen often graft the climbing clematis on to seedlings of *C. vitalba*. A better method is to layer plants in spring or early summer or to take cuttings of firm young growths in July or August and root these in silver sand in a propagating frame or by mist propagation. The herbaceous kinds can be increased by division of the roots at planting time.

CLEOME *klee-o-me* (Spider Flower). Half-hardy annual with pink flowers in summer. The only species grown is *C. spinosa*. It is 3 ft. tall.

Culture: Sow in March in a temperature of 60°. Prick off seedlings 2 in. apart into boxes and later pot individually in John Innes potting compost. Harden off for planting outdoors in late May or early June in good soil and a sunny position with plants spaced 5 in. to 18 in. apart.

CLERODENDRUM *kler-o-***den***-drum*. Shrubs and climbers, some hardy or nearly so, some tender and suitable only for warm greenhouse cultivation. Tender climbers with showy flowers include *C. thomsonae* which grows up to 12 ft. tall and has crimson and white flowers; *C. speciosum* with deep pink flowers, and *C. splendens* which has clusters of bright scarlet flowers. *C. fallax*, another shrubby type, is grown more commonly, probably because it is readily raised from seed. It has large heads of scarlet flowers.

Clianthus
formosus.

Clivia
miniata.

Cobaea
scandens.

Among the best hardy kinds are *C. bungei* with rose-purple flowers, a shrub growing to 6 ft. and *C. trichotomum* with white and brown flowers, a large shrub up to 10 ft. Both flower in late summer.

Culture of Tender Kinds: The climbing species can be grown in large pots or they can be planted in a border inside the greenhouse. The flowers are seen to their best advantage if the stems are trained under the greenhouse roof. To keep the plants growing healthily plenty of water must be given in the summer with occasional feeds of liquid manure. Much less water is needed in winter. After flowering the side growths should be pruned back fairly hard. Temperature: April to September, 60° to 70°; October to March, 55° to 60°.

Culture of Hardy Kinds: Plant October to March in good, loamy soil and sunny, sheltered position. Cut out dead or damaged growth of *C. bungei* each March. *C. trichotomum* needs no regular pruning.

Propagation: Apart from *C. fallax*, which is easily raised from seed in the spring, tender kinds are best propagated from mature shoots which are removed at pruning time and inserted into pots of sandy soil in a warm, moist propagating box. *C. bungei* can be increased by rooted suckers removed at planting time. *C. trichotomum* by suckers or cuttings in July.

CLIANTHUS *kli-an-thus* (Lobster Claw; Parrot's Bill). There are two species which have unusual flowers. *C. puniceus* is commonly called Parrot's Bill, because of the shape of the flowers which are scarlet in colour and there is also a variety with white flowers. They are tender climbing shrubs needing a frost-proof greenhouse but in mild districts in the west of the country they are often seen growing outside. The Glory Pea, *C. formosus* (syn. *C. dampieri*), is a more exotic looking species with large red flowers and an intense black-purple blotch in the centre of each one. It is a curious plant as it does not grow well on its own roots if sown and grown on in pots, but if seed is sown where the plant is to grow permanently it will

succeed. Another novel method of overcoming the difficulty is to graft clianthus seedlings on to seedlings of *Colutea arborescens*. This must be done at an early stage and good plants can be produced which are ideal for a hanging basket.

Culture: Plant or pot in March in John Innes potting compost. Water freely in spring and summer, sparing at other times. Minimum winter temperature, 45°. *C. puniceus* can be planted outdoors against sunny walls in mild districts.

Propagation: Plants of *C. puniceus* can be raised readily from seed or from heel cuttings in the spring or summer. They may be grown in large pots or they can be planted permanently in a border so that the stems can be trained up the greenhouse roof. Both species flower in the summer and light pruning of the growths can be undertaken afterwards.

CLIMBING HYDRANGEA, *see* Hydrangea and Schizophragma.

CLIVIA **kliv**-*ee-a* (Kafir Lily). Tender evergreen flowering plants with fleshy roots and showy heads of yellow or orange lily-like flowers in spring. Most of the plants seen are forms of *C. miniata*, or less commonly of *C. nobilis*. All carry their flower head upon a tall, stout stem rising from the centre of two rows of wide, strap-shaped leaves.

Culture: Pot in February in John Innes compost and place pots in a sunny position in a greenhouse. Water freely March to July, moderately August to October, sparing in winter. Temperature: September to May, 45° to 55°. May be kept in a sunny frame during summer. The dark green leaves suffer readily from browning at the tips, so the clivia is not really suitable as a permanent indoor plant. This is one of the plants that likes to be thoroughly pot-bound, and should be left in the same pot as long as possible, top-dressing in spring and feeding in summer.

Propagation: By division of roots at potting time. Seed sown in some heat when ripe germinates readily.

CLOCHE. Originally a glass shaped like a bell, but now cloches are made in various forms and of either glass or plastic. They are used for striking cuttings, seed raising, forcing early vegetables, hastening the ripening of strawberries, etc. Some cloches consist of sheets of glass (which can be packed flat

A glass cloche.

when not in use) held in position by stiff wire frames or clips. Others are made of plastic fixed to metal or wooden frames. All are light and easily portable so that they can be moved quickly from one crop to another.

CLUB-ROOT. This disease, also known as 'Finger and Toe' and 'Anbury', causes the roots of turnips, cabbages and other brassicas, wallflowers, and allied plants to become very swollen, distorted and almost devoid of fibres. It is caused by a soil fungus which enters the roots. Infected plants must be pulled up and burnt. Soils that have become acid or 'sour' are highly favourable to the development of club-root. Land that has borne a diseased crop should not be planted with any crop liable to be attacked for at least 4 years. The plot, as soon as cleared of the crop, should be given a dressing of lime at the rate of 1 lb. per sq. yd., and similar dressings can be given annually for 3 or 4 years. Seed beds in which brassicas or wallflowers are to be raised should be soaked with mercuric bichloride, 1 oz. to 10 gal. of water, prior to sowing, but this is a highly poisonous chemical which must be handled with the greatest care. A second treatment can be given when seedlings are 1 in. high and a little of this same solution poured into each hole at planting time. Another method of control is to dip the roots of the plants prior to planting into a paste made with 4 oz. calomel dust and water or to sprinkle calomel dust into the planting holes.

CLUSTERED WAX-FLOWER, *see* Stephanotis.

Clerodendrum trichotomum.

Clerodendrum bungei.

Club Root of brassicas.

COBAEA ko-bee-a (Cup and Saucer Vine; Mexican Ivy). Greenhouse and half-hardy climbing perennial, usually grown as an annual. Suitable for beds in greenhouses or against south or south-west walls outdoors and over arches or trellises. *C. scandens* is the species most commonly seen and it produces its large unusual flowers during the summer. These vary as they age from a greenish colour to shades of violet.
Culture: Pot March in a mixture of loam, leaf-mould and silver sand, or plant in good soil outdoors in late May or early June. Temperature: September to March, 45° to 50°. Water freely in summer, moderately at other times. When grown permanently in the greenhouse instead of being treated as an annual old stems should be cut hard back in late winter and when new shoots develop the weakest can be thinned out. The remainder should be allowed to ramble up the greenhouse roof or through a trellis.
Propagation: By seeds sown in light soil in a temperature of 65° in March.

COCHINEAL CACTUS, *see* Opuntia.

COCKCHAFER, *see* Chafer Beetles.

COCKROACH. This beetle-like pest, about 2 in. long and of a dark reddish-brown colour, is often troublesome in heated greenhouses where it may attack seeds, seedlings, and the foliage of plants. Where it occurs all possible hiding places such as accumulations of rubbish beneath the staging, should be eliminated, and a dust of either DDT or BHC should be applied around its haunts.

COCKSCOMB, *see* Celosia.

COCKSPUR THORN, *see* Crataegus.

COCONUT FIBRE. This material, found between the outer skin and the shell of coconut, has many uses in the garden. It is invaluable for plunging, mulching, the rooting of soft-wood cuttings and the protection of plants in winter. It is not imported now on the same scale that it once was, and so it has largely been superseded in the garden by peat.

CODIAEUM ko-*dee-um* (Croton; Cotton or South Sea Laurel). Tender evergreen shrubs with ornamental foliage. Leaves beautifully variegated with various colours. The greenhouse crotons are all varieties of *C. variegatum.*
Culture: Pot in March in a mixture of John Innes potting compost and some extra peat or leaf-mould and place pots in a warm greenhouse. Water freely March to September, moderately afterwards. To grow well they like a temperature of 60° to 70° in the summer and a moist atmosphere should be maintained by regular damping and syringing in the greenhouse. They are often used for room decoration but they are not good subjects for growing permanently in the average room because the atmosphere is likely to be too dry which will cause the leaves to fall. The colour of the leaves is more intense if the plants are given plenty of light and they should be stood in a good light place in the greenhouse. Feeds of liquid manure are beneficial to established plants during the growing

season but in winter feeding is not necessary and water should be given sparingly.
Propagation: By cuttings of the ends of shoots inserted singly in sandy soil at 75°, at any time; stem-rooting in March or April.

CODLING MOTH. This troublesome moth appears in May and June and lays its eggs on the sides of newly-formed apple fruits. The caterpillar enters the fruit often at the 'eye', and, after feeding within it for some weeks, emerges and lets itself down to the soil by means of a silken thread.

The trees should be sprayed with an insecticide such as DDT or arsenate of lead as soon as the petals have fallen and again at the middle and end of June. Place bands of hay or sacking around the tree trunks in June and examine these occasionally for sheltering caterpillars and cocoons. The bands should be removed and burned in winter.

COLCHICINE. A very poisonous drug obtained from the Autumn Crocus (*Colchicum autumnale*). It has the effect of altering the number of chromosomes in the cells of plants, with the result that changes in character occur. For instance, seeds soaked in a weak solution of it may produce dwarf and distorted plants, although these in turn may produce plants which vary in a different way from the original form, sometimes being much larger.

COLCHICUM kol-*chi-kum* (Autumn Crocus; Meadow Saffron). Hardy bulbous flowering plants, suitable for moist beds or rock gardens, shrubberies, borders, or for naturalising in short grass near shade of trees. *C. autumnale* grows about 4 in. high and *C. speciosum* 8 in. to 9 in. Both are purple but have white varieties.
Culture: Plant bulbs 3 in. deep and 6 in. apart in good loamy soil in July or August. Foliage dies down in June and July and does not appear until after plants have produced their crocus-like flowers during September or October.
Propagation: By seeds sown in pans of light soil in a cold frame in late summer, transplanting seedlings 3 in. apart when 2 years old. Division of bulb clusters

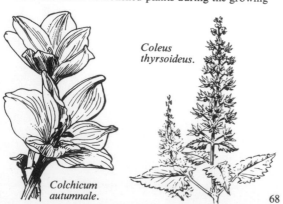

Coleus thyrsoideus.

Colchicum autumnale.

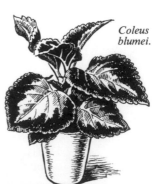

Coleus blumei.

Columnea banksii.

68

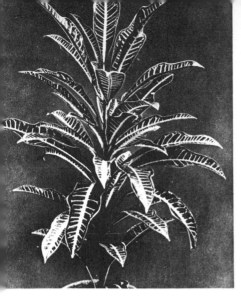

Colchicum speciosum album.

Codiaeum
(Croton).

Codling Moth
damage.

in July or August. Seedling bulbs do not flower until 4 or 5 years old.

COLD GREENHOUSE. In a greenhouse of this sort, which provides protection from the elements but is only heated by the sun, there is obviously less scope than in an artificially heated one. During the summer, however, there is little difference between the two, as most plants will succeed without artificial heat from about April to October; and if they must be started earlier than this, and only a few are required, it is often more economical to buy young plants than to heat the greenhouse. During the winter, of course, only frost-resisting subjects can be grown, but even so there is a wide range, including shrubs, herbaceous plants, annuals and bulbs, which can provide an effective display.

COLEUS ko-*lee-us* (Flame Nettle; Nettle Geranium). *C. blumei* is a popular tender perennial with ornamental foliage variegated with many bright colours. *C. thyrsoideus* and *C. frederici* are grown for their long, slender spikes of blue flowers in winter. **Culture:** Pot February or March in John Innes compost and keep in a well-heated greenhouse in winter (60° to 70°) and in an unheated, lightly shaded greenhouse in the summer. Water very moderately September to March, freely afterwards. Young plants of *C. blumei* should have their shoots pinched off in early stages of growth to ensure dwarf, bushy habit.

Coleus revel in warm, moist and shaded conditions. Any check in growth because of chills, dryness or draughts will cause the leaves to fall. Plants are often used for room decoration in the summer, but they do not live for long if kept permanently in a living room as they do not like dry atmosphere and fluctuating temperatures.
Propagation: By seeds sown in light soil in a tem-

perature of 60° to 65° in February, March or April; cuttings of young shoots inserted in light soil in a propagating frame at any time. Old plants of *C. blumei* are often rather difficult to overwinter but young plants raised from August cuttings overwinter more easily.

COLLAR ROT, *see* Neck Rot.

COLLINIA, *see* Neanthe.

COLLOIDAL COPPER. A form of copper fungicide which mixes readily with water and makes a very even protective film over stems and leaves of plants on which it is sprayed. It is used to control numerous diseases including black spot of roses, potato blight and various rusts.

COLLOIDAL SULPHUR. A form of sulphur used as a fungicide. It mixes readily with water and when sprayed on plants forms a very fine and even protective film over leaves and stems. It should be used according to manufacturers' instructions.

COLORADO SPRUCE, *see* Picea.

COLOURED MARGUERITE, *see* Pyrethrum.

COLUMBINE, *see* Aquilegia.

COLUMNEA kol-**um**-ne-a. Several species have very beautiful flowers, particularly *C. gloriosa*. Long trailing stems are produced from which bright red and yellow flowers appear in profusion during the winter. *C. banksii* is similar in habit, but the leaves are glossy and the flowers are of a reddish-orange colour. Another attractive species is *C. microphylla* which has very small leaves and attractive orange-red flowers.

Making compost.

Painting boxes with copper naphthanate.

A concrete greenhouse.

Culture: The columneas are idea for growing in hanging baskets. These should be lined with moss and young plants can be put fairly close to one another around the rim. As the stems develop they hang down from the basket and when in flower the plants are a magnificent sight. The baskets can be filled with a mixture of turfy loam, moist peat and a little coarse sand. A minimum temperature in winter of 55° is needed, but it can rise to 75° in summer, provided the atmosphere is kept moist. Light shade from strong sunshine should be given in summer.

Propagation: Cuttings made from pieces of stem cut into lengths of a few inches root readily if they are placed in a warm, moist propagating box in April.

COMPOST. Any mixture of soils, manures, fertilisers, etc., that may be applicable to the needs of certain crops or pot plants. The term is also applied to any garden refuse rotted down to form manure and piles of such refuse in the process of decay are known as compost heaps. Various chemicals are available to hasten decay and improve the quality of the resultant compost, the chief requisite being something that supplies freely available nitrogen. Decay is also improved if the compost heap is turned occasionally (*see also reference to* John Innes Composts).

CONCRETE GREENHOUSE. These are usually made of precast strips or units which can be readily assembled or dismantled. They have the advantage of being very durable without much maintenance, but against this they are not quite so attractive in appearance as those made of more conventional materials and the replacement of broken panes may prove difficult for the amateur. This last problem does not arise, of course, where the concrete construction serves only as a framework for wooden-framed glass, for example, Dutch Lights.

CONDENSATION. The water formed when warm, moist air condenses on a cold surface—can be a nuisance in the greenhouse, where it commonly forms on the glass. Apart from causing drip it may lead to decay of the woodwork on to which it runs, particularly as it is often difficult to get this dry enough to paint satisfactorily. Where the growing conditions required by the plants permit ample ventilation, this will keep condensation down considerably, although in a heated greenhouse in winter there is always bound to be a certain amount.

Where seeds are sown in boxes or pots and covered with glass condensation occurs so the glass should be turned over daily to get rid of the moisture which might possibly lead to damping off.

CONE-FLOWER, *see* Rudbeckia.

CONIFER. Any tree which produces its seeds in cones. Many useful evergreen trees and shrubs are conifers, including pines, firs, spruces, junipers, cypresses and yews. There are, however, deciduous conifers as well, notably the larches and also taxodium and metasequoia.

CONSERVATORY. Although in effect a greenhouse the conservatory is often a feature added on to the dwelling-house, although where architectural circumstances do not permit this it may be a separate structure. Unlike the greenhouse it is used more for the display of plants than for growing them, and a common practice is to bring them into it only when they are approaching their best. Permanently planted subjects, either in central beds or on the walls, are, however, often used very effectively, and where these or other plants are growing their cultural management is much the same as that required in the ordinary greenhouse. In the conservatory the layout of paths, stagings and so on is usually more decorative than in more business-like structures, and in general the main aim should be to maintain a well-kept attractive and fully stocked appearance all the year round.

CONVALLARIA *kon-val-***lair**-*ee-a* (Lily of the Valley). Hardy herbaceous perennial with white or pale pink fragrant flowers in spring, suitable for cultivation in the shade of trees, walls, fences, etc. There is only one species, *C. majalis.* Crowns may be potted and forced in greenhouses in winter for early spring flowering.
Outdoor Culture: Plant single crowns in autumn 2 in. or 3 in. apart with points just below the surface, in a well-nourished, fairly light soil. Heavy ground should be improved by the liberal addition of leaf-mould. Lift and replant when the bed becomes crowded. Mulch the bed annually in February with decayed manure or compost.
Greenhouse Culture: Although sturdy crowns from outdoor plants can be used, it is possible to purchase retarded crowns specially for forcing. These can be purchased all the year round from bulb specialists and flowers can be expected within a month of planting the crowns. Boxes, 4 in. deep, should be used and filled with John Innes potting compost or soil and leaf-mould. The crowns can be placed fairly close together leaving the tops of them just exposed above the level of the soil. A temperature of 60° and a moist atmosphere are desirable. The plants should be kept shaded until they are about 6 in. high when they can be given more light, although they must never be stood in direct sunlight.
Propagation: By seeds sown ¼ in. deep in light soil outdoors in March; division of crowns in September or October.

CONVOLVULUS *kon-***vol***-vu-lus.* *C. tricolor, C. major* and its varieties are hardy annuals up to 1 ft. high with blue, pink, crimson or white flowers in summer. Suitable for sunny beds or borders. *C. cneorum* is a slightly tender shrub, 2 ft. to 3 ft. high with silvery leaves and white or pinkish flowers in summer (See also Ipomoea).
Culture of Annuals: Sow in April or May in ordinary soil and sunny, sheltered position where plants are to flower. Thin seedlings to 9 in. apart. *C. major* should be given more space and a fence or trellis up which to climb.
Culture of Shrubs: Plant in autumn or spring in a sheltered sunny place in well-drained soil. A sunny rock garden or rock bank is a suitable place.
Propagation: *C. cneorum* by seed sown in a greenhouse in spring or by cuttings in a propagating frame in summer.

COPPER, COLLOIDAL, *see* Colloidal Copper.

COPPER NAPHTHANATE. This has largely replaced creosote as a wood preservative in the garden and particularly in confined spaces such as greenhouses and frames where the fumes from creosote may be harmful to plants. In its horticultural grades copper naphthanate is harmless to plants and may safely be used on seed-boxes, frames, stakes and so on, while in the erection of greenhouses it is useful for treating the joints before assembly. The best method of applying it is by impregnation under pressure, but in the garden the only two practical methods are immersion and painting; the former is most satisfactory.

Convallaria majalis.

Convolvulus tricolor.

Convolvulus cneorum.

COP

COPPER SULPHATE, *see* Sulphate of Copper.

CORAL BERRY, *see* Symphoricarpos.

CORAL PLANT, *see* Russelia.

CORAL-TREE, *see* Erythrina.

CORDON. A fruit tree restricted to 1 or 2 stems grown upright, horizontally, or obliquely. A useful form of training, especially for apples and pears, where space is limited. Cordons are generally very productive; they enable the small grower to plant a greater number of varieties than would be possible with trees of other shapes, and they are more easily attended to than most. Gooseberries are also grown as cordons when very large fruits are required. Apples or pears to be trained as cordons must be worked on suitable dwarfing stocks such as Malling Type IX or Malling Type VII for apples and Quince for pears. The term cordon is also extended to cover other artificial restrictions of plants to single stems. Thus 'cordon sweet peas' are sweet peas from which all side growths have been removed.

COREOPSIS *kor-ee-op-sis* (Tickseed). Hardy annual and perennial herbaceous plants suitable for sunny, well-drained beds and borders. The annuals are frequently catalogued as calliopsis and have yellow or brownish-purple flowers. The perennials, varieties of *C. grandiflora* and *C. lanceolata*, have yellow flowers. All are summer flowering.
Culture: Plant perennials in ordinary well-drained soil and in an open position in October or March. Annuals are raised from seed sown in March or April in a sunny, open position where the plants are to flower, seedlings being thinned to 9 in. or 12 in.
Propagation: Perennials by seed sown outdoors in April, transplanting seedlings when large enough to handle to permanent positions; cuttings of firm young growths in sandy soil in a frame in April.

CORFU LILY, *see* Hosta.

CORM. A short, fleshy subterranean stem used by the plant for food-storage, as in crocus and cyclamen. Corms are not true bulbs, though often treated as such. Corms are often annual, as in gladioli, but before dying produce buds which develop into the flowering corms for the following year. Numerous buds may be produced, each turning into a young corm and thus providing easy propagation.

CORN MARIGOLD, *see* Chrysanthemum.

CORNELIAN CHERRY, *see* Cornus.

CORNEL TREE, *see* Cornus.

CORNFLAG, *see* Gladiolus.

CORNFLOWER, *see* Centaurea.

CORNUS *kor-nus* (Bunch Berry; Cornelian Cherry; Cornel-tree; Dogwood; Dogberry; Skewerwood). Hardy deciduous flowering trees and shrubs, some with ornamental foliage or bark. Spring and early summer flowering. From a garden standpoint Dogwoods may be considered in four groups: those grown primarily for the red colour of their young stems such as *C. alba* and *C. sanguinea;* those grown for their handsomely variegated foliage such as *C. alba spaethii;* those grown for their white or pink flowers (they are really coloured bracts surrounding the inconspicuous flowers) such as *C. kousa, C. florida* and *C. nuttallii;* and those grown as ground cover such as *C. canadensis.* With the exception of the last named all will make large shrubs or small trees.
Culture: Plant October to February in sandy peat on rock gardens or banks for dwarf species; ordinary soil in open or shady shrubberies or as specimens on lawns for tall species. No regular pruning required.
Propagation: Shrubby kinds by cuttings of firm shoots inserted in sandy soil outdoors in November; layering shoots in spring; some kinds by suckers removed in November and replanted at once; seeds sown in frame or greenhouse in spring; *C. canadensis* by division in spring.

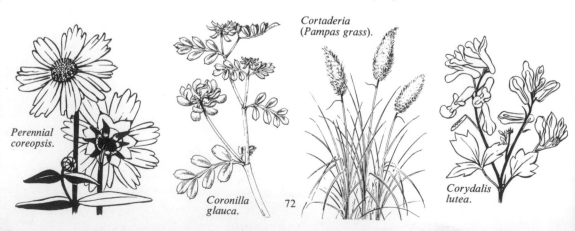

Perennial coreopsis.

Coronilla glauca.

Cortaderia (Pampas grass).

Corydalis lutea.

72

CORONILLA *kor-o-**nil**-a.* *C. glauca* is the species most commonly cultivated. It is a half-hardy evergreen shrub with yellow, pea-like flowers which appear mainly in the spring and summer. During the day the flowers are fragrant. Plants will succeed in a frost-proof greenhouse and during the summer they can be stood outside or in sheltered places they may be planted outdoors permanently, preferably trained against a sunny wall.

Culture: Re-potting of greenhouse plants is best undertaken in March or early April using John Innes potting compost. At the same time any straggly growths can be pruned back to keep the plants bushy and compact. Plenty of water is needed in the summer and the plants will benefit from feeding with liquid manure. When grown outdoors plant in March in good loamy well drained soil and, if necessary protect with sacking in winter.

Propagation: Cuttings of partly matured shoots, taken in late summer, will root readily in a cold frame or cool greenhouse in spring. *C. canadensis* by division in spring.

CORTADERIA *kor-ta-**dee**-ree-ah* (Pampas Grass; New Zealand Silvery Reed Grass). Hardy perennial grasses, flowering September to November, with ornamental foliage and silvery flower plumes. Gather plumes for winter decoration directly fully developed; female plumes are the most durable. The species commonly grown is *C. selloana*, better known as *C. argentea*.

Culture: Plant March or April in light, rich soil in sheltered shrubberies or on lawns. Water freely in dry weather. Leave foliage to wither, then pull away with gloved hands. Never cut green foliage.

Propagation: By seeds sown $\frac{1}{16}$ in. deep in sandy soil in well-drained pots or pans under a cloche in temperature of 55° to 60° in spring. Transplant seedlings outdoors in August or September. Also by careful division at planting time.

CORYDALIS *kor-id-**a**-lis.* Hardy herbaceous plants with finely divided ferny foliage and small sprays of flowers in summer. The species most commonly grown, *C. lutea*, is about 12 in. high and has yellow flowers.

Culture: Plant in spring or early autumn in ordinary soil and sunny or partially shady places on banks, rock gardens or in dry walls.

Propagation: By seed sown in spring where the plants are to grow or by division at planting time. Once established *C. lutea* often spreads by self-sown seedlings and may even become a nuisance because of the freedom with which these appear.

COSMOS **kos**-*mos* (Purple Mexican Aster; Cosmos). Half-hardy annuals with pink, red, or white daisy-like flowers in summer and fine, feathery foliage. The species commonly grown is *C. bipinnatus*.

Cordon apples.

Gladiolus cormlets.

Cornus nuttallii.

73

Culture: Sow seeds in light soil in temperature of 60° to 65° in March; prick off seedlings 2 in. apart in deep seed boxes and harden off in a frame for planting outdoors 1 ft. to 1½ ft. apart in May in ordinary soil in warm, dryish border.

COTINUS *kot-***eye**-*nus* (Smoke-tree; Wig Tree). Hardy deciduous shrubs grown for their foliage which colours brilliantly in autumn and *C. coggygria* also for the curious inflorescences composed of masses of silk-like hairs or filaments which are at first purplish-brown but age to grey. It is this that gives it the name Smoke-tree. Both this and *C. americana* grow 12 ft. to 15 ft. high. These shrubs are often known in gardens by their former names *Rhus cotinus* and *R. cotinoides*.
Culture: Plant November to March in ordinary well-drained soil and open, sunny position. No regular pruning required.
Propagation: By cuttings of well-ripened growth inserted in sandy soil in a frame or sheltered place outdoors in October.

COTONEASTER *ko-toe-nee-***ass**-*ter* (Rose Box). Hardy evergreen and deciduous shrubs bearing scarlet fruits in winter. Suitable for open or shady shrubberies, trailing species against walls, or growing over tree roots and rocks or bare ground under trees. There are many species varying greatly in habit. Among the best are *C. adpressa*, completely prostrate

and deciduous; *C. horizontalis*, horizontal branching and able to mould itself to a rock or wall, deciduous; *C. microphylla*, rather similar to the last but evergreen; *C. dielsiana*, slender arching branches to 8 ft., deciduous; *C. franchetii*, stiffer, to 10 ft., evergreen; *C. simonsii*, erect, to 10 ft., semi-evergreen; and *C. frigida*, tree-like, to 25 ft., deciduous.
Culture: Plant October to February in ordinary soil. No regular pruning required.
Propagation: By seeds sown 1 in. deep outdoors in March, cuttings inserted in sandy soil outdoors in October or in a propagating frame in July; layering shoots in spring.

COTTON LAUREL, *see* Codiaeum.

COTTON THISTLE, *see* Onopordon.

COTYLEDONS. The seed-leaves which form before the true leaves appear. They are contained in the seed before germination and may be either in pairs (dicotyledons) or single (monocotyledons). The former are readily seen on tomato and many other plants after germination, while the onion presents a good example of the latter.

COWSLIP, *see* Primula.

CRAB APPLE, *see* Malus.

CRANESBILL, *see* Geranium.

CRATAEGUS *kra-***tee**-*gus* (May; Hawthorn; Quick; Cockspur Thorn; Glastonbury Thorn; Thorn). Hardy deciduous flowering trees, some varieties producing brilliant crops of scarlet berries in the autumn. There are many species and varieties. Among the best for the garden are the varieties of the common hawthorn, *C. oxyacantha* with double pink and double scarlet flowers. Both make densely branched spiny trees to 20 ft. in height.
Culture: Plant October to March in ordinary soil and open, sunny positions. Regular pruning is not necessary, but overgrown specimens may be reduced in size and thinned out in February.
Propagation: Species by seed sown ½ in. deep outdoors in March. Choice varieties and double-flowered thorns, by grafting in March or budding in July on to seedlings of the common hawthorn.

CREEPING FORGET-ME-NOT, *see* Omphalodes.

CREEPING JENNY, *see* Lysimachia.

CREOSOTE. An oily liquid obtained from wood tar. It is an excellent wood preservative, but as the fumes from it are harmful to plants over a long period it has largely been replaced for garden purposes

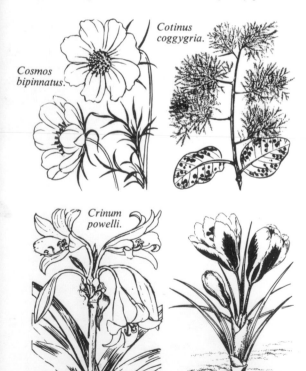

Cotinus coggygria.

Cosmos bipinnatus.

Crinum powelli.

Crocus chrysanthus E. A. Bowles.

74

by copper naphthanate solutions.

CRESYLIC ACID. As liquid carbolic acid this has long been used as a soil steriliser, but although it is effective against soil pests it has little effect on fungi. It is sold as an almost pure solution which must be diluted by adding 39 parts of water to each part of solution. It is then used at the rate of 1 gal. to each bushel of soil, after which the soil should be covered for 48 hours before being spread out to dry. It is ready for use 3 weeks later. The acid must be kept off hands and clothes.

CRIMSON FLAG, *see* Schizostylis.

CRINUM kri-*num* (Cape Lily). Tender and nearly hardy bulbous-rooted perennials with pink or white lily-like flowers. *C. longifolium* and *C. powelli* are both good species for outdoor culture in sheltered places.
Culture: The hardy crinums will grow in any deep, well-worked and freely drained soil, but their flowers will be much better if the soil is rather rich. Plant in March in a sunny sheltered position such as near the base of a south wall. The bulbs are very large and need to be planted so that their tips are just covered with soil. In cold districts a little dry straw may be spread over the surface in the autumn as a safeguard. Most species other than *C. longiflorum* and *C. powellii* are definitely tender and must be grown in the greenhouse. These can be potted in March in a good compost of loam, peat and sand and should be watered moderately at first but more freely as growth commences. In the autumn when foliage dies down, watering should be discontinued gradually, and the pots containing the bulbs stored on their sides beneath the greenhouse staging in a temperature of about 50°. The plants are restarted into growth in the spring when a temperature of about 60° to 65° is desirable.
Propagation: By seed sown in a warm greenhouse in the spring, and by offsets removed from the parent bulbs when these are lifted.

CROCUS kro-*kuss.* Hardy bulbous-rooted perennials. The well-known Dutch crocuses are much used as edgings to beds and borders and are also suitable for naturalising in grass. The species are delightful for rock gardens. There are autumn-flowering kinds such as *C. speciosus, C. sativus* and *C. zonatus;* others that flower in winter such as *C. imperati* and *C. chrysanthus;* early spring-flowering species such as *C. biflorus, C. tomasinianus, C. sieberi* and *C. susianus* as well as the more familiar spring-flowering crocus varieties which are hybrids. Colours include all shades from white and palest lilac to deep purple and violet and from pale yellow to deep orange-yellow.
Culture: The soil should be open and well-drained, but not liable to dry out badly in summer. Add leaf-mould or peat and some sharp sand for the choice

Cotoneaster franchetii.

species. Plant spring-flowering varieties in early autumn and autumn-flowering species in July. The corms should be planted 3 in. deep and about the same distance apart. It is not necessary to lift and replant annually, but if flowers show a deterioration in numbers and quality, corms should be carefully dug up as soon as the foliage dies down, and should be placed in shallow trays in a dry, airy shed until planting time.
Propagation: By offsets removed from the parent corms when the latter are lifted, and also by seeds sown as soon as ripe in an unheated greenhouse or frame.

CROTON, *see* Codiaeum.

CROWFOOT, *see* Ranunculus.

CROWN. A term often applied to the junction of root and stem on herbaceous plants and others of similar growth, particularly those of rosette-like habit.

CROWN IMPERIAL, *see* Fritillaria.

CRYPTANTHUS *krip-***tan-***thus.* These are dwarf bromeliads which make low rosettes of often wavy leaves which remind one of starfish. *C. bromelioides tricolor* is the most spectacular with brilliant pale pink and cream variegation. *C. zonatus* and its variety *zebrinus* have transverse bands of white and brown on the leaves, while *C. bivittatus* has longitudinal buff and red stripes. *C. beuckeri* has pink and light green stripes.

Culture: Cryptanthus are easily grown in porous orchid-type compost and will stand very adverse conditions, though they prefer a warm, moist atmosphere. They are very useful for bowl gardens or the front of greenhouse stagings, but may be difficult to place satisfactorily in a jardinière or similar container owing to their flatness. Re-pot when necessary in March.

Propagation: By removal of rooted offsets in March.

CRYPTOMERIA *krip-toe-***me***-re-a.* Evergreen cone-bearing trees grown for the beauty of their foliage. The best is *C. japonica elegans* with feathery foliage, green in summer turning bronzy-red in winter. It will reach a height of 30 ft.

Culture: Plant October to April in good, loamy soil and a sunny but not too exposed position.

Propagation: Species by seed sown in a greenhouse or frame in spring. Garden varieties by cuttings in July in sandy soil in a propagating frame.

CTENANTHE, *see* Maranta.

CUCKOO SPIT. This insect is fairly common in gardens during the summer months. Its presence is clearly indicated by small patches of froth appearing on the shoots of roses, carnations, etc. Under the protection of this covering the creamy-white larvae pierce the shoots and suck the sap. They make their appearance in early summer. On a small scale hand picking is the most effective method of getting rid of this pest but where the attack is widespread the infected shoots should first be syringed with water to clear away the froth and then given a thorough spraying with an insecticide such as BHC, malathion or nicotine. This is also known as froghopper.

CUCUMBER. Can be grown either in heated greenhouses or in frames, on a hot-bed, but the best and biggest crops are obtained from greenhouses.

For this purpose seed should be sown singly in small pots in a temperature of 65° to 70° at intervals from January until the end of April. As soon as the plants make one rough leaf each they should be transferred singly to small pots of John Innes compost. Water rather freely throughout. The fruiting beds should be prepared either on the floor of a low span-roofed greenhouse or on a flat staging in a taller structure. In either case the rooting medium should be rich compost of fibrous loam, leaf-mould, and well-rotted manure. A ridge of compost about 15 in. wide and 7 in. deep in the centre is sufficient for young plants. When roots appear on the surface they should be covered with a thin layer of rich, light compost similar to that used in the preparation of the ridge. The plants should be from 3 ft. to 5 ft. apart, and the shoots must be tied to wires strained lengthwise along the house.

Main growths may be allowed to run until they reach the apex of the roof. Side growths are trained horizontally and are pinched at the first or second leaf joint beyond the first fruit that sets. The plants should be syringed daily with tepid water and must be shaded from strong sunshine. Weak liquid manure can be applied as soon as the first fruits begin to develop.

In heated frames cucumbers can be planted in April and in unheated frames at the end of May or early in June. For this purpose seed should be sown as for indoor cucumbers but in March.

Ridge cucumbers, which are much hardier than any other kind, can be planted outdoors, in early June, on ridges of good soil built up in a sunny sheltered place. They should be watered freely during hot weather. Seed of ridge cucumbers should be sown in April.

CUCUMBER TREE, *see* Magnolia.

CUP AND SAUCER VINE, *see* Cobaea.

CUP FLOWER, *see* Nierembergia.

CUPHEA **kew**-*fee-a* (Mexican Cigar Flower). Throughout the summer *C. ignea*, a bushy evergreen

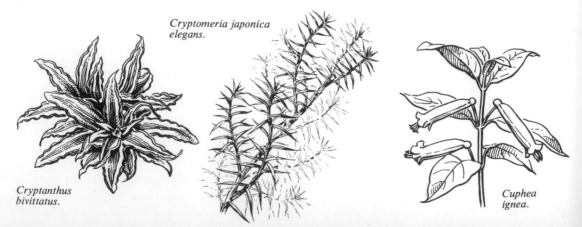

Cryptomeria japonica elegans.

Cryptanthus bivittatus.

Cuphea ignea.

Newly planted cucumbers.

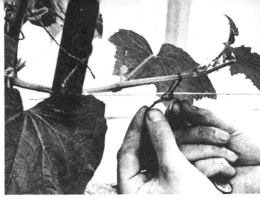

Tying cucumber side shoots.

Female (left) and male (right) cucumber flowers.

Cutting a cucumber.

plant 12 in. in height, produces scarlet and white tubular flowers.

Culture: It should be kept fairly dry during the winter in a temperature of about 50°. In spring the plants are cut hard back to induce new growths, some of which may then be taken off and rooted in a propagating frame with a temperature of about 70°. When rooted they should be potted on singly into 3 in. pots and again into 4½ in. ones, using the John Innes No. 2 compost for both pottings. Two or three stoppings are necessary to produce bushy, well-shaped plants, which during the summer should be kept in a temperature of about 60°. Frequent syringing is helpful during the summer.

Propagation: Apart from cuttings, already described, *C. ignea* may also be increased by seed sown in about 70° in early spring. After being pricked out the seedlings can then be potted up and grown on in the same way as the cuttings.

CUPRESSUS *ku-pres-us* (Cypress). Quick-growing evergreen trees some of which are used to form hedges and windbreaks. *C. macrocarpa*, the most popular, suffers from the disadvantage of .being subject to damage by wind and frost even when fully matured. *C. leylandii* is much hardier but not so easy to obtain. It is a hybrid between *C. macrocarpa* and *Chamaecyparis nootkatensis* and its correct name is *Cupressocyparis leylandii* but in gardens the more manageable name, *C. leylandii* is commonly used. All species may also be grown as isolated specimens for which purpose *C. leylandii* and *C. arizonica* are especially desirable.

Culture and Propagation: As for chamaecyparis, ex-

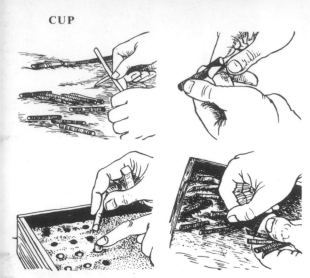

Root Cuttings: Cutting roots into 2 in. lengths (top left); trimming the base of each cutting (top right); inserting the cuttings either vertically (bottom left) or horizontally (bottom right).

Preparing a hardwood cutting.

cept that *C. macrocarpa* transplants rather badly and is best grown in a young state in pots, so that it can be finally planted with a minimum of root disturbance.

CURRANT, BLACK.
Plant November to March in good, rich, well cultivated, rather moist soil and sunny or partially shaded positions, spacing bushes at least 6 ft. apart. After planting cut all stems back to within 4 in. to 6 in. of ground level. In subsequent years prune annually after fruit has been gathered, cutting out as many as possible of the branches that have borne fruit but retaining all the strong, young, non-fruiting stems. Mulch each February with well-rotted manure or compost. Keep well watered in dry weather. There are many varieties varying in size of berry and the time at which they ripen. Recommended varieties for a succession are Boskoop Giant, Baldwin, Mendip Cross, Seabrook's Black and Amos Black.
Propagation: By cuttings of firm young stems 8 in. to 12 in. long inserted in ordinary soil outdoors in sheltered positions in October.

CURRANT, RED AND WHITE.
Plant November to March 4 ft. to 6 ft. apart each way in good, well-cultivated soil; sunny position for early crops; shady for late ones. Cut all branches back to about 6 in. after planting. In subsequent years shorten all side shoots to within 4 leaves of their base in June or July. Keep centres of bushes well open by removing badly placed or overcrowded branches in autumn. Mulch with decayed manure or compost each February. There are numerous varieties differing in size of berry and time of ripening. Recommended varieties are Fay's Prolific, Raby Castle, Laxton's No. 1 and White Dutch.

CUTTING.
A portion of growth severed from a plant for the purpose of producing another specimen of the same kind. Cuttings vary widely in character according to the class of plant from which they are taken, and are known as hard-wood cuttings, half-ripe cuttings, soft-wood cuttings, leaf cuttings, or root cuttings.

Hard-wood Cuttings are made from the growth of shrubs or trees which has become thoroughly ripened and firm. They are usually made between October and February. Shoots of the current year's growth from 6 in. to 12 in. long are suitable. The tips, which are almost always soft and unripened, should be removed, and the base of each trimmed with a sharp knife immediately below a joint or growth bud. There are some shrubs which root better if small side growths are taken with a 'heel'. If such laterals are held firmly, low down, and are simply pulled with a tearing motion from the parent branch, they will come away with a portion of older wood attached, and it is this that is referred to as a 'heel'. The torn-off strip of bark should be trimmed cleanly with a sharp knife close to the base of the cutting. The cuttings are lined out in a shallow trench 3 in. to 4 in. deep in a sheltered part of the garden. The soil should be made thoroughly firm around the cuttings with the foot. Evergreen shrubs may be propagated in the same way but it is wise to give the choicer varieties the protection of a frame.

Leaf Cuttings provide a means of propagating such plants as streptocarpus, gloxinia, *Begonia rex*, saintpaulia and ramonda. The practice with *B. rex* is simply to crack the midribs of the leaves by doubling them over and using pressure with the finger and thumb. The leaf is then laid flat in a well-drained pan filled with peat, loam and sand. Small pebbles are used to press the cracked portions of the leaf ribs close against the compost, and the pan is then placed in a warm propagating frame, kept closed to reduce the need for watering to a minimum. Streptocarpus and gloxinia leaves may be treated in a similar manner. Ramondas do not require artificial heat to root them, but should be placed in a shady frame. Nor are the leaves cracked but are pressed into the soil stalk end first, a method also used for saintpaulias, which,

Taking a softwood cutting   *Trimming the cutting below a joint.*   *Inserting the cuttings in sandy soil.*

however, need warmth. Choose foliage grown and firm and showing no signs of decay.

Root Cuttings are principally used for thick-rooted perennials such as anchusa, oriental poppies and *Statice latifolia*, but even some fibrous-rooted plants may be so propagated, including phlox and gaillardia. Romneyas, all the sumachs, aralias, and such tender plants as *Nicotiana affinis*, Zonal pelargoniums, and bouvardias are a few other subjects which may be increased in this way. Vegetables include seakale and horse-radish. In all cases short pieces of root are placed in sandy soil in winter or just before their normal season of growth. Ornamental plants are usually started in a frame or greenhouse, the tender kinds in warmth, but root cuttings of horse-radish and seakale can be inserted outdoors where they are to grow.

Soft-wood Cuttings are made from young shoots. They provide the most efficient means of propagating a great variety of plants such as pelargoniums, fuchsias, hydrangeas, pentstemons, violas, heliotropes, salvias, dahlias, and chrysanthemums. Closely allied to this type of cutting is the half-ripened cutting frequently used for propagating shrubs and prepared from firm side-shoots in June, July and August. The cuttings, whether soft-wooded or half-ripe, are prepared by trimming the base of each cleanly through with a sharp knife just below a joint and removing the lower leaves. The cuttings should be inserted in sandy soil or even pure sand, vermiculite or pumice powder. They should not be put deeper than is necessary to hold them erect without moving. Shade is advisable and the cuttings are best rooted in a propagating frame. They must be kept moist and one efficient method of rooting them is by mist propagation.

CUTWORM. A general name given to various species of caterpillar which live in the soil and attack the roots or collars of plants often causing their

A begonia leaf cutting.

collapse or checking growth severely. Cutworms are exposed to birds by cultivation or may be killed by watering the soil with BHC or raking in a BHC or aldrin dust at any time of year. They can also be poisoned with Paris green mixed with bran as a bait but this is also poisonous to birds and domestic animals.

CYCLAMEN sik-*la-men* (Sowbread). Hardy and greenhouse perennial flowering plants with tuberous roots. The greenhouse varieties, derived from *C. persicum*, produce their large white, pink or red flowers in winter. *C. coum*, *C. neapolitanum*, *C. repandum* and *C. europaeum* are good species for outdoor cultivation. They have much smaller flowers produced mainly in summer and early autumn.

Culture: The hardy cyclamen should be planted

during August or September in cool, shady places and in soil well supplied with peat or leaf-mould. Just cover the corms with soil and thereafter leave them undisturbed for as long a period as possible as these species do not like root disturbance and take rather a long time to settle down after transplanting.

The greenhouse cyclamen are best grown from seed sown in April or August in a greenhouse. Sow very thinly in well-drained pans filled with porous compost, and germinate in an even temperature of about 60°. Water very carefully as overwatering may cause the seeds to decay. Transfer the tiny plants singly to small pots filled with John Innes compost and thereafter keep them growing steadily in a temperature of 55° to 60° and pot them on into larger receptacles as the smaller pots become filled with roots. At all times the top of the tuber must be kept just clear of the surface. Well grown plants will eventually need pots 5 in. to 6 in. in diameter and should start to flower the autumn of the year after that in which seed was sown. Remove pots to a shady frame in May and give little water during summer. Re-pot in August and gradually increase the water supply bringing back into the greenhouse at the end of September.

Propagation: Hardy cyclamen may also be raised from seed sown in a cool greenhouse or frame in spring. Alternatively old clusters of tubers can be lifted, separated and replanted in August or September.

CYDONIA, see Chaenomeles.

CYMBALARIA, see Linaria.

CYMBIDIUM sim-**bid**-ee-um. In this group of orchids many fine hybrids have been raised and most of these are quite easy to grow where a minimum winter temperature of 45° can be maintained. The range of colours is enormous and, as the plants flower in early spring, they make an invaluable addition to the greenhouse.

Culture: The best compost for cymbidiums is a light, fibrous loam with a little sphagnum moss and, although they do not need the free drainage of some other orchids, it is best to crock the pots reasonably

well. The thick, fleshy roots need plenty of room and as they grow quite quickly the plants must be re-potted every second year. This is done after flowering when the young shoots are about 3 in. long. Established plants need plenty of water and light shade in the summer, but rather less water is needed after flowering and in the winter, although the plants must never be allowed to become too dry. To get a good number of the flower stems, which grow about 30 in. tall, it is best to keep the plants undivided year after year.

Propagation: By division or by re-potting the pseudo-bulbs in March.

CYPERUS si-**per**-us (Umbrella Plant). The radiating leaves on long stiff stems which form the almost permanent flowerheads of the greenhouse cyperus give them the name of Umbrella Plants. The two species usually grown, and suitable for rooms, are C. alternifolius and C. diffusus; both have variegated forms.

Culture: Plants are easily grown in a cool greenhouse or rather cool room, in a moist atmosphere if possible, using rich but porous soil. Relatively small pots are recommended and they can stand in a saucer containing water in hot weather; like most of the sedge family they are marsh plants.

Propagation: By seeds sown in heat; by division of clumps; or by rooting the leafy flower rosettes in moist sand or even water.

CYPRESS, see Cupressus.

CYPRIPEDIUM si-pre-**pee**-de-um (Lady's Slipper; Slipper Orchid). This orchid is known as the Lady's Slipper on account of the shape of the pouched lip of the flower. The name cypripedium is applied rather loosely to a large family comprising nearly 100 species and innumerable hybrids of mostly terrestrial orchids. This family is divided into four sections, of which the Paphiopedilum group may be considered the most popular for greenhouse work. Although some of the hardy species can be grown satisfactorily out-of-doors they are really better in a frost-proof greenhouse for the winter. The cypripediums of the

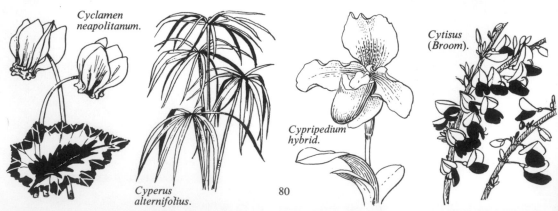

Cyclamen neapolitanum.

Cyperus alternifolius.

Cypripedium hybrid.

Cytisus (Broom).

Potting young greenhouse cyclamen.

Re-potting an old cyclamen tuber.

Cymbidium hybrid.

paphiopedilum group mostly possess large, leathery leaves, often mottled, and the flowers are excellent for cutting, but they need a winter temperature of between 55° and 65°. Two of the easiest to grow are *C. insigne*, with purple-spotted greenish-yellow flowers, and its variety *C. i. sanderae*, yellow and white, both of which grown to about 10 in. high and flower in winter.

Culture: All cypripediums can be grown in well-crocked pans of equal parts peat and fibrous loam mixed with sphagnum moss and broken brick, and during the summer they are best plunged outside. Once established, after being potted in the spring, they must never be allowed to become dry. Alternatively the hardy kinds can be planted outdoors in moist, peaty soil and sheltered, partially shaded places.

Propagation: By dividing the plants at potting time in spring, when the plants should go into a compost of 2 parts coarse peat and 1 of sphagnum moss, with a liberal sprinkling of sand and chippings. Plenty of water is needed at all times but rather less in winter, and shade from hot sun is advisable in summer.

CYTISUS *si-*tiss*-us* (Broom). Hardy and half-hardy deciduous flowering shrubs. In addition to the common yellow-flowered species, *C. scoparius*, there are numerous garden varieties with very brightly coloured flowers. All grow 5 ft. to 6 ft. high and flower in May and June. The greenhouse pot plant commonly known as *Genista fragrans* is correctly *Cytisus fragrans*.

Culture: These are essentially shrubs for sunny places—the larger hardy kinds in the shrub border, the smaller hardy varieties in the rock garden or on dry walls, and the half-hardy species in pots in a sunny greenhouse. They are not particular as regards soil, and they resist drought well. All resent root disturbance and so the hardy kinds should be planted out from pots. Firm staking is important for the same reason. November to March is the best season for planting hardy kinds, while the tender varieties can be re-potted as soon as the flowers fade. All may be lightly cut back immediately after flowering to prevent them from becoming straggly.

The greenhouse kinds should be kept in a minimum temperature of 45° in winter, but may be placed outdoors in a sunny position from June to September. The final potting into 5 in. pots of John Innes No. 2 compost is normally carried out in the spring following propagation, and during the second summer and winter great care is necessary at all stages, otherwise

Left: *Preparing a dahlia cutting.* Centre: *Planting dormant dahlia tubers in late April.* Right: *Staking and tying a dahlia.*

either the leaves or the flowers fall. Definitely not a good plant for the beginner!

Propagation: Species by seeds sown in a frame in March, April or as soon as ripe in summer. Choice varieties by cuttings with a heel in July or August in a propagating frame. Cuttings of the greenhouse kinds are usually taken in early spring and grown on very slowly in the greenhouse right through the year, with frequent stoppings to produce well-shaped plants.

DABOECIA *dab-o-ee-see-a* (Irish Heath; St. Dabeoc's Heath). A dwarf heather-like shrub for rock gardens, open banks and beds or in wild, heathy places. Purple or white flowers June to September. The only species grown is *D. cantabrica.*

Culture: The daboecia has an aversion to lime and the ideal soil is sandy peat and loam. Plant in spring and treat in the same way as the dwarf hardy heathers.

Propagation: By cuttings during summer in sandy soil in a propagating frame or by layering in May.

DAFFODIL, *see* Narcissus.

DAHLIA correctly **dar**-*lee-a* but commonly pronounced **day**-*lee-a*. All the numerous types of dahlia

are tuberous-rooted tender perennials. Included in the popular range are the dwarf bedding types, the single and collerette varieties, decoratives in various sizes with double flowers having relatively broad petals, and cactus varieties also double in various sizes but with narrow petals. Show and pompon dahlias have ball-like flowers and there are also orchid-flowered and anemone-flowered types. All flower from July until October or later if there is no frost and all have a most extensive colour range including white, pink, red, crimson, yellow, orange, apricot and purple also two colours in the same flower.

Culture: A reasonably rich well-dug soil is essential. Planting cannot be attempted until all danger of frost has passed, from early May in the south-west to June in Scotland. 3 ft. to 4 ft. each way is required by the largest varieties, but the bedding types may be planted from 1 ft. to 18 in. apart. These latter do not require any staking but this is essential with all the taller types. Most of the small flowered types can be allowed to make their own natural growth. The large flowered varieties should be thinned to half-a-dozen or so main stems per plant even when grown for garden decoration and for large flowers the buds should be restricted to one per flowering stem,

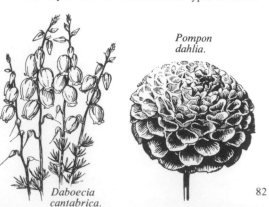

Daboecia cantabrica.

Pompon dahlia.

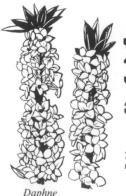

Daphne mezereum.

Daphne burkwood

82

Left: *Disbudding dahlias for large flowers.* Centre: *Storing dahlias for the winter in a frost-proof place.* Right: *Damping down in a greenhouse.*

small side buds being removed and the terminal buds retained. Water freely during dry spells, and feed with weak liquid manure or fertiliser when the flower buds show.

Lift roots when top growth has been blackened by frost in October or November. Cut stems back to within 6 in. of the tubers, place in a greenhouse or frost-proof shed to dry for a few days and then store in a cool, dry but frost-proof shed or room.

Propagation: Cuttings provide the ideal means of increasing stock. The tubers can be started into growth in February in boxes filled with a compost of loam, leaf-mould and sand. If moderately watered and kept in a temperature of 55°, they will soon produce shoots which are severed as cuttings as soon as they reach 2 in. or 3 in. in length. Trim each cutting beneath a joint, remove the lower leaves and insert in sandy compost in a propagating frame preferably with bottom heat.

As soon as rooted the young plants should be potted singly in John Innes compost and gradually hardened before going out to a cold frame.

Division of the roots is a simple means of increase when only a few plants are required. Growth buds appear at the base of the old stems, so start the old tubers into growth as for cuttings and then divide with a sharp knife when it can be seen where the new shoots are. Each division must have at least one tuber and one shoot, preferably more. They may then be boxed up or potted and hardened in the same way as cuttings.

Seed, if sown in February in a temperature of 60° to 65° will also produce plants to bloom the same summer. The seedlings must be potted singly as soon as they are large enough to handle, and are then treated in exactly the same manner as recommended for cuttings.

DAME'S ROCKET, *see* Hesperis.

DAME'S VIOLET, *see* Hesperis.

DAMPING DOWN. The process of increasing humidity in the greenhouse by wetting floors, walls and staging. In hot weather it has the effect of lowering the temperature and of reducing the rate of transpiration from the leaves of the plants. It should not be practised in winter except where tropical plants are being grown in a high temperature. On hot, sunny days in summer most plants may be included in the wetting, provided ample air is admitted.

DAMPING-OFF. A disease, mainly of seedlings grown under glass, which causes them to decay at or just above soil level and topple over. It can spread rapidly under damp, warm, badly ventilated conditions or among overcrowded seedlings. Thin sowing, early pricking-off, the use of sterilised soil, good ventilation, correct temperatures and careful watering, will all keep damping-off in check. If it does occur, watering with Cheshunt Compound, which can be purchased as a powder ready for mixing with water, will prevent its spread.

DAPHNE daf-*nee.* Evergreen and deciduous shrubs and rock plants many of which have very fragrant flowers. Among the best deciduous kinds are *D. mezereum,* 3 ft. to 4 ft., white, January to March, and *D. burkwoodii,* 3 ft. to 4 ft., pink, May. Good evergreen shrubs are *D. odora,* 2 ft., rose, January to March; *D. collina,* 3 ft., purple, May; *D. cneorum,* 1 ft., pink, May; *D. blagayana,* prostrate, creamy-white, May; and *D. retusa,* 3 ft. to 4 ft., rosy-purple, May. For the rock garden a real gem is *D. petraea,* also known as *D. rupestris,* 4 in. rose-pink, April.

Culture: Plant October to April in good loamy soil well-drained but not dry. *D. odora* should have a sheltered position. *D. petraea* is suitable for ledges in a sunny place in the rock garden.

DAP

Propagation: By cuttings in sandy soil in July in a propagating frame; species by seed sown in a frame or greenhouse in March.

DATE PALM, *see* Phoenix.

DATURA *da-***tu**-*ra* (Angel's Trumpet). Half-hardy annuals, shrubs and trees with large trumpet-shaped flowers, white in *D. suaveolens, D. arborea,* and *D. cornigera,* scarlet in *D. sanguinea,* yellow in *D. chlorantha.*
Culture: Plant towards the end of May or early June in rather rich well-drained soil and sheltered sunny positions. Water freely during the growing season. Lift in late September and place in a greenhouse with temperature of 45° to 50°. Water spraringly at this period. If grown throughout in pots in the greenhouse the plants should be grown in John Innes No. 2 compost and be gradually potted on into 12 in. pots, using a light, sandy soil. During the summer they need plenty of warmth and water, but in winter they should be kept fairly dry and little more than frost-proof. Pruning is done in March, when the side-shoots are cut back almost to the main branches.
Propagation: By cuttings prepared from young shoots 6 in. in length inserted in sandy soil in a

propagating frame in spring or early summer. Temperature required, 65° to 70°.

DAVIDIA *dav-***id**-*ee-a* (Ghost Tree; Handkerchief Tree; Dove Tree). Handsome deciduous trees the greenish flowers of which are surrounded by large white bracts which hang like handkerchiefs in May. The species grown, *D. involucrata,* is 50 ft. high.
Culture: Plant November to March in good, loamy soil and sunny but not too exposed position. No pruning desirable.
Propagation: By seed sown in a greenhouse or frame in March.

DAY LILY, *see* Hemerocallis.

DD. A petroleum by-product used for the control of root-knot eelworm in soils. It is injected into the soil and after treatment from 4 to 6 weeks must elapse before planting is carried out.

DDT. An abbreviation for dichloro-diphenyl-tri-chloroethane, a synthetic insecticide that can be used as a dust, spray or smoke. It can be used on all plants except cucumbers, melons and marrows, for controlling whiteflies, thrips, capsid bugs, caterpillars, leatherjackets and wasps. DDT works chiefly through the residual toxic deposit left on the plant, where it kills many insects which come into contact with it.

DEAD NETTLE, *see* Lamium.

DELPHINIUM *del-***fin**-*e-um* (Larkspur). Hardy herbaceous perennials and annuals. There are many species, but for the gardener these are not so important as the garden hybrids connected with *D. elatum* and *D. belladonna,* otherwise known as *D. cheilanthum.* There are a great many varieties of the 'elatum' type ranging from 3 ft. to 7 ft. in height and in colour from white, palest mauve and lavender to intense purple. The flowers are produced in long, dense spikes. The 'belladonna' varieties are less numerous, 3 ft. to 4 ft. high, freely branched and with their flowers in loose sprays. All flower in June and July. The annual larkspurs, obtained from *D. ejacis,* produce graceful spikes of bloom 2 ft. to 4 ft. high during the summer. The colour range includes blue, pink and white.
Culture: All the perennial delphiniums like good, rich, well-drained soil. The ground must be deeply dug and liberally enriched with manure or compost. Good drainage must be ensured. Planting, except on light, sandy soils, is best done in early spring. During the summer water freely in dry weather and feed when the flower spikes show. Reduce main stems of the 'elatum' varieties to 5 or 6 per plant and stake the taller varieties securely. Precautions must be taken against slugs.
Most of the species require a sheltered and sunny

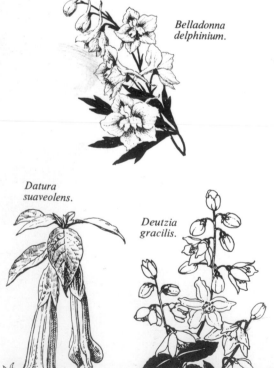

Belladonna delphinium.

Datura suaveolens.

Deutzia gracilis.

position and an exceptionally well-drained soil. They are usually fairly short plants, 2 ft. to 3 ft. in height and colours include in addition to the 'elatum' and 'belladonna' range yellows and bright reds.

The annuals larkspurs will thrive in any reasonably good garden soil. Seed should be sown outdoors where the plants are to flower, either in August, early September or during March and April. Autumn-sown plants are usually finer than spring-sown specimens. Seedlings should be thinned to at least 15 in. apart.

Propagation: The ideal method of increasing stocks of the large flowering delphiniums and varieties of *D. belladonna* is by cuttings, taken in early spring before the young shoots have become hollow. If inserted firmly in sandy soil in a cold frame they root readily. Division in spring affords a simple method of increase. All perennial delphiniums can also be raised from seeds which may be sown as soon as ripe in August or in spring in a cold frame or greenhouse. Seedlings are particularly subject to attack by slugs.

DERRIS. A substance obtained from the roots of certain tropical plants. It is non-poisonous to warm-blooded animals but a powerful poison to almost all insects. It may be either employed dry, the powder being blown on to the foliage with special bellows, or as a spray prepared according to manufacturer's instructions. It is deadly to fish and should never be allowed to come into contact with water containing them.

DEUTZIA doyts-*ee-a* (Japanese Snow-flower). Hardy deciduous shrubs with white, pink or purplish flowers in early summer. One species, *D. gracilis*, is sometimes grown as a greenhouse pot plant. The species most commonly grown outdoors is *D. scabra* a vigorous shrub reaching a height of 7 ft. to 8 ft. The flowers, produced in early summer, are white or purplish-rose.

Culture: Plant in ordinary soil and a sunny position in autumn or spring. Regular pruning is not required but thin out old growths occasionally after flowering. Where *D. gracilis* is grown in pots the plants should be potted in November and plunged in an ash bed out of doors until thoroughly established, after which they may be forced into bloom in a temperature of 65° to 70°.

Propagation: Cuttings of half-ripened wood taken in July root readily in sandy soil in a propagating frame or cuttings of fully ripe growth can be rooted outdoors in autumn in sandy soil.

DEVIL-IN-A-BUSH, *see* Nigella.

DIANTHUS die-**an**-*thus* (Pink; Indian Pink; Sweet William). This is a big genus of plants and one which has given the garden a number of highly popular and decorative plants, including the border

Davidia involucrata.

Dusting peas with DDT.

Thinning delphinium shoots.

carnation and the perpetual flowering carnation. For the sake of convenience carnations are described separately in this encyclopaedia under their own name and here only the garden pinks, annual pinks, sweet williams and rock garden dianthus will be found.

The common garden pink is derived from *D. plumarius* but other species have been crossed with it to produce greater variety and pinks have also been crossed with perpetual flowering carnations to produce *D. allwoodii*, a race of pinks with a longer flowering season and greater range of colour than the common garden pink and with border carnations to produce finer flowers. All these are hardy perennials suitable for beds and borders and all flower in summer. They vary in height from about 9 in. to 18 in., all flower from late May onwards and colours include white, pink, rose and crimson.

The annual pinks are mainly derived from *D. chinensis*, the Indian pink. They are half-hardy and summer flowering but must be renewed from seed each year. Colours are mainly in shades of pink, rose and crimson. Height 12 in. to 18 in.

The sweet william is derived from *D. barbatus*, flowers in early summer and in favourable places is a perennial, but is almost invariably treated as a biennial to be renewed annually from seed. Again there are hybrids with other species or races of dianthus some of which are decorative and useful garden plants. Colours include pink, scarlet, maroon and white. Height 18 in. to 24 in.

The rock garden dianthus are mostly wild species flowering in spring or early summer, small tufted plants such as *D. neglectus* or trailing ones such as *D. deltoides*, but there are also small garden hybrids which are best grown in the rock garden or on a dry wall. Colours include white, pink, rose, red and crimson.

Culture of Annual Pinks: Sow in sandy soil in a greenhouse at 60° to 65° in February or March. Prick off into boxes and harden off for planting out in late May or early June in ordinary, well-drained soil and open sunny position.

Culture of Perennial Pinks: Plant in March, April, or October in well-drained ordinary soil and open,

sunny positions. All do well in soils containing lime or chalk. Renew plants from cuttings or division every few years as they tend to deteriorate fairly quickly.

Culture of Sweet William: Sow outdoors or in a frame in May. Plant in June or July, 6 in. apart in rows 1 ft. apart in a nursery bed of good, well worked soil and transfer to flowering quarters in September or March. They like fairly good soil and an open, sunny position.

Culture of Rock Garden Pinks: Plant from pots at practically any time of year or from open ground in spring in light, well-drained soil and open, sunny positions. Particularly suitable for ledges in the rock garden and the tops of dry walls.

Propagation: Perennial pinks by cuttings of non-flowering shoots in early summer rooted in sandy soil in a frame. Also seed sown in a greenhouse or frame in spring. All rock garden species can be raised from seed in this way, some can be increased by cuttings as described for pinks and some can be divided in spring.

DIBBER. As used in the greenhouse this is a small piece of wood about 6 in. long and varying in thickness from that of a pencil to about ¾ in., with one end tapered to a blunt point. It is used for the pricking out of small seedlings by first making a hole with it for the roots and then placing the seedling in position before inserting the dibber at an angle and levering the adjacent soil up against the roots. Also used for inserting cuttings. Dibbers for outdoor use are much thicker, often made from old spade or fork handles rounded or pointed at the end. They are used for planting seedlings of various kinds and are particularly useful for brassicas and leeks.

DICENTRA *die-cen-tra* (Bleeding Heart). Hardy herbaceous perennials with rose or pink and white flowers in early summer. Suitable for sunny or shady beds or borders. The species commonly grown are *D. eximia*, 1 ft. tall; *D. formosa*, 15 in. and *D. spectabilis*, 2 ft. to 3 ft. The last is also grown as a pot plant for flowering in the greenhouse in spring.

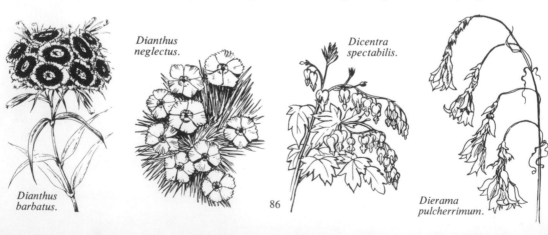

Dianthus neglectus.

Dicentra spectabilis.

Dianthus barbatus.

Dierama pulcherrimum.

Pricking out seedlings with a dibber.

Dieffenbachia picta.

Culture: Plant in ordinary soil in October, March or April. *D. spectabilis* may be potted in October in John Innes compost and grown in a greenhouse, temperature, 45° to 60°, until after flowering, when pots are best placed in a frame or shady place outdoors.

Propagation: By division at planting time.

DIDYMELLA *did-ee-***mel**-*a*. The fungus *D. lycopersici* was at one time a troublesome cause of Tomato Stem Rot or Canker, but this disease is not of common occurrence nowadays. Its effect is seen as a shrinking and cracking of the base of the stem, followed by a covering of small black spots, and if left unchecked it can cause serious losses. It can be controlled by steam sterilisation of the soil before planting, or in isolated cases by watering the soil with Cheshunt Compound after removing the affected plants.

DIEFFENBACHIA *die-fen-***bak**-*ee-a* (Dumb Cane; Mother-in-Law Plant). Really warm greenhouse plants, the dieffenbachias are also used for temporary purposes such as exhibitions and shop windows. Leaves are large, more or less oblong, and in the varieties usually grown—mainly forms of *D. picta*—are spotted with white to a greater or lesser degree. The plants eventually grow several feet tall, on substantial stems. All parts of the plant contain an acrid sap which is poisonous and must not get near the eyes or mouth. In the mouth, indeed, it causes the tongue to swell and may cause choking and inability to speak—hence the old name Dumb Cane and the unkind modern name of Mother-inLaw Plant.

Culture: Pot in March in John Innes compost. Water freely in spring and summer, moderately autumn and winter. Temperature: April to September, 60° to 70°; October to March, 55° to 60°.

As long as the conditions are warm and reasonably equable dieffenbachias often put up with rather dry air, though it must be emphasised that they really prefer a moist atmosphere. In the average living room, draughts and changing temperatures in winter are likely to play havoc with the leaves.

Propagation: Pieces of stem 2 in. or 3 in. long, containing at least one bud, will root and sprout readily if dried for a couple of days after cutting and then placed in sand kept warm and moist.

DIERAMA *die-er-***am**-*a* (Wand Flower). *D. pulcherrimum* is a hardy perennial with long, narrow, grass-like leaves and slender flower stems bearing numerous short trails of purple or white flowers in June or July. The plant makes corms.

Culture: Plant in March in good, loamy soil well-drained, but not dry, in a sunny but reasonably sheltered position.

Propagation: By seeds sown in a frame or greenhouse in spring. Seedlings should be planted out as soon as they are a few inches high in a sheltered nursery bed and should not go to their permanent positions until the following year. Can also be increased by division of the clusters of corms in March.

DIERVILLA, *see* Weigela.

DIGITALIS *dig-it-***a**-*lis* (Foxglove). Hardy biennial and perennial herbs. Suitable for borders or naturalising in woodlands and wild gardens. *D. purpurea* is the biennial species commonly grown. It is 4 ft. to 5 ft. tall and typically has rose-purple flowers but there are garden varieties in a considerable colour range. The 'Excelsior' varieties hold their flowers out all round the stem instead of hanging them on one side as in the common form. Modern strains of foxglove are extremely handsome and are highly serviceable for dry borders and sunless situations.

Culture of Perennial Species: Plant October or April

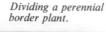
Disbudding rose buds.

Dioscorea discolor.

Dividing a perennial border plant.

in ordinary soil and sunny or shady places.

Culture of Biennial Species: Sow seeds in shady borders outdoors in April. Transplant seedlings 3 in. apart in a shady bed when large enough to handle. Transfer plants to flowering positions in October.

Propagation: Perennials by division of plants in March; seeds sown as directed for biennials.

DIMORPHOTHECA *die-mor-foth-ek-a* (Star of the Veldt). Hardy annuals with daisy-like flowers all summer in a variety of shades of orange, apricot, buff salmon and yellow. Height 12 in.

Culture: Sow seed in March or April in ordinary well-drained soil and sunny positions where plants are to flower. Thin seedlings to 9 in.

DINOCAP. This fungicide is a very useful control for powdery mildews which attacks roses and other garden plants.

DIOSCOREA *die-os-kor-ee-a*. The Yam family includes two plants sometimes grown in greenhouses for their large, handsomely marked, heart-shaped foliage purple beneath. These are *D. discolor*, in which the leaves, in different shades of green and purple, have a white line along the mid-rib, and *D. multicolor*, in which the dark green of the leaf is spotted with paler green. The latter has several varieties in which bronze, silver and yellow combine with green.

Culture: When growing, dioscoreas need warm, humid conditions, with rich compost containing rotted manure, and plenty of water. As the shoots die down in autumn the water supply is curtailed and in winter they should be kept perfectly dry and on the cool side. The tuberous roots can be left in their pots or stored in dry sand during the winter. *D. discolor*. is sometimes sold as a house plant and should survive for some time in summer if kept in an airy place out of direct sun and sprayed overhead.

Propagation: By dividing the tubers in winter.

DISBUDDING. The practice of removing side buds from clusters of flower buds in order to allow the main bud to produce a larger flower. Disbudding is frequently practised with roses, dahlias, chrysanthemums and carnations. The term is also used for the gradual removal of unwanted side growths on wall-trained fruit trees such as peaches, nectarines and Morello cherries.

DIVISION. One of the simplest methods of increasing many perennial plants, particularly those of herbaceous habit. Roots are lifted and divided into numerous pieces, each of which is then replanted separately to grow on into a new plant. Many plants can be divided by hand simply by pulling them apart. Tougher roots may need two small forks thrust in back-to-back and then levered apart. Occasionally a knife may be needed to cut through hard pieces. Each division should have both shoots and roots. The best time for division is usually the normal planting or potting time for the plant.

DIZYGOTHECA *dis-ee-***goth***-ek-a.* The plants with this dizzy name used to be called Aralia, and it is possible that they are stabilised juvenile forms of aralia species. This need not worry the grower, however. They are primarily foliage plants for the warm greenhouse, but can be used in rooms if warm, equable conditions, not too dry and stuffy, can be maintained. Anything untoward, such as a draught or a chill, will cause dropping of the leaves, which consist of narrow, toothed leaflets radiating from long stems. *D. elegantissima* has white mid-ribs; *D. veitchii* glossy leaflets with red undersides; and *D. kerchoveana* wavy-edged leaflets.
Culture: All like rich, acid soil with plenty of peat or leaf-mould. They should be potted in March in well-drained pots just large enough to accommodate the roots comfortably. Water fairly freely in summer, rather sparingly at other times. Temperature: April to September, 65° or more; October to March, 55° to 60°.
Propagation: By cuttings in heat.

DNC. An abbreviation for dinitro-ortho-cresol, an insecticide used as a winter wash for fruit trees. It will kill the eggs of red-spider mites, capsid bugs, aphides, apple suckers and some caterpillars.

DOGBERRY, *see* Cornus.

DOG'S-TOOTH VIOLET, *see* Erythronium.

DOGWOOD, *see* Cornus.

DOLPHIN FLY, *see* Aphis.

DORMANT. Most plants have a resting period when they are not in active growth and are described as dormant. During this period they need little or no water and, if grown in pots, should be stored in conditions appropriate to the particular plant. Some bulbous or tuberous rooted plants are commonly lifted and stored quite dry and without soil while dormant, e.g. tulips, hyacinths, gladioli and dahlias.

DORONICUM *dor-***on***-ik-um* (Leopard's Bane). Hardy herbaceous perennials with yellow daisy-flowers in spring. The species commonly grown, *D. plantagineum*, is 3 ft. tall. Suitable for borders, banks, or under shade of trees.
Culture: Plant autumn or early spring in ordinary soil. Lift, divide, and replant when becoming crowded.
Propagation: By division of roots in October or March.

DOUBLE MAY WEED, *see* Matricaria.

DOVE TREE, *see* Davidia.

DRACAENA *dra-***see***-na.* Many of the dracaenas and related cordylines (two pretty-well confused families) produce long, arching leaves which make them very decorative plants for the warm greenhouse, although they are seldom successful as house-plants. There are both green-leaved and variegated forms, and of the latter one of the best is *D. fragrans* Victoria with yellow and green stripes.
Culture: All do best in a mixture of loam, peat and sand. Most will do well in a 6 in. pot; as growth increases larger pots must be used but the dracaenas do not like to be over-potted. A warm, humid atmosphere and frequent watering, syringing and sponging of the leaves are all necessary to produce good plants and the variegated leaved ones, in particular, must be given full light. During the winter the plants still need fairly liberal watering but not overhead as the water tends to damage the leaves then. Temperature: April to September, 60° or more; October to March, 55° to 60°.
Propagation: Usually by pieces of stem or root inserted in a warm propagating frame in spring. The tops of old plants may also be rooted in this way.

DRAGON'S HEAD, *see* Physostegia.

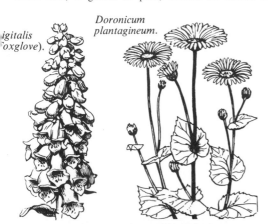
igitalis (Foxglove).
Doronicum plantagineum.

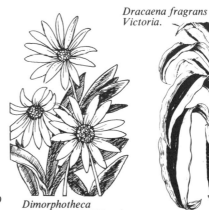
Dimorphotheca (Star of the Veldt).

Dracaena fragrans Victoria.

DRAINAGE. Before erecting a greenhouse, and particularly where the plants are to be grown in beds, the site must first be well-drained if there is any tendency to waterlogging. Three-inch pipe drains, put 2 ft. down and leading to a suitable outfall, provide the best method, but a trench partly filled with rubble, covered-in first with turf and then with soil, is usually quite effective on a small scale.

It is sometimes necessary to take similar steps to drain open land particularly where it lies low or is very heavy. Bad drainage will result in dead roots and poor growth or even the complete death of the whole plant.

In pots drainage is achieved by placing broken pieces of pot, known as 'crocks' concave side downwards over the drainage hole. Large pots may require as much as a 2 in. layer but normally $\frac{1}{2}$ in. of crocks is ample, and for pots below the $3\frac{1}{2}$ in. size no crocking is actually necessary although a handful of rough peat is sometimes used. Particular attention must be paid to the crocking when cacti, bromeliads and bulbous plants are being grown.

DRAWN. A descriptive term applied to plants which have become abnormally long and thin, with too widely-spaced joints. This type of faulty growth is usually caused by lack of light due to overcrowding or to growing the plants too far from the glass in greenhouses and frames, but it may also be caused by using too much heat in relation to the available light. The means of prevention are obvious.

DROPWORT, *see* Filipendula.

DRYAS dri-*ass* (Mountain Avens). Hardy evergreen trailing plants suitable for sunny rock gardens or banks. The species commonly grown is *D. octopetala* with white flowers rather like single roses.
Culture: Plant October, November or March in ordinary soil and open places. Will succeed in chalky soils.
Propagation: By seeds sown $\frac{1}{16}$ in. deep in a frame, April or May; by pegging down the trailing shoots in spring or early summer into sandy soil and detaching when well rooted.

DRY SET. A condition of tomato flowers in which the ovary in the centre does not enlarge to form a normal fruit but dries up and remains small, often no larger than $\frac{1}{8}$ in. in diameter. It is caused by faulty pollination and usually occurs where the atmosphere is too dry, although it may also occur on plants making excessive vegetative growth. It can be prevented by frequent overhead damping of the plants, particularly in hot weather, and by aiming at a steady, balanced growth.

DUMB CANE, *see* Dieffenbachia.

DUSTY MILLER, *see* Senecio.

DUTCHMAN'S PIPE, *see* Aristolochia.

DWARF CORNEL, *see* Cornus.

EARTHING-UP. The practice of drawing soil up in mounds or ridges around some plants. Potatoes are earthed-up to encourage the formation of tubers and prevent the tubers becoming green through exposure to light. Celery and leeks are earthed-up to blanch the stems. Sometimes broccoli and winter kales are earthed-up to give them greater security against winter gales.

EARWIGS. These familiar insects can do a great deal of damage to the leaves and flowers of some plants and are particularly troublesome with dahlias. They can be trapped in hollow bean stalks or inverted flower pots stuffed with hay and they can be killed by spraying or dusting with DDT or BHC.

ECCREMOCARPUS *ek-re-mo-***kar**-*pus* (Chilian Glory-flower). Half-hardy climbing plants with scarlet or orange-red flowers in summer. The only species grown is *E. scaber*.
Culture: Plant in May or June in ordinary, well-drained soil against south or south-west walls or to grow over sheltered arches. Protect the fleshy roots in October with a layer of cinder ashes and the base of the plant in severe weather with mats, dry straw or bracken.

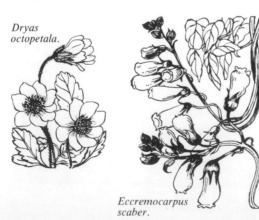

Dryas octopetala.

Eccremocarpus scaber.

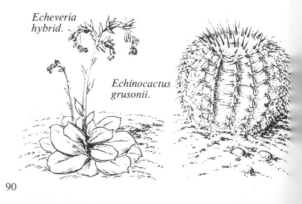

Echeveria hybrid.

Echinocactus grusonii.

Propagation: By seeds sown $\frac{1}{16}$ in. deep in well-drained pots of light, sandy soil in temperature of 60° to 65° in March or April.

ECHEVERIA *ek-ev-eer-ee-a*. These attractive succulents are suitable for greenhouses or rooms, needing only a sunny ledge or windowsill and protection from frost in winter. Although they will stand warmer conditions, dry air may cause the flowers to wither.

Most commonly seen as a pot plant is *E. retusa*, with large glaucous rosettes and tall stems carrying quantities of the waxy, orange-red, urn-shaped flowers in winter. *E. harmsii*, often sold under the name *Oliveranthus elegans*, has very large elongated bells, red with yellow tips, in late spring, on shorter stems; while the hybrid Worfield Wonder is a very compact plant with neat green rosettes and small, orange flowers, also in spring. *E. secunda*, with rosettes of grey-green leaves and short spikes of orange flowers in summer is often grown as a summer bedding plant particularly as a formal edging to beds or borders.

Culture: Most species are attractive and easily grown. They need a rich, open compost (John Innes potting compost is suitable), plenty of water in summer and relatively little in winter. In winter a temperature of 45° or more should be maintained; in summer natural temperatures are sufficient. When grown for summer bedding *E. secunda* is hardened off in a frame in May for planting out in early June and is returned to a frost-proof greenhouse in late September.

Propagation: Cuttings made from almost any part of the plant will root.

ECHINACEA *ek-in-ace-ee-a* (Purple Cone-flower). Hardy herbaceous perennial with purple flowers in late summer. The species grown, *E. purpurea*, is 3 ft. to 4 ft. tall.

Culture: Plant October or March in good, well-worked soil in well-drained sunny borders. Cut down flower stems when flowers fade.

Propagation: By division in March.

ECHINOCACTUS *ek-i-no-kak-tus* (Hedgehog Cactus). Greenhouse succulent plants. Very thick and fleshy, almost globose in some kinds, very spiny. There are numerous species, of which one of the most popular is *E. grusonii*, which makes such a large, rounded plant that it is sometimes called the Barrel Cactus.

Culture: Plant in well-drained pots in a sunny greenhouse or window, using a mixture of 2 parts fibrous sandy loam, 1 part brick rubble, old mortar, and sand. Re-pot every 3 or 4 years in March. Water scarcely at all September to April, whenever dry afterwards. Temperature: September to March, 50° to 55°. Natural temperature rest of the year.

Propagation: By seeds sown $\frac{1}{8}$ in. deep in well-drained pans of sandy soil in a temperature of 70° in March.

Earthing up celery.

Laying land drains.

ECHINOPS *ek-in-ops* (Globe Thistle). Hardy perennials with globular heads of blue flowers which may be dried for use as everlastings. The most popular species are *E. bannaticus*, 3 ft.; *E. humilis*, 4 ft.; *E. ritro*, 3 ft., and *E. sphaerocephalus*, 5 ft. to 6 ft. All are summer flowering.

Culture: Plant autumn or spring in ordinary soil in sunny, well-drained borders. These plants do well on chalky soils.

Propagation: By seeds sown $\frac{1}{8}$ in. deep in sunny positions outdoors in April; division of roots in October or March; by root cuttings in January or February.

ECHIUM ek-*ee-um*. There are perennial, biennial and annual echiums, but the most important for the garden are the hardy annuals which are hybrids. These grow 12 in. high and have heads of rose, lavender or blue flowers in summer.
Culture: Sow in March or April in light well-drained soil and open, sunny positions where plants are to flower. Thin seedlings to 8 in. or 9 in.

EDELWEISS, *see* Leontopodium.

EELWORMS. Minute more or less transparent worms which live within the tissues of some plants, notably daffodils, onions, phlox and chrysanthemums, causing the plants to become swollen or deformed and, in chrysanthemums, leaves to wither and growth to cease. Potatoes are attacked by an eelworm which produces tiny white cysts on roots and tubers, turns leaves yellow and checks growth. Eelworms are difficult to control though in some cases immersion of plants or bulbs for specified periods in water at exactly 110° will effect a cure. In general it is wise to destroy all eelworm infected plants and not to replant the same kind of plant on this ground for several years. Steam sterilisation is the normal large-scale method in greenhouses, while metham-sodium and DD are effective chemical materials.

EICHHORNIA, *see* Aquatic.

ELAEAGNUS *el-ee-ag-nus* (Oleaster). *E. pungens* is a hardy evergreen shrub with ornamental foliage. There are several varieties with leaves variegated with cream or yellow. Suitable for open borders and shrubberies. It makes a plant 8 ft. to 10 ft. tall and as much through.
Culture: Plant October to March in ordinary well-drained soil and sunny or partially shady places. No regular pruning is necessary but specimens can be reduced in size, if necessary, in April.

Propagation: By cuttings of firm young growth inserted in sandy soil in a propagating frame in July or August.

ELEPHANT'S TOOTH CACTUS, *see* Mammillaria.

ELK'S-HORN FERN, *see* Platycerium.

ELODEA, *see* Aquatic.

ENDIVE. A vegetable, rather like lettuce in appearance, grown for use as salad. Endive is grown from seed sown at intervals from April to mid-August in good, rich well-dug soil and an open situation. Thin seedlings to 9 in. apart. When plants are well grown cover each with an inverted plate or piece of wood to exclude light and blanch the leaves. This will take about 6 weeks. Late sown endive is best protected with a frame or cloches in autumn and for the last few weeks the glass can be whitewashed to secure a sufficient measure of blanching.

EPACRIS *ep-ak-ris*. For about 100 years these were very popular as winter-flowering pot-plants and many fine hybrids were raised from seed, but they seem to have gone out of favour these days, possibly because the plants are not too easy to grow. Owing to their heath-like character and long spikes of small flowers of white, pink or red, they are often known as the Australian Heaths, although actually they belong to a different family altogether, and like some of the greenhouse heaths they are nearly hardy.
Culture: A frost-proof greenhouse is all they need and in mild districts they may be successfully grown in a cold one. After flowering they should be cut hard back and then re-potted in sandy peat as soon as new growth starts. Good drainage and firm potting are essential. During the summer they are best plunged in a cold frame, but careful watering is necessary as too much will spoil them. Full sun is required to ripen the shoots to the flowering stage and when housed in September they should still be given plenty of light and air.

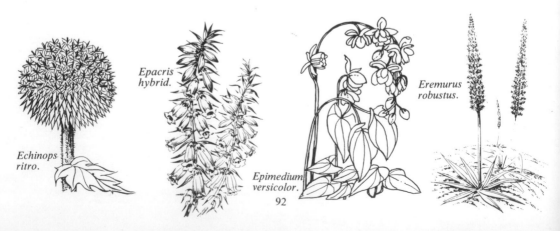

Epacris hybrid.

Eremurus robustus.

Echinops ritro.

Epimedium versicolor.

Echium fastuosum.

Elaeagnus pungens aurea.

Epiphyllum crenatum.

Propagation: By seed sown in gentle heat in March, or cuttings about 1 in. long may be inserted in bottom heat in spring.

EPIMEDIUM *ep-e-***mee***-de-um* (Barrenwort; Bishop's Hat). Hardy herbaceous perennials. Leaves green, margined with coppery-bronze becoming more highly coloured in autumn. Suitable for a cool, shady border or rock garden; will do well under trees. The variety most commonly seen in gardens is *E. versicolor sulphureum*, 9 in. high, with pale sulphur flowers in spring.
Culture: Plant autumn or spring in ordinary soil and open or shady places.
Propagation: By division in autumn.

EPIPHYLLUM *ep-e-***fi***-lum* (Orchid Cactus). These uncactus-like cacti have long, almost spineless stems, often flattened, which are sometimes mistaken for leaves. On these, in due season—usually spring—they carry large, spectular flowers, usually red, pink or white; most of them are hybrids.
Culture: They enjoy a warm, humid greenhouse—they differ in their needs from most cacti, being of jungle origin—but stand room conditions well. Compost: 2 parts turfy loam, 1 part peat or leaf-mould, 1 part coarse sand, with a sprinkling of hoof-and-horn meal. Position: light, warm greenhouse or window September to June, sheltered place outdoors or cold frame June to September. Water moderately October to February, freely other times. Shade from bright sun in summer and feed occasionally with weak liquid or soluble fertiliser. Spray overhead on hot days. Temperature: November to March, 50° to 60°; natural rise at other seasons.
Propagation: By cuttings of individual stem segments inserted singly in 2 in. pots filled with sandy soil and brick dust in March or April.

Blanched endive.

EPIPHYTE ep-*if***-ite.** A plant which grows on others, often trees, but not as a parasite. Epiphytic orchids grow on or are suspended from the branches of trees with long aerial roots which gather moisture from the atmosphere.

EPSOM SALTS, *see* Sulphate of Magnesium.

ERANTHIS *e-***ran***-this* (Winter Aconite). Low growing hardy tuberous-rooted perennial, with bright yellow flowers from January to March. Suitable for shady borders, beds, lawns, under trees or on rock gardens. The species grown is *E. hyemalis*.
Culture: Plant tubers in ordinary soil 2 in. deep and 2 in. to 4 in. apart in September or October. These should not be lifted, but left permanently in the soil where they will gradually increase and cover considerable areas with a carpet of green leaves studded in winter with the yellow, buttercup-like flowers.
Propagation: By division of tubers at planting time.

EREMURUS *er-e-***mu***-rus* (Foxtail Lily). Hardy herbaceous perennials with fleshy roots and tall, often

93

massive, flower spikes in early summer. Species commonly grown are *E. bungei*, 4 ft., orange yellow; *E. himalaicus*, 5 ft., white; *E. elwesii*, 5 ft., pink, and *E. robustus*, 8 ft., pink. There are also numerous hybrids.

Culture: Plant young roots in September or October in light, deep, rich soil in sunny well-drained beds or borders. Take great care not to crack the brittle roots. Water freely in hot weather. Protect in winter by a covering of bracken, dry litter, or sharp sand.

Propagation: By seeds sown as soon as ripe in September, in sandy soil in a frame. Seeds are often slow and irregular in germinating.

ERICA er-*ik-a* or er-**eye**-*ka* (Heather; Heath). Hardy and tender evergreen flowering shrubs. The British heathers are mostly low-growing plants, but there are hardy species up to about 8 ft. in height. In all cases the flowers are quite small and usually urn-shaped or tubular. A notable feature of the family is that there are hardy kinds to bloom during practically every month of the year without protection. Among the best kinds are *E. carnea*, 9 in. to 12 in., white, pink or carmine, late winter; *E. darleyensis*, 12 in. to 18 in., pink, winter; *E. cinerea*, 1 ft. to 2 ft.. white to crimson, early summer; *E. tetralix*, 1½ ft. to 2 ft., white to purple, summer; *E. vagans*, 1 ft. to 2 ft., white to purple, late summer and autumn; *E. arborea*, 7 ft. to 8 ft., white, early spring; *E. mediterranea*, 6 ft. to 10 ft., white to rosy-red, late winter. The tender heaths are of South African origin and make attractive pot plants, but are a little difficult to grow well. Forms of *E. gracilis* produce their pink, reddish, or white flowers from November to March, and *E. hyemalis*, the most popular, has pinkish-white flowers between December and February.

Culture of Hardy Kinds: Almost all, with the exception of *E. carnea* and *E. darleyensis* are lime-haters but will grow in any reasonably well-drained soil that is free from lime. Leaf-mould or peat may be worked in if soils lack natural humus. October and April are the best months for planting but pot-grown plants can be put in at almost any time. In almost all cases an open, sunny position should be chosen, but some of the so-called tree heaths, and notably *E. arborea*, is liable to damage by frost in severe winters, and should be given rather sheltered places. If the dwarf varieties of heather become straggly, they can be trimmed with shears immediately after flowering, but should not be cut back into hard, old wood.

Culture of Tender Kinds: A very peaty compost with lime-free loam and sharp sand should be used. Potting should be firm and is best done as soon as new growth commences in the spring. From July until the end of September the pots should be plunged to the rims in ashes in a sunny, sheltered place outdoors. Even in winter artificial heat is only required to keep out the frost and to keep air circulating. Only give water (which must be lime-free) when the soil is drying out, but then apply sufficient to soak right through the ball of soil in the pot. Strong growing kinds may be pruned to shape immediately after flowering.

Propagation: All the species can be raised from seed sown very thinly in a frame or cool greenhouse during February or March. The garden varieties can be increased by cuttings of side shoots rooted in sand or very sandy soil in a close frame. Summer is the best time for taking cuttings of the hardy kinds, but the tender heaths should be propagated when young shoots are available. The dwarf hardy heathers may also be increased by layering in early summer.

ERIGERON er-*idg-er-on* (Flea-bane). Hardy herbaceous perennials with blue or mauve daisy-like flowers in summer. Very free flowering and serviceable border plants, preferring sun, but doing quite well in partial shade. Most of the varieties grown in gardens are hybrids 1½ ft. to 2½ ft. in height.

Culture: Plant October or March in ordinary soil. Cut back stems after flowering.

Propagation: By division of roots in October or March.

ERODIUM er-*o-dee-um* (Heron's Bill). Hardy perennial herbs, closely allied to the hardy geraniums. They are suitable for rock gardens and for carpeting sunny banks. Mostly pink flowers spring and summer.

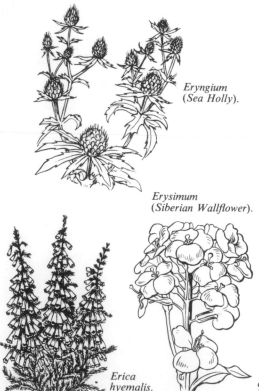

Eryngium (Sea Holly).

Erysimum (Siberian Wallflower).

Erica hyemalis.

94

Among the best kinds are *E. chamaedryoides roseum*, prostrate, pink, spring and summer; *E. guttatum*, pink, 6 in., early summer; *E. chrysanthum*, yellow, 6 in., summer; *E. corsicum*, pink, 4 in., summer, and *E. manescavii*, rosy-purple, 1 ft. to 1½ ft., summer.

Culture: Plant March or April in ordinary well-drained soil and sunny places. Transplant very seldom as the tough roots of old plants do not readily form fresh fibres.

Propagation: By seeds sown in pots of sandy soil in a frame or greenhouse in March or April, transplanting seedlings outdoors in June or July.

Erodium corsicum.

ERYNGIUM *er-in-***gee***-um* (Sea Holly). Hardy perennial herbs with ornamental foliage and flower heads in summer, surrounded by spiny, coloured bracts. These may be dried for use as everlastings. The eryngiums are good plants for seaside gardens. Among the best kinds are *E. alpinum*, 3 ft.; *E. amethystinum*, 2 ft.; *E. oliverianum*, 2 ft.; *E. tripartitum*, 3 ft., and *E. violetta*, 3 ft. *E. giganteum*, 4 ft. to 6 ft., white, is often grown as a biennial.

Culture: Plant early autumn or spring in light, well-drained soil in sunny borders. Disturbance of established plants is inadvisable.

Propagation: By seeds sown in sandy soil in a cold frame in April or May; by root cuttings formed from 2 in. long pieces of stout thongy roots inserted in trays of sandy soil in January or February, placing these in a cold frame.

Erica carnea.

ERYSIMUM *er-***iss***-im-um* (Alpine Wallflower; Siberian Wallflower). Hardy biennials and perennials. *E. asperum* is the plant commonly grown in gardens as *Cheiranthus allionii* or Siberian Wallflower. *E. linifolium*, a mauve-coloured rock and wall plant is also more generally known as *Cheiranthus linifolius*. All are like the familiar wallflower on a smaller scale and flower in spring and early summer.

Culture: Plant March or April in ordinary soil in dryish sunny beds or rock gardens. All thrive best on near-starvation diet, dislike transplanting, and cannot tolerate stagnant moisture.

Propagation: Biennials by seeds sown in sunny places outdoors in June, transplanting seedlings to flowering positions in August or September; perennials by seeds sown as advised for biennials, also by cuttings inserted in a frame in sandy soil in summer.

Erigeron hybrid.

ERYTHRINA *er-***rith***-***ri***-na* (Coral-tree). *E. crista-galli*, with its scarlet pea-shaped flowers carried on stems up to 4 ft. long, makes a fine early summer display in the cool greenhouse, or even a cold one if it can be given a little extra protection in winter.

Culture: Erythrina grows from a thick rootstock which should be kept practically dry through the winter and then soaked in spring. This should start into growth when it may be re-potted into any rich soil and stood in full sun. Plenty of water is needed

Erythrina crista-galli.

Espalier-trained apple tree.

Erythronium dens-canis.

Eucharis grandiflora.

up to and during the flowering period, but then it should be allowed to dry off and die down gradually. When there is no fear of frost it may be stood outside for the rest of the summer.

Propagation: Cuttings about 3 in. long root readily in bottom heat in spring.

ERYTHRONIUM *er-ee-***thro**-*ne-um* (Dog's-tooth Violet; Trout Lily). Hardy bulbous perennials, suitable for sheltered rock gardens, beds, borders, or under the shade of trees. The most familiar species is *D. dens-canis*, 6 in., rose. Other good kinds are *E. americanum*, 6 in., yellow; *E. revolutum*, 12 in., cream and purple, and *E. tuolumnense*, 12 in., yellow. All are spring flowering.

Culture: Plant bulbs in autumn 2 in. deep and 3 in. apart in cool, partially shaded places and soils with plenty of humus which may be added, if necessary, as peat or leaf-mould. Transplant very seldom. Top-dress annually with peat or leaf-mould.

Propagation: By removal of offsets at planting time.

ESCALLONIA *es-ka-***lo**-*nee-a* (Chilian Gum Box). Hardy or slightly tender evergreen or deciduous flowering shrubs, suitable for open gardens in the milder districts, especially near the sea. May also be planted against walls. Pink, red or white flowers in summer. Among the best species are *E. langleyensis*, 6 ft. to 8 ft., rose; *E. macrantha*, 6 ft. to 8 ft., crimson, and *E. edinensis*, 6 ft. to 8 ft., pale pink, but there are also many garden varieties.

Culture: Plant October, November, March or April in ordinary well-drained soil. Prune straggly shoots only in April.

Propagation: By cuttings inserted in sandy soil in a propagating frame in July or August.

ESCHSCHOLTZIA *esh-***kolt**-*se-a* (Californian Poppy). Hardy annuals with poppy-like flowers in many bright colours in summer. Foliage finely cut and glaucous. All will thrive in hungry soil and sun-baked situations, but do not do well in damp, shady quarters. All are derived from *E. californica*.

Culture: Sow seeds in March, April or early September where plants are to bloom. Thin seedlings to 8 in. or 9 in. apart. Keep seed pods picked off to maintain flowering as long as possible.

ESPALIER *ess-***pal**-*ee-er*. A fence or framework made with a series of upright posts supporting several wires strained horizontally for the purpose of securing trained fruit-trees. An espalier-trained tree is restricted to pairs of branches stretching horizontally from the trunk, which are secured to the strands of the espalier for support. Apples and pears are frequently grown in this form and can be very decorative as well as prolific.

EUCALYPTUS *eu-kal-***ip**-*tus* (Australian Gum; Blue Gum). Greenhouse and slightly tender evergreen trees with ornamental foliage. Leaves mostly blue-grey with the pungent odour characteristic of the oil extracted from these plants. The most popular kind for the greenhouse is *E. globulus* and for outdoors planting *E. gunnii* which will eventually grow 50 ft. or more high. In favourable places these trees grow very rapidly.

Culture: Pot March or April in John Innes potting compost in the smallest pots that will contain the roots comfortably. Place pots in a greenhouse in a temperature of 45° to 50° in winter, or in sunny beds outdoors in summer. In sheltered places some kinds such as *E. gunnii*, *E. coccifera*, *E. dalrympleana* and *E. parvifolia* can be grown outdoors all the year round in ordinary well-drained soil. Water plants in pots moderately October to April, freely afterwards. Pruning not required.

Propagation: By seeds sown in sandy soil in a temperature of 65° in February or March. Young plants should be raised annually for pot culture as they soon get too large for convenience.

EUCHARIS *eu-kar-is* (Amazon Lily). If you can afford to keep a winter temperature of 65° in the greenhouse the Amazon Lily, *E. grandiflora*, is certainly worth growing, for it blooms twice a year, although its normal flowering period is winter or spring. The large white drooping flowers, each about 5 in. across, are carried on stems about 2 ft. long.

Culture: Potting up of the bulbs is best done in spring, when six strong ones should be placed in a 10 in. pot containing a rich loam with some leaf-mould and cow manure. The bulbs should not be completely covered until they have started into growth. Plenty of water is needed once growth starts and feeding as soon as the flower stems appear. There is no need to re-pot the plants until they have quite filled their pots but an annual top-dressing of good soil should be given. In the autumn the plants are rested by reducing the water supply, although this must never be cut off completely or the foliage will die and weaken the bulbs.

Propagation: By division, but it should only be done when really necessary.

EUCOMIS *eu-ko-mis* (Pineapple Flower). Though some species are hardy in mild districts they must usually be grown in a cool greenhouse. In early summer they produce stout stems carrying spikes of greenish-white flowers ending in a dense tuft of leaves. *E. pallidiflora*, *E. undulata* and *E. comosa*, also known as *E. punctata*, are often grown.

Culture: Mature bulbs are best potted in autumn, when each one should be given a 4½ in. pot of rich, well-drained compost. Little water is required in winter but plenty should be given in spring and summer. Re-potting is only necessary every third year or so. Temperature: October to March, 45° to 50°; natural rise at other seasons.

Propagation: By offsets detached in March and potted individually as for mature bulb but in small pots.

EUCRYPHIA *eu-krif-e-a*. Slightly tender evergreen or deciduous shrubs with white flowers, rather like single roses, in summer. Some of the choicest of flowing shrubs for favourably sheltered gardens. The best kinds are *E. cordifolia*, evergreen, 30 ft. to 40 ft.; *E. glutinosa*, deciduous, 12 ft. to 18 ft.; *E. nymansay*, evergreen, 30 ft. to 40 ft.

Culture: Plant in autumn in good lime-free soil in warm sheltered shrubberies or against south or west walls.

Propagation: By cuttings of firm young shoots in sandy soil in a propagating frame in July.

EULALIA, *see* Miscanthus.

EUONYMUS *eu-on-e-mus* (Spindle-tree). Hardy deciduous and evergreen shrubs. Good seaside shrubs. Several, like the native *E. europaeus*, and *E. latifolius*, bear clusters of orange and scarlet fruits in autumn. Both shrubs are 6 ft. to 8 ft. tall. The evergreen *E. japonicus* is a useful hedge plant which will grow 12 ft. to 15 ft. high, and another evergreen kind, *E. radicans* has two distinct forms, one climbing or spreading, the other bushy and about 2 ft. high.

Culture: Plant November to March in ordinary soil. Prune evergreen kinds grown as hedges in summer.

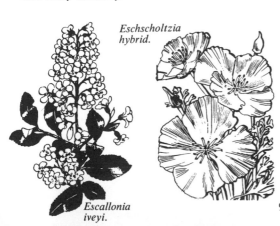

Eschscholtzia hybrid.

Escallonia iveyi.

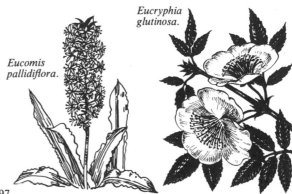

Eucomis pallidiflora.

Eucryphia glutinosa.

Other kinds need no regular pruning. The naturally spreading or creeping form of *E. radicans* may be grown against walls up which it will then climb without additional support.

Propagation: By cuttings of firm young shoots inserted in sandy soil in a frame in September to October; the creeping form of *E. radicans* by division at planting time.

EUPATORIUM *eu-pat-or-e-um.* Several species of eupatorium make useful additions to the autumn and winter display in the warm greenhouse. These include *E. atrorubens*, with reddish flowers on 2 ft. stems, and the white-flowered *E. riparium* (2 ft.), *E. micranthum* (2 ft. to 4 ft.) and *E. vernale* (2 ft. to 3 ft.).

Culture: During the summer the simplest way of growing the plants is to plant them outside in rich soil, where they can remain until they are lifted with a good ball of soil and potted up in September. For each one a 6 in. or 8 in. pot will be required according to its size. After flowering the plants should be cut back to induce new growth.

Propagation: Cuttings inserted in a close, warm frame in spring root fairly easily and afterwards they should be grown on without any stopping. This will produce a single terminal flowerhead but the following year the plants can be pinched out to produce more bushy specimens.

EUPHORBIA *eu-for-be-a* (Spurge; Caper Spurge; Poinsettia). Tender and hardy flowering shrubs and herbs. Beauty of foliage is characteristic of the family; the flowers are often in quiet shades of yellow, amber and green, but *E. fulgens*, also known rather fancifully as the Scarlet Plume, has small scarlet flowers which are clustered along arching branches and may be anything up to 3 ft. long if left unstopped, and the poinsettia, *E. pulcherrima* has enormous scarlet 'flowers', sometimes a foot or more across if grown on single stems, although a greater number of smaller flowers can be produced by pinching the plants.

Culture of Tender Species: Pot in March in John Innes compost. Place in sunny dry part of greenhouse, water moderately September to January; keep almost dry January to May; water freely afterwards. Temperature: January to May, 50° to 55°; May to September, 65° to 75°; September to January, 55° to 65°. Prune *E. fulgens* in June, cutting shoots back to within 1 in. of base.

Culture of Poinsettia: Compost as above. Place old plants in temperature of 65° to 75° in May. Remove young shoots when 2 in. to 3 in. long, insert singly in 2 in. pots filled with sandy loam and peat, and plunge to the rims in a propagating frame with bottom heat. When rooted, place singly in 4 in. pots, plunge again in bottom heat for a few days, then remove to shelf near glass. As soon as pots are well filled with roots transfer to 6 in. or 8 in. pots. Keep near the glass for week or so, then gradually harden off. Place in cold, sunny frame until September, when remove to greenhouse, temperature 55°. Water freely and syringe twice daily. Ventilate freely on fine days. Raise temperature to 60° to 65° end of September. Water moderately. Apply liquid feed twice a week. After flowering, remove to a temperature of 40° to 45°, keep roots quite dry, and store pots on their side under staging. Prune shoots, unless required for producing cuttings, to second dormant bud from base, end of April. When new shoots are 1 in. long, turn plants out of their pots, remove old soil from roots, cut off the straggling ends of latter, and re-pot in pots just large enough to take roots and a little fresh compost. Place in temperature of 65° to 75° from pruning time. Re-pot in larger size when small pots are filled with roots. Place in cold, sunny frame during July and August. Water and syringe freely. Remove to temperature of 55° to 60° in September.

Culture of Hardy Species: Plant in spring or autumn in ordinary soil in dry borders, banks, or sunny rock gardens.

Propagation: Tender species by cuttings of young shoots; hardy species by cuttings inserted in sandy soil in a cold frame in summer; seeds sown in dryish positions outdoors in April; division of plants in October or April.

EURYA *eu-re-a.* The almost hardy *E. japonica* is related to the camellia and is normally grown for its

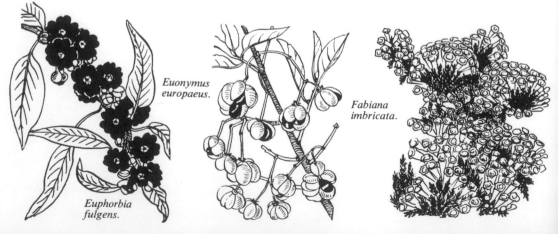

Euonymus
europaeus.

Euphorbia
fulgens.

Fabiana
imbricata.

Eupatorium atrorubens.

Euphorbia pulcherrima.

Eurya japonica.

Exacum affine.

glossy camellia-like leaves, the flowers being insignificant. It is usually grown in its cream-variegated form.

Culture: Pot in March in leafy, acid soil, and grow in a cool, airy place with good indirect light. Water freely spring and summer, moderately at other times. No regular pruning essential but plants can be trimmed or reduced as necessary for convenience in spring.

Propagation: Summer cuttings inserted in sandy soil in heat root readily.

EVENING PRIMROSE, *see* Oenothera.

EVERLASTING FLOWER, *see* Helichrysum.

EVERLASTING PEA, *see* Lathyrus.

EXACUM ex-*a-cum*. Flowering in late summer and autumn, *E. affine* comes in very useful when other plants are getting a bit scarce, but it needs a fair amount of warmth. The fragrant flowers, carried on a plant anything from 6 in. to 1 ft. high, are normally a pale blue, but there is a richer-coloured variety in *E. a. atrocaeruleum*.

Culture: Being a biennial it does best when sown in August and grown on in 3 in. pots through the winter, after which it should be potted on into 5 in. pots, but smaller plants can be obtained by sowing in March for flowering the same year. A suitable compost is equal parts peat and soil, with enough sand to keep it open. Good drainage and careful watering are essential as the plants are inclined to damp off rather easily, and shade from hot sun is also advisable. For plants sown in late summer a winter temperature of 60° is necessary.

FABIANA *fab-ee-*a-*na* (False Heath). This genus comprises about 20 species, although only two of these are in cultivation. These are *F. imbricata* and *F. violacea*, both evergreen rather tender shrubs growing to about 5 ft. high. In very mild districts they will succeed in the open, but in most parts of the country greenhouse protection is necessary in winter. *F. violacea* with pale mauve, tubular flowers in June is the hardier of the two, but the white-flowered *F. imbricata* is equally good as a greenhouse plant.

Culture: Both species will do well in a warm, sandy soil with plenty of water in summer and rather less in winter. During the summer they should be stood outside in full sun until they are housed in September.

Propagation: Cuttings root readily in a warm propagating frame in July and August.

FAIR MAIDS OF FRANCE, *see* Ranunculus.

FAIR MAIDS OF KENT, *see* Ranunculus.

FALSE ACACIA, *see* Robinia.

FALSE CASTOR-OIL PLANT, *see* Fatsia.

FALSE CYPRESS, *see* Chamaecyparis.

FALSE HEATH, *see* Fabiana.

FALSE HELLEBORE, *see* Veratrum.

FALSE INDIGO, *see* Baptisia.

FALSE MITREWORT, *see* Tiarella.

FAN PALM, *see* Chamaerops.

FASTIGIATE *fas-**tij**-ee-ate.* This term denotes a tree or shrub having branches all erect and more or less parallel with the main stems, as in the Lombardy poplar and *Prunus serrulata erecta.*

FATSHEDERA *fats-**hed**-er-a. F. lizei* is a hardy plant, a hybrid between *Fatsia japonica* and the Irish Ivy, *Hedera hibernica.* The only English name bestowed on it is an irreverent rendering of the Latin—Fat-headed Lizzie. It has five-lobed leaves rather like

those of ivy, up to 8 in. or 10 in. across, all the way up stiff erect stems which may reach a considerable height. There is an attractive cream-variegated form which grows more slowly and is reputed to be a little harder to succeed with. Pinching out the growing point encourages side shoots to form.

Culture: This is a very tolerant plant, standing quite warm conditions and sun or part shade; but dry, hot air and fluctuating temperatures may cause the leaves to go yellow and fall. However, if this happens the stem can be cut back hard and will sprout afresh from the base.

Propagation: By cuttings which will root readily without heat in summer, preferably in a close atmosphere. The top of the plant, and sections of stem about 6 in. long, are suitable materials.

FATSIA fat-*se-a* (False Castor-oil Plant). Hardy or nearly hardy evergreen shrubs. The green and variegated forms of *F. japonica* (widely known as *Aralia sieboldii*) make very serviceable plants for the dwelling-house and the cool conservatory.

Greenhouse Culture: Pot or plant in spring in John Innes compost. Water moderately October to March, freely April to September. Temperature: October to March, 40° or more; natural rise in summer. Shade from strong direct sunshine.

Outdoor culture: Plant October to March in ordinary well-drained soil in sheltered sunny or partially shaded positions. Requires protection in severe weather.

Propagation: By cuttings of firm young shoots inserted in sandy soil in late summer in a propagating frame with bottom heat.

FEATHER HYACINTH, *see* Muscari.

FELICIA *fel-is-**ee**-a* (Blue Daisy; Blue Marguerite). *F. amelloides* is a bushy little plant 12 in. to 18 in. high with narrow leaves and blue daisy flowers produced more or less continuously in summer. It is a little tender.

Culture: Plant in spring in well-drained soil and sunny sheltered places. Alternatively pot in March in John Innes compost and grow in a sunny greenhouse

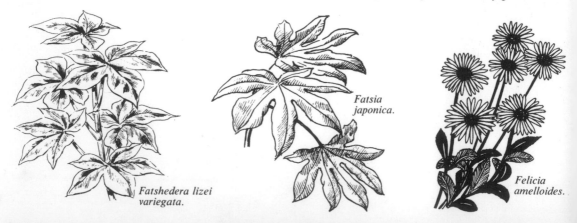

Fatshedera lizei variegata.

Fatsia japonica.

Felicia amelloides.

Fastigiate type of growth (Lombardy poplar).

Potting Ficus elastica.

with a minimum winter temperature of 40°.
Propagation: By seed sown in a warm greenhouse in February or March.

FENNEL-FLOWER, *see* Nigella.

FERTILISER. Any substance which may be used to feed plants. Fertilisers may be grouped as inorganic or organic, chemical or natural, and also according to the particular food or foods they supply. 'Complete' fertilisers usually supply nitrogen, phosphorus and potash, sometimes with the addition of other chemicals such as magnesium, manganese and iron. Among the most commonly used fertilisers in gardens are sulphate of ammonia, nitrate of soda, nitro-chalk, dried blood and hoof and horn meal (all supplying nitrogen), superphosphate of lime and bone meal (phosphorus) and muriate of potash and sulphate of potash (potash). Epsom salts (sulphate of magnesium) may be used to supply magnesium and sulphate of iron or chelated iron (iron sequestrol) to supply iron.

FICUS fi-*cus* (Fig-tree; India-rubber Plant). Greenhouse and hardy deciduous and evergreen trees and shrubs with ornamental foliage. Everyone knows the India rubber plant, *F. elastica*, with its big ovate leaves, usually grown in the form *decora* with dark red undersides to the young leaves, and a pink sheath to the terminal bud. It has a variegated form, sometimes called *F. doescheri*. More or less similar in appearance are *F. benghalensis*, the Banyan, *F. chauvieri*, and *F. heterophylla* (usually listed as *F. panduriformis*). *F. lyrata*, the aptly named Fiddle-leaf Fig, has very large leaves, pale green, with a distinct 'waist'. *F. australis* is a bushier plant with rounded leaves, brownish below, and *F. diversifolia* is a bushy shrublet with small leaves and small round 'figs' most of the time. One of the most attractive is *F. benjamina*, with spreading branches and hanging, glossy, pale green leaves after the manner of a weeping willow. Quite distinct are *F. pumila* (syn. *F. repens*), the almost hardy small-leaved creeping fig, and *F. radicans*, another trailer with rather larger leaves, which has a silver-variegated form. (The fruit-bearing fig is *Ficus carica* and its culture is described under Fig.)

Culture of Tender Species: Pot or plant February, March, or April in John Innes potting compost. Place creeping species such as *F. pumila*, in beds where shoots can cling to walls, rocks, etc. Water moderately October to March, freely afterwards. Syringe daily February to August. Temperature: October to April, 50° to 60°; May to September, 60° to 70°. Shade in summer.

The tree and bush species of ficus are all more or less suitable for room conditions though low or fluctuating temperatures and hot, stuffy air are liable to cause brown or yellow marks on the leaves and eventual leaf fall, as is overwatering in winter. Over-potting also readily leads to stagnant root conditions which give rise in turn to leaf fall. *F. pumila* must be kept very cool and dampish in a room.

Propagation: By cuttings of firm, young shoots inserted in a temperature of 75° in spring or summer. *F. elastica* and its kind by cuttings of a short piece of stem with a leaf struck in much heat (75° to 80°). *F. pumila* and *F. radicans* need less heat but close, humid conditions.

FIG. This can be grown outdoors in the milder parts of the country or under glass anywhere. Position outdoors should be as sunny and sheltered as possible as, for example, against walls facing south or south-west. Plant in March or April in a border 2 ft. deep and 3 ft. wide enclosed with brick or concrete wall, in a mixture of 2 parts fibrous loam, 1 part brick rubble and old mortar. Fruits may be borne along the entire length of previous year's shoots, but only one crop at the base of the young shoots is borne out-doors in England. Prune April or October, simply removing damaged, dead, or weak branches. Pinch points of vigorous young shoots in July. Apply liquid manure once in August to trees bearing heavily. Pick off figlets size of filberts in September or October as these are unlikely to produce usable fruits in Britain. Protect branches in December with straw or mats, removing these in April.

Culture of Fig under Glass: Compost, position, time of planting as above. Branches should be trained up roof or against wall. Fruits are borne on shoots of previous year's growth for first crop; those of current year for second crop. Prune and pinch as above. Disbud young shoots when too many are forming. Water and syringe freely in summer. Apply liquid manure occasionally in summer.

Propagation: By cuttings of firm young shoots in autumn, inserted singly in pots filled with sandy soil and plunged in a frame or cool greenhouse.

FIG MARIGOLD, *see* Mesembryanthemum.

FIG TREE, *see* Ficus.

FILIPENDULA *fil-ee-pen-due-la* (Meadow Sweet; Dropwort; Queen-of-the-Prairie). Hardy herbaceous perennials, formerly known as spiraea. The Meadow Sweet, *F. ulmaria*, is a common British wild plant with plumes of creamy flowers on 3 ft. stems in summer and in gardens usually represented by its double-flowered form. Similarly, it is the double-flowered form of the Dropwort, *F. hexapetala*, with smaller heads of ivory-white flowers in summer that is generally planted. It is 2 ft. high. Other good kinds are the Queen-of-the-Prairie, *F. rubra*, with plumes of pink or carmine flowers on 5 ft. stems in July to August, and *F. palmata*, 2 ft., with pale pink flowers in summer.

Culture: Plant October to April in fairly rich soil. Most like a rather moist situation and *F. ulmaria* naturally grows beside streams, but *F. hexapetala* favours the drier chalk downs in nature and will put up with quite a lot of dryness in the garden.

Propagation: By division in March.

FINGER AND TOE, *see* Club-root.

FIR, *see* Abies.

FIRETHORN, *see* Pyracantha.

FISHBONE PLANT, *see* Maranta.

FITTONIA *fit-o-ne-a*. Small, creeping plants. the fittonias are colourful in shady parts of a warm, humid greenhouse, but they are unsuitable for rooms, drying up at once in a stuffy atmosphere. They have oval leaves netted with white veins in *F. argyroneura* and red veins in *F. verschaffeltii*. The small flowers are carried in quaint upright rectangular spikes.

Culture: Grow in shallow, well-drained pans of porous, leafy soil, or establish on the soil at the base of larger plants in pots, or even in the gravel on the greenhouse staging. Pinching of the growing point will ensure bushy growth, which is desirable as the plants are naturally rather straggling. Plenty of water is needed. Temperature: April to September, 65° to 75°; October to March, 60° to 65°.

Propagation: Cuttings root readily with bottom heat.

FLAG, *see* Iris.

FLAME FLOWER, *see* Tropaeolum.

FLAME NETTLE, *see* Coleus.

FLAMINGO FLOWER, *see* Anthurium.

FLAX, *see* Linum.

FLEA BEETLE, *see* Turnip Flea Beetle.

FLEA-BANE, *see* Erigeron.

FLEUR-DE-LIS, *see* Iris.

Fittonia argyroneura.

Filipendula rubra.

FLOSS FLOWER, *see* Ageratum.

FLOWER OF THE FIELD, *see* Sternbergia.

FLOWER OF THE WEST WIND, *see* Zephyranthes.

FLOWERING CURRANT, *see* Ribes.

FLOWERING FERN, *see* Osmunda.

FLOWERING MAPLE, *see* Abutilon.

FLOWERING NUTMEG, *see* Leycesteria.

FLOWERING RUSH, *see* Butomus.

FLY, CARROT, *see* Carrot Fly.

FLY, CELERY, *see* Celery Fly.

FOAM FLOWER, *see* Tiarella.

FOOT ROT (MELONS, CUCUMBERS). A somewhat similar trouble to damping-off, but one which usually occurs at a later stage of growth, when the base of the stem decays and the plant collapses. Planting on a mound, so that the base of the stem does not become too wet, helps to avoid it, but if it does appear copper-lime dust should be applied to the base of the stems. Spraying with Bordeaux mixture has also been found effective. This trouble is also known as canker.

FORCING. The art of inducing plants to produce flowers or fruit, or vegetables to attain usable size, before their normal season. The more usual method

Young cucumbers affected by foot rot.

is to utilise artificial heat in a glass-house specially equipped for the purpose. Sometimes roots, bulbs, or plants are prepared for forcing by subjecting them to a prior period of vernalisation in which the cold conditions of autumn and winter are artifically reproduced before the plant is required to make its new growth. Rhubarb roots may be lifted in November and left on the surface for a few days exposed to frost before they are brought into a warm place.

FORGET-ME-NOT, *see* Myosotis.

FORMALIN. A powerful disinfectant containing 40% of pure formaldehyde. To prepare this for use as a soil steriliser, it is further diluted with 49 times its own bulk of water. The soil is then thoroughly soaked with this and covered with sacks for 2 or 3 days to trap the fumes. The same solution may be used for the sterilisation of boxes, pots, canes and so on. Nothing which has been treated with formalin should be used until all traces of the smell have gone, usually in about a fortnight. The fumes are deadly to plant life and are not exactly good for humans, so it is best to breathe them in as little as possible.

FORSYTHIA *for-sye-the-a* (Golden Bells). Hardy deciduous shrubs with yellow flowers in early spring. Suitable for sunny or partially shaded shrubbery, or *F. suspensa* may be trained against walls. The most

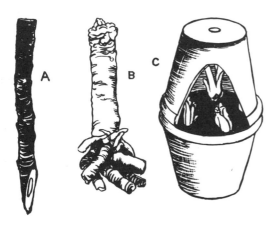

Forcing Seakale: (a) a suitable thong prepared for planting; (b) a sturdy crown lifted for forcing; (c) the top pot is cut away to show crowns being blanched.

popular kind is *F. intermedia spectabilis*, which makes a fine bush 8 ft. to 10 ft. high.

Culture: Plant October to March in ordinary soil. Prune immediately after flowering, cutting out as much as possible of the wood that has just borne flowers but retaining all the young, non-flowering stems.

Propagation: By cuttings of firm young stems in sandy soil in a frame or outdoors in October.

FOXGLOVE, *see* Digitalis.

FOXTAIL LILY, *see* Eremurus.

FRAGRANT OLIVE, *see* Osmanthus.

FRAME. This can be of great service both as a substitute for a greenhouse and as an auxiliary to it. Frames can be warmed in various ways: with electric cables; by standing them on hotbeds of trodden fresh horse manure, etc. If a temperature of 55° to 60° can be maintained many seeds of half-hardy plants can be germinated in early spring or early crops of potatoes, lettuce, etc., can be produced. Unheated frames are useful for slightly later sowing, for cuttings at almost any time of year, for protection of slightly tender plants, such as penstemons and bedding calceolarias in winter, and for hardening-off greenhouse-raised plants before they are planted outdoors in spring or early summer.

Frames are of many patterns but the traditional frame with a 'light', i.e. a glazed and removable top, 6 ft. by 4 ft., is still one of the most generally useful. The sides of the frame may be of wood, brick, concrete, or asbestos sheeting. For seeds and cuttings it will be sufficient if the front wall of the frame is about 12 in. high, and the back wall 18 in., but for some large pot plants deeper frames are more convenient.

Another type of frame light is that known as the Dutch light. This takes a single sheet of glass 56 in. by 28¾ in., and is much lighter to handle than the traditional 6 ft. by 4 ft. light with its numerous panes of glass and several glazing bars. A drawback of the Dutch light is that breakages are costly to replace.

Propagating frames are usually much smaller, though there is no standard size. They are often made to stand inside the greenhouse, probably on the staging, and their purpose is to maintain a very even temperature and rather moist atmosphere, in which cuttings will root readily and seeds will germinate rapidly.

When frames are used for hardening off, every opportunity should be taken on fine days to give increasing ventilation until eventually the lights can be left off most of the time.

FRANCOA *fran-ko-a* (Maiden's Wreath; Bridal Wreath). *F. ramosa* is a slightly tender perennial with ornamental foliage and spikes of white flowers late in summer. There is also a very similar, but pink-flowered species, *F. sonchifolia*. Both make ideal plants for the frost-proof greenhouse, where they will flower the second year after sowing the seed.

Culture: Pot March or April in well-drained pots of John Innes potting compost. Place in cool greenhouse, frame, or window. Water moderately October to April, freely afterwards. Apply liquid feed to plants in flower. Temperature: October to April, 40° to 50°; April to September, natural warmth with free ventilation.

Propagation: By seeds sown in a temperature of 50° to 55° in February, March or April; division of plants at potting time.

FREESIA *free-se-a*. Tender cormous plants with fragrant flowers. Modern hybrids of *F. refracta* embrace many lovely shades of colour. All flower in winter or spring.

Culture: Pot August to flower in January, and in successional batches until November to flower until April. Plant corms 1 in. deep and 2 in. apart in 5 in. pots in John Innes compost. Stand pots in cool position in greenhouse, frame or window. Water freely when growth is well advanced and until plants have flowered, then gradually decrease supply, keeping soil quite dry till July. Early staking to prevent the flopping of the foliage is important, and so too is plenty of light. Temperature not lower than 40°. Re-pot

Francoa ramosa.

Forsythia suspensa.

Freesia hybrid.

Fritillaria imperialis.

Picking pot-grown french beans.

Pruning forsythia immediately after flowering.

Fritillaria meleagris.

Garden frame.

annually. Specially prepared freesias are available for planting outside in mid-April. They flower in late summer and need a sunny, sheltered position.

Propagation: By seeds sown in pots or pans of light sandy soil in greenhouse; temperature: 60° to 65° in February or March; by offsets at potting time. Do not transplant seedlings first year. They will flower the same winter earlier than plants grown from corms and this is so satisfactory a method of growing freesias that many gardeners use it regularly, treating the plants as annuals and discarding the corms after flowering.

FRENCH BEANS. Ground should be well prepared by digging, the addition of rotted manure or compost and a good sprinkling of a compound fertiliser a week or so before sowing. Sow in late April and early May, 1 in. deep in drills 18 in. apart, spacing the seeds singly 6 in. apart in the drills. Gather beans regularly as soon as they attain usable size, and do not allow any to mature and produce seed as this checks

further cropping. Early crops can be produced by sowing in January or February, 5 or 6 seeds in a 6 in. or 7 in. pot, in John Innes compost and keeping in a greenhouse or frame in which a temperature 55° to 65° is maintained. Only two-thirds fill the pots at first and then top-dress with more John Innes compost as the plants grow.

Climbing French beans are grown in exactly the same way except that rows should be at least 3 ft. apart, and pea sticks should be stuck in firmly along the rows for support. There is a purple-podded variety which cooks green and is easy to grow; it also crops well. Bean sticks are needed for support.

FRENCH MARIGOLD, see Tagetes.

FRINGE FLOWER, see Schizanthus.

FRITILLARIA *frit-il-lair-ee-a* (Fritillary; Crown Imperial). Hardy bulbous plants. *F. meleagris,* the Snake's head Fritillary with nodding flowers chequered

Fumigating the greenhouse.

Gaillardia hybrid.

in pale and deep purple on slender 1 ft. high stems is suitable for borders or naturalising in turf; other species, well-drained open borders; sunny or partially shaded borders for *F. imperialis*, the Crown Imperial. It is much more robust in growth than most, 3 ft. high with clusters of nodding orange or yellow flowers on stout stems. All are spring flowering.

Culture: Plant 2 in. to 3 in. deep in fairly rich soil. Bulbs of *F. meleagris* should be about 6 in. apart; those of *F. imperialis* 12 in. Do not disturb bulbs as long as they maintain vigour and flower freely.

Propagation: By offsets removed at planting time.

FRITILLARY, *see* Fritillaria.

FROGHOPPER, *see* Cuckoo Spit.

FUCHSIA few-*she-a*. Tender and hardy deciduous flowering shrubs. After a period of neglect following its popularity in Victorian times the fuchsia—too well-known to need any description—has made quite a 'come-back', and this is hardly surprising as it is one of the most useful and attractive of all plants. It makes an ideal pot-plant as either a bush or standard. It comes in useful for window-boxes, hanging baskets, and bedding, and it can also be grown as a permanently planted greenhouse climber or trailer. It is not, however, a very good room plant, as buds are liable to fall in such conditions. Its long flowering period, from about June to autumn, makes it invaluable too.

Culture Under Glass: Pot old plants in February or March, young ones as they fill their pots with roots. Use John Innes No. 2 potting compost. Prune old plants in February. Water moderately March to May, freely May to October, very little at other times. Temperature: October to February, 40° to 45°, increasing as the year advances, reducing again in autumn. Apply liquid feed or fertiliser to healthy plants showing flower. Pinch out points of shoots frequently in spring and early summer to induce bushy growth.

Standards are produced by rubbing out all the side-shoots from young plants until the main stem is of the required height; the top is then pinched out and allowed to grow more or less as a bush, although any further growths which appear on the main stem must be continually removed.

Summer Culture in Beds: Plant out in June. Water freely during dry weather. Lift, pot and store plants in greenhouse in September.

Culture of Hardy Varieties: Plant October or April in ordinary well-drained soil in sheltered positions in sun or partial shade. Protect in winter with layers of dry litter or sharp cinders over crowns of plants. In April, cut off all top growth damaged by frost. This may necessitate cutting back to ground level in some cases, but plants usually throw up strong new shoots from the crowns and these flower the same year.

Propagation: By cuttings 2 in. to 3 in. long of young shoots inserted in sandy soil in temperature of about 60° in spring or summer.

FUMIGATION. A method of destroying insect pests and some fungi in greenhouses, by exposing them to poisonous fumes. Many different preparations are available for use as fumigants. In all cases it is essential to seal up the glass-house as tightly as possible during the period of fumigation. All ventilators and doors should be closed and covered with wet sacks, to prevent loss of fumes. Houses should be vacated the moment the fumigating compound is set in action, and should be ventilated freely for a while when fumigation is complete. Insecticides, such as DDT and BHC, are available in special smoke generators which have only to be ignited in the house, and a fungicide can also be obtained in the same form.

FUNGICIDE. Any chemical which will control or cure plant diseases caused by fungi, e.g. mildews, rusts, grey mould, leaf spot, etc. Popular fungicides include Bordeaux mixture, lime sulphur, colloidal sulphur, flowers of sulphur, colloidal copper, karathane and captan.

FUNKIA, *see* Hosta.

FURZE, *see* Ulex.

GAILLARDIA *gal-***lar**-*de-a* (Blanket Flower). Hardy annual and perennial plants with showy flowers in summer, often contrasting shades of red and yellow. The perennial gaillardias are derived from *G. aristata*, and are about 3 ft. in height, the annuals from *G. pulchella* and are 1½ ft. to 2 ft. tall. There are numerous garden varieties of both.
Culture: Plant perennial kinds 12 in. to 18 in. apart in March or April in ordinary soil in sunny well-drained beds or borders. Renew fairly frequently as old plants tend to die in winter. Annual species sown in shallow boxes of light soil in temperature of 55° to 65° in April, transplanting seedlings outdoors in May or, alternatively, seed may be sown outdoors in April where plants are to flower. Plant or thin to 12 in. apart. Soil and situation as for perennial kinds.
Propagation: Perennial kinds by division of plants in March or April; cuttings of roots laid in shallow boxes of sandy soil in February or March; seed sown in open ground in May, transplanting to flowering quarters in September.

GALANTHUS *gal-***an**-*thus* (Snowdrop). Hardy bulbous flowering plants, blooming in winter and spring, suitable for margins of beds, groups in open or shady borders, banks, rock gardens, or for naturalising in turf. The common snowdrop, *G. nivalis*, is 6 in. tall. Some other species, such as *G. byzantinus* and *G. elwesii*, are twice that height. All have white flowers marked with green.
Culture: Plant bulbs 2 in. deep and 3 in. apart September to November in ordinary soil. Bulbs should be lifted only when they show signs of deterioration, and are then best transplanted in spring immediately after flowering.
Propagation: By offsets treated as bulbs or by lifting and dividing old clumps of bulbs as soon as flowers fade in spring.

GALEGA *ga-***lee**-*ga* (Goat's Rue). Hardy perennial herbaceous plants bearing small, but plentiful, spikes of white, lilac, or mauve-pink flowers in summer. The plants will thrive in sunny or partially shaded borders. The species commonly grown, *G. officinalis*, is 3 ft. to 4 ft. tall.
Culture: Plant October to March 2 ft. apart in ordinary soil. Cut down flower stems in October. Replant every 2 or 3 years.
Propagation: By division in October to March.

GALL WEEVIL, *see* Turnip Gall Weevil.

GALTONIA *gawl-***toe**-*ne-a* (Spire Lily; Giant Summer Hyacinth). Hardy bulbous plant with white flowers. *G. candicans*, the only kind commonly cultivated, is 3 ft. to 4 ft. tall, flowering in August and September.
Culture: Plant October to March, placing bulbs 6 in. deep and 1 ft. apart in ordinary, well-drained soil in open, sunny borders. Lift and replant only when bulbs show signs of deterioration.
Propagation: By offsets removed at planting time.

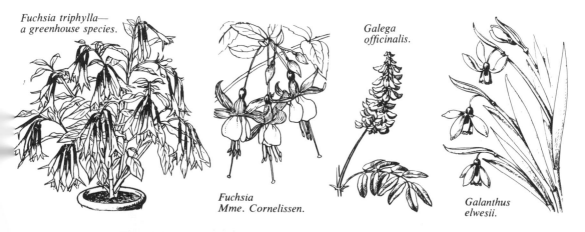

Fuchsia triphylla—a greenhouse species.

Fuchsia Mme. Cornelissen.

Galega officinalis.

Galanthus elwesii.

GAR

GARDENIA *gar-dee-ne-a* (Cape Jasmine). Tender evergreen shrubs with fragrant white flowers during spring and early summer. The double flowered forms of *G. jasminoides* are commonly grown.

Culture: Pot or plant February or March in well-drained pots or beds in greenhouse in John Innes compost. Prune into shape February or March. Temperature: March to September, 70° to 75°; September to March, 55° to 65°. Water moderately October to February, freely afterwards. Syringe daily, except when in bloom and in winter. Apply liquid feed to healthy plants when coming into flower. Plants 1 to 2 years old produce the best blooms, but older specimens flower profusely. Gardenias are 'dirty' plants and constant syringing is necessary to guard against greenfly, mealy bug and scale.

Propagation: By heel cuttings inserted in February in a close propagating frame with a bottom heat of about 70°. When rooted the cuttings are potted up into 3 in. pots and finally into 5 in. or 6 in. ones. One pinching-out is necessary to produce bushy plants, and then with plenty of heat and water they should flower later in the year.

GARLIC. A well-drained, rather light, but reasonably rich soil, and open, sunny position should be chosen. The bulbs are planted in February 2 in. deep and 6 in. apart, in rows 8 in. apart. Beyond regular hoeing, no further attention is required until July or August when the bulbs are lifted and stored in a cool airy place. They are often tied in small bunches, and suspended from a nail or beam in a shed.

GARRYA *gar-ree-a*. Hardy evergreen shrubs with ornamental foliage and beautiful pendulous catkins in winter. Male and female catkins are borne on separate trees, the male catkins are more decorative. The species grown is *G. elliptica*, and it will make a bush 8 ft. to 12 ft. high or cover a wall several feet higher than this.

Culture: Plant October or March to May in ordinary well-drained soil and a position sheltered from cold winds but open to sunshine. Plants may also be trained against sunny walls. No regular pruning required, but, when trained against walls, unwanted and badly placed shoots can be cut out in spring.

Propagation: By cuttings of firm shoots inserted in sandy soil in a propagating frame July or August.

GAZANIA *gaz-ay-nee-a* (Treasure Flower). More or less tender perennials, suitable for summer bedding in dry positions fully exposed to hot sunshine. Also excellent for seaside planting, where they will usually survive English winters. The plants are trailing with showy daisy-flowers in shades of yellow and orange often with a maroon or nearly black zone. They flower more or less continuously all summer.

Indoor Culture: Pot March or April in well-drained pots in John Innes compost and keep in sunny part of greenhouse. Water very little October to March, moderately other times. Temperature: September to March, 45° to 55°.

Outdoor Culture: Plant early in June in light, well-drained soil in sunny positions, either in beds, on sloping banks, or trailing over ledges in rock gardens. Lift in October and place in pots in a frost-proof greenhouse or frame for the winter except in seaside or other mild places where plants may survive a winter outdoors.

Propagation: By cuttings inserted in sandy soil in a cold frame July to September; cuttings may remain in cold frame during winter if protected from frost.

GENISTA *jen-is-ta* (Broom). Hardy deciduous flowering shrubs, usually with yellow flowers which are often fragrant. Tall species suitable for shrubbery; rock gardens for dwarf kinds. Among the best species are *G. aethnensis*, 12 ft. to 15 ft., July; *G. virgata*, 10 ft. to 12 ft., June to July; *G. lydia*, 2 ft. to 3 ft., May to June; *G. tinctoria*, 6 in., June; and *G. hispanica*, often called Spanish Gorse, 2 ft. to 3 ft., May to June. (See also Cytisus.)

Culture: Plant October to March in light, well-drained soil and sunny, sheltered positions. Prune lightly after flowering if necessary.

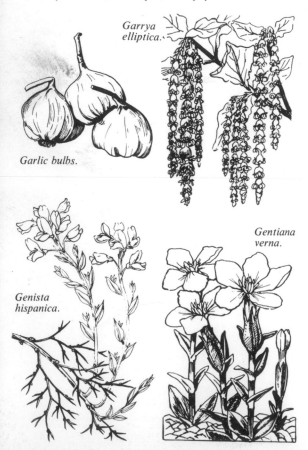

Garrya elliptica.

Garlic bulbs.

Gentiana verna.

Genista hispanica.

Propagation: By seeds sown ¼ in. deep in greenhouse or frame in March or April. Grow seedlings on in pots as most kinds resent much root disturbance.

GENTIAN, *see* Gentiana.

GENTIANA *jen-tee-***ar**-*na* (Gentian; Gentianella). Hardy perennials. Tall kinds suitable for sunny borders; sunny rockeries for dwarf kinds; all to be fairly dry in winter and moist in summer. Some are of easy culture, but others are among the more difficult plants. Among the best are *G. acaulis*, deep blue, spring; *G. verna*, bright blue, spring; *G. freyniana*, *G. lagodechiana*, and *G. septemfida*, all purplish blue, summer; *G. farreri*, *G. sino-ornata* and *G. macaulayi*, blue and white, autumn.

Culture: Plant September, October, March or April in a mixture of 2 parts loam, 1 part peat, and 1 part grit or coarse sand. Top-dress in March with a little peat or well-rotted leaf-mould. Water freely on dry soils in summer.

Propagation: By seeds sown in well-drained pots or pans of sandy loam in greenhouse or frame in March; division of plants March or April. Seeds sometimes take 1 or 2 years to germinate.

GENTIANELLA, *see* Gentiana.

GERANIUM *jer-***ay**-*ne-um* (Cranesbill; the bedding plants commonly referred to as 'geraniums' are really pelargoniums). Hardy herbaceous perennials. Dwarf kinds are suitable for planting in the rock garden. Flowers mostly rather fragile and saucer-shaped produced mainly in early summer. Among the best species are *G. pratense* and *G. grandiflorum*, both purplish-blue, 2 ft.; *G. armenum*, magenta, 2 ft.; *G. endressii*, pink, 1 ft.; *G. ibericum*, purple, 1 ft. to 1½ ft.; *G. sanguineum*, magenta and its variety *lancastriense*, pink, both 6 in.; and *G. subcaulescens*, magenta, 6 in.

Culture: Plant in spring or autumn in ordinary soil and open or partially shaded positions. *G. pratense* is one of the best perennials for planting on chalky land, and all species are tolerant of lime in the soil.

Propagation: By division of the roots at planting time; seed sown in a frame in March.

GERBERA *jer-***ber**-*a* (Barberton or Transvaal Daisy). In a very warm spot the showy *G. jamesonii*, and the hybrids partly derived from it, can be grown outside, but elsewhere they are only suitable for greenhouse cultivation. The large, daisy-like blooms, sometimes as much as 4 in. across, are splendid for cutting, with stems up to about 15 in. long, and although the type plant is limited to yellow and orange shades, there is a much bigger range in the hybrids including terracotta, salmon and red.

Culture: Grow in John Innes compost with some extra sand or grit in a light, airy greenhouse, tempera-

Gardenia grandiflora.

Gazania hybrid.

Geranium grandiflorum.

ture: 45° to 50° from November to May; without artificial heat afterwards. Water sparingly from November to April, freely afterwards. Re-pot annually in spring, but be careful not to over-pot. The roots should almost fill the pots from the start. No shade required. The plants are not usually at their best until 3 years old.

Propagation: By seeds sown in sandy soil in March in temperature of 55°. Cuttings can also be taken from non-flowering shoots at potting time in spring and rooted in pure sand or very sandy soil in a propagating frame.

GERMAN CATCHFLY, *see* Lychnis.

GERMINATION. The emergence of the young plant from the seed, in which it has previously remained as an embryo. The main factors in producing germination are warmth, moisture and air; although some seeds have special requirements, e.g. those of high alpine plants which often germinate best after being frozen. The most common cause of poor germination is lack of moisture after growth has started.

GEUM jee-*um* (Avens). Hardy herbaceous perennials with showy red, yellow or orange flowers in summer. The taller species are suitable for sunny borders, dwarf kinds on sunny rock gardens. *G. coccineum* is the species from which most garden varieties have been developed. It grows about 2 ft. high. *G. reptans* is a nearly prostrate plant with yellow flowers; *G. forisii*, a hybrid, 1 ft. high with orange-red flowers, and *G. rivale*, a moisture-loving species, 1½ ft. to 2 ft. high with old-rose flowers.

Culture: Plant October to April in ordinary well-drained soil, with the exception of *G. rivale*, the Bog Avens, which does well in the moist soil near the margins of pools and streams. Cut down flower stems when flowers have faded, thus relieving the plants of the strain of developing seed.

Propagation: By seed sown in light soil in a cold frame in March or April, or in sunny positions outdoors April or July, division of plants October to April.

Ginkgo biloba.

GHOST TREE, *see* Davidia.

GIANT SUMMER HYACINTH, *see* Galtonia.

GINGER LILY, *see* Hedychium.

GINKGO gink-*go* (Maidenhair Tree). *G. biloba* is a deciduous tree closely allied to the conifers, and with most attractive leaves each of which resembles a single segment of a maidenhair fern leaf on a greater scale. It will eventually reach a height of 70 or 80 ft., but most forms grown in Britain are rather erect in habit so that they do not take up a lot of room. It is a good town tree.

Culture: Plant October to April in ordinary soil and open, sunny position. No regular pruning is desirable.

Propagation: By seed sown in a greenhouse or frame in March.

GLADIOLUS glad-ee-**o**-*lus* (Cornflag; Sword Lily). Half-hardy cormous flowering plants. There are several distinct types in general cultivation: the

Gerbera hybrid.

Geum Mrs Bradshaw.

Gladiolus primulinus.

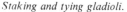
Staking and tying gladioli.   *Gladiolus colvillei rubra.*   *Removing gladioli cormlets.*

large flowered, with spikes of big flowers closely set on long stems; hybrids, of the smaller and daintier *G. primulinus*, with hooded flowers fairly widely spaced; the early flowering varieties, for the most part hybrids of *G. colvillei*, which are grown chiefly under glass for cutting; miniature gladioli, often with elegantly ruffled flowers, which are sometimes collectively described as 'nanus varieties'; 'Butterflies' which resemble the large-flowered in height but have smaller flowers usually with sharply contrasted colours, and various species which are mainly grown by specialists. Today varieties are innumerable and their colour range is extremely varied. Most flower from late July to September and are from 3 ft. to 5 ft. tall, but the early flowering varieties are smaller, seldom exceeding 2 ft., and they flower in May and June.

Culture Outdoors: Good drainage is essential and a sunny, open position. Soil should be deeply worked and reasonably enriched, but do not use fresh manure. Plant in March, April and May about 4 in. deep and 6 in. to 8 in. apart. Water freely during dry weather. Stake individually when the spikes begin to form. Lift the corms before severe frost, cut away foliage, and dry off in a frost-proof shed or greenhouse. Before storing remove and discard old shrivelled corms from the base of the new ones formed during the season. Store in shallow trays in a cool, airy place secure from frost.

Culture Under Glass: Practically all forms of gladioli may be successfully grown under glass. One corm of the large-flowered type is sufficient for a 6 in. pot, in which it should be potted 2 in. deep in a rich well-drained compost. Potting up may be done in January or February, but until the flower-spikes appear and the plants are removed to the greenhouse, the pots are best stood in a cold frame with a covering of straw

or litter in severe weather. The corms may also be planted at the same time in the soil of a cold greenhouse where, if set 3 in. deep and 4 in. apart, they will provide some early blooms.

The large-flowered gladioli resent forcing but some of the dwarf forms, such as the *colvillei* and *nanus* types, may be flowered in gentle heat in spring if potted up three to a 6 in. pot in autumn.

After potting the pots should be plunged in ashes or peat in a cold frame, where they should be completely covered until plenty of roots have formed. They will then soon come into bloom in a greenhouse, in a temperature of about 50° if given plenty of light and water. After flowering gradually reduce the water supply until foliage dies down, when the corms may be cleaned and stored in trays.

Propagation: Mainly by corms, but cormlets or spawn which appear around the base of the corms may be planted in spring in nursery beds of light soil. They will flower in 2 to 3 years.

GLASS. Greenhouse glass is sold in various standard sizes but, for the normal type of greenhouse, sheets about 2 sq. ft. in area are the most suitable; 20 in. by 14 in. is thus a suitable size. Smaller sizes than this mean too much loss of light, owing to the number of glazing bars and larger ones are costly to replace. The thickness of the glass is measured by weight per sq. ft., and 24 oz. should be regarded as the minimum, this is the weight commonly sold as horticultural glass. For Dutch lights a single sheet of glass 56 in. by $28\frac{3}{4}$ in. is used, and although this is costly to replace the ease with which this operation can be carried out does offset the expense. These Dutch light sheets are merely slid into grooved wood with no puttying.

GLASTONBURY THORN, *see* Crataegus.

GLOBE ARTICHOKE, *see* Artichoke, Globe.

GLOBE FLOWER, *see* Trollius.

GLOBE THISTLE, *see* Echinops.

GLORIOSA *glor-ee-o-sa* (Glory Lily). Tender tuberous-rooted climbers with gaily marked, spotted and striped flowers, the petals being narrow, waved, and recurved like those of some true lilies. Mostly natives of Tropical Africa, these very showy lilies, which climb to about 6 ft. by means of tendrils emitted from the tips of the leaves, are superb plants for the warm greenhouse but the bulbs seem to be seldom listed. It is, however, possible to raise them from seed, and that of the crimson *G. rothschildiana*, and the orange and red *G. superba*, is readily obtained.
Culture: Pot *bulbs* in February in well-drained pots, placing *tubers* 2 in. deep, one in a 6 in. or several in an 8 in. or 12 in. pot using John Innes No. 2 compost. Train shoots to roof or trellis. Water moderately till growth is well advanced, then freely. After flowering gradually withhold water and keep soil quite dry till potting time. Temperature: February to April, 70° to 85°; September to January, about 55°.
Propagation: By seed which should be sown singly in small pots in good, moist bottom heat in January, after which the seedlings should be transferred without root disturbance to 7 in. pots. By offsets removed at potting time, but great care must be taken not to damage the parent bulbs, which are very brittle.

GLORY LILY, *see* Gloriosa.

GLORY OF THE SNOW, *see* Chionodoxa.

GLOXINIA *gloks-in-ee-a*. Tender tuberous-rooted plants with showy flowers in many bright colours in summer. These plants, which are actually derived from *Sinningia speciosa*, are popular greenhouse subjects.
Culture: Cultivation from tubers is easy. They are boxed or potted-up with the crowns just showing, in either John Innes No. 1 potting compost or a mixture of leaf-mould and peat with a small amount of soil, cow manure and sand. This is done at any time from February to April as long as a temperature of at least 60° can be maintained. Kept barely moist the tubers will soon produce growth, and as soon as this is 2 in. high the plants should be transferred to 5 in. pots and eventually to 7 in. or even 8 in. ones, using either the mixture already mentioned or John Innes No. 2 compost. A humid atmosphere, plenty of water and shade from hot sun are needed during the summer, but the temperature should be on the low side when the plants are in flower. After flowering the tubers should be dried off slowly and stored for the winter in a temperature of not less than 50°.
Propagation: By seed, but this requires care as the seed is very fine indeed, but good plants can be raised to flower the same year from a sowing made in early spring; or by sowing in June, when it is easier to keep up the necessary temperature of 70° required for germination, small tubers can be produced for flowering the following year. The plants may also be increased by means of leaf-cuttings in summer.

GOAT'S BEARD, *see* Aruncus.

GOAT'S RUE, *see* Galega.

GODETIA *god-ee-sha*. Hardy annuals, with variously coloured flowers in summer. There are numerous garden varieties, some with single some with double flowers. Heights range from 9 in. to 2½ ft.
Culture: Sow seed thinly outdoors in spring or early September where the plants are to flower, and thin seedlings 6 in. to 8 in. apart. Godetias thrive in any ordinary soil and open or partially shaded places.

GOLD DUST, *see* Alyssum.

GOLDEN BELLS, *see* Forsythia.

GOLDEN CHAIN, *see* Laburnum.

GOLDEN ROD, *see* Solidago.

Gloriosa rothschildiana.

Gloxinia hybrid.

Godetia.

GOOSEBERRY. Plant October to March in good, well-cultivated soil and open positions, spacing the bushes at least 5 ft. apart. After planting cut all stems back to about 6 in. In subsequent years prune in October thinning out overcrowded, thin, damaged or old branches. In particular keep the centres of the bushes reasonably open to facilitate fruit picking. Some varieties have a weeping habit which can be corrected by pruning each such branch to an upward pointing bud at about the apex of the arch. Mulch each February with well-rotted manure or compost. Thin fruits in late May and early June when they are large enough for cooking and leave remaining fruits to ripen. There are numerous varieties differing in time of ripening and colour of fruits. Good kinds are Early Sulphur, yellow, early; Careless, white, mid-season; Lancashire Lad, red, mid-season; Leveller, yellow, mid-season, and Keepsake, green, late.
Propagation: By cutting of firm young stems 6 in. to 9 in. long inserted in light soil in October. All but the top three buds should be removed.

GOOSEFOOT PLANT, *see* Syngonium.

GORSE, *see* Ulex.

GRAFTING. The art of uniting a portion of one plant with a portion of another. Grafting is very largely used in the propagation of top fruits, such as apples and pears and also for some choice shrubs and ornamental trees. A form of grafting known as 'root grafting' is used for the propagation of double-flowered gypsophila and a few other herbaceous plants, while grafting is occasionally used in propagating some choice cacti. In all cases the essential thing is to bring the cambium layer (situated between the bark and wood) of the two portions into close contact. This is done by cutting both and then binding the cut surfaces together. That portion of a graft which is to supply the top growth is known as the scion, and that part which is to supply the roots is known as the stock.

A great many different types of graft are employed, and these are designated by various terms, such as 'whip grafting', 'rind grafting', 'cleft grafting', 'saddle

Pruning a gooseberry bush.

Preparing gooseberry cuttings.

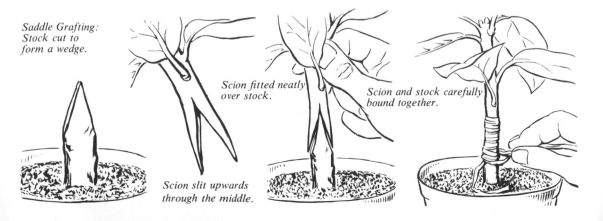

Saddle Grafting:
Stock cut to
form a wedge.

Scion fitted neatly over stock.

Scion and stock carefully bound together.

Scion slit upwards through the middle.

Stopping the laterals of a vine.

Thinning greenhouse grapes.

'grafting', etc., but in essentials the process is the same whatever the method employed. When grafting outdoors it is essential to cover the whole of the wounded surface with grafting wax or something else to keep out air, but this is not invariably required when grafting in a propagating frame under glass. The most favourable time for grafting is usually in the spring just as growth commences, but it is usually advisable to take steps to retard the scions so that they are more backward than the stocks at the actual time of grafting. For example, fruit scions are gathered when pruning in winter and are then heeled-in, in a cool, shady place, such as under a north-facing wall until they are required in March.

GRAPE HYACINTH, *see* Muscari.

GRAPE VINES. These can be grown both out-doors, trained against sunny walls or over trellis, or wires, or under glass in heated or unheated glass-houses. Outdoors ripening tends to be uncertain and selection is limited to certain very hardy varieties, such as Royal Muscadine, Brandt, Pirovana 14, and Pearl of Czaba. Under glass any varieties can be grown and ripened successfully though some are more difficult than others. Specially recommended are Black Hamburgh, Gros Colmar, Madresfield, Court and Muscat of Alexandria.

Vines need good, rich soil and good drainage. Borders specially prepared for them should be at least 3 ft. deep and the full width of the greenhouse. Hard rubble should be placed in the bottom for drainage, a layer of turves on top of this and then the border should be filled with good, loamy soil, well sprinkled with wood ashes and coarse bone meal

and with a little well-rotted manure all thoroughly mixed in.

Vines are best planted in late February or early March, roots should be well spread out and made thoroughly firm. Either one vine can be trained to fill a whole house with numerous stems or else, the more usual method, each vine can be restricted to one main rod when the vines should be 5 ft. to 6 ft. apart. The first year the newly planted vine is only allowed to make one main growth and this is trained upwards towards the ridge of the house for single rod culture or horizontally along the eaves for multiple stem culture.

In subsequent years side growths are allowed to form every 15 in. to 18 in. on each side of each main rod of single stem vines. Multiple rod vines are per-mitted to form a main growth every 5 ft. along the horizontally trained stems and these are trained to the ridge, each being subsequently treated like the main rod of a single-stem vine.

The side growths carry the flowers and bunches of grapes, not more than one to each side growth which is stopped two leaves beyond the flower cluster or when it is 2 ft. to 3 ft. long. All secondary growths which appear are stopped at the first leaf. All these side growths are carefully tied to wires strained hori-zontally about 9 in. below the glass.

Each winter the side growths are cut back to within 1 or 2 dormant growth buds of the main rods or the woody 'spurs' which in time form on them. In January the main rods are untied and allowed to hang down to check uprush of sap but, when growth has started, are retied in their former positions. Allow only one side growth to form at each spur and rub off any others. Vines respond to fairly generous feed-

Greenfly on roses.

Greasebanding a fruit tree.

Tomatoes affected by Greenback.

ing. In winter the top 2 in. of soil can be carefully removed and replaced by a mixture of equal parts well-rotted manure, and good, loamy soil. Immediately after flowering the border can be further enriched by a top-dressing of a compound vine fertiliser at the rate recommended by the manufacturer.

Vines are started any time from January to March by closing ventilators and allowing temperature to rise to 50° to 60°. First the border should be thoroughly soaked. Daily syringing with clear water should be given, but should be discontinued while vines are in flower when temperature may rise a little, and flowers should be pollinated with a camel hair brush.

When berries are well formed they must be carefully thinned with pointed scissors. Water is necessary to keep soil moist, keep paths and walls damp to maintain a fairly humid atmosphere but allow air to become much drier and temperature to rise a little as grapes ripen. Outdoors, vines can be treated in much the same way as those indoors but it is best to plant them against a warm and sheltered wall.

Propagation: By 'eyes', or dormant growth buds cut from well-ripened side growths in autumn with a short piece of stem itself. These 'eyes' are laid horizontally, but uppermost, in John Innes compost in small flower pots, 1 per pot, and are started into growth in a propagating frame, temperature 60°.

GREASE-BANDING. A method of keeping down certain insect pests of fruit trees, particularly the winter moths. Broad bands of grease-proof paper are placed around the main trunks, or each of the main branches, of the fruit trees about mid-September and are coated with a sticky substance. This can be renewed from time to time during the winter. Any insects which attempt to crawl over the bands are trapped. The female winter moths are wingless and have to crawl up the trees in the autumn to lay their eggs on the branches or twigs. Hence the effectiveness of banding against these pests. Special bands and banding compounds can be purchased from dealers in horticultural sundries. Grease-banding is most serviceable in the case of apples and can also be used for pears, plums, and other large fruit trees. The bands should be at least 1½ ft. above ground level if they are to be effective.

GREENBACK. A common tomato disorder in which the fruits do not ripen completely but remain green near the stalk. It may be due to lack of potash or to hot sun reaching the fruits, prevention consists of ensuring that nitrogenous fertilisers are balanced by an adequate supply of potash and that the plants are allowed to keep sufficient foliage to provide, natural shade. In hot weather it may be necessary to shade the greenhouse lightly. If, even with these precautions, the trouble persists, a change of variety should be tried as some varieties are much less susceptible to the trouble than others. Potentate is apt to suffer badly but is popular, nevertheless, because it is a very heavy cropper.

GREENFLY. A popular name for certain species of aphides which attack plants, suck the sap from their leaves or young stems, and often cripple growth. They show a preference for the undersides of the leaves, which makes the efficient application of a spray a somewhat difficult matter in certain cases. Infested leaves may cockle or even curl up completely when badly attacked, and it is most difficult to destroy the pests by means of ordinary insecticides. Early spraying before curling has taken place is advisable. Nicotine and BHC are effective against all kinds of greenfly, but it may be necessary to repeat applications several times, at intervals of 3 or 4 days, to destroy successive broods which escape earlier treatment. The systemic insecticide menazon will give protection for about a month.

GREENHOUSE. Although this term is commonly applied to all types of glass-houses it should, strictly speaking, be used for those in which plants requiring a moderate temperature are grown in pots—other types of glass-house are the conservatory (in which some of the subjects may be planted out permanently and others are brought in for display for short periods), propagating house, stove house, and so on. Nowadays greenhouses are made in all sorts of designs and materials, but with all of them the main thing should be plenty of light· adequate ventilation, freedom from draughts and sound construction are also important points. For general purposes the best type is the span-roof, with the overhead glass forming an inverted V, as in this the plants get light from all sides; but the lean-to pattern, with the roof consisting of one slope only, is useful where the structure is to be built against a wall. From a cultivation point of view greenhouses are usually divided into two groups: the cold house, with no artificial heat, and the cool house, with enough to maintain a temperature of about 50° in winter.

Greenhouses may be made of wood, aluminium alloy, steel or concrete. Wood has the advantage of cheapness, and, if the wood is western red cedar, teak or one of the African hardwoods it will withstand damp conditions for many years. Aluminium alloys are rather expensive but cost little in upkeep as they need no painting.

The house may be glazed to ground level, which has the advantage if crops, such as tomatoes and chrysanthemums, are to be grown in beds or on the floor of the house, or they may have walls, usually about 2½ ft. high, of wood or brick which conserves more heat and is convenient if pot plants are to be grown on staging.

GREEN MANURING. The practice of growing rapid-maturing crops, such as mustard, vetches or rape and digging these in before they produce seed. This has been recommended as a substitute for manuring with dung. Vetches and other members of the pea family actually enrich the soil with nitrogen, but the principal value of other crops is that they supply extra humus and so improve the texture of the soil. To assist their rotting they should be dusted with sulphate of ammonia before turning in.

GREVILLEA grev-*il-ee-a* (Silk Oak; Silk Bark Oak). *G. robusta* is a multi-purpose plant, sometimes used as a dot or feature plant in summer bedding schemes and window boxes, but primarily valuable as a greenhouse or indoor foliage subject. It has finely-cut leaves of a silvery-bronze tone, shaped rather like those of some ferns. *G. rosmarinifolia* is a slightly tender shrub, to 6 ft. high with crimson flowers in summer; *G. sulphurea* is similar but yellow.
Culture: Cool, airy conditions are best for *G. robusta;* hot, stuffy air, draughts and dryness at the roots will make leaves fall. Plenty of water is needed in summer, when the plants should grow rapidly; they will make big specimens quite quickly. The near-hardy grevilleas should be planted outdoors in sunny, sheltered positions in any well-drained soil. No regular pruning is required.
Propagation: Either by cuttings of half-ripe tips of side growths in summer, struck in a close frame or under a jam jar; or by seeds, which sometimes take many months to germinate.

GREY MOULD, *see* Botrytis.

GROMWELL, *see* Lithospermum.

GROUND IVY, *see* Nepeta.

GROWTH SUBSTANCES. Various preparations which effect the growth of plants are available nowadays and the most common uses to which these are put are the rooting of cuttings, the suppression of weeds and the setting of fruit. They are all based on certain compounds known as hormones.

GUELDER ROSE, *see* Viburnum.

GUERNSEY LILY, *see* Nerine.

GUM CISTUS, *see* Cistus.

GUNNERA gun-*er-a.* Hardy herbaceous plants with immense leaves rather like those of a rhubarb,

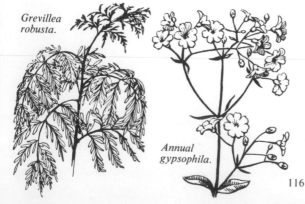

Grevillea robusta.

Annual gypsophila.

Grevillea sulphurea.

Gunnera manicata.

but on a greatly increased scale. *G. manicata*, the species commonly grown, will produce leaves 6 ft. across, the whole plant by mid-summer being 8 ft. or 9 ft. high. It is a handsome foliage plant for the waterside.

Culture: Plant in March or April in good, rich, loamy soil by the side of pools or streams. In autumn cover crowns with dry straw or bracken for protection or cut off the plant's own leaves and invert them over the crowns. Whatever is used must be secured in position with flexible branches thrust into the soil, wire netting or anything else convenient.

Propagation: By division at planting time.

GYPSOPHILA *gyp-**soph**-il-a.* Hardy herbaceous perennials and annuals suitable for sunny beds, and borders, and some small kinds for rock gardens and dry walls. All thrive in chalky soil. Flowers small, numerous, white or pink in summer.

The most popular species is *G. paniculata*, 3 ft. to 4 ft. high. *G. repens* is a trailing plant. The annual gypsophilas are also trailing or sprawling and are derived from *G. elegans*. The flowers are larger individually than those of the perennial kinds.

Culture: Plant perennial kinds October to April in ordinary well-drained soil. Do not disturb unnecessarily. Annual kinds: sow in March, April or September where they are to flower, and thin to 6 in. apart.

Propagation: By seed in a frame or greenhouse in March; cuttings in a propagating frame in July; double-flowered forms by root grafting in March or April on the seedlings of the common kinds.

A brick-based greenhouse.

HAEMANTHUS *he-**man**-thus* (Blood Flower; Red Cape Lily). Bulbous plants for the greenhouse. The species most commonly grown, *H. multiflorus*, makes a fine novelty, for its huge round umbels of scarlet flowers, carried on 1 ft. long stems, are quite out of the ordinary. Other species include the crimson *H. katherinae* and the white *H. albiflos*. They are all quite easy to grow indoors.

Culture: Bulbs should be potted up in spring in a

117

mixture of loam and sandy peat, with perfect drainage, in pots little more than large enough to take the bulbs which should be completely covered. After flowering growth should be maintained for a time, but then the bulbs should be completely rested until re-started into growth in spring. Re-potting is only needed every few years, when the plants may be increased by offsets, which flower 2 or 3 years later. Temperature: April to September, 60° to 70°; October to March, 50° to 60°.

HAMAMELIS *ham-am-el-is* (Witch Hazel). Hardy deciduous shrubs or small trees with fragrant flowers in winter. The petals are narrow and twisted, yellow in the most popular species, *H. mollis*, yellow and purple in *H. japonica*. They will grow from 12 ft. to 20 ft. high.
Culture: Plant November to March in good, loamy soil and a sunny, but reasonably sheltered position. No regular pruning is desirable, but if bushes get too big they can be thinned and branches shortened immediately after flowering.
Propagation: By removal of rooted suckers at planting time or by layering in spring.

HANDKERCHIEF TREE, *see* Davidia.

HANGING BASKETS. A basket of wire or strips of wood in which plants are grown and suspended either in a glass-house or outdoors in porches, verandahs, etc. Ivy-leaved pelargoniums, fuchsias, marguerites, trailing lobelia, *Campanula isophylla*, *Asparagus sprengeri*, *A. plumosus*, *Nepeta glechoma variegata* and *Lysimachia nummularia aurea* are among the most popular plants for hanging baskets. There are also tuberous-rooted begonias of drooping habit which are particularly valuable for the purpose. Most of these plants are grown in greenhouses in pots during the autumn and winter months and are placed in the baskets in March or April. The baskets themselves are well lined with sphagnum moss to give them an attractive appearance and to prevent soil from washing out when the plants are watered. The plants are then placed in position, and good soil, such as John Innes compost, packed around their roots.

As many of the plants commonly used in hanging baskets are tender, it is usually unsafe to put such baskets outdoors before the end of May. During the summer, plants in hanging baskets must be watered regularly and freely. They should be given a liquid feed every week or 10 days.

HARDENING-OFF. The process of gradually preparing for planting in the open air, such plants as have been raised, or over-wintered, under cover. More and more air and less heat are provided as the tissues harden, until eventually they are capable of enduring outdoor conditions. As a rule hardening-off starts in a greenhouse to which increased ventilation is given and is completed in a frame from which, eventually, the protective light can be removed altogether.

HARDY. A term applied to any plant which will normally endure our winters without protection. The term must sometimes be accepted as relative in value rather than absolute, local factors exerting an influence upon the behaviour of plants. It is commonly accepted that some subjects are hardy in the south of England and not hardy in the north. A number of shrubs and succulent plants will thrive near the sea-coast even in the north, though they cannot be regarded as fully reliable in the open in inland gardens, even in the south. There are districts in Scotland where, owing to the shelter of high mountains on one side and the influence of the sea on the other, sub-tropical plants flourish as well as in Cornwall. The life of many plants which are native to high altitudes, where keener frosts than ever occur in England are endured, is often jeopardised by the mild humidity of our winter climate which keeps the plants in growth when they should be dormant. Shelter from wind is often as important as protection from frost especially in seaside gardens.

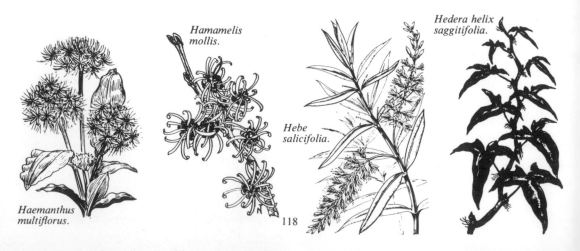

Hamamelis mollis.

Hebe salicifolia.

Hedera helix saggitifolia.

Haemanthus multiflorus.

118

HARDY PALM, *see* Chamaerops.

HART'S-TONGUE FERN, *see* Scolopendrium.

HAWTHORN, *see* Crataegus.

HEART'S-EASE, *see* Viola.

HEARTS ENTANGLED, *see* Ceropegia.

HEATHER, *see* Calluna and Erica.

HEBE hee-*bee* (Veronica). Hardy or slightly tender evergreen shrubs with blue, purple, red, or white flowers in early summer and early autumn. Formerly known as veronica. Specially suitable for sheltered, sunny shrubberies and borders. Particularly good near sea. Among the best kinds are the numerous varieties of *H. speciosa* with blue, purple, pink, or crimson flowers which grow 5 ft. tall; *H. traversii*, white, 5 ft.; *H. salicifolia*, white, 5 ft. to 10 ft.; *H. cataractae*, white or blue, 1 ft.; *H. cupressoides*, pale blue, 1 ft. to 3 ft., and *H. armstrongii*, old-gold foliage 1 ft. to 2 ft.
Culture: Plant October to March in ordinary well-drained soil. Protect slightly tender kinds, such as *H. speciosa* and varieties with sacking or wattle hurdles in winter. No regular pruning required, but bushes may be reduced in size in April.
Propagation: By cuttings of firm shoots in sandy soil in a frame, July to September.

HEDERA hed-*er-a* (Ivy). Hardy evergreen climbing plants with ornamental foliage, green and variegated, too well known to require description. They derive mainly (by sporting) from *H. helix*, the English ivy, which is, of course, perfectly hardy; but *H. canariensis*, the Canary ivy, is also grown, usually in its variegated forms, but is used as a greenhouse or house plant. The hardy *H. colchica* has also provided a few forms, such as *H. c. dentata*, mainly utilised outside owing to their robust growth.
Outdoor Culture: Plant October to April in ordinary soil and sunny or shady places. Trim with shears in April cutting off old leaves and straggling shoots. Ivies are self-clinging and so require no tying, but the bush ivies grown from flowering growth of the ordinary ivies, do not climb at all but are branching and chubby in habit. They can be grown as specimens in the open without support of any kind.
Indoor Culture: Because they are hardy the varieties of *H. helix* are excellent for cool, part-shady conditions, but they do not like draughts in a dark hall or stairway. Nor do they appreciate the dry stuffy air of a well-heated room in winter, which causes the leaves to wither and drop. Fresh air and coolness—below 50° in winter—are the desirable conditions, coupled with adequate, but never excessive, watering, though the soil must not dry right out even in the winter. *H. canariensis* likes warmer conditions, but

Lining a hanging basket with sphagnum moss.

Planting the sides of a hanging basket.

Filling in the centre with a fuchsia and trailing geranium.

Hardening off plants in a frame.

not fluctuating temperatures. All like an overhead spray from time to time.

Propagation: By cuttings of firm shoots inserted in ordinary soil and shady place September to November.

HEDGE. A hedge may be the outer boundary of a garden intended to give privacy, it may be planted primarily as a windbreak or for shelter, or it may simply be intended for ornament, or as a division between one feature in the garden and another. Boundary hedges must be sufficiently strong to serve their purpose, hence the popularity of privet, hawthorn, beech, holly and yew. Laurels and aucuba also make very strong hedges but take up rather a lot of room.

Windbreaks and shelter hedges are often formed with quick-growing conifers, such as *Chamaecyparis lawsoniana* or *C. leylandii*, *Thuja plicata* or *T. occidentalis*.

Dividing hedges within the garden can be of less robust shrubs. *Lonicera nitida* is popular and neat. Box was once much used but has fallen into disfavour. Flowering shrubs, such as *Berberis darwinii* or *B. stenophylla*, may be used, also lavender or freely branched roses, such as some of the hybrid floribunda varieties and hybrid musks.

Whatever is planted the ground for hedges should be well prepared. Dig a strip at least 3 ft. wide, work in rotted manure or compost and finish off with a dusting of bonemeal or superphosphate of lime to give the hedge shrubs a good start. It may help a lot to provide some shelter at first, as with wattle hurdles, or to attach each plant to a wire strained between posts.

Hedges must be kept neat by trimming, but too much trimming may do more harm than good. In general hard cutting back is best done in spring and during summer light trimming with shears is all that is necessary.

HEDGEHOG CACTUS, *see* Echinocactus.

HEDYCHIUM *hed-***ik**-*ee-um* (Ginger Lily). Half-hardy perennials 4 ft. to 5 ft. high with 1 ft.-long spikes of fragrant flowers in summer, which are lemon-yellow in the species usually grown, *H. gardnerianum*.

Culture: In very warm, sheltered gardens it is, in fact, hardy, but the more usual way of growing it is to treat it like a dahlia or canna and store the roots in winter after planting them out for the summer, or it may be grown as a pot plant in a greenhouse as long as the roots are protected from frost in winter. Almost any rich soil suits it but a moisture-holding one is advisable as the plants need copious supplies of water in summer, together with liberal feeding. Under glass the plants should be potted into a size larger pot each spring.

Propagation: By division in the spring.

HEELING-IN. The practice of covering the roots of plants temporarily until they can be planted permanently. The usual method is to dig out a rather wide, shallow trench, lay the plants at an angle, close together with their roots spread out in the trench, and then cover the roots with soil and make it firm. Plants heeled-in properly will remain in good condition for weeks or even months.

HELENIUM *hel-***een**-*ee-um* (Helen-flower; Sneezewort; Sneeze-weed). Hardy herbaceous perennials with yellow, bronze or crimson flowers in summer. There are numerous garden varieties, mostly derived from *H. autumnale*. They range in height from 2 ft. to 5 ft.

Culture: Plant autumn or spring in ordinary soil in sunny well-drained borders. Divide and transplant every third year.

Propagation: By division of roots in October or March.

HELIANTHEMUM *he-lee-***anthe**-*mum* (Sun Rose; Rock Rose). Dwarf hardy flowering evergreen shrubs with gaily coloured flowers in early summer. Suitable for sunny banks, rock gardens or dry walls.

There are numerous garden varieties mainly derived from *H. nummularium*, which grows only about 1 ft. high but may spread over several square feet of ground.

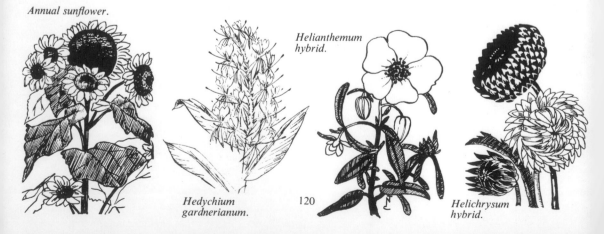

Annual sunflower.

Helianthemum hybrid.

Hedychium gardnerianum.

120

Helichrysum hybrid.

Heeling-in privet.

Helenium hybrid.

Culture: Plant autumn or spring in light, sandy soil. Prune into shape immediately after flowering.
Propagation: By seeds sown in sandy soil in a frame or greenhouse in March or April; cuttings of firm young shoots inserted in sandy soil in a frame in July or August.

HELIANTHUS *he-lee-***an**-*thus* (Sunflower). Hardy annual or perennial herbs usually of sturdy habit and with large yellow flowers in summer or early autumn. There are numerous garden varieties, the perennials derived mainly from *H. decapetalus*, 3 ft. to 5 ft. high and *H. rigidus*, 6 ft. to 8 ft. high; the annuals from *H. annuus*, 8 ft. to 12 ft. and *H. debilis*, 3 ft. to 4 ft.; *H. atrorubens*, better known as *H. sparsifolius*, is a particularly handsome perennial, 6 ft. to 7 ft. high, but it is less hardy than most.
Culture of Annual Species: Sow seeds $\frac{1}{4}$ in. deep in ordinary soil in sunny borders in April where plants are to flower, or in small pots in temperature of 55° to 60° in March, transplanting seedlings outdoors in May or June.
Culture of Perennial Species: Plant October, November, March or April in ordinary soil in sunny well-drained borders. Cut down stems in November; replant every third year. Lift roots of *H. atrorubens* in October, place in sandy soil in a frame for the winter and replant in April.
Propagation: Perennial species by division of roots October, March or April.

HELICHRYSUM *he-lee-***kry**-*sum* (Everlasting Flower; Immortelle). Half-hardy annuals with showy flower-heads surrounded by papery bracts in red, yellow, orange, and white, which can be dried for winter decoration and hardy or slightly tender perennials usually with grey leaves and silvery flowers. The annual varieties are derived from *H. bracteatum*, 2 ft. to 3 ft. high. Among the first of the perennial kinds are *H. bellidioides*, white flowers, silver leaves, trailing; *H. lanatum*, silver leaves, 3 ft.; *H. trilineatum*, silver leaves, 2 ft.
Culture of Annual Species: Sow seeds in temperature of 60°. In March prick off into boxes, harden-off and plant out in May in ordinary soil in sunny positions. Gather flowers for winter decoration directly they are fully expanded.
Culture of Perennial Species: Plant March or April in light soil in sunny well-drained borders or rock gardens. Protect in very severe weather.
Propagation: Perennial species by seeds sown in a greenhouse or frame in April, or cuttings in greenhouse or frame in spring.

HELIOPSIS *he-lee-***op**-*sis*. Hardy herbaceous perennials with yellow sunflower-like flowers in summer. There are several good garden varieties derived from *H. scabra*, 4 ft. to 5 ft. One, named *zinniaeflora*, has double flowers.
Culture: Plant October, November, March or April in ordinary soil in sunny, well-drained borders. Cut down in October.
Propagation: By division of plants October, March or April.

HELIOTROPIUM *he-lee-***tro**-*pee-um* (Heliotrope; Cherry Pie). Half-hardy perennials with fragrant purple flowers in summer. Several named varieties in various shades of blue are available. It may be grown as either a greenhouse plant or bedding subject

121

Helleborus orientalis.

Helxine soleirolii aurea.

and for the latter purpose specimens grown as standards are particularly valuable as pot-plants among lower-growing subjects. The heliotrope is, however, one of the most tender of the perennial bedding subjects and to maintain a stock it is necessary to give it a winter temperature of at least 50°.

Culture: Pot February to May in John Innes compost or plant in beds in a greenhouse with shoots growing loosely or trained to walls, pillars, or rafters. Plant outdoors in sunny beds in early June. The plants do well in any rich open soil in full sun, but should be pinched back occasionally to induce a bushy habit. Standards should be allowed to grow to the required height before being pinched out at the top, after which the stem should be kept clear of shoots and the top treated in the same way as a bush plant. Lift and re-pot September. Water freely March to October, moderately afterwards. Apply liquid feed to healthy plants in flower. Prune old plants closely in February. Temperature: February to October, 60° to 70°; October to February, 50° to 55°. Pot plants do best in a cold frame or sunny position outdoors in July and August.

Propagation: By seed sown $\frac{1}{16}$ in. deep in light soil in temperature of 65° to 70° in March; by cuttings of firm young shoots inserted in sandy soil in a propagating frame in a temperature of 65° to 70° in March, April, August or September.

HELLEBORUS *hel-le-bor-us* (Hellebore; Christmas Rose; Lenten Rose). Hardy perennials with white, green, purple or maroon flowers in winter and spring. Suitable for shady beds and borders. The Christmas Rose is *H. niger*. It grows 1 ft. tall and flowers in January. The Lenten Rose, *H. orientalis*, is 15 in. to 18 in. and flowers in March and April. *H. corsicus*, 3 ft., green flowers in January and February.

Culture: Plant October, November and March in rich loamy soil and cool, shady positions. Water freely in dry weather. Apply liquid manure occasionally May to September. Disturb roots as little as possible. Protect winter flowering kinds when in bloom.

Propagation: By seeds sown $\frac{1}{8}$ in. deep in shallow boxes of sandy soil in a cold frame, October to March, transplanting seedlings outdoors when a year old; by division of roots in March.

Hesperis (Double Flowered).

Heuchera (Garden Form).

Hibiscus syriacus.

Hemerocallis hybrid.

Hibiscus rosa-sinensis.

HELXINE *helks-***ee**-*ne*. Hardy creeping perennial suitable for pots suspended in windows, or for rock gardens in sun or shade—but can be very invasive. The only species, *H. soleirolii*, is grown for its dense almost moss-like carpet of small evergreen leaves.
Culture: Pot in John Innes compost in spring or plant out in ordinary soil in May. Water moderately those in pots. Do not place near small and choice plants which may easily be over-run. May also be used to carpet the soil beneath the greenhouse staging.
Propagation: By division at any time of the year.

HEMEROCALLIS *hem-er-***ock**-*al-is* (Day Lily). Hardy herbaceous perennials with yellow, orange, apricot or bronze-red flowers in summer. Each flower lasts for only one day, but a succession of flowers is maintained for several weeks. There are numerous garden varieties varying in height from 2 ft. to 3 ft.
Culture: Plant in March, April or October in ordinary soil and sunny or partially shady places.
Propagation: By division at planting time; offsets removed in summer from flowering stems and inserted in sandy soil in a frame.

HERBACEOUS. Having the character of a herb. A herbaceous perennial is a plant the roots of which live for several years, but the stems and foliage of which are soft and usually die down annually, though this is not invariably the case.

HERON'S BILL, *see* Erodium.

HESPERIS **hes**-*per-is* (Sweet Rocket; Dame's Violet; Dame's Rocket). Hardy perennial herbs with fragrant white or purple flowers in early summer. The species commonly grown is *H. matronalis*. It is 3 ft. tall.
Culture: Plant October, March or April in ordinary

rich, moist soil in sunny beds or borders. Cut down flower stems in October. Lift and replant double kinds every second year.
Propagation: Single kinds by seeds sown ¼ in. deep in sunny position outdoors in April transplanting seedlings in June or July; double kinds by cuttings of young shoots 3 in. long inserted in sandy soil in shady position outdoors in July to September, or in cold frame September or October, transplanting in March, or division of roots October to March.

HEUCHERA hoy-*ke-ra*. Hardy perennial herbs with pink or red flowers in summer and with ornamental foliage. Suitable for open, sunny well-drained borders. There are numerous garden varieties mainly derived from *H. sanguinea*. They average 2 ft. in height.
Culture: Plant October, March or April in ordinary light, well-drained soil.
Propagation: By division in March or April.

HIBISCUS hi-**bis**-*kus* (Rose Mallow; Tree Mallow). Tender evergreen and hardy deciduous shrubs and half-hardy annuals. Flowers of various colours in summer and early autumn. The hardy shrubby species grown is *H. syriacus*, of which there are several varieties, some with double and some with single flowers produced in August and September. All are 10 ft. to 12 ft. high. The principal annual species grown, *H. trionum*, is summer flowering and 2 ft. tall. *H. rosa-sinensis* is one that needs a warm greenhouse, where it makes a fine shrub up to 6 ft. with pink flowers up to 5 in. across in summer. There are several forms of it, with either single or double flowers in varying shades, and the variety *cooperi* has very colourful foliage.
Culture of Tender Species: Pot or plant February to March in well-drained pots in John Innes compost or in beds of fibrous peat, loam and sand. Prune into

123

shape February. Water abundantly March to October, moderately afterwards. Temperatures: March to October, 65° to 75°; October to March, 55° to 65°.

Culture of Annual Species: Sow in well-drained pans of sandy soil during February or March in temperature of 60° to 65°, and harden off for planting out in late May or early June in ordinary soil and sunny bed or border.

Culture of Hardy Shrubby Species: Plant October to March in rich, light loam in sheltered, well-drained border or shrubbery. Prune in spring, thinning out weak and dead wood only.

Propagation: Tender species by seed sown $\frac{1}{16}$ in. deep in well-drained pots of sandy peat, in temperature of 75°. In March by cuttings of firm shoots inserted in sandy peat in a propagating frame, in temperature of 75°. Hardy shrubby kinds by cuttings in July in a propagating frame; cuttings of well-ripened growth in October in sandy soil and sheltered places outdoors; layering in spring.

HIMALAYAN HONEYSUCKLE, *see* Leycesteria.

HIMALAYAN POPPY, *see* Meconopsis.

HIPPEASTRUM *hip-ee-**ass**-trum.* This relative of the Amaryllis (in fact it sometimes goes under this name) makes a fine summer-flowering plant for the cool greenhouse or even for a sunny window indoors, while in a warmer greenhouse it may be had in bloom quite early in the year. The hybrid forms are mostly grown and with these it is possible to get a magnificent show of the large, trumpet-shaped blooms, carried on stems 2 ft. high, in a wide range of colours from palest pink to scarlet and crimson. There are also white varieties but these are less common.

Culture: The bulbs should be potted up from December to March and kept warm and almost dry until growth is well under way, when watering can be gradually increased until by summer the plants are receiving liberal supplies. The size of pot used will depend on the size of the bulbs, which should be potted individually to half of their depth in a well-drained rather heavy soil. After flowering the plants

should be kept in full light and well watered until no more foliage is produced, when they may be allowed to die down and rest until starting time. Annual re-potting is not necessary, but the top soil should be renewed each year, when the plants are started into growth.

Propagation: By seeds sown in March which produce flowering plants in 2 or 3 years; off-sets which are taken off the parent plant when re-potting is done.

HIPPOPHAE *hip-po-**fay**-ee* (Sea Buckthorn). *H. rhamnoides* is a hardy deciduous shrub with orange berries in autumn and silver foliage. Male and female flowers are borne on separate plants; only the females bear berries, and then only if pollinated from a male bush nearby. Suitable for open shrubberies and specially suitable for seaside gardens. It eventually reaches a height of 15 ft. or more.

Culture: Plant October to February in ordinary well-drained soil. No regular pruning is necessary.

Propagation: By seeds sown $\frac{1}{2}$ in. deep outdoors in spring; layering shoots in autumn. The sex of the layered plants will be the same as that of the parent, but seedlings may be of either sex.

HOE. An implement used for stirring the surface soil. There are hoes of many patterns. The Dutch hoe has a rather narrow, flat blade set in practically the same plane as the handle. It is particularly useful for keeping down weeds during the summer months, as the user moves backwards across the ground and does not tread on the soil that has just been hoed. The draw hoe has a broader blade set at right angles to the handle, and is serviceable for breaking up rough ground, chopping out tough weeds and drawing soil towards plants, as in earthing-up potatoes. The Canterbury hoe has prongs in place of a blade, set at right angles to the handle and useful for breaking down rough soil and loosening the surface of hard soil. There are other patented types for which certain advantages are claimed by their manufacturers.

HOLLY, *see* Ilex.

HOLLYHOCK, *see* Althaea.

HOLLY-LEAVED OLIVE, *see* Osmanthus.

HONESTY, *see* Lunaria.

HONEY PLANT, *see* Hoya.

HONEYSUCKLE, *see* Lonicera.

HOOF AND HORN MEAL. This is used as a manure to supply nitrogen to the soil. A good sample should contain about 13% nitrogen. Being long-lasting it makes an excellent ingredient for fertilisers for pot plants. It is quicker in its effect upon plants'

Hippeastrum hybrid.

growth the more finely it is ground. An average application is 2 oz. per sq. yd. or 1 oz. per bushel of potting soil.

HOPS. The spent hops from breweries do not contain a great deal of plant food but they do make a good soil dressing either as a mulch spread on the surface with the main object of checking the rapid drying of soil in warm weather, or forked or dug in to improve the texture of soil and add humus to it. For these purposes hops may be used freely like manure or compost, a barrow load being spread over 6 to 12 sq. yd. of ground. Hop manure must be used much more sparingly, usually at rates of from 4 oz. to 6 oz. per sq. yd., because it has been fortified by the addition of chemical plant foods, such as sulphate of ammonia, superphosphate of lime and sulphate of potash. Manufacturers' instructions should be followed closely. Hops can be used at almost any time of year, but hop manure is most effectively used in spring or early summer.

HORMONES. The various substances which regulate plant growth, bud and root formation are referred to as plant hormones. These exist naturally in all plants, but some forms of them are available nowadays in synthetic preparations designed for specific purposes. (See under Growth Substances.)

HORNED RAMPION, *see* Phyteuma.

HORSE MANURE. One of the most valuable of the animal manures. It is rich in ammonia (nitrogen) and also contains smaller quantities of phosphate and potash. It is fibrous in texture and absorbent, quicker in action, drier, and hotter than either cow or pig manure, but it does not last so long in the soil and is better, therefore, for cool stiff loams than for light, sandy soil. As a fermenting manure for use in hotbeds, mushroom beds, etc., it has no equal.

HOSTA hos-*ta* (Plantain Lily; Corfu Lily). Hardy herbaceous flowering plants with ornamental foliage.

Hippophae rhamnoides.

Left to right: Wire hoe, swan-neck draw hoe, Dutch hoe, miniature hoe for close work, plain draw hoe.

Dipping calceolaria cuttings in hormone rooting powder.

Hosta undulata.

Hosta sieboldiana.

Large leaves, green or bluish, sometimes variegated with white and yellow. The genus is also known as funkia. The species commonly grown are *H. fortunei*, blue-grey leaves, 2 ft.; *H. lancifolia*, dark green leaves or banded with white, 2 ft.; *H. plantaginea*, green leaves, 2½ ft.; *H. sieboldiana*, blue grey leaves, 2 ft.; and *H. undulata*, green and white leaves. *H. plantaginea* has white, fragrant flowers. Flowers of the others named are lilac or lavender.

Outdoor Culture: Plant October or March in ordinary soil in sunny or shady beds or borders, or beside woodland paths and in wild gardens.

Propagation: By division at planting time.

HOTBED. A bed heated by fermenting dung or vegetation and usually covered by a glazed frame, its chief uses being to encourage the early growth of certain vegetables and fruits, to hasten germination of seeds, and to assist in the production of roots on soft cuttings. The best material for the purpose is fairly fresh, strawy horse dung. Place some of the longest strawy manure around the sides of the area to be occupied by the hotbed and then fill in the centre with a layer of shorter manure. Tree leaves in about equal proportions may be mixed with this. When the manure has been built up to a height of about 2 ft. to 3 ft. from the ground level the frame should be placed in position and a layer of soil from 6 in. to 9 in. deep put on it.

If a thermometer is thrust into the bed immediately it has been constructed it will probably quickly run up to a high figure. After a few days the heat should lessen considerably, and when it reaches a point at which it remains fairly steady the hotbed is ready for use. The lights should be placed in position from the outset, or heavy rain may soak the bed and upset the process of steady decomposition. A modern method of producing the same result is to bury special electric soil warming cable 6 in. deep in a frame and connect it to a mains voltage system. Alternatively, bare wire can be used with a 12-volt transformer. A temperature of 60° is ideal.

HOT WATER PLANT, *see* Achimenes.

HOUSE LEEK, *see* Sempervivum.

HOWEA *how-ee-a.* Perhaps the easiest of the palms are the howeas or kentias, whose main fate today seems to be the decoration of hotel lounges. *H. fosteriana* grows very quickly, but *H. belmoreana* is perhaps more attractive, and if anything, hardier. Both can become very large, with leaves up to 4 ft. long, but are unlikely to do so in pots, and the young plants usually sold are around 2 ft. tall.

Culture: Like other palms the howeas like plenty of water in summer and less in winter, when they should be kept cool; the leaves should be sponged from time to time, with special care to remove the scale insects to which they are prone.

They can remain in the same pots for years, once they have reached a sufficient size, being fed during the summer and top-dressed in spring. Temperature: October to March, 45° to 55°; April to September, 55° to 65°.

Propagation: By seed sown in considerable heat; germination may be erratic.

HOYA *hoy-a* (Honey Plant; Wax Flower). Tender evergreen climbing plants. Known as Wax Flowers on account of the appearance of their pale pink florets, carried in drooping clusters or umbels in late summer and autumn. *H. carnosa* makes a fine evergreen climber for the cool greenhouse and is the species commonly grown. *H. bella* is a smaller plant suitable for hanging baskets.

Culture: Pot February or March in John Innes compost or plant in well-drained bed in warm greenhouse. Shoots may be trained round trellises, up rafters, or against walls, and fully exposed to the light. Water freely March to September, moderately September to March. Temperature: 65° to 75°, March to October; 45° to 55° in winter. Prune into shape February.

Propagation: By cuttings of the previous year's growth taken about 4 in. long and inserted in spring in sandy soil with a bottom heat of about 75°; or by layers made by stripping a few of the leaves from any strong growth and pegging the bare part down into the same compost used for potting. When rooted the cuttings and layers should be potted up and eventually pinched out, but potting must not be overdone. Once in 8 in. pots the plants need only an annual top-dressing for the next few years.

HUMBLE PLANT, *see* Mimosa.

HUMEA *hue-mee-a* (Incense Plant; Amaranth Feathers). *H. elegans* is a half-hardy biennial with reddish, incense scented flowers borne in plume-like racemes, on graceful stems up to 8 ft. in summer. A well-grown plant may reach as much as 4 ft. in diameter. It is

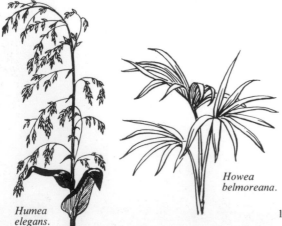

Howea belmoreana.

Humea elegans.

called Incense Plant on account of the scent which the whole plant exudes. In warm, sheltered gardens it makes a fine feature for beds or borders, but elsewhere it needs greenhouse protection even in summer.
Culture: Seed should be sown in July in a cold frame, and when the seedlings are up they should be potted on very carefully, without any check, until they are in 9 in. pots in a very rich compost such as John Innes No. 2. During the winter the plants must be kept dry and just frost-proof, and even in summer watering must be done carefully, particularly after potting, as they have a nasty habit of collapsing suddenly if over-wet. Where it can be safely done, planting out should take place in June, or later if the weather is bad. Temperatures: October to April, 45° to 55°; summer time, natural warmth. Discard plants after flowering.

HUMIDITY. The moisture content or humidity of the atmosphere is an important factor in glasshouse cultivation. It may be measured by means of a hygrometer but with a little experience it is soon possible to sense whether the air is moist enough or not. For most plants other than cacti and some succulants a moist 'growing' atmosphere is the one to aim at, and if the air is hot and dry it can be readily made more congenial by sprinkling or spraying water on the floor and staging of the greenhouse, a process described as 'damping down'.

HUMUS. The more or less brown powdery matter produced in the soil by decomposition of foliage, stems, roots, etc., and also from the decayed carcases of animals, birds, insects, etc. Its presence in reasonable proportion contributes largely to the fertility of soil by improving its texture, enabling it to retain moisture without becoming waterlogged and increasing the useful bacterial population.

HYACINTH, *see* Hyacinthus.

HYACINTHUS *hie-a-**sin**-thus* (Hyacinth). Hardy bulbous-rooted perennials with showy fragrant blue, pink, white and yellow flowers in the spring.
Culture Outdoors: A well-drained but rich soil produces the best results. Fresh animal manure is not advised, but the soil should be well dusted with bonemeal before planting, and a light dressing of a compound artificial fertiliser can be given in spring when growth first appears. Beds should always be dug deeply, well in advance of planting. September to November is the best time for planting outdoors. The bulbs must be covered with 3 in. to 4 in. of soil. In summer as growth dies down, the bulbs should be lifted carefully and stored in shallow trays in a cool dry, and airy but not sunny, place. There is usually slight deterioration from year to year, and so it is wise to keep the lifted bulbs for planting permanently in less important places.

A well-constructed hotbed.

Hoya carnosa.

Damping down the greenhouse staging to increase humidity.

Culture in the Greenhouse: Pot in September, or as soon as bulbs can be obtained, in John Innes compost, 1 bulb in each 4 in. pot or 3 bulbs in each 6 in. or 7 in. pot. The tip of the bulbs should be just above the surface of the soil. After potting place outdoors in a shady place and cover 4 in. deep with ashes or sharp sand. Leave in this plunge-bed for at least 10 weeks to form roots. Then bring in a few at a time, first to an unheated frame and then, a week or so later to a light airy greenhouse with a temperature of 60° to 65°. Water with increasing freedom as growth proceeds, and when the flower spikes appear substitute very weak liquid feed for clear water. Stake each spike carefully before it commences to bend. For Christmas flowering, bulbs which have been specially prepared for early flowering should be potted up as soon as they are received. Roman hyacinths potted up in August will flower from November onwards, but they are much less showy than the large-flowered type.

Culture in Bowls: Use special bulb fibre containing a proportion of crushed oyster shell and charcoal, to keep it sweet. Do not quite cover the bulbs with this fibre, and set them almost shoulder to shoulder in the bowls in August and September. Place in a dark, cool place and water very moderately until top growth is 2 in. in height. Then remove to a sunny window and water with increasing freedom.

Propagation: By offsets removed when bulbs are lifted.

HYBRID. Strictly speaking a hybrid is a plant that has been produced by crossing two plants belonging to different species but in gardens the term is often used to indicate any race of plants produced by cross-fertilisation.

HYDRANGEA hy-**drain**-jee-a. Hardy or slightly tender deciduous shrubby plants with white, pink, or blue flowers in summer. The familiar shrubby varieties seen in gardens and greenhouses are varieties of *H. macrophylla* (also known as *H. hortensis*) but there are other species, one of which, *H. petiolaris*, is a self-clinging climber with white flowers in summer.

It will grow to a height of 40 ft. or 50 ft. *H. paniculata* and *H. arborescens* are both shrubs to 10 ft. high, but usually considerably less, with white or creamy-white flowers in late summer. They are hardier than *H. macrophylla*.

Culture in Pots: Pot in autumn in John Innes No. 2 potting compost. Place pots in a cool greenhouse or frame, November to March; greenhouse, window or warm terrace, April to September. Water abundantly March to October, moderately November to February. Prune after flowering, cutting out weak shoots and shortening flowering stems to side growths or growth buds. Best blooms obtained on plants propagated by cuttings taken annually in March or April. Apply liquid feed weekly to plants showing flower. Blue flowers may be obtained by planting suitable varieties in a rather acid compost or by watering with one of the proprietary 'blueing' compounds sold for this purpose. Greenfly is a pest which demands frequent spraying and in winter the flower-buds should be protected from mildew by dusting them with flowers of sulphur and giving the plant just enough water to keep the buds plump.

Outdoor Culture: Plant October to April in fairly rich soil in sunny, or partially shady shrubberies or borders or on the edge of woodland. Prune straggling or dead shoots and remove previous year's flower trusses in March. Top-dress annually with decayed manure or compost. Varieties of *H. macrophylla* are good plants for seaside gardens particularly in the south and west of England. *H. paniculata* and *H. arborescens* may be grown practically anywhere in sunny borders or shrubberies or as specimens on lawns. *H. petiolaris* should be planted near a wall or at the base of a large tree up which it can climb.

Propagation: By cuttings of young shoots inserted in small pots of sandy soil in a propagating frame in a temperature of 55° to 65° in April, or August. If taken about 4 in. long and trimmed the cuttings will root readily in a sandy, peaty soil, either in a propagating frame or, more slowly on an open, shaded bench covered with polythene. When rooted they should be potted-on to 3 in. pots, of John Innes No. 1 potting compost and then into 5 in. pots of

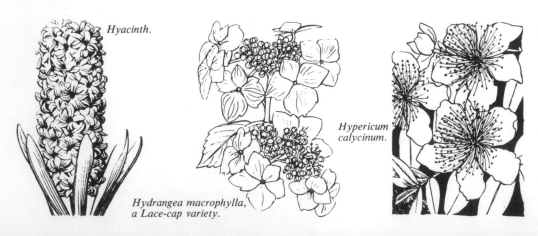

Hyacinth.

Hydrangea macrophylla, a Lace-cap variety.

Hypericum calycinum.

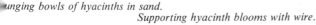
unging bowls of hyacinths in sand.

Supporting hyacinth blooms with wire.

Left: *Preparing hydrangea cuttings.* Centre: *Inserting hydrangea cuttings treated with rooting powder.* Right: *Covering hydrangea cuttings with polythene bag.*

John Innes No. 2 potting compost. For blue varieties, however, the chalk in these composts should be replaced by a proprietary hydrangea colourant, as their colour is usually poor if lime is present in the soil. As soon as the earliest plants are a few inches high pinch them out to encourage the production of side-shoots. Cuttings struck after the end of May are better grown on as single-headed plants without stopping.

HYPERICUM *hy-per-ik-um* (Aaron's Beard; Rose of Sharon; St. John's Wort; Tutsan). Hardy shrubs and rock plants, evergreen and deciduous, with yellow flowers in summer. *H. calycinum*, a prostrate evergreen shrub with large yellow flowers in summer, is suitable for dry banks and under shade of trees. Among the best shrubby kinds are *H. patulum*, deciduous, 3 ft. to 4 ft., July to August; *H.* Hidcote,

similar but sometimes nearly evergreen and with larger flowers; and *H. moserianum*, 1 ft. to 1½ ft., July and August. Good rock garden kinds are *H. coris*, 4 in. to 5 in., June; *H. fragile*, 6 in. to 9 in., June to July; *H. olympicum*, 1 ft., June to July; *H. polyphyllum*, 6 in., June to July; and *H. repens*, prostrate, June to July.

Culture of Shrubby Species: Plant October to March in ordinary soil in sunny shrubberies. Prune into shape February to March.

Culture of Rock Garden Species: Plant October, March or April in ordinary, well-drained soil in sunny rock gardens and dry walls.

Propagation: Rock garden species by seeds sown $\frac{1}{16}$ in. deep in sandy soil in a frame or greenhouse in March; some by division of roots in spring; shrubby species by cuttings of firm shoots in sandy soil in a propagating frame, July to August.

129

IBERIS eye-*ber-is* (Candytuft). Hardy annuals and evergreen perennials, with white, lilac, or purple flowers in spring and summer. The best perennial species are *I. saxatilis*, 6 in., and *I. sempervirens*, 9 in., both with white flowers in May and June. The annual varieties which flower in summer, are derived from *I. amara*, *I. umbellata* and other species and grow 8 in. to 12 in. high.

Culture of Annual Species: Sow seeds $\frac{1}{8}$ in. deep in March or April in ordinary soil in sunny beds or borders where plants are to flower. Thin out seedlings while small to 6 in. or 8 in.

Culture of Perennial Species: Plant autumn or spring in fissures or ledges of sunny rock gardens, dry walls, or margins of well-drained sunny borders in ordinary soil.

Propagation: Perennial species by seeds sown $\frac{1}{16}$ in. deep in sandy soil in a frame or cool greenhouse in March or April; cuttings of partially ripened shoots in a propagating frame July to August.

ICE PLANT, *see* Mesembryanthemum.

ILEX i-*lex* (Holly). Hardy evergreen trees and shrubs with ornamental foliage, usually spiny, and in some varieties variegated. Berries red, or sometimes yellow; autumn and winter. Sexes are usually found on separate trees, but there are hermaphrodite forms. Most of the hollies cultivated are varieties of *I. aquifolium* and will grow up to 40 ft. high.

Culture: Plant September to May in fairly rich soil in well-drained shrubberies, or as specimens in open or partially shady places. Prune April to secure shape and well-balanced growth.

Hedge Culture: Plant 18 in. apart September to May in ordinary well-dug soil. Trim into shape April and September.

Propagation: Common species by seed (berries) gathered in November, buried in sand outdoors until following October, then sown 1 in. deep in ordinary soil outdoors. Transplant seedlings when 2 years old. Selected varieties by budding on common species in August, grafting in March; cuttings of half-ripened

side shoots with heel of older wood inserted will root in sandy soil in a propagating frame, or under mist propagation but are not very easy.

IMPATIENS im-**pat**-*ee-ens* (Balsam; Busy Lizzie; Touch-me-not). Tender and hardy annuals and perennials with variously coloured flowers in summer. The garden balsam, *I. balsamina*, grows 2 ft. high and usually has double flowers. *I. holstii* and *I. sultani*, both known as Busy Lizzie, are greenhouse perennials with scarlet, pink or white flowers produced all summer. The fleshy, almost glassy stems carry at their tips large pink, red, orange or white flowers, flat and with a projecting spur. These and the translucent stems, and the great quantity of water they like in summer, give the plant the misleading name of Water Fuchsia which is occasionally heard. The flowers are carried continuously, at any rate during the summer; in a warm greenhouse or congenial room conditions flowering continues in winter. *I. roylei* is a hardy annual 4 ft. to 5 ft. high with purplish flowers in summer; *I. noli-tangere*, another hardy annual, 2 ft. with yellow and orange flowers in summer. It is called Touch-me-not because the ripe seeds are scattered explosively when the plant is touched.

Culture of Tender Species: Pot February or March in well-drained pots in John Innes compost and place in sunny greenhouse. Water very freely March to September, 55° to 65°; moderately October to February, 45° to 55°. In winter plants may become prone to rotting; if this happens they should be watered rather sparingly and above all given maximum light—though be careful that they do not get frosted if left near a window on a cold night. Plants may be pinched to keep them bushy. May be grown in the flower garden during the summer in sunny, sheltered borders.

Culture of Balsam: (*I. balsamina*) sow seeds $\frac{1}{8}$ in. deep in March or April in light soil in temperature of 65° to 70°. Transplant seedlings singly into 2 in. pots in John Innes compost. Place pots near glass in greenhouse not shaded. Transfer from 2 in. into 5 in. or 6 in. pots. Water freely and apply liquid feed to

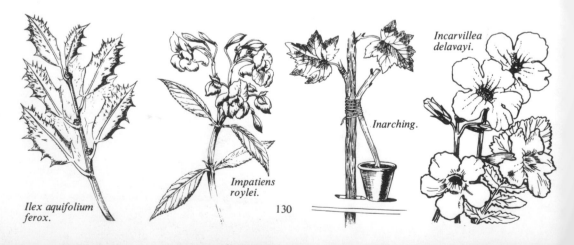

Ilex aquifolium ferox.
Impatiens roylei.
Inarching.
Incarvillea delavayi.

130

plants showing flower. Temperature: May to September, 55° to 65°. May be grown in flower garden during the summer, in sunny borders.

Culture of Hardy Species: Sow seeds in ordinary soil ⅛ in. deep in April where plants are to grow in sunny borders. Thin seedlings to 1 ft. apart when 1 in. high.

Propagation: Tender species by seeds sown 1/16 in. deep in light soil in temperature of 65° in March; by cuttings of side shoots inserted in sandy soil in temperature of 65°, March to August.

INARCHING. May be described as 'grafting by approach'. It differs from ordinary grafting in that the scion is still attached to the parent stem until it has united with the stock. It bears much the same relation to ordinary grafting as layering does to propagation by cuttings. The plants supplying both stock and scion must be growing close together. With pot plants, however, this difficulty is easily overcome.

INCARVILLEA in-kar-vil-ea. Hardy perennials with pink or rose flowers in May and June. The species commonly grown are *I. delavayi*, 1½ ft. to 2 ft. and *I. grandiflora*, 1 ft.

Culture: Plant in March or April in rich, well-drained soil in sunny sheltered borders. Protect crowns of the plant in winter by a covering of dry litter.

Propagation: By seeds sown in a temperature of 55° in March; by careful division of tuberous roots at planting time.

INCENSE PLANT, *see* Humea.

INDIAN BEAN, *see* Catalpa.

INDIAN CRESS, *see* Tropaeolum.

INDIAN FIG, *see* Opuntia.

INDIAN MALLOW, *see* Abutilon.

INDIAN PINK, *see* Dianthus.

INDIAN SHOT, *see* Canna.

INDIA-RUBBER PLANT, *see* Ficus.

INORGANIC. Any substance not belonging to the animal or vegetable kingdoms, or not containing the element carbon. Sulphate of ammonia and superphosphate of lime are inorganic chemicals used in gardens as fertilisers. Hoof and horn meal and bonemeal are organic substances supplying the same plant foods.

INSECTICIDE. Any preparation for killing insects. Useful insecticides for garden use include BHC, DDT, nicotine, derris and pyrethrum.

Iberis umbellata.

Ilex aquifolium, fructu-luteo.

Impatiens sultani hybrida.

Ipomoea tricolor.

Iris reticulata.

Iris (Bearded).

IPOMOEA *i-po-***mee**-*a* (American Bell-bind; Moon Creep; Morning Glory). Tender perennial and half-hardy annuals, all climbers. The best known ipomoea is *I. tricolor* (syn. *rubro-caerulea*) the blue Morning Glory, which is now correctly called *Pharbitis*. A half-hardy annual often grown to flower outside, it also makes a fine pot plant for the cool greenhouse, flowering from June to September or even later. The brilliant sky-blue flowers each last only part of a day, normally closing up during the early afternoon, but if the plant is shaded from mid-day sunlight they may last until evening. *I. learii*, a twining perennial, has deeper coloured blue-purple flowers in late summer. *I. horsfalliae*, another twining perennial has large, waxy magenta-crimson flowers in winter continuing to bloom into the summer.

Culture of Perennial Species: Pot or plant in spring in a mixture of fibrous loam, peat, and sand in a sunny greenhouse. They can be grown in large pots or tubs but are better in a border or bed of soil. Train shoots up roof or on trellis. Shorten over-long growths in February. Temperature: September to March, 45° to 55°; natural rise in summer.

Culture of Half-Hardy Annuals: Sow seeds in late March or early April, preferably singly in small pots, in as much heat as possible (at least 55°). They germinate best if chipped or soaked in water for 24 hours first. Acclimatise them to full light as soon as possible; spindly seedlings are very prone to damping off. Pot them on in rich soil to flower 1 in a 6 in. or 3 in an 8 in. pot, providing twigs, light trellis or wire for support—well grown plants can reach 8 ft. alternatively. Plant out in June in borders against sunny walls, training shoots to trellis or sticks.

Propagation: By seed sown in February to March, temperature 65°; or by stem cuttings in a propagating frame in spring or summer.

IRESINE *ire-is-***eye**-*ne*. Striking foliage plants, about 18 in. high, which deserve to be better known, as the large maroon, crimson or yellow leaves can make a vivid splash of colour in summer bedding schemes.

Culture: Pot rooted cuttings in spring in a good, porous mixture, grow-on in the greenhouse in a temperature of 60° to 65° at first, but gradually harden off in May for planting out in June in ordinary soil and a sunny position. They may also be used for greenhouse decoration if grown-on in 6 in. pots in John Innes potting compost.

Propagation: Cuttings root readily if inserted round the edge of a 5 in. pot in August and if they are kept dry and frost-proof during the winter they will provide further cuttings in spring.

IRIS **eye**-*ris* (Flag; Orris-root; Fleur de Lys). Hardy herbaceous perennials, some rhizomatous rooted, others bulbous rooted, and yet others fibrous rooted. In addition to a great number of species there are many garden varieties and hybrids. The most important of these are the June-flowering or bearded irises, *I. germanica*, flowering in May and June, 2 ft. to 3½ ft. tall and all rhizomatous rooted; the Japanese irises, *I. kaempferi* and *I. laevigata*, 2 ft. to 3 ft., flowering June and July, and more or less fleshy rooted; and the Spanish, English and Dutch irises, 1½ ft. to 2 ft., flowering in June and July, and all bulbous rooted. However, the genus abounds in different types and forms and is in flower almost through the year. The fibrous-rooted *I. unguicularis*, better known as *I. stylosa*, will bloom in mid-winter in a sheltered place, while such dwarf bulbous-rooted species *I. histrioides* and *I. reticulata* are in bloom during January and February. The Siberian Iris, *I. sibirica*, flowers in June, is 2½ ft. to 3 ft. tall and has

Dividing irises.

Replanting iris division.

smaller flowers than the varieties of *I. germanica*.
Culture: The June-flowering irises delight in sunny places and well-drained soil which should contain plenty of lime or chalk. All may be planted in early July, as soon as the flowers fade, or, alternatively, in March, early April or September; no animal manure should be used. Bulbous irises should be planted in September to October in ordinary well-worked soil enriched with a little bonemeal. A sunny position is best. Cover with 2 in to 3 in. of soil. It is not necessary to lift bulbs annually.

For *I. histrioides* and *I. reticulata* a much lighter soil should be used with plenty of sharp sand and a little leaf-mould or peat. They are ideal for sunny well-drained places in the rock garden. *I. reticulata* is also a good pot plant; use 3 or 4 bulbs in each 3 in. pot.

The Japanese irises are best planted in bog gardens or at the water's edge. The soil should be fairly rich and acid. The best times for planting are in spring or in summer immediately after flowering.

I. sibirica, and other fibrous-rooted kinds grow

successfully in ordinary soil, but need plenty of moisture during the summer months. Spring and early autumn are the best times for planting.

I. unguicularis should be planted in early autumn in light, well-drained and not over-rich soil and a sunny sheltered place, and should thereafter be left undisturbed so long as flowers are produced freely.
Propagation: The rhizomatous and fibrous-rooted irises can be increased by division at planting time. The bulbous-rooted kinds make offsets, or small bulbs, which can be removed when the parent bulbs are lifted in July. All can be increased by seeds sown in well-drained pots in a frame either as soon as ripe or in March. Several years elapse before seedlings attain flowering size.

IRISH HEATH, *see* Daboecia.

IRON SEQUESTROL. A special form of iron, also known as chelated iron, or iron chelate, used to supply iron to plants on alkaline (chalk or lime) soil. Iron is often deficient in such soils because it becomes locked up in insoluble compounds. The chelating agent enables the iron to resist this process.

IRON SULPHATE, *see* Sulphate of Iron.

IVY, *see* Hedera.

IXIA iks-*ee-a* (African Corn Lily). Half-hardy bulbous plants with flowers of many different colours in early summer.
Outdoor Culture: Plant September to November, 4 in. deep in sandy soil in sunny, well-drained borders. Lift and replant bulbs annually.
Pot Culture: Place half-a-dozen bulbs to a 5 in. pot from September to December. A mixture of loam, sand and peat in equal parts suits them, and the bulbs

Iresine herbstii.

Ixia (African Corn Lily).

133

should be buried about an inch deep. During the winter the bulbs are best kept cool and fairly dry in a cold frame, where although they are more or less hardy it pays to protect them from hard frost. As soon as the flower spikes appear in early spring move the plants to a light position in a cool greenhouse, where they will soon produce a good display of brilliantly-coloured star-like flowers on 18 in. stems. After flowering they should be kept watered and in full light until the foliage dies down, when they should be dried and stored until the autumn.

Propagation: By offsets removed in autumn and treated as advised for bulbs.

IXORA *iks-or-a*. For those with plenty of heat in the greenhouse the ixoras are well worth growing for their showy terminal clusters of flowers, carried on neat, evergreen plants. One of the most commonly grown is *I. fulgens* which may eventually reach about 3 ft. in a large pot and has orange-scarlet flowers in summer.

Culture: Ixoras need plenty of water and warmth in summer, but less of both in winter although the temperature then should not be allowed to drop lower than 60°. A rough, peaty soil suits them, and once the plants are in pots of a large enough size they may remain in them for several years provided they are

kept well fed in summer. Shading should not be given except in very hot weather.

Propagation: By cuttings rooted in spring in a close propagating frame at about 80°. When potted-on the cuttings should be pinched out as necessary to produce bushy plants.

JACOBINIA *jak-o-bin-ee-a*. A genus of about 40 species of which the most useful are the winter-flowering *J. ghiesbreghtiana*, scarlet; *J. carnea*, rose; *J. pauciflora*, red with yellow tips; and *J. penrhosiensis*, crimson. The last of these is perhaps the best for pot work, but *J. pauciflora* (syn. *Libonia floribunda*) will succeed in a lower temperature than the others, which need a temperature of between 50° and 60°.

Culture: All will grow well in 5 in. pots in a good, porous soil, but frequent pinching is required to get bushy plants. In the summer the best place for them is a sunny cold frame as unless the shoots are thoroughly ripened by exposure to sun and air they fail to flower satisfactorily. After flowering the plants should be cut hard back before being grown on for another year.

Propagation: Cuttings in spring which will root easily in pots of sandy soil if kept close.

JACOB'S LADDER, *see* Polemonium.

JAPANESE QUINCE, *see* Chaenomeles.

JAPANESE SNOW-FLOWER, *see* Deutzia.

JAPONICA, *see* Chaenomeles.

JASMINE, *see* Jasminum.

JASMINUM *jas-my-num* (Jasmine; Jessamine). Tender and hardy climbing and trailing plants, ever-green and deciduous, with white or yellow flowers in winter, spring and summer. Some kinds are very fragrant. The most popular hardy species are *J. nudiflorum*, yellow, winter, and *J. officinale*, white, summer, fragrant; or the best for cool conditions are the white, pink-flushed fragrant *J. polyanthum*, which is sometimes sold as a pot plant and the yellow *J. primulinum*.

Culture of Greenhouse Species: Pot or plant in February or March in loam, peat and a little sand. Train shoots up trellis, walls and rafters. Prune moderately February or after flowering if in bloom then. Water freely March to October, moderately October to March. Syringe daily during spring and summer.

Culture of Hardy Species: Plant autumn or spring in ordinary soil in well-drained borders at base of walls or arches. Prune *J. nudiflorum* moderately after flowering, removing only shoots that have flowered. *J. officinale* as a rule needs no pruning but can be cut back in spring if over-grown.

Propagation: By cuttings of firm shoots inserted in

Ixora fulgens.

Jasminum nudiflorum.

Jasminum officinale.

Above: *Ingredients for John Innes compost; (back, left to right) Coarse Sand, Peat, Sterilised loam; (front) Ground Limestone or chalk, base fertiliser.*

Jacobinia pauciflora.

sandy soil in a propagating frame in summer at a temperature of 60° to 70°; hardy species by cuttings in a cold frame or in sheltered borders outdoors, September to November; layering in spring or summer.

JERSEY LILY, *see* Amaryllis.

JERUSALEM ARTICHOKE, *see* Artichoke, Jerusalem.

JERUSALEM SAGE, *see* Phlomis.

JESSAMINE, *see* Jasminum.

JEW'S MALLOW, *see* Kerria.

JOHN INNES COMPOST. Standardised potting mixtures originally devised at the John Innes Horticultural Institute.

John Innes potting compost contains 7 parts medium sterilised loam, 3 parts peat and 2 parts coarse sand, all parts by loose bulk. To each bushel of this mixture are added $\frac{3}{4}$ oz. ground limestone, or chalk, and 4 oz. of a base fertiliser made from 2 parts by weight superphosphate (16% phosphoric acid) 2 parts hoof and horn meal ($12\frac{1}{4}$% nitrogen) and 1 part sulphate of potash. This makes No. 1 potting compost often referred to as J.I. No. 1. Stronger growing plants can go into No. 2 or No. 3 composts, made by doubling and trebling the quantities of fertiliser per bushel. For lime-hating plants such as heaths, azaleas, rhododendrons, and camellias the chalk is omitted.

John Innes seed compost consists of 2 parts medium sterilised loam, 1 part peat and 1 part coarse sand. To each bushel is added $1\frac{1}{2}$ oz. superphosphate and $\frac{3}{4}$ oz. ground limestone or chalk.

JONQUIL, *see* Narcissus.

JUDAS-TREE, *see* Cercis.

JUGLANS jug-*lans* (Walnut). Trees, all ornamental and some grown also for their edible nuts. Suitable for planting as isolated specimens in open places.
Culture: Walnuts dislike root disturbance and must be established while still quite young. Deep and reasonably rich soil and open, sunny situations are essential. Plant autumn or spring. The only pruning necessary is to remove misplaced or overcrowding branches in February.
Propagation: Choice varieties are increased by patch budding in summer on to stocks of the common walnut. The latter may be increased by seeds in a sheltered place outdoors as soon as the nuts are ripe in autumn.

JUNE BERRY, *see* Amelanchier.

JUNIPER, *see* Juniperus.

JUNIPERUS *joo-***nip-***er-us* (Juniper; Savin). Coniferous trees and shrubs. *J. communis compressa* is one of the dwarfest of all conifers and is suitable for planting in rock gardens. It makes a little column rarely exceeding 2 ft. in height. By contrast *J. communis hibernica* makes a column 10 ft. to 15 ft. high. *J. chinensis pfitzeriana* is a low growing horizontally-branched shrub and *J. sabina tamariscifolia* is almost completely 'prostrate. There are many other kinds.
Culture: Plant October to April in deep loamy, well-drained soil in which lime is not deficient. No pruning required.

Juniperus communis compressa.   *Kerria japonica fl. pl.*   *Kochia scoparia.*

Propagation: Species by seed sown in light soil in a frame in April; varieties by cutting of young shoots in sandy soil in a frame in September-October.

JUSTICIA, *see* Jacobinia.

KAFIR LILY, *see* Clivia.

KAINIT. A natural mixture of chemicals consisting of potassium sulphate, magnesium sulphate, magnesium chloride, and common salt. Kainit is a useful fertiliser for adding potash to the soil, particularly suitable for use in orchards. It should be applied in autumn, the usual rate of application being from 2 oz. to 3 oz. per sq. yd.

KALANCHOE *kal-an-*ko-*ee.* Tender succulent plants with red, pink, or yellow flowers in summer. There are numerous species, many attractive in their specialised way, but only one commonly grown for mixed greenhouse decoration, or as an indoor pot plant. This is *K. blossfeldiana*, a plant around 9 in. tall with glossy fleshy leaves and tight heads of small, bright red flowers. There are varieties of this—presumably tetraploid forms, much larger.
Culture: Pot in March in John Innes potting compost and place in light greenhouse. Temperature: October to March, 45° to 55°; natural rise in summer. Water moderately in spring and summer, very sparingly in winter.
Propagation: By seed sown in spring in well-drained pans of sandy soil, temperature 65°; cuttings from side growths, after the plants have flowered, rooted in sandy soil in a temperature of 65°.

KALE. There are a number of different kinds of kale including Asparagus, Cottager's, Curled, Hungry Gap, Russian and Thousand Headed, all useful green crops for use in winter and spring. They belong to the brassica family and have the same general needs. (*See* Brassica).
Culture: Sow in March or April and plant out in May or June in good, rich, well-worked but firm land. Plant at least 2 ft. apart in rows 3 ft. apart. Feed during summer with small top-dressings of a good compound fertiliser. Draw soil a little around stems in autumn to give additional anchorage. Remove leaves or shoots for use as required.

KALMIA kal-*mee-a* (Calico Bush). Hardy evergreen shrubs related to rhododendrons, and sharing similar tastes. With their clusters of pink flowers in early summer they make showy specimens in an open or partially shaded place. The most popular species is *K. latifolia*, which makes a dense rounded bush up to 10 ft. in height.
Culture: A lime-free soil is essential. Plant in March or April. Pruning, beyond removal of faded flowers, is unnecessary.
Propagation: By layering in spring; seeds sown in a cool greenhouse in February in a peaty compost.

KANGAROO VINE, *see* Cissus.

KENTIA, *see* Howea.

KERRIA ker-*re-a* (Jew's Mallow). Hardy shrub with bright yellow flowers in spring, usually grown as a climber trained against a wall. The double-

Laburnum vossii.

ing in height from 3 ft. to 6 ft. and flowering from July to September. *K. galpinii* is a smaller plant, 2 ft. high, with orange flowers in September. Other small species are *K. nelsoni*, *K. macowanii* and *K. rufa*.
Culture: Plant in October, March or April in deep, well-worked, fairly rich soil. Water very freely in dry weather, especially when plants are throwing up their flower spikes.
Propagation: By careful division of roots in March or April.

KNOT-WEED, *see* Polygonum.

KOCHIA *ko-she-a* (Summer Cypress). ·*K. scoparia* is a half-hardy annual grown for its ornamental foliage which, towards the end of the summer, changes from its original bright green to a rich purple-red. It makes a neat column of growth 1½ ft. to 2 ft. high.
Culture: Sow under glass in pans of sandy compost in March, temperature of 55° to 60°. The young plants should be potted on singly as soon as they are large enough to handle, and hardened-off for planting out end of May or early June in ordinary soil and sunny position, allowing 1 ft. to 2 ft. between plants.

flowered form, *K. japonica fl. pl.* is the variety generally cultivated.
Culture: Plant October to March in ordinary soil and sunny or shady positions. In early June cut out as much as possible of the older wood that has flowered, making room for young and more vigorous shoots which flower more freely.
Propagation: Division of established plants in March; cuttings of young wood in June in a propagating frame.

KING CUP, *see* Caltha.

KNIPHOFIA *nif-oaf-eea* (Red-Hot Poker; Torch Lily). Hardy perennial herbs with red, yellow or orange flowers in summer or early autumn. Suitable for sunny beds and borders. They grow exceptionally well in coastal areas. The most popular species is *K. uvaria* of which there are numerous varieties rang-

KOHL-RABI. A turnip-like vegetable belonging, like the turnip, to the brassica family and having the same general requirements. Unlike the turnip it is the stem above the ground that becomes swollen and edible not the root in the ground. Sow seed thinly in drills 18 in. apart in good, well-worked soil. Thin seedlings to 9 in. to 12 in. apart and keep well hoed and fed occasionally with small dressings of a compound vegetable fertiliser. Pull and use as soon as stems are of reasonable size.

LABURNUM *la-bur-num* (Golden Chain). Hardy deciduous ornamental trees. *L. vulgare*, the common laburnum, and *L. alpinum*, the Scotch laburnum, are the best known species but a hybrid between them, *L. vossii*, has longer flowering trails. All make small trees, 15 ft. to 25 ft. high.
Culture: These are all quick growing and easy trees unless soil is badly drained. Plant autumn or spring.

Kalanchoe blossfeldiana.

Kalmia latifolia.

Kniphofia uvaria.

Stake young trees; prune in February or March to secure shapely, well-balanced trees. On young trees remove seed pods when flowers disappear to relieve the strain of unnecessary seed bearing. The seeds are poisonous in the early stages of development.

Propagation: Species from seed sown outdoors in spring; choice varieties by layering in autumn or grafting on common seedlings in March, or by budding on to stocks of the common laburnum in July.

LACHENALIA *la-ken-*ay-*le-a* (Cape Cowslip). Greenhouse bulbous plants with fleshy, strap-shaped leaves. Of the many species and hybrids grown the two most commonly listed are *L. nelsonii* and *L. bulbifera*. Both produce long spikes of bell-like flowers, golden yellow on the former and bright coral red, with an edging of green and purple, on the latter, and their leaves, like those of many other lachenalias, are noticeably spotted—hence the other common name of the family, Leopard Lilies. The flowers are carried on stems about a foot high. The lachenalias require very much the same treatment as freesias.

Culture: The bulbs should be potted up in early August, 6 to a 5 in. pot, with $\frac{1}{2}$ in. of soil over them. A compost of 2 parts soil, and 1 part each of peat, sand and old manure suits them or John Innes potting compost may be used. After potting the plants should be stood in an airy frame and given very little water until the foliage appears, when they should be transferred to a cool house with a temperature of 45° to 50°. Too warm an atmosphere does more harm than good. More water is needed then and still more as the flowers open. After flowering reduce watering and allow the plants to die down, and ripen in full sun.

Propagation: Offsets detached from the parent bulbs and grown on in pans; seed sown in a temperature of 60° to 65°.

LADYBIRD. A genus of small beetles, too familiar to need description, of great value to the gardener because they and their larvae feed on aphides, currant mites, scale insects, etc. The females lay their eggs in the haunts of these pests so that the young may feed upon them as soon as they appear.

LADY'S SLIPPER, *see* Cypripedium.

LAGERSTROEMIA *lag-er-*stro-*me-a*. The two main cultivated species are *L. indica* and *L. speciosa*, both of which make handsome flowering shrubs under glass, although in nature they are quite large trees. *L. indica* will do well in a cool greenhouse and in very mild parts of the country it may even thrive in the open on a sunny wall, but *L. speciosa* is much more tender and needs a quite warm greenhouse.

Culture: Both species should be potted in March in large pots of well-drained, good soil with plenty of humus to retain moisture, and during the summer they should be given plenty of water and full sun. Less water is needed in winter. Pruning is done in February, when the shoots of the previous year's growth are cut back by about a third. Temperature: October to March, 45° to 55°; natural rise in spring and summer.

Propagation: Cuttings of the young shoots, 3 in. or 4 in. long, root easily in a close frame.

LAMB'S EARS, *see* Stachys.

LAMIUM lay-*me-um* (Dead Nettle). Most of the Dead Nettles are weeds but there is one species, *L. maculatum*, which is a useful carpeting plant for rough places. It grows a few inches high, has purple flowers in spring and dark green leaves each of which has a cream stripe down the middle.

Culture: Plant in spring or autumn in ordinary soil and sunny or shady position.

Propagation: By division at planting time.

LANTANA lan-ta-*na*. The hybrid lantanas are easily raised from seed and come in useful both as greenhouse and bedding plants. Most of them make shrubby plants about 4 ft. tall but there are dwarf forms of *L. camara* known as *L. hybrida nana*, which grows to no more than a foot. The roundish heads of small flowers in shades of red, yellow and purple are produced from June to September.

Culture: Lantanas grow best in a rich soil with plenty of syringing and watering in summer, but in winter they should only be kept wet enough to

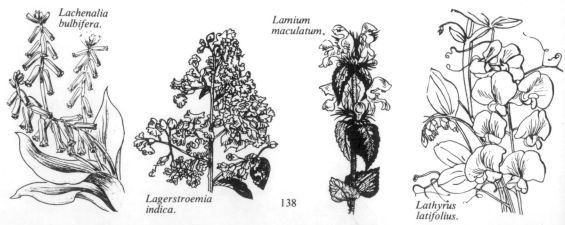

Lachenalia bulbifera.

Lagerstroemia indica.

Lamium maculatum.

Lathyrus latifolius.

Lantana camara.　　Preparing sweet pea trench.　　Layering sweet peas.

prevent the shrivelling of the stems. They must not be exposed to frost but an average winter temperature of 45° is sufficient with natural rise in spring and summer. They can be planted outdoors in a sunny place in June.
Propagation: Both hybrids and species can be propagated by means of cuttings taken in August and rooted in a close frame, and if these are grown on in 3 in. and then in 5 in. pots they make excellent plants. They should be pinched out occasionally to produce a bushy habit.

LAPAGERIA lap-a-**jeer**-ee-a (Chilean Bellflower). Half-hardy and greenhouse evergreen climbers which, in mild and sheltered places, can be grown out of doors on west facing walls. In most parts, however, they are best regarded as greenhouse plants. The only species is L. rosea, with pink bell-shaped flowers in autumn. It has a white variety.
Culture: Plant early in March in good, lime-free, loamy soil with which some peat has been mixed. Thorough drainage is essential, and for preference plants should be grown in the greenhouse border rather than in pots or tubs. Shade from strong sunshine. During spring and summer water freely and syringe growths daily. In winter little water is required, and temperatures should be between 45° and 50°. In March, remove weak and overcrowded growths. In the early stages slugs may be troublesome, but once the plants are well established the only serious pest is likely to be greenfly.
Propagation: By layers in spring or summer which may be easily obtained by pegging down the young shoots and covering them with soil. Roots will form at every joint, and layered shoots can be severed and potted when nicely rooted.

Lapageria rosea.

LARKSPUR, see Delphinium.

LATHYRUS lath-ee-rus (Sweet Pea; Everlasting Pea). The generic name of the sweet pea, perennial or everlasting pea, and various other species of the pea tribe, but not of the culinary kind. The garden sweet pea is derived from L. odoratus, a vigorous hardy annual climber of which there are numerous garden varieties in many colours, though without true yellow. There are also dwarf varieties sometimes known as Cupid sweet peas and growing only 8 in. or 9 in. high. The species of perennial or everlasting pea commonly grown is L. latifolius, a climber to 8 ft. or 9 ft., with rose, pink or white flowers in summer, but

L. grandiflorus, a smaller climber, 6 ft. high, with large rose-purple flowers in summer, is also grown.

Culture of Sweet Peas: Grown from seed sown direct in flowering quarters or in pots or boxes for transplanting. Outdoor sowings March or April, 2 in. deep, 3 in. apart, in deeply dug, rich soil. Support plants with hazel sticks or string or wire netting. Sow in pots or boxes in January or February, in temperature of 55° to 60°, or in early October in an unheated frame. Keep cool, but safe from frost: plant out in April. For finest flowers restrict each plant to a single stem, remove side shoots and tendrils and tie to a long cane. When plants grown in this 'cordon' fashion reach the top of their canes they can be untied, laid carefully along the row and tied to another cane further along so that they can ascend all over again.

Perennial Species: Plant autumn or spring. Provide supports for climbing kinds or allow them to ramble over banks or rough places.

Propagation of Perennial Species: By seeds sown in frame or greenhouse in spring, or by division of roots in spring, or by cuttings of young shoots in early spring rooted in sandy soil in a frame.

LAURUS *law-rus* (Bay-tree; Sweet Bay; Victor's Laurel; Poet's Laurel). Hardy evergreen tree with aromatic foliage used for flavouring. The species grown is *L. nobilis*. It can reach a height of 40 ft., but is usually much smaller.

Culture: Plant September, March or April in ordinary soil in sheltered but sunny places. Prune in April as much as may be necessary to keep specimens in shape. Bay is often used to produce mop-heads, pyramids and other topiary specimens.

Culture in Tubs: Plant in a mixture of 2 parts loam, 1 part leaf-mould and sand. Water very little October to April, freely afterwards.

Propagation: By cuttings of shoots 3 in. to 4 in. long inserted in sandy soil in a frame, August to September.

LAURUSTINUS, *see* Viburnum.

LAVANDULA *lav-an-du-la* (Lavender). Hardy flowering evergreen shrubs, flowers highly esteemed for their fragrance. The species commonly grown is *L. spica* with varieties ranging in height from 1 ft. to 3 ft. and in colour from white and pale lavender to deep purple. *L. vera*, the Dutch Lavender, is 3 ft. tall.

Culture: Plant March or September in well-drained soil; dry, sunny position. Lavenders do especially well on chalk or limestone soils. Prune straggly plants into shape as soon as flowers fade in August.

Propagation: By cuttings taken with a heel and inserted in sandy soil in a frame in August, or in a sunny position outdoors in September.

LAVATERA *lav-a-teer-a* (Mallow). Hardy flowering shrubs and annuals. The shrubby species most commonly grown is *L. olbia*, rose flowers, July to October, 5 ft. to 6 ft. The annual varieties are derived from *L. trimestris*, 2½ ft. to 3 ft., rose or white.

Culture of Annual Species: Sow seeds ⅛ in. deep in spring in any ordinary soil in sunny beds or borders where plants are required to grow. Thin seedlings to at least 1 ft. apart.

Culture of Shrubby Species: Plant late spring in ordinary soil in warm, dryish borders. Prune damaged shoots after hard winter.

Propagation of Shrubby Species: By seeds sown in pots of light soil in temperature of 55° to 60° in February or March; variegated species by cuttings of young shoots in sandy soil in a close frame during June or July.

LAVENDER, *see* Lavandula.

LAVENDER COTTON, *see* Santolina.

LAWN. There are three possible ways of making a lawn; by sowing grass seed in April or September, by laying turves in autumn or early spring or by planting tufts of a creeping grass such as *Agrostis stolonifera* in spring or early autumn. Seed has the advantage that special mixtures can be chosen to suit any soil, situation or purpose.

In all cases the site should be well dug and cleared of all perennial weeds first. The surface should be raked fine and level. Seed is sown at 1 oz. to 2 oz. per

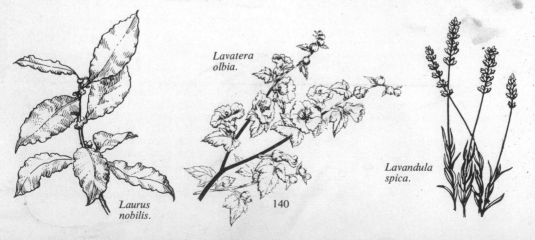

Lavatera
olbia.

Laurus
nobilis.

Lavandula
spica.

sq. yd. and either raked in or lightly covered with fine soil. Turves are laid so that the joins in adjacent rows do not coincide. The turves should all be of the same size and thickness and should be pressed down on to the soil with a wooden beater or the back of a spade.

Young grass should be mown when about 2 in. high with a sharp lawn mower set to cut about 1½ in. high. Later it can be gradually lowered to about 1 in.

Established lawns should be cut regularly March to October and should be fed in spring with a quick acting lawn fertiliser and in autumn with a slow acting lawn fertiliser and top-dressing. Weeds can be destroyed by watering occasionally in spring or summer with hormone weed killer. It is good policy to give a light dressing of lawn fertiliser 3 or 4 days before applying the weed killer and not to cut the grass during this intervening period.

Worm casts should be regularly removed by brushing, dead grass should be removed by raking with a spring-toothed rake, and in autumn, lawns which have received heavy wear or for other reasons become compacted, should be aerated by pricking with a fork or with a spiked roller. Use of an ordinary roller should be restricted except for lawns used for sport where a very true playing surface is required.

LAYERING. A method of propagation whereby a branch or shoot is bent downwards and pegged into the soil so that it may make roots. A layer is virtually a cutting struck while still attached to the parent plant. The best time to layer shrubs is in the spring or early summer, soft-wooded plants such as carnations in the summer. Half-ripened shoots as a rule make the best layers, and in most cases the buried portion of the stem is partially severed. The layer may be held firmly in place with a stone or bent wire. As soon as layers are well rooted they are severed from the parent plant and a week or so later are potted or planted out either in their permanent quarters or in a nursery bed.

Another method of layering is used where a branch cannot be brought down to the soil. A cut is made to encircle the branch, this is dusted with hormone rooting powder, a sleeve of polythene film is slipped over, filled with damp sphagnum moss and then bound tightly at each end. The moss inside the sealed polythene will remain moist for months and roots are formed into it. When the sleeve is fairly filled with roots, the stem is severed just below the place of rooting. This is known as air-layering.

LEADWORT, *see* Ceratostigma; Plumbago.

LEAF CURL. A fungal disease of peach, nectarine and almond which causes the leaves to curl, become thickened and red or purple. It is usually worse in spring and is aggravated by cold weather. Spray with lime sulphur or captan when the flower buds show pink in late February.

141

Layering a rhododendron, making the cut.

Pegging down the layer.

Earthing-up and staking the layer.

LEAF MINERS. The larvae of various flies which actually tunnel into the tissue of the leaves of chrysanthemums, cinerarias, celery, etc., are known as 'leaf miners'. In very severe cases it is advisable to remove and burn the badly attacked leaves. When attacks are first noticed it may be possible to check them by running each leaf between the fingers, feeling for the grub within and killing it with the point of a penknife. If this fails spray with malathion, nicotine, BHC or DDT.

LEAF-MOULD. Leaves reduced to the consistency of a dark brown crumbly mould by decay. Autumn leaves stored in an open-air heap and occasionally turned over will make usable leaf-mould in a year, but the older mould found beneath the fallen leaves in woods is even finer. The best leaf-mould is that yielded by the leaves of hardwood trees (oak, beech, hornbeam). Leaf-mould is rich in plant foods, notably nitrogen; it is a good moisture retainer, but if used in excess is liable to cause damping off, especially among seedling plants.

LEAF SCORCH. A general term used to describe various troubles which cause browning of the foliage. Apple leaf scorch can be checked by application of sulphate or muriate of potash in the autumn at the rate of 1 oz. per sq. yd. Rose leaf scorch, which is caused by a fungus, can be kept in check by spraying with Bordeaux mixture, but in bad cases the most severely attacked leaves should be removed and burned.

Grape vines under glass suffer from a form of leaf scorch, in which the young leaves take on a shrivelled appearance. It is usually caused by too high a temperature, particularly in the early morning, and can be prevented by gradually admitting air as the sun strengthens. Other causes of leaf scorch on plants under glass are fumes from heating equipment and the use of unsuitable sprays or fumigants.

LEAN-TO. A greenhouse or other structure in which the roof slopes one way only from a wall. On a south wall this type of greenhouse is ideal for such fruits as peaches and nectarines which need plenty of sun, or the wall may be used for the growing of many fine tender flowering subjects, including zonal pelargoniums, and heliotropes, provided the greenhouse is heated. The disadvantages of the lean-to are the difficulty of obtaining sufficient height and the more or less one-way lighting, but against these there is the fact that it costs less to heat. For general work, however, the span-roof type of greenhouse is to be preferred.

LEATHER-JACKET. The larvae of the crane-fly or daddy longlegs, leather-jackets are troublesome pests. They are an inch or so in length, dirty, greyish-black in colour with tough, leathery skins. Most usually found in grass, they also feed on the roots of many flower and vegetable plants. On cultivated ground a soil insecticide, such as aldrin, may be applied in winter or spring. Infested soil may be watered with dieldrin at any time.

LEBANON CANDYTUFT, *see* Aethionema.

LEEK. A deep, rich, well-manured soil is necessary to produce the best results. Seed should be sown in January in a warm greenhouse for an early crop, or outdoors in March in rows 1 ft. apart. Seedlings raised under glass must be pricked out into boxes as soon as they can be handled, and any required for exhibition may have a further shift singly into small pots. Hardening off should be completed in time for planting in May. Outdoor sown leeks are usually planted in June. In both cases the plants should be 8 in. or 9 in. apart in rows about 18 in. apart. Hoe frequently during the summer and water freely in dry weather. Feed as advised for onions. As growth proceeds the stems must be earthed up gradually to ensure blanching. An alternative method is to plant in holes bored with a stout bar so that only the tips of the leaves show above the rim, but this is not suitable for exhibition purposes. A third method, suitable where small leeks are preferred, is to thin the outdoor sown leeks in their seed bed instead of transplanting them. Then earth is gradually drawn up around them to blanch the stems.

LEMON SCENTED VERBENA, *see* Lippia.

LENTEN ROSE, *see* Helleborus.

LEONTOPODIUM *lee-on-to-*po*-de-um* (Edelweiss). Hardy perennial suitable for rock gardens. The species grown, *L. alpinum*, is 6 in. high, has grey, woolly leaves and white, woolly bracts around the small flower heads in summer.
Culture: Plant March or April in well-drained soil. Protect from heavy rains in autumn and winter by tilting a sheet of glass a few inches above the plants.
Propagation: By seeds sown in March, in a well-

Leontopodium alpinum.

Leptosyne.

Lifting leeks.

Leptospermum hybrid.

drained pan filled with loam, leaf-mould and granite chips and placed in a cold frame.

LEOPARD LILY, *see* Lachenalia.

LEOPARD'S BANE, *see* Doronicum.

LEPTOSPERMUM *lep-to-*sper-*mum* (South Sea Myrtle). Half-hardy evergreen shrubs suitable for sheltered gardens or against a south wall in colder districts. The species commonly grown is *L. scoparium,* 8 ft. to 15 ft. tall, with white flowers in June. The variety *nichollsii* has carmine red flowers.
Culture: Plant in April or May in a mixture of peat, loam and sand. Prune slightly in April, if bushes become straggly.
Propagation: By cuttings in sandy peat in a close frame in July or by seeds sown in similar soil in a cold greenhouse or frame in spring.

LEPTOSYNE *lep-to-*sy-*ne.* Hardy annuals with yellow, starry flowers in summer. The species commonly grown, *L. stillmanii,* is 8 in. tall; *L. maritima* is 12 in. to 15 in.
Culture: Sow in April or early May in sunny, well-drained beds or borders, or earlier under glass for transplanting in April or May.

LETTUCE. There are two main types of lettuce, the cabbage and cos, and a great many varieties of each differing in colour, crispness, size and season.
Lettuce like a well-dug, rather rich, well-manured soil. It is frequently treated purely as a catch crop, and good yields can be obtained from sowings made on the ridges of celery trenches or between rows of peas.

Leaf Miner on chrysanthemum.

For earliest crops a sowing can be made in pots or boxes of sandy soil under glass in February. Prick out the seedlings as soon as they can be handled and plant out in a sheltered border in late March or early April when thoroughly hardened. Outdoor sowings can be made at fortnightly intervals from early March onwards until mid-August. Seedlings can be thinned where they stand and thinnings can be transplanted elsewhere to give a slightly later supply. Space the large varieties 1 ft. apart in rows 1 ft. apart; small varieties such as Tom Thumb 8 in. apart in 1 ft. rows. For winter culture in frame or greenhouse sow late September. For this purpose special varieties, such as Cheshunt Early Giant or May Queen are best.

LEUCOJUM *lew-*ko-*jum* (Snowflake; Summer Snowdrop). Hardy bulbous plants, suitable for

Lewisia tweedyi.

Leucojum autumnale.

borders, woodlands or rock gardens. Both summer snowflake (*L. aestivum*), 18 in. high and spring snowflake (*L. vernum*) 6 in. high have white, green-tipped flowers, and may be naturalised in grass. The autumn snowflake (*L. autumnale*) has pink-tinged flowers and is a more fragile plant.

Culture: Plant bulbs 4 in. deep and 3 in. apart, July or August, for autumn snowflake; September or October, for other kinds. Leave undisturbed for several years.

Propagation: By offsets removed at planting time.

LEWISIA *lew-is-ee-a* (Bitterwort). Hardy rock plants flowering in May and June and suitable for crevices of sunny rock gardens. Among the most popular kinds are *L. howellii*, 8 in. high with salmon-pink flowers and *L. tweedyi*, 6 in., pink.

Culture: Plant autumn or spring in a mixture of sandy loam, peat and sand in about equal parts. Water in dry weather in spring. Lewisias like good drainage and often do best growing in crevices in a more or less vertical rock face or wall.

Propagation: By seeds sown in well-drained pans of sandy loam and peat in spring.

LEYCESTERIA *lay-ses-teer-ee-a* (Himalayan Honeysuckle; Flowering Nutmeg). Hardy deciduous shrub with white and purple flowers in late summer succeeded by purple berries. The species grown, *L. formosa*, grows 7 ft. to 8 ft. tall.

Culture: Plant autumn or spring in ordinary soil in sun or shade. Cut out some of the older stems in February.

Propagation: By seeds sown $\frac{1}{16}$ in. deep in light soil in temperature of 45° to 55° in March or April; cuttings or side shoots inserted in light soil and similar temperature in April, also of firm shoots inserted in sandy soil under handlight in September or October. Rooted suckers or offsets can be detached in spring or autumn.

LIATRIS *li-at-ris* (Button Snake Root; Blazing Star). Hardy perennial herbs with spikes of reddish-purple flowers in summer. The species commonly grown are *L. spicata*, 18 in.; and *L. pycnostachya*, 3 ft.

Culture: Plant September or spring in light, rich soil in open, sunny beds or borders. Water freely in dry weather.

Propagation: By division in March or April.

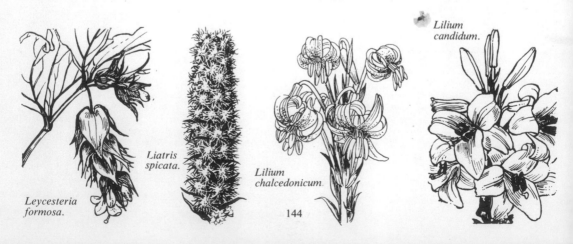

Lilium candidum.

Liatris spicata.

Lilium chalcedonicum.

Leycesteria formosa.

144

Planting lilies on a base of sharp sand.

Lilium davidii.

Cutting back lilies after flowering.

LIGUSTRUM *li-***gus**-*trum* (Privet). Hardy deciduous and evergreen shrubs. Common species suitable for shrubberies, under shade of trees, in open, or as hedges; other kinds in open shrubberies. The common species used for hedges is *L. ovalifolium* and its golden-leaved form. It will grow up to 15 ft. tall.

Culture: Plant in ordinary soil from October to March. Prune deciduous kinds in autumn, evergreens in April.

Hedge Culture: Plant privet (1 ft. to 3 ft. high) 6 in. to 9 in. apart, October to April, in ordinary soil which has been well dug. Prune half way back after planting. Trim annually from June to August.

Propagation: By cuttings of firm shoots 8 in. to 12 in. long inserted in sheltered position September to November. Cuttings of the golden privet will often root more readily if inserted during March or April.

LILAC, *see* Syringa.

LILIUM *lil-*ee-*um* (Lily). Numerous species and hybrids of hardy and half-hardy bulbous flowering plants. Many lilies thrive in thin woodland or planted among fairly low growing shrubs which will shade their roots while allowing their stems to grow up into full sunlight. Many lilies dislike lime soil but some will tolerate lime. Those that can be described as very lime tolerant are: *L. amabile, candidum, carniolicum, chalcedonicum, concolor, henryi, martagon, monadelphum, pomponium, testaceum.* Fairly lime-tolerant species are: *L. brownii, bulbiferum, croceum, callosum, centifolium, cernuum, davidii, hansonii, hollandicum, longiflorum, marhan, pardalinum, parryi, pyrenaicum, regale, szovitsianum* and *thomsonianum.* Most lilies can also be grown in pots under glass.

Culture: In habit of growth there are two distinct groups of lilies—the stem rooters (which form a second and distinct set of roots on the stems above the bulbs) and the non-stem rooters. The first should be planted deeply with at least 6 in. of soil between the bulbs. Shade for the lower parts of the stems, such as provided by dwarf shrubs, is also helpful. The non-stem rooters plant 2½ times the depth of the bulbs themselves, except *L. candidum* and *L. testaceum* which plant only an inch deep. *L. giganteum* plant with tips of the bulbs peeping through the surface. In every case good drainage is the first essential; soil must be deeply worked and, if heavy, leaf-mould, peat and coarse sharp sand mixed in. To ensure local drainage surround each bulb with a handful or so of clean, sharp sand. Plant either October to November or March to April. Do not subsequently disturb unless unavoidable. Remove flower heads after flowering to prevent seeds forming.

Culture Under Glass: The most popular kinds for greenhouse culture are *L. auratum, longiflorum* and *speciosum.* These will stand gentle forcing. Pot in a mixture of 2 parts fibrous loam, 1 part old leaf-mould or peat, and some coarse sand and charcoal, in autumn, as soon as the bulbs are available, putting one bulb in a 5 in to 8 in. pot or 3 or 4 together in a bigger pot. The pots should be only partly filled at first and the bulbs set fairly low down, covered with an inch of soil, so that top-dressing with soil can be carried out later to encourage the stem roots formed by many kinds. Most lilies should be started in cool conditions, preferably in a frame, and when growth is well advanced they can be brought into more heat—up to 60° if available. One exception is the huge *L. auratum* which can be placed straight into a temperature of 55° after potting.

Little water is needed until some growth has been made and even then the compost should be kept only just moist. Plenty of ventilation is needed at all times, and although lilies like the sun it is advisable to shade the base of the stem to encourage rooting. Liquid manure can be given occasionally until the buds show colour, when no more feeding is desirable; at this stage also the plants should be kept cooler—not above 50°—as this will make the flower last longer.

After flowering watering should be cut down gradually until the stems wither, when the pots may be placed in a cold frame until it is time to start the plants again.

Propagation: Seeds may be sown in well-drained pans of sandy soil in cold frames as soon as ripe. Transplant seedlings to an outdoor bed when one year old. Also, by stem bulbs or bulbils planted in outdoor nursery beds 2 in. apart each way; by scales detached from the parent bulb in autumn or winter, and placed in trays filled with a compost of sand, loam and chopped sphagnum moss. Lilies may also be increased by division of the bulb clusters in autumn.

LILY, *see* Lilium.

LILY OF THE VALLEY, *see* Convallaria.

LIME. Horticulturally, the term includes calcium carbonate (chalk or limestone) in addition to calcium oxide or quicklime and calcium hydroxide, or hydrated lime. One of the main essentials for soil fertility; lime corrects acidity and 'sourness' in the soil and accelerates the decay of organic material. It will also check slugs and, by coagulating the finer particles in clay soil, render them coarser in texture, less retentive of excessive moisture, and more workable. Plants which thrive under acid conditions resent lime in any form. These include rhododendrons, azaleas, heathers, and most members of the heather family as well as many gentians and lupins. As a general rule hydrated lime is used for winter dressings on stiff soil and powdered chalk or limestone for lighter sands.

Lime has the effect of liberating ammonia in compounds and must not, therefore, be mixed with animal manures or with such nitrogenous artificials as sulphate of ammonia and Nitro-chalk. The same remark applies to basic slag, which contains a large proportion of free lime. Usual dressings are: hydrated lime, 2 oz. to 4 oz. per sq. yd.; ground chalk or limestone, 4 oz. to 6 oz. per sq. yd.

LIME SULPHUR WASH. A fungicide used in the control of apple and pear scab, gooseberry mildew, and various other diseases. It is also useful for checking the ravages of the black currant bud mite. Lime sulphur is purchased as a concentrated solution ready for mixing with water. It is used in various strengths according to the purpose for which it is intended and time of year at which it is applied, and on these points manufacturers' instructions should always be followed.

LIMNANTHES *lim-nan-thes* (Meadow Foam). The only species grown, *L. douglasii,* is a low growing hardy annual with pale yellow and white flowers in May and June. Bees are very fond of it.

Culture: Sow in March or early September in ordinary well-drained soil and sunny positions where the plants are to flower. Thin seedlings to 6 in.

LINARIA *lin-air-ee-a* (Toad-flax). Hardy perennials, rock plants and annuals with variously coloured flowers in summer. The perennial species commonly grown are *L. dalmatica,* 4 ft., yellow; and *L. purpurea,* 3 ft., purple. The annual species in a variety of colours are derived from *L. maroccana,* 8 in. to 12 in. The rock plants commonly grown are *L. alpina,* 6 in., purple or pink; *L. aequitriloba,* prostrate, mauve; *L. pallida,* 2 in., mauve, but the two last are correctly named *cymbalaria.*

Culture of Perennial Species: Plant autumn or spring in ordinary soil; *L. dalmatica* in sunny beds or borders; *L. alpina* in sunny rock gardens in gritty, well-drained soil; *L. aequitriloba* and *L. pallida* in dry walls and in the crevices between paving stones.

Culture of Annual Species: Sow seeds $\frac{1}{16}$ in. deep in ordinary soil in March or April where the plants are to flower. Thin seedlings to about 6 in.

Propagation: Perennial species by seeds sown in sandy soil in pots or pans in a frame or greenhouse in spring; division in October or April.

LINDANE. Owing to the tainting properties of the ordinary BHC insecticide a refined form known as Gamma BHC or Lindane has been produced. This is

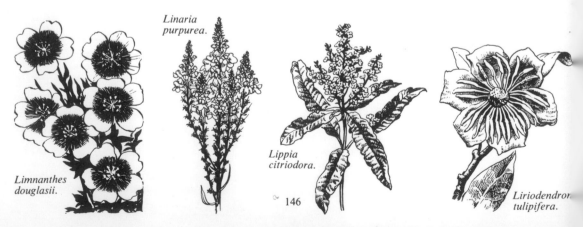

Linaria purpurea.

Limnanthes douglasii.

Lippia citriodora.

Liriodendron tulipifera.

available in dust, spray and smoke forms, but normally only the last two are used under glass. These are effective against most pests apart from some caterpillars, but care is needed in their use where cucumbers, vines, hydrangeas, and roses are grown, and the maker's instructions should be closely followed.

LING, *see* Calluna.

LINSEED OIL PLANT, *see* Linum.

LINUM ly-*num* (Flax; Linseed Oil Plant). Hardy annuals, perennials and one small shrub with yellow flowers in June, *L. arboreum*, suitable for the rock garden. The annual species commonly grown is *L. grandiflorum*, 1 ft., scarlet, summer. If a white flax is required *L. g. album* is a good variety. The most popular perennials are *L. perenne*, 18 in., blue, summer. *L. narbonense*, similar but 2 ft., and *L. flavum*, 2 ft., yellow, summer.
Culture of Annual Species: Sow seed ⅛ in. deep in ordinary soil and sunny position in March, April or September where plants are to flower. Thin to 6 in.
Culture of Perennial Species: Plant autumn or spring, on warm, sheltered rock gardens or dry walls, or *L. perenne* and *L. narbonense* in sunny beds or borders in ordinary, well-drained soil. Prune straggly shoots of shrubby species into shape March or April.
Propagation: Perennial species by seeds sown ½ in. deep in a frame in April, also by division in March or April; shrubby species by seed as above or by cuttings of young shoots inserted in sandy soil in a close frame during June or July.

LIPPIA lip-*ee-a* (Lemon Scented Verbena). Rather tender deciduous shrub with fragrant foliage. The species grown is *L. citriodora* which grows to 10 ft.
Culture: Pot or plant in March in John Innes potting compost. Position sunny windows or greenhouses. Alternatively, plant in autumn or spring in ordinary soil and very sheltered positions outdoors such as against south walls. Water pot plants freely March to September, little afterwards. Prune shoots in February to within an inch of their base.
Propagation: By cuttings of firm young growths inserted in sandy soil in a close frame during late spring or summer.

LIQUID MANURE. Any manure or fertiliser applied to plants in liquid form. Liquid manure can be made by steeping well-rotted stable or farmyard manure in a tub of water and diluting the liquor to the colour of pale straw. More usually, nowadays, specially compounded chemical liquid or soluble fertilisers are used which only need to be added to water at the rate prescribed by the manufacturer. Liquid manures are often used to feed plants in full growth or when forming flowers or fruits. They are then applied every week or 10 days.

Linum grandiflorum album.

LIQUIDAMBAR lik-wid-**am**-*bar* (Sweet Gum). Hardy deciduous trees with ornamental foliage, turning crimson in autumn. The species usually grown, *L. styraciflua*, will attain 60 ft. or 70 ft.
Culture: Plant November to March in loamy soil on lawns, or in open places. No pruning is normally required.
Propagation: By seeds sown ⅛ in. deep in sandy soil outdoors in March or April. Seeds may not germinate until the following year; by rooted suckers lifted in autumn or winter.

LIRIODENDRON lir-ee-o-**den**-*dron* (Tulip Tree). Hardy deciduous tree with fragrant yellow flowers and ornamental foliage. The species commonly grown, *L. tulipifera*, will attain 70 ft. to 80 ft.
Culture: Plant October to February in deep, loamy soil in sunny places as specimens on lawns or in similar open positions. No pruning normally required.
Propagation: By seeds sown in sandy soil in a frame in spring, but germination is usually slow and may be spread over 2 or 3 years.

LITHOSPERMUM lith-o-**sper**-*mum* (Gromwell). Hardy trailing evergreen flowering shrubs and perennials with blue flowers. Suitable for margins or borders or on ledges of rock gardens. The species commonly grown is *L. diffusum*, better known as *L. prostratum*, prostrate, blue, May to June. A good form of *L. diffusum* is Grace Ward.
Culture: Plant autumn or spring in gritty, well-drained soil and sunny open positions.
Propagation: By seeds sown in well-drained pots of sandy soil in a frame or greenhouse in March or

April; cuttings of firm shoots inserted in sandy soil in a close frame in July or August.

LOAM. Though the word loam is loosely used to mean any kind of soil, it is more specifically used in connection with soils in which clay, silt and sand are present in similar proportions, together with between 2% and 7% of humus, and with a somewhat acid reaction. For greenhouse work the term is usually applied to such soils when prepared in a certain way. This consists of cutting turves 4 in. to 5 in. thick and stacking them in single layers, with manure and lime used alternately between each layer. When building the stack plenty of water is needed to ensure thorough breaking down of the turves. The heap is best built between April and June, when the turves are most grassy, and if it is covered when completed, the loam should be dry and ready for use 6 months afterwards.

LOBELIA *lo-bee-le-a* (Cardinal Flower). Hardy and herbaceous perennials and half-hardy annuals. Tall kinds for borders, dwarfs for edging summer beds. The perennial species commonly grown are *L. cardinalis*, 3 ft., scarlet, summer; *L. fulgens*, similar but with purple foliage; and *L. syphilitica*, 3 ft., blue or purple, summer.
Outdoor Culture of Hardy Species: Plant March or April in rich soil in sunny, moist borders. *L. cardinalis* and *L. fulgens* are best lifted in October, placed in pots or boxes and stored in cold frames till March when they may be replanted outdoors.
Culture of Annual Species: Sow seeds in a temperature 60° in February, transplant 2 in. apart in boxes, harden off in a cold frame and plant out in May, 4 in. to 6 in. apart in ordinary soil and sunny beds or borders.
Pot Culture: Pot in spring in John Innes potting compost, or trailing kinds in hanging baskets, and place in greenhouse or sunny window. Water freely in summer, moderately other times. Apply stimulants to plants in flower.
Propagation: Hardy perennial species by seeds sown $\frac{1}{16}$ in. deep in sandy loam and leaf-mould in cold frame September or October, or in temperature of 55° in March; division in March.

LOBSTER CLAW, *see* Clianthus.

LOCUST TREE, *see* Robinia.

LOGANBERRY. The cultivation of this fruit is in every respect identical with that of the blackberry.

LONDON PRIDE, *see* Saxifraga.

LONICERA *lon-iss-er-a* (Honeysuckle). Hardy and half-hardy deciduous and evergreen shrubs and climbers. The best of the climbing honeysuckles are *L. periclymenum* in its two varieties, *belgica*, the Early Dutch Honeysuckle, and *serotina*, the Late Dutch Honeysuckle with fragrant yellow and purple flowers in summer; *L. japonica* partially evergreen and its varieties *halliana* and *aureo-reticulata*, the last with yellow netted leaves; and *L. tragophylla* with large yellow unscented flowers in summer. The most familiar shrubby species is *L. nitida*, an evergreen to 6 ft. to 7 ft. much used for hedge making. *L. fragrantissima* and *L. purpusii* are deciduous shrubs to 8 ft. with fragrant creamy-white flowers in winter.
Culture of Twining Species: Plant October to April in rich soil against warm walls or fences for evergreen kinds; fences, walls, or arbours in any aspect for deciduous kinds. No pruning essential but shoots of previous year's growth may be shortened if desired to within 3 in. of base in February.
Culture of Shrubby Species: Plant October to March in ordinary soil. Prune away weak growths only, after flowering. Mulch with decayed manure February or March. *L. nitida* suitable for hedge-making. Plant 1 ft. to 1½ ft. apart and clip in June and July.
Propagation: By cuttings of firm shoots about 8 in. long, inserted in sandy soil in a frame in September or October; layering shoots in May or June.

LOVE LIES BLEEDING, *see* Amaranthus.

LOVE-IN-A-MIST, *see* Nigella.

LUCULIA *luk-u-le-a.* Until recently the only species of this genus worth growing was *L. gratissima*, an evergreen shrub with large, fragrant trusses of pink flowers in autumn, but a beautiful white flowered variety has now been introduced from Bhutan. This is *L. grandifolia*, which differs chiefly from the other in having much larger leaves.
Culture: The luculias need plenty of room and are best planted out in a well-drained, peaty soil in the greenhouse, with a winter temperature of about 55°. Plenty of water is needed in summer but much less in winter, particularly after the plants are cut hard back after flowering.
Propagation: Cuttings are slow and unreliable and seed sown in a warm greenhouse in spring provides the better method.

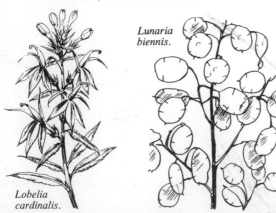

Lunaria biennis.

Lobelia cardinalis.

Lithospermum diffusum Grace Ward.   *Lonicera periclymenum.*   *Lupinus polyphyllus hybrid.*

LUNARIA *loo-***nair***-ee-a* (Honesty; Money Flower; Satin Flower). *L. biennis* is a biennial flowering plant of which the seed pods contain a parchment-like partition useful for drying for winter decorations.
Culture: Plant August to November in ordinary soil in partially shaded borders or margins of shrub-beries. Discard plants after flowering.
Propagation: By seeds sown in shallow drills in sunny positions in April or May.

LUNGWORT, *see* Pulmonaria.

LUPIN, LUPINE, *see* Lupinus.

LUPINUS *lu-***pie***-nus* (Lupine or Lupin). Hardy shrubs, herbaceous perennials and annuals suitable for sunny shrubberies or open, sunny borders in lime-free soil. The familiar herbaceous lupins, 2½ ft. to 4 ft. high and June flowering in many colours, are varieties of *L. polyphyllus*. The so-called tree lupin is *L. arboreus*, a shrub to 8 ft. with yellow or white flowers in June or July. The annual varieties are derived from *L. hartwegii*, 2 ft. to 3 ft., various colours, summer.
Culture of Shrubs: Plant October or April in well-drained, sunny position. Prune after flowering.
Culture of Herbaceous Perennials: Plant, preferably in spring, in ordinary soil and open, sunny positions. Cut down flower stems after flowering.
Culture of Annual Species: Sow seeds in March or April where required to flower. Thin seedlings 6 in. to 12 in. apart.
Propagation: Perennial species and shrubs by seeds sown thinly outdoors in April or May; cuttings of young growth taken in March before they have become hollow, and rooted in sandy soil in a frame.

Luculia gratissima.

LYCHNIS **lik**-*nis* (Campion; German Catchfly; Rose Campion). Hardy perennials with pink, rose or white flowers in summer. Among the best kinds are *L. chalcedonica*, 3 ft., scarlet, July to August; *L. coronaria*, 3 ft., crimson, June to July; and *L. viscaria splendens plena*, 1 ft., purplish-red, June to July.
Culture of Perennial Species: Plant in March or April in ordinary, well-drained soil, taller kinds in sunny beds or borders, dwarf kinds in sunny rock gardens, or on banks and dry walls.

Propagation: By seeds sown in light soil in a frame or greenhouse in March or April; division of plants March or April.

LYSICHITUM *lie-se-***kite***-um* (Skunk Cabbage). Hardy herbaceous plants suitable for very moist places such as in bogs and at the side of pools or slow moving streams. They have large, shining green leaves and arum-like flowers in April and May. The two species commonly grown are *L. americanum*, yellow and *L. camtschatcense*, white.
Culture: Plant in April or May in good loamy soil and very moist position but not where plants are liable to be flooded with more than an inch or so of water during wet weather.
Propagation: By division at planting time.

LYSIMACHIA *lis-ee-***mak***-ee-a* (Yellow Loosestrife; Creeping Jenny; Yellow Pimpernel). Hardy erect or creeping herbaceous perennials. Among the best kinds are *L. clethroides*, 3 ft., white, summer; *L. punctata*, 3 ft., yellow, summer; *L. vulgaris*, 4 ft., yellow, summer; and *L. nummularia*, creeping, yellow, spring. The last has a pretty golden-leaved variety.
Culture: Plant in autumn or spring in ordinary rich soil in moist shady borders or at margins of pools or streams, or *L. nummularia* (Creeping Jenny) in moist, shady rock gardens by the water side or in hanging baskets.
Propagation: By division carried out in autumn or spring.

LYTHRUM **lith***-rum* (Purple Loosestrife). Hardy herbaceous perennials with spikes of magenta flowers in summer. Suitable for moist, shady borders or margins of ponds ·or streams. The two species commonly grown are *L. salicaria*, 3 ft. to 4 ft., magenta, July to August; and *L. virgatum*, similar but with smaller flowers.
Culture: Plant in autumn or spring. Water freely in dry weather.
Propagation: By division in October or April.

MADAGASCAR JASMINE, *see* Stephanotis.

MADWORT, *see* Alyssum.

MAGNESIUM. An essential plant food which may occasionally be in short supply in the soil. Lack of magnesium shows in poor leaf colour which may be pale or actually white or cream between the veins. The symptoms are similar to those caused by iron deficiency. Magnesium is usually applied as sulphate of magnesium (Epsom salts) to the soil or sprayed on the foliage. (*See* Sulphate of Magnesium).

MAGNOLIA *mag-no-***lee***-a* (Cucumber Tree; Yulan). Hardy deciduous and evergreen trees and shrubs with showy white, pink or purple flowers in spring or summer. Some species also have ornamental foliage. *M. stellata*, *M. conspicua*, and *M. soulangeana* are the most popular deciduous species and *M. grandiflora* is a favourite evergreen kind often trained against sunny walls. *M. sieboldii* and *M. wilsonii* have smaller but very fragrant white and purple flowers in early summer.
Culture: Plant March to April in rich, deep, well-drained and preferably lime-free soil. When necessary prune evergreen species in spring; deciduous species after flowering, but as a rule no regular pruning is required. Be careful not to injure roots which are often very near the surface.
Propagation: By seeds sown $\frac{1}{8}$ in. deep in spring or autumn in sandy soil in a cold frame or greenhouse; layering in summer or autumn.

MAHONIA *ma-ho-***ne***-a*. Hardy evergreen shrubs with yellow flowers in winter or spring. Suitable for sunny or partially shady, sheltered shrubberies. The most popular kinds are *M. aquifolium*, 3 ft. to 5 ft., February to May; *M. bealei*, 6 ft. to 7 ft., February to March; *M. japonica*, similar but with widely spread flower sprays, and *M. lomariifolia*, 8 ft. to 10 ft., spring.
Culture: Plant October to April in ordinary soil. No regular pruning required but evergreen specimens may be cut back a little after flowering.

Magnolia stellata.

Lychnis chalcedonica.

Mahonia bealei.

Malope.

Propagation: By seed sown in a greenhouse in March; by cuttings of firm young growth in autumn in a frame; *M. aquifolium* by careful division in spring or autumn.

MAIDEN. A term applied to roses and fruit trees in their first year of growth after grafting or budding. Thus if a maiden tree or bush is purchased it should be one year old.

MAIDENHAIR FERN, *see* Adiantum.

MAIDENHAIR TREE, *see* Ginkgo.

MAIDEN'S WREATH, *see* Francoa.

MALATHION *mal-a-thy-on.* An insecticide effective in the destruction of many insects including aphides, leaf miners, whitefly, thrips, red spider mite, scale insects, capsids, leaf hoppers and mealy bug. May be used as a dust, a wet spray or as an aerosol for greenhouse use. It should not be used on food crops within 10 days of harvesting and it is liable to injure ferns, crassulas and petunias.

MALCOMIA *mal-ko-me-a* (Virginia Stock). *M. maritima* is a pretty hardy annual with variously coloured flowers, like confetti, on 8 in. stems in summer.
Culture: Sow in spring in ordinary soil and open positions where plants are to flower. If sown thinly little subsequent thinning of seedlings should be necessary.

MALLOW, *see* Lavatera.

MALLOW-WORT, *see* Malope.

MALOPE *mal-o-pe* (Large-flowered Mallow-wort). Hardy annuals with showy magenta flowers in summer. Suitable for sunny beds in masses in borders. The garden varieties are derived from *M. trifida*; all are about 1 ft. in height.
Culture: Sow in March, April or September in ordinary soil and sunny positions where plants are to flower. Thin seedlings to about 1 ft. apart.

MALUS *may-lus* (Crab Apple). Ornamental trees flowering in spring, and some kinds producing decorative fruits in late summer and autumn. Among the most popular kinds are *M. baccata*, the Siberian Crab, white flowers, cherry-like red fruits; *M. floribunda*, pink and white; *M. lemoinei*, deep crimson; and fruiting crabs such as Dartmouth, Golden Hornet and John Downie. All these make trees from 20 ft. to 40 ft. high.
Culture: The ornamental species and varieties are perfectly hardy, will grow freely in any ordinary garden soil and open position, and require little attention after planting beyond a certain amount of

Lythrum salicaria.

Lysichitum americanum.

Magnolia soulangeana.

Malus Golden Hornet.

Mammillaria bocasana.

thinning out each winter. Planting can be done at any time from late October until March provided the weather is not unduly wet or frosty. Trees should be firmly staked immediately after planting.

Propagation: The species by seeds (pips) sown in a sheltered border outdoors during March. Selected garden varieties and hybrids by grafting in March or April or by budding in July and August either on to the stocks used for apples or on to seedlings of the type species.

MALVA mal-*va* (Musk Mallow). Hardy perennial flowering plants with pink or white flowers in summer. The most popular kinds are *M. alcea*, 2 ft., rose or white; and *M. moschata*, 1 ft. to 2 ft., pink or white.

Culture: Plant October or March in ordinary soil in sunny or partially shady beds or borders.

Propagation: By seeds sown ⅛ in. deep in light, sandy soil in a temperature of 55° in March or April, or by cuttings inserted in cold frame in July and August.

MAMMILLARIA *mam-mi-*lar*-ee-a* (Nipple Cactus; Elephant's Tooth Cactus). Tender succulent perennials. Stems leafless, cylindrical, or globular, bearing at even distance over their surface small tubercles crowned with rosettes or stars of spines. There are over 200 species.

Culture: Pot March or April in well-drained pots just large enough to accommodate roots, in John Innes potting compost with some extra sand or brick dust. Place pots in sunny, airy greenhouse or window. Repot every third or fourth year only. Water moderately March to September; occasionally, to prevent total dryness, September to November, none after-

wards. Ventilate freely in summer. Temperatures: April to September, natural; September to April, 40° to 50°.

Propagation: By seeds sown ⅛ in. deep in well-drained pans or pots of sandy soil in a temperature of 70° in March; by cuttings of the tops of the plants inserted in small pots of sandy, gritty soil in spring.

MAPLE, *see* Acer.

MARANTA mar-*an-ta* (Arrowroot Plant). Tender herbaceous perennials with ornamental foliage. Under this name one can conveniently group the various ornamental members of the Arrowroot tribe, including calathea, ctenanthe and stromanthe. The nomenclature of the group is confused and plants with the same specific (second) name can be found under more than one generic name. This botanical confusion should not put one off, for there are some attractive small plants in the group. The commonest is *M. leuconeura kerchoveana*, the Prayer Plant, with pale green leaves with oblong purple markings which darken to brown and start life neatly rolled up. Its half-brother, *M.l. massangeana*, has silvery lines and mid-rib on dark green, which give it the name Fishbone Plant. *M. zebrina* has dark green alternating with light green. *Calathea oppenheimiana* combines green, white and pink, and *C. ornata* has pink lines on bronze. The most exciting is *Calathea*, or *Maranta makoyana*, with a fascinating but indescribable pattern.

Culture: Pot February to March in well-drained pots in a shady greenhouse in John Innes potting compost. Water abundantly March to September, moderately September to November; keep nearly dry December

Matricaria Golden Ball.

MATRICARIA *mat-ree-**kar**-ee-a* (Double May Weed). *M. maritima plenissima* is a hardy annual, 12 in. to 18 in. high producing finely cut bright green foliage and small double button-like flowers of pure white or rich yellow.

Culture: Sow in temperature of 60° to 65° in February or March. Prick off into boxes of John Innes compost and harden off for planting outdoors in late May in sunny places and ordinary soil. Space 12 in. to 18 in. apart.

MATTHIOLA *mat-ee-o-la* (Ten-week, Brompton, Night-scented and Intermediate Stocks). Half-hardy annuals and biennials. With the exception of the Night-scented Stock, which is *M. bicornis,* 12 in., rosy lavender, summer, fragrant, all the several classes and many varieties of stock are derived from one species, *M. incana.* Most popular are the Ten-week Stocks, 12 in. to 18 in., many colours, summer flowering, fragrant. The Brompton Stocks are more branched, winter or spring flowering, and so are the Intermediate Stocks which are hybrids between Brompton and Ten-week.

Culture of Ten-week Stock: Sow seeds $\frac{1}{16}$ in. deep in light soil in a temperature of 55° to 60° in March. Prick out seedlings into boxes and harden off for planting outdoors in deep, rich, well manured soil in open, sunny beds or borders end of May; or sow in cold frame in April for planting out in June. Plant dwarf kinds 9 in. and tall kinds 12 in. to 15 in. apart each way.

Culture of Brompton and Intermediate Stocks: Sow seeds $\frac{1}{8}$ in. deep in light soil in a cold frame in June or July. Pot seedlings singly in 2 in. pots, keep in cold frame and plant out in March.

Culture Under Glass: Although Ten-week and Brompton Stocks may be grown under glass, the East Lothian and Intermediate types are the most suitable for pot work. These should be sown about the end of July, in boxes or pots of the John Innes seed compost in a cold frame. As soon as the seedlings are large enough pot them up singly in 2 in. pots, using the John Innes No. 1 potting compost or any good soil dressed with lime. During the winter the plants

to February; syringe daily March to September. Apply weak liquid feed occasionally during the summer. Temperature: spring to autumn, 60° to 75°; October to February, 55° to 60°. Repot annually. Not the easiest of plants, they may wither in winter for want of a combination of warmth and humidity, but a constant temperature around 55° to 60° and absence of draughts go a long way. If they do die down, do not despair; new growth often appears later when watering can be resumed.

Propagation: By division in February or March.

MARGUERITE, *see* Chrysanthemum.

MARROW, *see* Vegetable Marrow.

MARSH MARIGOLD, *see* Caltha.

MASTERWORT, *see* Astrantia.

Maranta leuconeura kerchoveana.

Malus lemoinei.

Matthiola, Brompton Stock.

may be grown-on in a cold frame as long as they are protected from severe frost, and then in spring they should be potted up into 6 in. pots of John Innes No. 1 compost. Cool treatment and plenty of light are necessary at all times.

Brompton Stocks may be treated similarly but should be sown a month earlier. With all stocks avoid over-watering in winter or damping off may occur.

MAY, *see* Crataegus.

MAZUS may-*zus***.** Hardy dwarf perennial herbs with purple flowers in summer. Suitable for sunny rock garden or for planting in the crevices between paving slabs. The species commonly grown are *M. pumilio,* pale blue and *M. reptans,* purplish-blue.
Culture: Plant in spring in moist, sandy loam.
Propagation: By division in spring.

MEADOW FOAM, *see* Limnanthes.

MEADOW RUE, *see* Thalictrum.

MEADOW SAFFRON, *see* Colchicum.

MEADOW SWEET, *see* Filipendula.

MEALY BUG. This is a pernicious greenhouse pest, belonging to the same family as the scale insect and related to the aphides. The insects in general resemble tiny wood-lice and are covered with white, waxy, wool-like material, which protects them against water. Though capable of movement they usually settle down in one place when adult, sucking plant sap through a piercing mouthpiece like the aphides. They can multiply at great speed and, in a warm greenhouse, breeding is continuous. The root mealy bug, a common pest of cacti, is similar in appearance.

Small colonies are best dealt with by hand, using a stiff paint brush dipped in insecticide. Spraying with derris, malathion, nicotine or white oil emulsion is effective. Repeated attention is often necessary to ensure that no young appear from eggs which have escaped treatment. Where root mealy bug occurs the

soil must be shaken off the roots and destroyed, the worst infections cut away, and the roots dipped into insecticide before re-potting.

With vines remedies consist in removing loose bark in the winter and painting rods and spurs with a petroleum emulsion insecticide. All woodwork should be thoroughly scrubbed with hot, soapy water.

MECONOPSIS *mek-on-***op***-sis* (Welsh Poppy; Himalayan Poppy; Blue Poppy; Prickly Poppy; Nepal Poppy). Hardy monocarpic and perennial herbs with variously coloured flowers in spring or summer. Among the most popular species are *M. betonicifolia,* 3 ft. to 5 ft., blue, July to August; *M. integrifolia,* yellow, 3 ft., summer; *M. napaulensis,* 4 ft. to 6 ft., pale blue and *M. cambrica,* yellow, 12 in. to 18 in.
Culture: Sow seeds $\frac{1}{16}$ in. deep in light, sandy soil in a temperature of 55° to 60° in March or April. Transplant seedlings when large enough to handle into a cold frame and plant out in a permanent position as soon as they have formed tufts of 7 or 8 leaves each. Use a mixture of loam, sand and leaf-mould or peat in sunny or partly shaded borders or rock gardens. Water freely in summer; keep as dry as possible in winter. Monocarpic species flower when 2 to 4 years old and afterwards die, but perennial species may continue for several more years, though they are seldom long lived. The Welsh Poppy, *M. cambrica,* will often naturalise itself, scattering its seed and coming up in any sheltered, fairly well-drained place.

MEDINILLA *med-in-***el***-a.* A family of warm greenhouse plants mostly remarkable for their large, pendant bunches of bright flowers, large leaves and peculiar 'winged' stems. The species commonly grown is *M. magnifica,* with pink flowers on an ever-green plant to 3 ft. high.
Culture: Medinillas need a winter temperature of about 60° and a humid atmosphere. They should be grown in a good soil consisting largely of humus. Re-pot occasionally.
Propagation: By half-ripe cuttings inserted in a warm, close frame in spring.

MELON. Seeds should be sown singly in small pots in a temperature of 65° to 70° at any time from January till the end of April. The plants are grown on ridges of rich soil either on the floor of a low green-house or on the staging of a taller structure. The bed should be about 2½ ft. to 3 ft. in width with 6 in. depth of soil spread over it, and in addition, a narrow ridge, a further 6 in. deep, towards the back. On this plants will be set 18 in. apart. The compost should be good fibrous loam mixed with a little good leaf-mould and well-rotted manure. The plants are trained as single stems to wires strained from one end of the house to the other 6 in. from the roof glass. When each plant is about 30 in. in height pinch off the top.

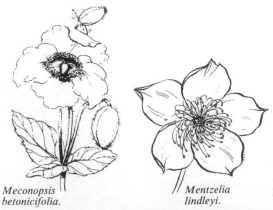

Meconopsis betonicifolia.

Mentzelia lindleyi.

Side shoots will soon grow and 2 per plant should be retained. On each, female flowers will form distinguishable by the small embryo fruit immediately behind the flower. These must be fertilised with the pollen from the male flowers, and all the female flowers of one plant should be fertilised at one time. Usually 2 fruits per plant are sufficient, but 3 or 4 fruits can be allowed to form on exceptionally strong plants.

When the young melons begin to swell, all sub-lateral shoots should be pinched out. Water should be given freely at all times until the plants are nearly ripe and begin to emit their characteristic smell, and the atmosphere must be kept humid. Melons can be fed freely with weak liquid manure from the time the fruits commence to swell.

Melons may also be grown in frames. Seed should be sown early in May and the plants set out in June. Two plants can be accommodated in a frame 6 ft. by 4 ft. The plants should be stopped at the second rough leaf and two side growths retained for flowering and fruiting. Subsequent culture is the same as for melons in greenhouses. It helps if the frames stand on a hot bed or are soil-warmed with electric cables.

The most troublesome disease is foot rot.

MENAZON. A systemic insecticide principally for use against aphides. It has a very low toxicity to human beings and domestic animals and can be used even on fruits up to 3 weeks before picking and all other food crops up to 1 week before harvesting.

MENTHA men-*tha* (Mint; Peppermint; Pennyroyal; Spearmint). Hardy perennials with aromatic foliage, suitable for sunny or partially shady borders. *M. requienii* is an excellent creeping plant for covering surface of soil in moist places but it is slightly tender and not suitable for planting in cold, exposed places. **Culture of Spearmint and Peppermint:** Plant roots 2 in. deep in rows 9 in. apart in rich, moist, ordinary soil in February or March. Mulch with decayed manure in March. Keep potassic chemicals and wood ash away from mint beds; they are detrimental rather than helpful. Water freely in dry weather. Cut off stems close to ground in September and cover beds with 2 in. of soil. Lift and replant every 3 years. Gather shoots for drying when flowers first open in October to March. Keep soil moist. Some roots may be lifted and placed in seed boxes filled with old potting soil. In a frame or greenhouse they will produce early shoots and leaves. **Culture of Other Species:** Plant March or April in light, rich soil. *M. pulegium gibraltarica* (Gibraltar Mint) should be wintered in a cold frame and planted out in April or May. **Propagation:** By division of roots at planting time.

MENTZELIA ment-**zeel**-*ee-a*. The only species grown, *M. lindleyi*, is a showy hardy annual, 18 in. high, with bright yellow, poppy-like flowers all

Medinilla magnifica superba.

Mealy Bug on codiaeum.

Melons trained-up the greenhouse roof.

summer. It is often known in gardens as *Bartonia aurea*.

Culture: Sow seed in March or April in ordinary, well-drained soil and sunny positions where plants are to flower. Thin seedlings to 9 in. to 12 in.

MERCUROUS CHLORIDE, *see* Calomel.

MESEMBRYANTHEMUM *mes-em-bree-**an**-the-mum* (Fig Marigold; Ice Plant). Commonly used name for many years of half-hardy succulent plants, mostly perennials but some, such as *M. criniflorum*, are annuals. There are a great many species but many, familiar to gardeners as mesembryanthemums, have been removed by botanists to other genera.

Culture of Perennial Kinds: Pot March to May in well-drained pots using John Innes potting compost. Water freely April to September; keep nearly dry during winter. Temperature: October to March, 40° to 50°. Many species may be planted in sunny beds or rock gardens in June: lifted, re-potted and placed in a greenhouse in September; or in mild places and especially near the coast some kinds can be planted out permanently.

Culture of Annual Species: Sow seeds $\frac{1}{16}$ in. deep in March in a greenhouse in a temperature of 60° to 65°. Prick off into boxes and harden off for planting out in late May or early June in well-drained soil and warm, sunny places.

Propagation: By seeds sown in spring in a greenhouse; by cuttings inserted in sandy soil in a temperature of 55° to 65°, March to September.

METALDEHYDE *mee-**tal**-dee-hide*. A chemical used to kill slugs and snails. For this purpose 1 oz. of finely powdered metaldehyde is mixed with 3 lb. of bran and either scattered over the surface of the soil or placed in small heaps near plants liable to be attacked.

METHAM-SODIUM. A powerful soil sterilising material of fairly recent introduction, used to control eelworms and other organisms and also effective in destroying soil fungi and germinating weed seeds. It is applied as a solution 4 to 8 weeks before planting, after which the soil is flooded to keep the fumes in the soil. Maker's instructions should be carefully followed.

MEXICAN CIGAR FLOWER, *see* Cuphea.

MEXICAN IVY, *see* Cobaea.

MEXICAN ORANGE-FLOWER, *see* Choisya.

MEXICAN SOAP PLANT, *see* Agave.

MICE. These can be very destructive in the garden and greenhouse devouring many bulbs, corms and tubers and nibbling the bark of young trees and shrubs. Remedies include trapping and the use of poisons such as phosphorous paste and Warfarin.

MICHAELMAS DAISY, *see* Aster.

MIGNONETTE, *see* Reseda.

MILDEW. A group of diseases all of fungal origin and attacking a great variety of plants. The surface of the leaves, and possibly also the stems, are covered with whitish or greyish patches that often appear to be mealy. Mildew is most likely to occur when the atmosphere is very moist and the soil is rather dry and is common in August and September. Remedial measures include dusting the leaves with flowers of sulphur and spraying with a fungicide such as kara-thane, lime sulphur or Bordeaux mixture. Under glass mildew can be kept in check by giving increased ventilation and using artificial heat to keep air dry and circulating. Ample spacing between the plants, even to the extent of lifting some of them up on inverted plant-pots, will also help to create un-favourable conditions for the fungus by allowing a free circulation of air.

MILFOIL, *see* Achillea.

MILKWEED, *see* Asclepias.

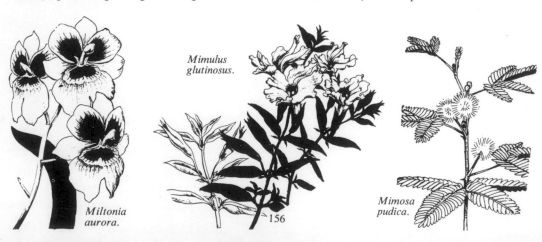

Mimulus glutinosus.

Miltonia aurora.

Mimosa pudica.

Mesembryanthemum criniflorum.

Rose leaves affected by Mildew.

Millepedes.

MILLEPEDE. Soil pests with long, more or less cylindrical bodies and numbers of small legs. They are usually greyish or blackish in colour and some kinds have a habit of coiling themselves up like watch-springs when disturbed. They feed on the roots of many plants and have a particular liking for those with fleshy roots. Millepedes can be destroyed by forking in soil insecticides, such as aldrin or dieldrin, at almost any time of the year.

MILTONIA *mil-***tone***-ee-a* (Pansy Orchid). Handsome orchids with pansy-like flowers, often rich purple or crimson in colour marked with white or yellow, produced mainly in spring and early summer.
Culture: A winter temperature of 55° to 60° is necessary rising to 70° or more in summer with shade and abundant atmospheric moisture. Pot in September in a compost of equal parts chopped sphagnum moss and osmunda fibre. A little dried cow dung rubbed through a sieve can be added with advantage but is not essential. Water sparingly at first, more freely as growth starts in spring. Rest in winter but do not keep quite dry even at this season.
Propagation: By division at potting time. The plants make pseudo bulbs and some of these can be split away and be potted separately.

MIMOSA *mim-***o***-sa* (Sensitive Plant; Humble Plant). Tender perennials with ornamental foliage. The species commonly grown, *M. pudica* is not the florists 'mimosa' (*Acacia dealbata*) but a quite different plant growing to about a foot high. Although a perennial it is usually treated as an annual. The main attraction of this plant is not its round heads of purplish flowers, which are not very showy but its peculiar habit of drooping when touched—which accounts for its common name of Sensitive Plant.

Culture: Pot February to March in well-drained pots of John Innes potting compost. Water freely March to September, moderately afterwards. Temperature: March to October, 65° to 75°. Scarcely worth winter storage as they are best renewed annually from seed.
Propagation: By seeds sown $\frac{1}{16}$ in. deep in light soil in a temperature of 65° to 75°; February or March cuttings of young shoots inserted in sandy·soil in a temperature of 65° to 75° at any time.

MIMULUS **mim**-*u-lus* (Monkey Flower; Musk). Greenhouse and hardy annual and perennial herbs with gaily-coloured flowers in summer. The perennial species mostly 12 in. to 18 in. high with yellow flowers in summer are mostly suitable for damp places in the garden by streams or pools but a number of the colourful musks with their large bright flowers make attractive pot plants in cool or even cold greenhouses.

These include *M. cardinalis*, *M. cupreus*, *M. luteus* and *M. ringens*. *M. glutinosus*, is the Bush Musk of California, and though closely related is quite different in habit. It is a half-hardy evergreen shrub which grows to about 5 ft. high and bears in summer, large trumpet-like flowers varying in colour from pale buff to deep orange. The annual musks grow about 12 in. high, have variously coloured flowers and are said to be derived from *M̂. tigrinus*.

Culture of Annuals: Sow seeds on surface of light soil, slightly cover, and place in a temperature of 55° to 65° in February, March or April. Transplant seedlings where 3 leaves have formed 1 in. apart in shallow boxes. Harden off for planting outdoors in late May or early June in fairly rich soil. Water freely in dry weather.

Culture of Perennials: Plant in spring in moist soil near margins of pools, streams, etc., or in ordinary soil kept well watered.

Culture of M. glutinosus: This makes a fine plant for the frost-proof greenhouse, where it may be either pinched out to form a bush or allowed to grow more or less as a climber on a suitable trellis. It should be potted on as required. Plenty of sun and water are needed in summer and even in winter the plants should not be allowed to become too dry.

Propagation: Perennial kinds may be increased by division at planting time. *M. glutinosus* by cuttings which root readily in moist sandy soils in April.

MINT, *see* Mentha.

MISCANTHUS *mis-***kan**-*thus* (Eulalia; Zebra Grass). *M. sinensis* is a handsome ornamental grass with numerous varieties differing in the breadth and colour of their leaves which may be $\frac{1}{4}$ in. and green in *gracillimus*, 1 in. and longitudinally striped silver or gold in *variegatus*, 1 in. and horizontally banded yellow in *zebrina* the Zebra grass! All are 3 ft. to 5 ft. tall.

Culture: Plant October to April in ordinary well-drained soil and open, sunny positions. May also be grown in pots for greenhouse or room decoration. Pot in March in John Innes potting compost, water freely from April to October, moderately at other times. No artificial heat is required.

Propagation: By division at planting or potting time.

MIST PROPAGATION. Although leafy cuttings, if kept constantly moist, will root comparatively quickly if exposed to full sunlight in a closed frame, the method involved a good deal of risk owing to the need of frequent watering and spraying. Much of the risk can be eliminated by a technique known as mist propagation used in conjunction with adequate bottom heat if necessary. The main feature of this technique is the automatic provision of a fine-mist spray which not only covers the leaves and stems with a film of water but also reduces the temperature of the frame so that exposure to maximum light may be safely given. The duration and frequency of the mist is either controlled electrically by means of an 'electric leaf', which operates somewhat on the lines of the thermostat used for heat control but in response to the degree of moisture present or by a simple time switch which gives a short burst of spray, perhaps a second or so, at intervals of a few minutes. The rooting medium for mist propagation is always extremely porous, often pure sand or powdered pumice stone or horticultural vermiculite and as none of these contain any plant food the cuttings must be carefully moved to a more normal compost as soon as they are well rooted. Mist propagation is most suitable for spring and summer cuttings.

MITES. A group of minute animals, related to the spider. There is an enormous number of different species, and these include some notorious plant pests, of which the most serious glasshouse one is red spider, which despite its name is not a true spider. (*See* Red Spider).

MOCK ORANGE, *see* Philadelphus.

MOLE. These well-known animals do much good by devouring wireworms, leather jackets, and other soil pests, but unfortunately at the same time do a great deal of damage to lawns, seedlings, etc., by

Monarda didyma.

Monstera deliciosa.

Miscanthus sinensis zebrina.

Equipment for mist propagation.

Putting down a mole trap.

burrowing just beneath the surface of the soil and throwing up loose mounds of soil (molehills) at frequent intervals. Moles can be caught in special steel mole-traps which can be purchased from dealers in horticultural or agricultural sundries. These traps must be set in the runs, preferably in those leading to water as these are likely to be in constant use. It is advisable to wear gloves when setting traps, as moles have a keenly developed sence of smell and are liable to be frightened off by the scent of human beings. Moles can also be killed by fumigation with calcium cyanide, but this is a dangerous poison which should only be handled by thoroughly responsible persons. A safer method is to place a few lumps of calcium carbide in each of the runs, as the smell of this will drive out the moles.

MONARCH OF THE EAST, *see* Sauromatum.

MONARDA *mon-ar-da* (Bergamot; Bee Balm; Oswego Tea). Hardy herbaceous perennials Leaves scented and red, pink, or mauve flowers in whorls in August. The garden varieties are all derived from *M. didyma*, 3 ft. tall.
Culture: Plant autumn or spring in ordinary soil and sunny positions.
Propagation: By division of roots in early autumn or spring.

MONEY FLOWER, *see* Lunaria.

MONKEY FLOWER, *see* Mimulus.

MONKEY PUZZLE, *see* Araucaria.

MONKSHOOD, *see* Aconitum.

MONSTERA **mon**-*ster-a* (Shingle Plant; Swiss Cheese Plant). Tender evergreen climbers, with large handsome, perforated, dark green leaves. A really well-known plant of *M. deliciosa* is one of the wonders of nature, for the leaves, up to 18 in. across are slashed at the edges and much perforated in the centre, while from the stems develop huge aerial roots. Unfortunately it needs moist heat and above all an extensive root run to achieve this, and the plants normally sold have smaller, shield-shaped leaves with a row of deep slits along each edge. So different does it appear that it has been called *Philodendron pertusum*, but this is only an immature form. Unfortunately, even this form is prone to producing leaves with fewer and fewer slits, eventually with none, when they look very like those of *Philodendron scandens*. The holes give the plant the name Swiss Cheese Plant, while the *deliciosa* comes from the curious edible fruit, seldom produced in rooms but occasionally seen in expensive shops.
Culture: Pot in March or April in John Innes No. 2 compost and grow in warm greenhouse or rooms. Water freely March to October, moderately afterwards. Syringe twice daily March to September, once daily afterwards. Temperature: October to April, 55° to 65°, natural rise during summer. No pot large enough to be convenient indoors will overcome the tendency to produce smaller, less perforated leaves but warm, moist conditions frequent repotting in rich soil and regular feeding will all help.
Propagation: By cuttings of the stem inserted in light soil in a temperature of 70° to 80° any time.

MONTBRETIA *mont-**bree**-shee-ah*. Hardy or slightly tender perennials. The flowers are produced in slender spikes in late summer and are mostly in shades of yellow, orange, and crimson.

Culture: Plant corms or growing tufts during March or April in well-drained ordinary soil in sunny borders or on banks. Lift choice varieties in October and place in an unheated frame until planting time. Practically no water required until growth recommences in February. The common kinds are much hardier and usually survive the winter without difficulty in well-drained soil.

Propagation: By division at planting time.

MOON CREEP, *see* Ipomoea.

MORNING GLORY, *see* Ipomoea.

MORUS *more-us* (Mulberry). Hardy deciduous trees with handsome foliage and edible fruits. The best species for garden planting is *M. nigra*, the Black Mulberry, which usually makes a wide-spreading tree, 25 ft. high or a little more. *M. alba*, the White Mulberry, is the species mainly planted to supply leaves for feeding silkworms. It is much taller and less spreading.

Culture: Plant November to March in good, rich, loamy soil and sunny, sheltered situations. Mulberries do not like cold and exposed places and are more suitable for the south of Britain than for the north.

Propagation: By layering in spring or by seed sown in a greenhouse or frame in spring.

MOSAIC. A general name for a group of plant diseases, all caused by viruses, which infect the sap and reveal their presence in mottled or crippled foliage of young stems. No cure has yet been discovered, and in most cases plants should be burned at the first sign of disease. Infected sap is often carried from plant to plant on knife blades or fingers and also by various sucking insects, notably aphides. Any measure that will keep down these pests will also lessen the likelihood of infection by mosaic diseases.

MOSS. The common name for a group of primitive plants. In the garden sphagnum moss is often used as one of the ingredients for orchid composts.

It is also employed for lining hanging baskets and for packing around the roots of plants that are to be despatched, by rail, post, etc. Moss on lawns can be a serious weed. Its growth is often encouraged by poor drainage or lack of nutriment in the soil. Insufficient aeration of the soil and sourness are other contributary causes, and can be rectified by puncturing the surface and brushing in sharp grit. Special spiked rollers are made to facilitate the former operations. Various chemicals are manufactured to kill moss, the most effective are based on mercuric compounds.

MOTHER-IN-LAW PLANT, *see* Dieffenbachia.

MOTHER OF THOUSANDS, *see* Saxifraga.

MOTHS, *see* Cabbage Moths; Winter Moths.

MOUNTAIN ASH, *see* Sorbus.

MOUNTAIN AVENS, *see* Dryas.

MOUSTACHE PLANT, *see* Caryopteris.

MOWRAH MEAL. This is often used as a worm killer on lawns. The meal is sprinkled over the surface at the rate of 4 oz. per sq. yd., and is then watered in very freely preferably with a hose. Worms will soon come to the surface and die. Treatment is most effective in spring or early autumn when the weather is mild and the soil is moist.

MULBERRY, *see* Morus.

MULCH. Any fairly bulky substance, spread on the surface of the soil to retain moisture, check weed growth or supply plant food. Well-rotted farmyard or stable manure will serve all three purposes. Straw serves the first two but supplies little food and the same is true of peat and sawdust. Other substances commonly used are spent hops and grass clippings. Mulches may be applied at any time of year but are especially useful in spring while the soil is still moist from winter rain.

MULLEIN, *see* Verbascum.

MURIATE OF POTASH (Potassium chloride). An inorganic fertiliser containing up to 50% of potash. It is more liable to damage delicate plants than sulphate of potash, but is cheaper and widely used in the preparation of compound fertilisers. Normal rate of application is $\frac{1}{2}$ oz. to 1 oz. per sq. yd.

MUSCARI *mus-kar-i* (Grape Hyacinth). Hardy bulbous plants with blue flowers in spring. Suitable for sunny beds, borders or rock gardens. The most popular species is *M. botryoides*, 6 in. high. *M. comosum monstrosum* is a very different plant in

Muscari—Grape Hyacinth.

Montbretia.

appearance with a large feathery flopping spike of blue flowers. It is sometimes called the Feather Hyacinth.

Outdoor Culture: Plant August to November, 2 in. to 3 in. deep and 3 in. to 4 in. apart in good well-drained soil and sunny positions. *M. comosum monstrosum* looks particularly effective on a sunny ledge in the rock garden. Lift, divide and replant when overcrowded.

Propagation: By offsets from old bulbs removed when lifting and planted as advised for full-sized bulbs.

MUSHROOM. Mushrooms can be grown in any well-ventilated outbuildings or cellars where a temperature of around 60° can be maintained. Frames can also be used, and even glasshouses, during the autumn and winter, or quite a good early autumn crop can be obtained in specially prepared outdoor beds.

Culture: The first essential is a supply of good, fresh stable manure. Only that obtained from stables where the horses are bedded in straw is suitable and the sample should not contain any appreciable proportion of wood chips, shavings, or similar material, neither must manure be used from horses under medical treatment. The manure must be stored under cover and carefully turned every 2 or 3 days for about a fortnight. There should be no smell of ammonia by the time it is ready for use, while a sample taken from the centre of the heap should contain just sufficient moisture to bind it together when squeezed in the hand.

The beds should be laid down to a depth of about 9 in. with a slight slope from back to front, and patted down quite firmly with a fork. A soil thermometer should be thrust into the bed and after about 10 days the temperature should have fallen to around 70°, when spawning can commence.

Sterilised spawn is broken into pieces each about the size of a walnut and these are inserted 1 in. deep at 10 in. intervals all over the bed.

Within 7 days to 10 days fine white threads should be apparent on the surface. A casing of soil must then be applied. Finely sifted soil of a loamy nature, containing a fair proportion of lime is best, and should be laid on to a depth of 1 in. and be firmed lightly with the back of a spade.

Cropping, as a rule, begins within about 6 weeks to 8 weeks. Watering is not advisable until the mushrooms appear. To maintain a reasonably humid atmosphere walls and paths should be moderately damped. The only watering necessary at any time is sufficient to prevent the casing soil becoming bone dry.

Outdoor beds are usually built up in the form of ridges. July is the ideal time for spawning these, and it is advisable to protect the beds from direct sunlight before covering with clean straw.

Special chemicals are also available for turning

Mosaic disease on raspberry.

Planting mushroom spawn.

Covering spawn with a newspaper.

The start of the mushroom crop.

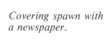

straw or chaff into mushroom composts, and these should be used according to manufacturers' instructions.

MUSK, *see* Mimulus.

MUSK MALLOW, *see* Malva.

MUSTARD. Outdoor sowings can be made at intervals from early March until the end of August in an open border. The seeds may either be covered with light soil or with mats or boards until germinated. Indoor sowings should be made on the surface of shallow boxes filled with light soil and covered with a sheet of paper, and provided a temperature of 55° or thereabouts can be maintained, can be made at practically any time of the year. Mustard is ready for use more quickly than cress, and the cress should therefore be sown 3 days in advance if these two crops are required simultaneously.

MYOSOTIS *my-o-***so**-*tis* (Forget-me-nots; Scorpion Grass). Hardy perennials often grown as biennials, with blue, pink or white flowers in spring. There are numerous garden varieties varying in height from 6 in. to 12 in. *M. alpestris* is an alpine forget-me-not of compact habit suitable for the rock garden and *M. palustris* is the water forget-me-not suitable for damp places.
Culture: Plant in autumn 4 in. to 6 in. apart in ordinary soil in partially shaded beds or borders, *M. alpestris* in rock gardens. *M. palustris* by streams or pools.
Propagation: By seeds sown $\frac{1}{16}$ in. deep outdoors in June or early July, seedlings being transferred to a nursery bed as soon as they can be handled conveniently; division of roots in March or October, but the common forget-me-not is best renewed from seed annually, once established it often renews itself by self-sown seed.

MYRTLE, *see* Myrtus.

MYRTUS mir-*tus* (Myrtle). Greenhouse and half-hardy evergreen shrubs with fragrant white flowers May to July and ornamental foliage. The species usually grown is *M. communis* which will reach 15 ft. in favourable places.
Culture in Greenhouses: Plant February or March in well-drained pots or tubs or in beds with shoots trained to walls, in light, sunny airy greenhouses, using John Innes potting compost. Place pot plants in sunny position outdoors, June to September. Prune into shape February. Water freely March to October, moderately afterwards. Syringe daily March to October. Apply weak liquid feed once a week May to September to healthy plants only. Temperature: September to March, 45° to 50°; natural rise in summer.
Outdoor Culture: Plant October to March in ordinary soil in well-drained borders against sheltered south walls in the milder parts of the country. Protect October to March in severe winters with mats of straw.
Propagation: By seeds sown $\frac{1}{8}$ in. deep in sandy soil in a temperature of 60° to 70° in autumn or spring; cuttings of young shoots inserted in sandy soil in a propagating frame in a temperature of 65° to 75° in spring and summer; cuttings of firm shoots inserted in sandy soil in cool greenhouses June or July.

NAPHTHALENE. Although not so effective as some of the modern insecticides, flaked or whizzed naphthalene is fairly effective as a deterrent against soil pests such as wireworms, leather-jackets and so on. To destroy them it must be used at $\frac{1}{4}$ lb. per sq. yd. or at a heavier rate still if the infestation is severe, but even at a much lower rate it serves to protect plants if forked into the top few inches of soil.

NARCISSUS *nar-***siss**-*us* (Daffodil; Jonquil). Hardy bulbous plants. The name narcissus is commonly applied to the small-cupped varieties, derived from *N. incomparabilis*, *N. poeticus*, *N. tazetta*, and others. The larger trumpet kinds derived from *N. pseudo-narcissus*, being known as daffodils, but narcissus is the correct botanical name for all. The genus is divided into a number of sections according to the general formation and colour of the flowers, in each of which there are innumerable varieties. Those

Myosotis alpestris.

Myrtus communis.

Narcissus cyclamineus.

Planting narcissi with special tool.

Narcissus tazetta hybrid.

with long central crowns or trumpets are known as trumpet daffodils, while the short-crowned kinds are small-cupped narcissi. The poet or pheasant-eye narcissi are small-cupped but the colour of the cup is peculiar, being ringed with red. There are narcissi with double flowers and others which carry a number of small flowers on one stem. Some species, such as *N. cyclamineus* and *N. bulbocodium*, are very small and suitable for planting in the rock garden.

Culture: Plant from August to November but the earlier in this season the better. For best results choose open, sunny positions and good, deeply worked soil. Plant 4 in. to 6 in. deep in permanent plantations, leave bulbs undisturbed until they show signs of overcrowding. In bedding schemes it is usually necessary to lift immediately after flowering, replanting the bulbs in spare ground to finish growth. Narcissi may also be planted in grassland and a special tool is obtainable for this purpose which gouges out small cylinders of turf which can then be replaced neatly on top of the bulbs. To obtain a natural effect the bulbs should be planted in irregular drifts of varying size.

Narcissi also make splendid pot plants for the cool greenhouse and some will also stand forcing. Pot during August and September in John Innes potting compost. Plunge out of doors in an ash-bed to encourage root growth and do not bring into the greenhouse until top growth is about 2 in. in length. A temperature of 45° to 50° is quite sufficient, but early flowers can be obtained from forcing. varieties by increasing this to 65°, when the flower buds are clearly visible. A damp atmosphere is essential. A few varieties such as King Alfred, will stand rather

more forcing; catalogues will give information on this point. Water freely when growing strongly and when buds form feed with weak liquid manure. After flowering stand pots out of doors in a sheltered place until the foliage dies down, when bulbs can be replanted in the open.

Narcissi may also be grown in ornamental bowls, using specially prepared bulb fibre which has been thoroughly moistened. Keep in shade in a cool room until top growth shows, when move to a sunny window. Keep moderately moist until flower buds form, after which water more freely.

Propagation: Offsets are produced and can be detached from the parent bulbs at planting time and put out in a nursery bed until they reach flowering size. Seedlings are also quite easy to rear, but they seldom flower in less than 7 years from the date of sowing.

NASTURTIUM, *see* Tropaeolum.

NEANTHE *ne-***an**-*the*. Palms are not everyone's cup of tea but if one wants a palm tree the most attractive is undoubtedly *N. elegans* (syn. *N. bella*). It has also been called Collinia and *Chamaedorea elegans*. This is a small plant, seldom exceeding about 4 ft. with graceful arching foliage even when young— unlike so many palms. The leaves are composed of long, narrow opposite leaflets, on a mid-rib up to 2 ft. long.

Culture: It is quite easy to grow but will show its distaste for draughts, cold nights, or hot, dry air by withering at the tips. Like most palms it can be left

Neanthe elegans.

Nemesia hybrid.

in the same pot for several years, with annual top-dressing, occasionally feeding in summer. Grow in John Innes potting compost and maintain a minimum winter temperature of 45°.

Propagation: By seed sown in a warm greenhouse in spring.

NECK ROT. Also known as Collar Rot. A rather vague term referring to the blackening and decay of the base of the stem on many plants. It is most likely to occur if the soil round the stem is kept too wet.

NECTARINE, *see* Peach.

NEMESIA *nem-ee-zee-a.* Half-hardy annuals, useful for summer bedding or for greenhouse culture. Modern strains embrace many lovely colours, and varying height from 6 in. to 12 in. All are derived from *N. strumosa.*

Culture of Outdoor Bedding: For early flowering sow in February in a temperature of 50° to 55°. Grow on and harden off for planting early March. Nip out any precocious flower buds which appear. For summer flowering sow in March. Plant 4 in. to 6 in. apart in well-prepared sunny, open positions.

Culture Under Glass: Sow in July or August for winter flowering. September for spring flowering. January to flower in May and June, and March for summer blooms. Sow in a temperature of 55°, prick off when large enough to handle, and water. Pot singly in 3 in. or 4 in. pots or 3 plants in a 5 in. pot. Keep close to glass and in a cool temperature. Final potting is into 5 in. pots in John Innes potting compost. Cool treatment is essential if the plants are to be kept bushy.

NEMOPHILA *nem-off-ill-ah* (Californian Blue-Bell). *N. menziesii*, better known as *N. insignis* is a hardy trailing annual with blue flowers, suitable for planting in sunny beds or borders.

Outdoor Culture: Sow seeds $\frac{1}{16}$ in. deep in ordinary soil in March or April for flowering in summer; in early September for flowering in spring. Thin seedlings to 4 in. to 6 in. apart.

NEPAL POPPY, *see* Meconopsis.

NEPENTHES *nep-en-thees* (Pitcher Plant). A fascinating family cultivated chiefly for the novel and decorative effect of the pitcher-like growths at the end of the leaves. These usually develop a lid at the mouth and their purpose is to trap the insects which are part of the plants 'food'. The pitchers are often quite large and brightly coloured as in the case of *N. sanguinea*, unfortunately one of the more difficult species to grow. On this plant the pitchers are red or reddish-green and up to 10 in. long.

Culture: Nepenthes are better grown in baskets or orchid pots than in ordinary plant pots. The compost should consist of 2 parts rough, peaty soil and 1 part sphagnum moss. Little water is needed after potting until the plants are well established, when it can be gradually increased until eventually liberal supplies are being given. Shade from hot sun and frequent syringing will help to produce good growth, and to get large pitchers, the ends of the shoots should be pinched out when they have made several leaves, so that the energy of the plant is thrown into the last pitchers formed. Although in general the nepenthes are not difficult to cultivate they are definitely not plants for the cool house, and unless a winter temperature of at least 60° can be maintained it is hardly worth attempting them.

Nepeta hederacea variegata.

Propagation: Cuttings or seeds, but a temperature of at least 80° is needed for both.

NEPETA *nep*-**e**-*ta*, popularly *nep*-**ee**-*ta* (Catmint; Ground Ivy). Hardy herbaceous perennials. *N. mussini*, more correctly known as *N. farsenii*, is a bushy plant with slender spikes of lavender flowers in summer much used for margins of herbaceous borders. *N. hederacea variegata* is a trailing plant with green and white heart-shaped leaves. Popular as a greenhouse plant for edges of staging or hanging baskets as a house plant, or in window boxes.

Culture: Plant October to March in ordinary soil in sunny beds, borders, or rock gardens. *N. hederacea variegata* also makes a pretty basket or pot plant for a cool greenhouse or window. Grow in John Innes potting compost, water fairly freely spring and summer moderately at other times. No artificial heat required.

Propagation: Division of roots October to March; cuttings of basal or auxillary shoots inserted in sandy composts in a frame in summer.

NERINE *nee*-**ry**-*nee* (Guernsey Lily). Greenhouse bulbous plants, flowering from August well on in to the autumn. In this family are some of the finest bulbous plants for flowering in the cool greenhouse in autumn. There are about 18 different species including the almost hardy *N. bowdenii*, but most of these offered in catalogues are hybrids. These cover a considerable range of pink, red and orange and their glistening flowers, carried in umbels of up to a dozen blooms, make a superb show with very little re-potting of the bulbs.

Culture: Potting up should be done between July and September when the bulbs are dormant, and one bulb is usually sufficient for a 4 in. pot. A fairly plain compost of well-drained fibrous loam suits them best and after potting they should be kept almost dry in a cold frame until growth appears, when they should be transferred to a frost-proof greenhouse and watered liberally. After flowering watering should continue until the leaves turn yellow, when the plant should be gradually dried off and rested in a cool place. The chief cause of failure with these plants is over-potting and they seldom flower well until pot bound.

Culture Outdoors: Plant August to November, 2 in. to 3 in. deep in light, well-drained soil enriched with a little decayed manure in sunny borders at bases of south walls. Protect November to April with covering of dry litter. Top-dress annually in August with leaf-mould or decayed manure. Lift and replant every 4 or 5 years.

Propagation: By offsets removed when re-potting and treated as old bulbs (during July and September) after about the fourth year.

NERIUM *nee*-**re**-*um* (Oleander; Rose Bay). Greenhouse evergreen shrubs, up to 10 ft. or more high, with terminal clusters of large, showy flowers and handsome willow-like foliage. *N. oleander*, the common 'Oleander', grows outside in very mild districts, but in general the neriums are subjects for the cool greenhouse, where they will make fine specimens in tubs or large pots, flowering from June to October. *N. oleander* and *N. odorum* are the two species most commonly grown, and both are available in various

Nemophila menziesii.

Nepeta farsenii.

Nepenthes 165
sanguinea.

Nerine hybrid.

shades of white to deep pink, with either single or double flowers.

Culture: Pot February or March in John Innes compost or plant in well-drained beds of loamy soil in light, sunny greenhouse. Place pot plants outdoors June to September. Prune immediately after flowering or in October, shortening firm shoots to within 3 in. or 4 in. of their base. Temperature: September to March, 45° to 55°; normal warmth in summer. Water copiously March to September, moderately September to November; keep nearly dry November to March. Apply liquid feed once or twice weekly May to September. Remove young shoots that issue from base of flower trusses as soon as they appear. No shade required. Syringe twice daily March to June.

Propagation: By cuttings of firm young shoots 3 in. to 6 in. long inserted singly in 2 in. pots of sandy soil and placed in a propagating frame in a temperature of 60° spring or summer; or cuttings of mature wood may be placed in bottles of water in full sun in summer and potted up very carefully as soon as the roots form.

NETTLE GERANIUM, see Coleus.

NEW ZEALAND DAISY BUSH, see Olearia.

NEW ZEALAND SILVERY REED GRASS see Cortaderia.

Nigella damascena.

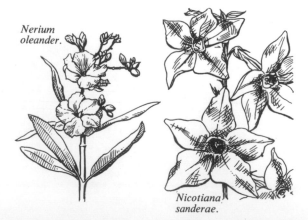

Nerium oleander.

Nicotiana sanderae.

NICOTIANA *nik-oh-te-**ar**-na* (Tobacco Plant; Sweet-scented Tobacco). Half-hardy annuals with white, pink, or crimson flowers in summer. Suitable for sunny or shady beds and borders. The numerous garden varieties are derived from *N. grandiflora*, the Jasmine Tobacco or Sweet-scented Tobacco and *N. sanderae*, the red-flowered tobacco. They grow 3 ft. to 4 ft. tall.

Culture: Sow seed in a temperature of 60° February to April. Prick off seedlings into boxes, harden off and plant outdoors in late May or early June 1 ft. apart.

NICOTINE. A poisonous alkaloid obtained from tobacco leaves. Nicotine is a powerful insecticide especially deadly to aphides (greenfly, blackfly, etc.) thrips, capsid bugs, frogflies, apple sawfly, and young caterpillars. Horticultural liquid nicotine is always sold in very dilute form and should be mixed strictly in accordance with manufacturers instructions. 'Pure' nicotine (95% to 98%) is prepared for use by diluting in water at the rate of $\frac{1}{4}$ fluid oz. to 5 gal. It is a dangerous poison to handle. Nicotine is available in spray, fumigant, and dust forms, all of which are most effective in a temperature of 65° or above. Nicotine is a contact poison, killing by means of the vapour it gives off, and in its dust form it is often effective against pests which are too protected by rolled or curled leaves to be dealt with by spray. Both the dust and spray forms are sold mixed with a spreader, such as kaolin or soft soap respectively, to ensure good coverage.

NIDULARIUM *nid-u-**lair**-ee-um*. Most of the species of this genus of bromeliads produce large flattish rosettes of foliage, often brightly coloured in the inner part, with a small central cluster of bloom. On the purple-flowered *N. acanthocrater* this rosette may be as much as 3 ft. across. *N. innocentii*, with leaves 12 in. to 15 in. in length and dark green and purple in colour is one of the most popular.

Culture: To grow these plants a winter temperature of at least 60° is desirable and a humid atmosphere must be provided at all times, though they will sometimes succeed in rooms. Pot in March in a mixture of equal parts peat, coarse sand and osmunda fibre with the addition of some leaf-mould and old cow manure. Water moderately from April to September, sparingly October to March; allow water to collect naturally in the 'cup' or 'vase' of leaves in the centre of the plant. No shade is required.

Propagation: By offsets taken off and potted up in rich leafy soil in moist heat.

NIEREMBERGIA *neer-em-**ber**-gee-a* (Cupflower). Hardy and half-hardy mostly creeping perennial herbs with white or blue flowers in summer. Suitable for sunny, moist borders or ledges of rock gardens.

166

Nidularium acanthocrater.

Nierembergia rivularis.

The two most popular species are *N. hippomanica*, 9 in. blue, usually grown as an annual, and *N. rivularis*, creeping, white, grown as a perennial.
Culture: Plant in spring in a mixture of sandy loam and leaf-mould. Water freely in dry weather. Top-dress annually in March with sandy peat. Protect in severe weather with a covering of litter.
Propagation: By seeds sown in light, sandy soil in a greenhouse February or March. *N. hippomanica* is usually renewed annually in this way; cuttings inserted in sandy soil in a propagating frame in August transferring when well-rooted to 2 in. pots.

NIGELLA *ny-***jel***-la* (Fennel-flower; Devil-in-a-Bush; Love-in-a-Mist). Hardy annuals. Blue flowers in summer surrounded by a green feathery involucre. Foliage green, graceful and feathery. The species commonly grown, *N. damascena*, is 18 in. high.
Culture: Sow in spring or early September, in ordinary soil in open, sunny beds or borders, where plants are to flower. Thin seedlings to 1 ft. apart.

NIGHT-FLOWERING CACTUS, *see* Cereus.

NIPPLE CACTUS, *see* Mammillaria.

NITRATE OF POTASH. This chemical, commonly known as saltpetre, is sometimes used as a fertiliser for pot plants in full growth, but is too expensive for widespread use. It contains $12\frac{1}{2}\%$ nitrogen and 40% potash and is usually dissolved in water at $\frac{1}{2}$ oz. per gal., and applied once every week or so in place of ordinary water.

NITRATE OF SODA. A very quick-acting fertiliser containing about 16% nitrogen. It must not be mixed with superphosphate of lime as the mixture tends to set into a solid cake. It is generally used by itself as a top dressing to plants in growth to give

them a quick fillip. For this purpose it is used at $\frac{1}{2}$ oz. to 1 oz. per sq. yd. or dissolved in water $\frac{1}{4}$ oz. to $\frac{1}{2}$ oz. per gal.

NITRO CHALK. A proprietory granular fertiliser which supplies both nitrogen and lime to the soil. It is very suitable for rapid stimulation of growth in spring and summer particularly on soils that are inclined to be acid. Rate of application is 1 oz. to 2 oz. per sq. yd. It is also useful for hastening the decay of vegetable refuse for which purpose it can be sprinkled freely over each 6 in. thick layer of refuse as it is built up into a compost heap.

NORFOLK ISLAND PINE, *see* Araucaria.

NORWAY SPRUCE, *see* Picea.

NYMPHAEA nim-*fee-a* (Water Lily). Tender and hardy, aquatic, tuberous-rooted perennials. Flowers of many colours in summer. There are numerous species but it is the hybrids such as *N. marliacea* in its various colour forms that are most popular.
Culture of Hardy Species: Plant March to June in open, sunny pools or lakes in a mixture of 2 parts rich loam, 1 part well-decayed manure. Depth of water 2 ft. to 3 ft. for strong-growing kinds, such as *N. alba*, and *N. gladstoniana*, 1 ft. to 2 ft. for varieties of medium strength such as *N. marliacea*, 4 in. to 6 in. for weaker-growing species, such as *N. tetragona* white and its pale yellow variety *helvola*. Place plant in a small basket containing above compost and lower to the bottom of pond or lake; alternatively place large mounds of compost at the bottom of pond when dry, plant one water lily in centre of each afterwards submerging with water, which can be added a little at a time as the plants grow.
Culture of Tender Species: Plant February to April, immersed 8 in. to 12 in. below surface of water, in

tanks or tubs, fully exposed to light using a mixture of 2 parts rich turfy loam and 1 part well-decayed manure. Temperatures of atmosphere: March to September, 65° to 75°; September to March, 50° to 60°. Temperatures of water: March to September, 65° to 75°; September to March, 55° to 65°. Replant annually.

Propagation: Tender species by seeds sown $\frac{1}{8}$ in. deep in pots of rich soil immersed in water heated to a temperature of 65° to 75°, March or April. Hardy species by seeds sown $\frac{1}{4}$ in. deep in rich soil in shallow basket and immersed in ponds or lakes in spring; division of roots April or May.

OBEDIENT PLANT, see Physostegia.

ODONTOGLOSSUM *o-dont-o-***gloss**-*um*. One of the loveliest genera of orchids suitable for moderately heated greenhouses. *O. crispum* and the many hybrids connected with it produce long, arching stems of rather flat flowers which may be white or variously tinged and blotched with yellow, pink or purple. *O. grande* is more erect in habit, few flowered with larger individual blooms yellow banded with chestnut.

Culture: Pot in March in a mixture of equal parts chopped sphagnum moss and osmunda fibre. Water sparingly at first more freely as growth takes place. Maintain as near as possible a temperature of 60° both summer and winter. Shade fairly heavily May to September and syringe and damp down frequently to maintain a moist atmosphere and prevent too great a rise in temperature. Keep only just moist in winter when the plants are at rest.

Propagation: By division at potting time.

OENOTHERA *een-***oth**-*er-a* by custom, correctly *en-oth-***ee**-*ra* (Evening Primrose; Sun Drops; Tree Primrose). Hardy biennials and herbaceous perennials. The biennial species most grown is the native Evening Primrose, *O. biennis*, 4 ft. to 5 ft. tall with pale yellow flowers in July and August. Among the best of the perennial kinds are *O. fruticosa*, 18 in. to 24 in. high with bright yellow flowers in July and August, and *O. missouriensis*, prostrate, grey leaved with yellow flowers in late summer.

Culture of Biennial Species: Sow seeds $\frac{1}{16}$ in. deep in shady position outdoors in April, transplanting seedlings when 1 in. high 3 in. apart each way in sunny beds or borders, again transplanting into flowering position following September or March.

Culture of Perennial Species: Plant autumn or spring in light, sandy loam in sunny borders, beds, or rock gardens.

Propagation: Perennial species by seeds sown in light soil in a cold frame in March or April, transplanting outdoors end of May or June; cuttings of young shoots inserted in sandy soil in a frame in spring or summer; division of roots in the case of tufted herbaceous kinds, March or April.

OLD MAN, see Artemisia.

OLD MAN'S BEARD, see Clematis.

OLEANDER, see Nerium.

OLEARIA *o-lee-***air**-*ee-a* (New Zealand Daisy Bush). Hardy and half-hardy evergreen flowering shrubs, with small, daisy-like flowers. The best kinds are *O. scilloniensis*, 4 ft. to 6 ft., white, May; *O. stellulata*, similar but white, lavender or pink; *O. haastii*, 6 ft. to 8 ft., white, July and August, the hardiest species.

Outdoor Culture: Plant September to November or in April in well-drained soil. Protect the more tender kinds in winter. Pruning not required except to remove dead or unhealthy shoots in April.

Propagation: By cuttings of firm young shoots, 2 in. to 3 in. long, inserted in well-drained pots of sandy soil in a frame in summer.

OLEASTER, see Elaeagnus.

OLIVERANTHUS, see Echeveria.

OMPHALODES *om-fa-***lo**-*des* (Venus's Navelwort; Rock Forget-me-not; Creeping Forget-me-

Oenothera fruticosa.

Olearia haastii.

Omphalodes luciliae.

Nymphaea alba.

Odontoglossum grande.

not). Hardy perennials with blue flowers in spring or early summer. Dwarf or spreading habit. The easiest to grow is *O. verna*, 8 in. to 9 in., April to May. *O. luciliae* is a choicer plant, with blue-grey foliage, 6 in. high flowering in May.

Culture: Plant autumn or spring in ordinary soil in partially shaded, well-drained borders or rock gardens. Water freely in dry weather. *O. luciliae*, thrives best in a mixture of loam, sand and stone chippings in a sunny, open rock garden and must be carefully guarded against damage by slugs.

Propagation: By seeds sown ⅛ in. deep in light, rich soil in semi-shaded position in April; division of roots, March or April.

ONCIDIUM *on-sid-ee-um* (Butterfly Orchid). One of the popular and comparatively easily grown genera of orchids. Many oncidiums produce their rather small flowers in large, branching sprays but one species, *O. papilio*, the Butterfly Orchid, has much larger flowers produced as a rule only one at a time on a stem though there may be a succession of flowers over a period. The typical oncidium colour is yellow often marked with brown.

Culture: Pot in early spring in a mixture of equal parts chopped sphagnum moss and osmunda fibre. Water fairly freely in spring and summer, give light shade only and maintain a temperature of 65° to 70°. In autumn and winter keep rather dry and let the temperature drop to 50° to 55°.

Propagation: By division at potting time.

ONION. Soil should be deep, well-worked, and crumbly. Prepare it as early as possible in advance, preferably in the autumn, so that the soil may be broken up thoroughly by winter frost. Well-rotted farmyard or stable manure, worked in deeply, will improve the quality of the crop. Wood ashes can be incorporated freely with the top soil. Seed can be sown in January or February under glass in a tem-

Thinning onions.

Ripening onions.

169

perature of 60°, in March outdoors, where the plants are to mature, or in late August or early September in sheltered nursery beds outdoors.

Seedlings from early sowings under glass are pricked out when 1½ in. tall and later may be placed singly in small pots. In these they are hardened off for planting out about the middle of April. Seedlings from April sowings are thinned out where they stand. Seedlings from autumn sowings are transplanted in March. In all cases the bulbs should be 6 in. apart in rows 1 ft. apart unless they are required for exhibition, when a little more space should be allowed.

Hoe frequently during the summer, water freely during dry weather, and during June and July feed every 10 days or so either with very weak liquid manure or with a reliable artificial fertiliser.

Bend over the tops when growth slackens in summer. This will encourage the swelling of the bulbs. Lift when fully developed, lay the bulbs out to dry in the sun, and then store in a cool, dry place.

ONION FLY. The white maggots of this fly attack the young bulbs of onions eating into them and destroying them. The first indication of attack is that the foliage assumes a leaden hue and flags. Effective remedies are to sprinkle aldrin dust around the young plants in May and June and hoe it in; to water with dilute dieldrin.

ONOPORDON *on-o-***por**-*don* (Cotton Thistle; Scotch Thistle). Hardy biennial herbs with ornamental white or grey foliage, suitable for wild gardens, gaps in shrubberies and herbaceous borders. The species commonly grown are *O. acanthium* and *O. tauricum*. Both will reach a height of 7 ft. or 8 ft.
Culture: Sow seeds ⅛ in. deep in ordinary soil in sunny position outdoors March or April. Transplant seedlings September where required to flower. Remove faded flower heads before seed is scattered, unless self-sown seedlings are required.

OPUNTIA *o-***pun**-*tee-a* (Indian Fig; Prickly Pear; Cochineal Cactus; Barbary Fig). Greenhouse succulent plants. Stems fleshy, flat, bristly. The species of

which there are over 250 are divided according to the character of their stems, which may be either cylindrical, globose or flattened. Most are more or less spiny, some have hairs, and all have insidious tiny barbs called glochids which it is advisable to avoid. A few have rudimentary leaves. Few of the opuntias flower until they are of a good age.
Culture: Pot March or April in pots filled ⅛ of depth with crocks and just large enough to accommodate roots, using John Innes No. 2 compost with some extra grit. Place pots in sunny, airy greenhouse or window without shading at any time. Repot every 3 or 4 years only. Water freely May to September; sparingly September to November; little afterwards. Ventilate freely in summer. Temperature: September to March, 50° to 55°; natural warmth in summer.
Propagation: By seeds sown ⅛ in. deep in well-drained pots or pans of sandy soil in temperature of 75° in March; cuttings of portions of stems exposed for a few days to dry then inserted in small, well-drained pots of loam and brickdust in temperature of 65° to 75° in summer; delicate species by grafting on robust kinds in April.

ORANGE-BALL TREE, *see* Buddleia.

ORCHID. A large family of flowering plants containing over 500 genera, great numbers of species and almost innumerable varieties and hybrids. Some are hardy and can be grown in rock gardens, cool borders or bog gardens but most are tender plants to be grown in greenhouses. From the standpoint of temperature they may be grouped in 3 classes, the cool house orchids which thrive in a minimum winter temperature of 45°, intermediate kinds requiring 55° in winter and hot house kinds which must have a minimum of 65° even in winter. Some are terrestial plants growing in soil mixed with peat and chopped sphagnum moss but many of the most popular greenhouse kinds are epiphytic plants deriving most of their nourishment from the air. These require no soil and are grown in sphagnum moss and peat, sometimes with the addition of osmunda fibre (*see* Potting).

Oncidium papilio.

Ornithogalum thrysoides.

Osmanthus delavayi.

Osmunda fern.

Orchids are not difficult to grow but they require quite different treatment from most greenhouse plants and so do not mix well with them. Anyone contemplating taking up the cultivation of these beautiful and interesting plants should try to devote a greenhouse entirely to them and should read a book on the subject of orchid cultivation and visit some orchid collections or orchid nurseries before commencing.

ORCHID CACTUS, *see* Epiphyllum.

ORNITHOGALUM *ore-ne-***thog***-a-lum* (Star of Bethlehem; Chincherinchee). Hardy and greenhouse bulbous plants with white flowers in summer. The species most commonly grown are *O. umbellatum*, 12 in., white, June; *O. nutans*, 12 in., white, June; and *O. thrysoides*, the Chincherinchee, 2 ft., white, summer, 'everlasting' flowers.
Outdoor Culture: Plant August to November, *O. thrysoides* in spring, 3 in. to 4 in. deep, in ordinary soil in sunny borders or rock gardens. Annual replanting is neither necessary nor desirable, except for *O. thrysoides* which rarely survives the winter in Britain and must usually be renewed annually. However bulbs can be lifted in October, stood in a cool dry place like gladioli, and replanted in March or April.
Indoor Culture: Pot September to February, placing several small or 1 large bulb in a 5 in. or 6 in. pot, using John Innes compost. Grow in a sunny greenhouse or window. Water moderately at first, freely when in full growth, gradually withholding water when foliage turns yellow, and keeping dry till new growth begins. Repot annually.
Propagation: By offsets removed from old bulbs and re-potted September to February.

ORRIS-ROOT, *see* Iris.

OSMANTHUS *oz-***man***-thus* (Fragrant Olive; Holly-leaved Olive). Hardy and half-hardy evergreen flowering shrubs, some with white fragrant flowers in spring. The most popular kinds are *O. aquifolium*, 20 ft. but usually much smaller, summer flowering, and *O. delavayi*, 5 ft. to 6 ft., April, very fragrant.
Culture: Plant September, October or April in good loamy soil and sheltered places. Prune in April, or after flowering, when necessary, but regular pruning is not usually required.
Propagation: By seeds sown in a frame or greenhouse in spring; by cuttings of firm young shoots inserted in sandy soil in a propagating frame in summer.

OSMUNDA *oz-***mun***-da* (Royal Fern; Flowering Fern). Hardy deciduous fern, with very large and handsome fronds. The species commonly grown is *O. regalis*, 6 ft. tall.
Culture: Plant during March or April in a mixture of 1 part each loam, leaf-mould and sand, 2 parts

Opuntia herrfeldtii.

peat, in sheltered, moist rock gardens or margins of ponds in shade or partial shade. Top-dress annually in April with compost of peat, leaf-mould and loam. Remove dead fronds in March. Water plants growing otherwise than on the margins of ponds freely in dry weather.
Propagation: By spores sown on the surface of sandy peat and leaf-mould in well-drained pans covered with a sheet of glass, in a shady part of a cool greenhouse at any time; offsets from established plants in April.

OSMUNDA FIBRE. Derived from the roots of various osmunda ferns, this material is an invaluable component of orchid potting composts, in which it is used in different proportions according to the species.

OSWEGO TEA, *see* Monarda.

OXALIS *ox-***al***-is* (Wood Sorrel). Greenhouse and hardy annuals, herbaceous perennials, and bulbous-rooted plants. Flowers white or pink. Among the most popular hardy kinds are *O. adenophylla*, 3 in., rosy-lilac, summer; *O. enneaphylla*, 3 in., white, summer; and *O. rosea*, 9 in., pink, summer.
Culture of Greenhouse Species: Pot autumn-flowering kinds in August, winter-flowering kinds in September or October; spring-flowering kinds January or February, and summer-flowering kinds March or April. Place bulbs ½ in. deep and ½ in. apart in well-drained pots of John Innes compost in

Oxalis enneaphylla rosea.

Paeonia officinalis plena.

sunny greenhouse or window. Water moderately till leaves appear, then freely. Gradually withhold water when flowers fade, and keep dry and cool till growth begins. Re-pot annually.

Culture of Hardy Species: Plant in well-drained soil as edgings to sunny borders or on rock gardens. Cool deep soil and partial shade for *O. enneaphylla* and *O. adenophylla*, plant August to November; other species in March or April.

Propagation: By seeds sown $\frac{1}{16}$ in. deep in light, sandy soil in temperature of 55° to 65° in spring; division of roots or offsets at potting or planting time.

OX-EYE DAISY, *see* Chrysanthemum.

OXLIP, *see* Primula.

OYSTER SHELL. Although not used to any extent in the greenhouse this is a useful ingredient of potting composts for many cacti and succulents, as it provides the necessary lime and at the same time improves the drainage.

PAEONIA *pee-o-nee-a* (Paeony; Peony). Hardy herbaceous and shrubby perennials, suitable for

sunny positions. The shrubby kinds (of which the tree peony, *P. suffruticosa* in many varieties with large single or double flowers in June on 4 ft. to 6 ft. bushes, is typical) require shelter from cold winds. Established plants of all kinds of peony should remain undisturbed as long as possible. The herbaceous peonies, of which there are a great many garden varieties, are mainly derived from *P. officinalis*, the common peony with crimson, pink or white flowers in May, and from *P. albiflora*, the Chinese peony with fragrant flowers in many colours in June. Both are 2½ ft. to 3 ft. tall. There are also numerous species ranging in height from 1½ ft. to 5 ft.

Culture of Tree Peonies: Plant October or March in good, loamy soil. If plants have been grafted, bury point of union between stock and scion 2 in. below surface. Mulch in spring with garden compost or well-rotted manure. Protect in severe weather with covering of bracken or straw.

Culture of Herbaceous Peonies: Plant October to April in good, loamy soil. Top-dress annually with well-decayed manure or garden compost, lightly forked into surface in October or November. Mulch on dry soils in April. Water freely in dry weather.

Propagation: All species by seeds sown in a green-

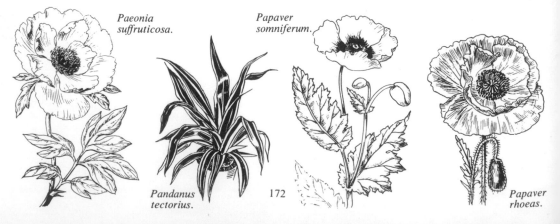

Paeonia suffruticosa.

Papaver somniferum.

Pandanus tectorius.

172

Papaver rhoeas.

Storing parsnips in sand.

house or frame in March or September. Herbaceous peonies by division of roots in March or April. Tree species by grafting on the fleshy roots of *P. albiflora* or *P. officinalis* in August; layering in autumn or spring.

PAEONY, *see* Paeonia.

PAINTED DAISY, *see* Pyrethrum.

PAMPAS GRASS, *see* Cortaderia.

PAN. Plant-pots which are wider than they are high are usually described as pans. They are often used for the raising of small quantities of seed and they are better than seed-boxes for very slow-germinating ones, such as those of certain rock-plants, as they do not deteriorate. Pans are often used, too, for the growing of the more tender alpine plants, and very fine mature specimens can be grown in them. They are usually sold in the same diameters as pots.

PANDANUS *pan-dan-us* (Screw Pine). Trees and shrubs, many of which produce thick aerial roots which develop into almost trunk-like growths. The spiral arrangement of the long, narrow leaves give the plants their common name. They are all natives of the warmer parts of the world and need fairly high temperatures, although a few species such as *P. baptistii*, with yellow striped leaves, and *P. sanderi*, with green and gold variegations, are used as house plants in their young stage. Apart from these one of the most widely cultivated is *P. tectorius*, with green leaves abruptly tapering to a long, slender point.
Culture: Pot in March in John Innes compost. Water freely April to September, sparingly October to March. Temperatures: October to March, 55° to 65°; April to September, 65° to 75°.
Propagation: By offsets detached at potting time.

PANSY, *see* Viola.

PANSY ORCHID, *see* Miltonia.

PAPAVER *pap-ah-ver* (Poppy). Hardy annual and perennial herbs. Suitable for sunny beds, borders, or rock gardens. *P. alpinum* and *P. nudicaule* are best grown as annuals or biennials. The most popular perennial poppy is *P. orientale*, 3 ft., scarlet, pink or white, June. The annual poppies are derived from *P. rhoeas*, the Shirley poppies being in many shades from white and pale pink to crimson, and from *P. somniferum*, more robust, with grey-green leaves and large flowers in colours from white, lavender and pink to purple and crimson. All summer flowering.
Culture of Annual Species: Sow seeds $\frac{1}{16}$ in. deep in March or April in patches where required to grow for flowering in summer; September for flowering in spring in good ordinary soil. Thin seedlings to 6 in. to 8 in. when $\frac{1}{2}$ in. high.
Culture of Perennial Species: Plant October, March, or April in well-drained ordinary soil. Remove faded flowers and withering or yellowing leaves.
Propagation: Annual species by seeds as above; perennial species by seeds sown outdoors in March or April; division of roots in March or April; by root cuttings in sandy soil in late winter.

Iceland poppy

PARLOUR PALM, *see* Aspidistra.

PARROT'S BILL, *see* Clianthus.

PARSLEY. For a continuous supply three sowings should be made annually, one in early March, a second towards the end of May, and a third in August. Position should be open and soil reasonably good and well dug. Sow in drills $\frac{1}{4}$ in. deep and 1 ft. apart or use as edging to a bed. Thin seedlings to 6 in. Gather leaves a few at a time, so that plants are not weakened unduly. Some seedlings from August sowings can be transferred in October to a frame for winter use, or alternatively plants may be covered where they grow with cloches.

PARSNIP. This crop needs deeply-worked soil that is in good condition but has not been freshly manured. A compound vegetable fertiliser should be scattered over the ground at 4 oz. per sq. yd. prior to sowing. Sow in March, April or early May in drills 1 in. deep and 18 in. apart. Drop the seeds in twos or threes 6 in. apart and later thin them to one at each cluster. Allow a little more space for exhibition. Parsnips are hardy and can be left in the ground all winter, to be lifted as required, but it is usually convenient to lift some roots in November and bury them in sand or peat in a shed or sheltered place as it may be difficult to dig parsnips when the ground is frozen hard.

PARTHENOCISSUS *par-then-o-sissus* (Virginia Creeper). Self-clinging climbing plants, with brilliant

173

autumn colouring. *P. quinquefolia* (Virginia Creeper), *P. henryana* and *P. tricuspidata veitchii* (*Ampelopsis veitchii*) are the species commonly grown.

PASSIFLORA *pas-see-***flor**-*a* (Passion Flower). Tender and nearly hardy climbing plants with flowers of uncommon character and beauty in summer. The Passion Flowers are so named because of the fancied resemblance of parts of the flower to certain features of the Crucifixion. They are natives of South America and most of the species cultivated in this country, such as *P. racemosa*, *P. quadrangularis* and *P. edulis* are suitable only for the warm greenhouse, although *P. caerulea* will grow outside in sheltered positions. This last, is the most commonly grown Passion Flower and its large flowers, of which the most re-markable feature is the prominent 'corona' of blue-tipped filaments, are well-known. Although these flowers are very fleeting, lasting only a day or so, they are produced so freely that there is a constant display from June to September and very often they are followed by the edible bright orange fruits.

Culture of Greenhouse Species: Pot February or March in well-drained tubs or large pots in John Innes compost or plant in beds of good, loamy soil. Train shoots up rafters or walls. Prune February, thinning out weak shoots and shortening strong ones by ⅓. Water freely March to September, moderately afterwards. Syringe daily April to September. Apply liquid feed occasionally to healthy plants when in flower only. Temperature: October to March, 45° to 60° according to species; normal rise in summer.

Outdoor Culture of Passiflora Caerulea: Plant October or March in ordinary well-drained soil against south or south-west wall or fence. Prune in April, only removing dead, tangled or surplus growth. Water freely in dry weather. Protect base of plant with straw or dry bracken during severe weather.

Propagation: By seeds sown ¼ in. deep in sandy soil in temperature of 60° to 65° in spring; by cuttings of young shoots inserted in sandy soil in propagating frame in temperature of 65° April to September.

PASSION FLOWER, *see* Passiflora.

Passiflora quadrangularis.

Passiflora caerulea.

PAULOWNIA *paw-lo-nee-a.* Hardy deciduous trees with violet flowers in summer and large orna-mental leaves. The species usually grown is *P. tomen-tosa*, 30 ft. to 50 ft. tall. It is often known as *P. imperialis.*

Culture: Plant October to February in rich, well-drained loam in sunny, sheltered places. Prune shoots annually in February to within 2 in. or 3 in. of their base if only foliage is desired; leave unpruned for flowering, except for removal of soft wood injured by frost.

Propagation: By seeds sown ⅛ in. deep in sandy soil in a frame in spring; by cuttings of roots inserted in sandy soil in frame in February.

PEA. These require good, rich, well-manured and well-dug soil. Prepare it during autumn or winter and make first outdoor sowings as early in March as soil and weather will permit. Sowing can commence in February with the protection of cloches. Subse-quently, sowing may be continued every fortnight or so until early June for succession. Seed may either be sown in drills 2 in. deep or in shallow, flat-bottomed trenches about 2 in. deep scooped out with a spade, in which case 2 or 3 lines of seed may be sown in each trench. Space the seeds 2 in. or 3 in. apart.

There are many varieties of peas, and these may be classified in various ways: as early, mid-season and late; as tall, medium or dwarf; and as round-seeded or wrinkle-seeded (marrowfat). The round-seeded peas are hardier, but the wrinkle-seeded peas are sweeter. Dwarf peas need not be supported though they are better for a few short, bushy sticks. Medium and tall peas must always be supported with pea-sticks (usually hazel branches) or netting. Early peas take about 12 weeks from sowing to first gathering; mid-season peas 14 weeks; late peas 16 weeks or more.

Successive rows of peas should be spaced roughly according to the height of the peas; 2 ft. peas in rows 2 ft. apart; 4 ft. peas in rows 4 ft. apart, and so on.

Gathering should be done a little at a time as the pods fill up. It is the lower pods that fill first.

PEACH AND NECTARINE. Both can be grown outdoors, but only a few varieties such as Hale's Early, Peregrine and Early Rivers will fruit satisfactorily without the protection of a sheltered wall. They need a good soil with plenty of old mortar rubble or lime and a liberal sprinkling of bonemeal. Plant fan-trained trees 10 ft. to 12 ft. apart in Novem-ber. At first prune weak shoots and shorten leaders in November, to build up a strong framework of growth, but when the trees fill up their space do most pruning during the summer months. Remove young shoots a few at a time until only 2 are left, 1 at the tip and 1 near the base of each fruit-bearing side growth. Then in November cut out the old side growth and train the young side growth retained near its base in its place.

• *Paulownia tomentosa.*

An early sowing of peas in pots.

Pinching out lateral shoots on a peach tree.

Water freely in dry weather. Fruits must be thinned when about the size of walnuts about 9 in. apart each way. Mulch with well-rotted manure or compost each February.

Propagation: By seeds (stones) sown in March (but varieties do not come true to type from seed); by budding in summer on to plum stocks or seedling peaches.

PEAR. (Ornamental varieties *see* Pyrus). Pears require a rather lighter soil and warmer position than apples; they resent cold, wet clays and do not produce fruits of high quality on poor, sandy or gravelly soil. The choicest varieties should, for preference, be trained against a sunny wall or fence, but there are many kinds which can be grown quite satisfactorily in the open, either as bushes or standards. Trained trees are usually grown as cordons or espaliers.

Pears can be planted at any time from early November until about the middle of March. Preparation of the soil should be very thorough, and if it is naturally heavy it is advisable to improve the drainage. Dig in moderate quantities of farmyard or stable manure.

Pruning is practically the same as that advised for apples, but pears form spurs even more readily than apples, and so are particularly well adapted to the more restricted forms of training such as single-stem cordons, or horizontally trained trees (espaliers). These should be pruned in summer shortening laterals a few at a time during July and early August to five leaves. This should be supplemented by winter pruning, at which season the laterals may be further shortened to 2 buds each, leading growths being cut back about a third. The fruits require thinning, but this must not be done too drastically as some will fall before they are fully grown.

Propagation: By grafting in March or April or by budding in July and August. Seedling pears are used as stocks for large trees, but trained trees should be worked upon the quince stock.

PEAT. The fibrous mould common to most heaths and moorlands and also to bogs and made up, for the

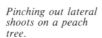

Thinning pears.

Picking a good crop of pears.

175

most part, of decayed vegetable matter. Peat varies considerably in its composition. For horticultural purposes it is samples of a fibrous or granular texture and of moderate acidity which are most useful. Such peat has very largely taken the place of leaf-mould for potting mixtures, as it serves the same purpose of keeping the compost open and reasonably retentive of moisture, and with it there is practically no danger of introducing disease spores or weed seeds. Before use for potting or seed sowing, peat should be put through a $\frac{1}{2}$ in. sieve to ensure an even texture and even distribution, throughout the compost. It must also be moist, although not wet, as, if used in a dry state it is difficult to wet again. Some plants, such as rhododendrons, azaleas and heathers, thrive specially well in peaty soils and dislike chalky or alkaline soils. When making peat beds in calcareous soil outdoors it is essential to isolate them in some way from the surrounding soil, or lime will soon find its way into the peat.

PELARGONIUM *pel-ar-go-nee-um* (Geranium). Greenhouse evergreen shrubby and sub-shrubby perennials. There are many types of pelargoniums in cultivation, chief among them being the zonals, commonly called 'geraniums'; regal pelargoniums with larger flowers in more diverse colours grown as greenhouse pot plants; climbing ivy-leaved varieties suitable for beds, hanging baskets and for training up sunny walls; and a number of species with leaves that are fragrant when bruised or crushed.

Culture of Zonal Pelargoniums: Cuttings should be taken in August and September, potted up when rooted and wintered in a cool, dry greenhouse. The plants should be pinched occasionally to ensure a bushy habit. John Innes compost is suitable. Water sparingly during winter, and maintain temperature between 45° and 55°. When growth restarts in spring increase water supply and feed when flowering with weak liquid manure or fertiliser. If required for summer bedding plant out in late May or early June, when damage by frost is past. After flowering, plants can be cut back, re-potted in spring when growth becomes active, and grown on to make large specimens. Plants may be induced to bloom in winter by

pinching main growths and removing all flower buds throughout summer and maintaining a winter temperature of about 60°.

Culture of Regal Pelargoniums: Insert cuttings in July or August in a frame or greenhouse. When rooted, pot individually and keep close to the glass in a temperature of 45° to 55°. Pinch out tips of shoots occasionally to make them bushy. About January transfer to 5 in. pots. Water only moderately during winter, freely from March to July and apply liquid manure or fertiliser when flower buds show. After flowering plunge the pots outdoors in a sunny place and prune shoots to within 1 or 2 joints of their base in July. When growth restarts, re-pot, shaking away as much soil as possible, and re-house in September. About the turn of the year another shift should be given to 6 in. or 8 in. pots. A similar compost to that advised for the zonals will suit. The minimum winter temperature required is 45° to 55° with a natural rise in the spring months.

Culture of Ivy-leaved Varieties: Root cuttings in August or September, and grow plants on in cool greenhouse, minimum temperature 45°, close to the glass. In February or March transfer to 4 in. pots and nip off the point of the main shoots. In April or May re-pot in 5 in. pots or plant in hanging baskets. In the former case train the shoots to stakes. Water freely during the summer, sparingly at other seasons. Feed with liquid manure when in flower. Prune back old plants during February and March. Climbers need only have laterals cut back. Plants in hanging baskets, prune severely to encourage fresh growth. Re-pot each specimen as soon as growth restarts. Compost required is similar to that recommended for zonals. Culture of ivy-leaved pelargoniums out of doors is as advised for zonals except that shoots may be pegged to surface of soil to give ground cover or may be tied to canes to provide dot plants.

Culture of Fragrant-leaved Pelargoniums: This is, to all intents and purposes, the same as that advised for zonals for summer flowering except that there need be no period of rest outdoors in summer.

Propagation: The correct time for taking cuttings of the different types has been outlined in each case. Cuttings in every instance are made from firm growth.

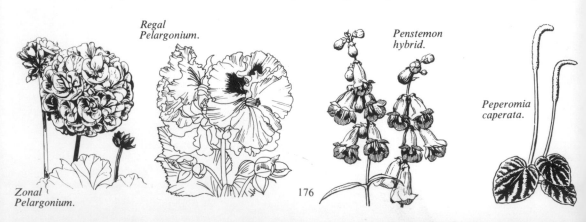

Regal Pelargonium.

Penstemon hybrid.

Peperomia caperata.

Zonal Pelargonium.

Taking a regal pelargonium cutting.   Inserting the cutting.   Pruning regal pelargonium.

Rooting will be rapid if a fairly close atmosphere is maintained and the cuttings are shaded for a week or two. A temperature of 50° to 55° is ample.

PENNYROYAL, *see* Mentha.

PENSTEMON *pen-***stem***-on.*   Hardy and half-hardy herbaceous and some shrubby perennials. The innumerable varieties of florists' penstemons are hybrids, amongst the showiest of summer flowering plants, but most can only be considered half-hardy; although they thrive for years in mild districts, a severe winter will kill them. Many of the dwarf species such as *P. heterophyllus,* 12 in., blue, summer; and *P. scouleri,* 12 in., lavender, summer, are much hardier and splendid plants for the rock garden. A wide range of colours-excluding yellow.

Culture: For the finest spikes the florist varieties are best raised annually from cuttings. Plant early May in good, rich soil. Pinch out leading shoots to encourage branching habit. The rock garden species, plant during March or April in well-drained soil on sunny ledges where they will have some protection from north winds.

Propagation: The florist varieties should be propagated annually from cuttings. Select firm, young shoots about 4 in. long in August and September and insert in a sandy compost in a frame. Winter in this frame and harden off in preparation for planting in spring. Cuttings may also be taken of the rock garden species or they may be raised from seed sown in a temperature of 55° to 60° in February or March.

PEONY, *see* Paeonia.

PEPEROMIA *pep-er-***o***-me-a* (Pepper Elder). Some kinds of peperomia are now sold as foliage

Potting regal pelargonium.

house plants, but while they are quite decorative for this purpose they are not too easily managed except for a short time, at any rate in winter. The species include both trailing and upright types but apart from *P. scandens* the latter are the most commonly grown. Among these *P. magnoliaefolia variegata,* with smooth, fleshy leaves of gold and green on a plant up to 12 in. high, is one of the hardiest, and *P. caperata* one of the most showy, with deeply-furrowed green leaves and 'pipe-cleaner' flowerspikes of pure white.

Culture: They need a quite humid atmosphere and a temperature of about 70° with shade from hot sun

Philodendron scandens.

Pernettya mucronata.

except in winter, when they need all the sun they can get. With peperomias over-watering is the main thing to guard against and even in summer they do not need a lot. The use of cold water is harmful too, so water that has been aired should always be used.

Propagation: By cuttings consisting of short pieces of stem, each with a leaf attached. These should be inserted in sandy peat in a temperature of about 75°, but not in a propagating frame as this often leads to damping off. When rooted the cuttings should be potted up into small pots of equal parts of peat and sandy soil.

PEPPER ELDER, *see* Peperomia.

PEPPERMINT, *see* Mentha.

PERENNIAL. A plant that lives for several years and does not naturally die immediately after flowering and seeding. Usually classed as hardy, half-hardy, and tender. A herbaceous perennial is a plant that lives for several years and has soft, in contrast to woody, growth which usually dies back to ground level before winter.

PERIWINKLE, *see* Vinca.

PERNETTYA *per-***net**-*ee-a* (Prickly Heath). Hardy low-growing evergreen berry-bearing shrubs with crimson, blue, black, rose or white berries in autumn. The species cultivated, *P. mucronata*, grows from 3 ft. to 5 ft. tall.

Outdoor Culture: Plant September to November or March to May in peaty soil and sunny or half-shady position.

Propagation: By seeds sown ¼ in. deep in bed of peaty soil outdoors in autumn; layering shoots in March or April.

PERMANGANATE OF POTASH. This is sometimes used at the rate of 1 oz. to 4 gal. of water as a precaution against the damping-off of seedlings and cuttings, but its value is largely over-rated. It has, however, some value as a mild fungicide and there is no harm in putting a few crystals in the water tanks—sufficient to make the water pink—as a precautionary measure.

PEROVSKIA *per-***of**-*skee-a* (Russian Sage). Hardy deciduous, semi-woody shrubs suitable for sunny borders or shrubberies. The species usually grown, *P. atriplicifolia*, grows 6 ft. to 7 ft. tall and has lavender flowers in late summer.

Culture: Plant November to February preferably from pots in groups of 3 or 4 in good, well-drained soil. Cut away all dead growth in early spring.

Propagation: By cuttings of half-ripened growth in July, inserted in sandy soil in a propagating frame and transferred singly to pots when rooted.

PERUVIAN LILY, *see* Alstroemeria.

PETUNIA *pet-***u**-*ne-a.* Half-hardy annuals with flowers of many different colours in summer. There are a great many varieties and at least 3 distinct types, the large-flowered or 'grandiflora', the bedding or 'multiflora' and the 'double-flowered'.

Culture: Sow in February, March or April in a temperature of 60°. Prick-off seedlings 2 in. apart in boxes and harden off for planting outdoors 9 in. apart in late May or early June in a sunny situation and good well-drained soil. The large-flowered and

Phlomis fruticosa.

double-flowered petunias also make admirable pot plants for the greenhouse or window ledge in summer for which purpose they should be started in just the same manner as for summer bedding but should be potted singly in April or May in 4 in. or 5 in. pots in John Innes compost.

PHACELIA *fa-see-le-a.* Hardy annuals with blue flowers, good for bees. *P. campanularia* is one of the finest blue-flowered annuals for summer bedding.
Culture: Sow in April in ordinary soil, where required to grow, in sunny or partially shaded beds or borders. Thin seedlings, as soon as large enough to 6 in.

PHILADELPHUS *fill-a-dell-fuss* (Mock Orange). Hardy deciduous flowering shrubs, mostly with white flowers, some very fragrant in summer. Among the most popular kinds are *P. lemoinei*, 6 ft. to 8 ft., and all the hybrids and garden varieties connected with it. Other good kinds are *P. coronarius*, 10 ft. to 12 ft.;

P. microphyllus, 4 ft. to 5 ft.; and *P. purpureo-maculatus*, 4 ft. to 5 ft.
Culture: Plant October to February in good ordinary soil and open positions. Prune immediately after flowering, thinning out shoots that have bloomed but retaining all young stems.
Propagation: By cuttings of well-ripened growth in October or November inserted in sandy soil and sheltered positions outdoors.

PHILODENDRON *fil-o-den-dron.* Although growing naturally to an enormous size in their native tropical America, some of the philodendrons make excellent and easily grown plants for the house or warm greenhouse. They are climbing plants grown chiefly for their foliage, and even when young are interesting for the comparatively large aerial roots they throw out. The plant sometimes called *P. pertusum* is really *Monstera deliciosa*. *P. scandens*, with pear-shaped leaves, is the species most commonly sold and it does well almost anywhere except in full sun provided that it is given plenty of water and syringing in summer and kept well away from frost in winter.
Culture: A compost of about equal parts peat and sandy soil suits all the philodendrons. Pot in March. Water freely in spring and summer, moderately at other times and shade from direct sunlight. Temperature 50° to 60° in winter, natural rise in summer. Syringe freely in spring and summer. When growing indoors it is an advantage to train stems up bark or cork and keep this moist to encourage the aerial roots which will be freely formed on the stems.
Propagation: By cuttings consisting of about 3 joints. These root easily in sandy soil in a temperature of about 80°.

PHLOMIS *flo-mis* (Jerusalem Sage). Hardy perennials and shrubs of which the best for garden display is *P. fruticosa*, an evergreen shrub with whorls of yellow flowers in summer.
Culture: Plant October to April in ordinary soil or a sandy loam and sunny position. No regular pruning required.

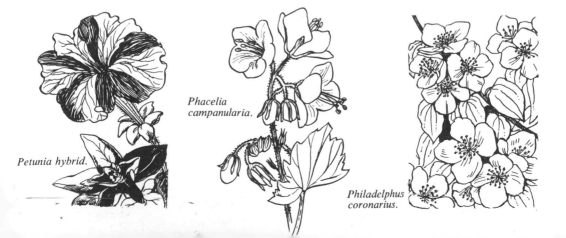

Petunia hybrid.

Phacelia campanularia.

Philadelphus coronarius.

Propagation: By seeds sown in warm greenhouse in March or also by cuttings inserted in a frame in August.

PHLOX *floks*. Half-hardy annuals and hardy perennials. Phloxes for garden cultivation are divided into three main classes: alpines such as *P. subulata*, *P. nivalis* and *P. divaricata*, varying from 2 in. to 18 in., may be planted as edgings to sunny borders, on ledges or rock gardens and in dry walls; herbaceous summer-flowering, varieties mainly derived from *P. paniculata*, varying from 1 ft. to 4 ft., suitable for sunny or partially shaded beds or borders; annuals derived from *P. drummondii*, height about 1 ft., useful for summer bedding.

Culture of Alpine Species: Plant in spring in light, well-drained soil and sunny positions. Lift and divide in March only when grown too large for the position they occupy.

Culture of Herbaceous Varieties: Plant autumn or spring in deep, rich, moderately heavy loam. Mulch with decayed manure in March or April. Water freely in dry weather. Cut down stems in October. Lift, divide, and replant every third year.

Culture of Annual Species: Sow seeds $\frac{1}{16}$ in. deep in light soil in temperature of 60° in March. Transplant seedlings 2 in. apart in boxes, gradually harden off, and plant outdoors 6 in. apart in good soil in sunny position in June. Nip off point of main shoot after planting to induce bushy growth. Water freely in dry weather.

Propagation: Herbaceous phloxes by careful division either in March or September; by root cuttings in a frame February or March. Alpine phloxes by cuttings of firm young growth during August in sandy soil in a frame; by seeds sown in a frame or greenhouse in March.

PHOENIX **fee-***niks* (Date Palm). This genus of feathery-leaved palms provides us not only with dates, but also with a few fine subjects for the cool greenhouse, and there is one species, *P. canariensis*, which even grows out of doors in the extreme south of Britain. Under glass, probably the most common species is *P. rupicola*, with bright green rather limply

drooping leaves, but another species, *P. dactylifera*, ought to be equally common for it can be easily grown from date stones.

Culture: Pot in March in John Innes No. 2 compost or a mixture of 2 parts of good loam and 1 each of peat and sand. Over-potting should be guarded against. During the summer the soil should be kept evenly moist, but in winter, when the plants must be kept out of frost, little watering is needed. Minimum winter temperature 45°; natural rise in summer. Syringe frequently in summer or sponge leaves with water containing a few drops of milk.

Propagation: By seeds sown in spring in John Innes potting compost in temperature of 60° to 65°.

PHYGELIUS *fie-***jee-***lee-us* (Cape Figwort). Half-hardy herbaceous perennial with orange-scarlet flowers in late summer. Suitable for sunny, well-drained borders in sheltered places. The species grown, *P. capensis*, is 3 ft. to 4 ft. tall but will reach 2 or 3 times that height against a wall.

Culture: Plant March or April in ordinary, well-drained soil. Protect in winter by a covering of ashes or dry bracken.

Propagation: By division of roots, March or April.

PHOSPHATE fos-*fate*. One of the essential plant foods in the soil which exerts a great influence on the production of roots. Chemically, a salt of phosphoric acid. Important phosphatic fertilisers include basic slag, superphosphate and bonemeal.

PHYLLOSTACHYS, *see* Arundinaria.

PHYSALIS *fie-***say-***liss* (Winter Cherry; Cape Gooseberry). Hardy perennial herbs producing inflated bladder-like orange seed vessels which are used for winter decoration. One of the best kinds is *P. franchetii*, 18 in. tall.

Culture: Plant March or April in rich soil in sunny, well-drained borders. Gather stems bearing fruit in September and dry for winter decorations.

Propagation: By seeds sown in a frame or greenhouse in March; by division of roots at planting time.

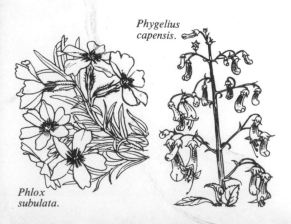

Phlox subulata.

Phygelius capensis.

Physalis franchetii.

Physostegia virginiana.

PHYSOSTEGIA *phy-sos-***tee**-*jee-a* (Dragon's Head; Obedient Plant). Hardy herbaceous perennials with pink or carmine flowers in late summer. Suitable for sunny beds and borders. The most familiar species, *P. virginiana*, is 4 ft. tall but there is a dwarf (15 in.) variety of this named Vivid.
Culture: Plant October to April in ordinary soil.
Propagation: By division at planting time.

PHYTEUMA *fie-***tew**-*ma* (Horned Rampion). Hardy perennial herbs with blue or white flowers in May or June. Suitable for sunny, well-drained rock gardens. Among the best species are *Phyteuma comosum*, 4 in. to 6 in., purple; *P. orbiculare*, 1 ft., blue; and *P. hemisphaericum*, 3 in. to 4 in., blue.
Culture: Plant March or April in good loam mixed with limestone grit and leaf-mould or peat. Lift, divide and re-plant only when overgrown as these plants dislike disturbance. Top-dress with a mixture of peat and limestone grit annually in February or March. Water freely in dry weather.
Propagation: By seeds sown in sandy soil in a cold frame in March; division of plants in March or April.

PICEA *pice-***ee**-*a* (Spruce; Christmas Tree). Hardy evergreen cone-bearing trees mostly too large for garden planting, although a few species are popular. The Christmas Tree or Norway Spruce, *P. abies*, grows rapidly and will reach a height of 100 ft. or more. It can be useful as a windbreak. More ornamental is the Colorado Spruce, *P. pungens*, especially in its very 'blue' needled forms such as *glauca*, *kosteriana* and *moerheimii*. These are all much slower growing and may take many years to reach 50 ft.
Culture: Plant October to April in ordinary, well-drained soil and sunny positions. No pruning is desirable.
Propagation: By seed sown in peaty soil in spring. Selected garden forms usually by grafting in spring on to seedlings of the related species.

PIE, *see* Clamp.

PIERIS **peer**-*is*. Hardy evergreen shrubs with white lily-of-the valley-like flowers in spring. Suitable for sheltered shrubberies or thin woodlands in lime-free soil. The most popular are *P. floribunda*, 4 ft. to 6 ft.; *P. japonica*, 7 ft. to 10 ft.; and *P. forrestii*, 8 ft. to 10 ft. The young growth of the last is brilliant red.
Culture: Plant October to March in lime-free loamy soil with some peat or leaf-mould. Water freely in dry positions during summer. No regular pruning necessary.
Propagation: By layering shoots in spring; seeds sown in peaty soil in a greenhouse or frame in spring.

PILEA *pie-***lee**-*a* (Artillery Plant). Most of the members of this family are hardly worth cultivating,

Herbaceous phlox.

Picea pungens glauca pendula.

Pieris japonica.

but two of interest are *P. muscosa* and the recently introduced *P. cadierei*. *P. muscosa* forms a neat little plant about 6 in. high with small heads of flowers which have earned it the name of Artillery Plant, from the way in which they obviously discharge their pollen when shaken. *P. cadieiri* has become quite popular as a foliage house plant, a purpose for which it is quite effective with its heavily silver-marked green leaves.

Culture: *P. cadierei* grows quite rapidly to its maximum size of a foot or so but it should be fed rather than potted-on as it grows. A moderate temperature, 55° to 65°, with fairly liberal watering all the year round, suits it and provided the soil is kept moist it does not mind full sun. *P. muscosa* grows well under similar conditions and is, if anything, rather hardier. Both plants will thrive in John Innes potting compost.

Propagation: Both species by cuttings, which root readily in a warm frame at almost any time.

PIMPERNEL, *see* Anagallis.

PINCHING. The process of removing the tips of shoots with the finger and thumb. It is usually done to prevent the upward or outward growth of the shoots so that a more bushy habit is developed, but on certain plants, such as the chrysanthemum it is done with the idea of getting a certain number of blooms at a given time (*see* Stopping).

PINCUSHION FLOWER, *see* Scabiosa.

PINEAPPLE, *see* Ananas.

PINEAPPLE FLOWER, *see* Eucomis.

PINK. A name given in gardens to forms of *Dianthus plumarius* (*see* Dianthus).

PIPES. In the low-pressure hot-water systems used in greenhouses the hot water from the boiler is conveyed round the structure by means of cast iron pipes, usually 4 in. in diameter. These are supplied in short lengths and are joined either by permanent joints made of cement and tow or by 'expansion joints' sealed by rubber rings. The latter have the advantage that they can be easily assembled or dismantled if it is necessary to remove or alter the pipes. Positioning of the pipes should be done so that the heat is distributed as evenly as possible, and to ensure a good circulation there must be a continual rise, with no sags, from the boiler to the terminal point. This rise should be not less than 1 in. in 12 ft. There is no actual need to paint the pipes, but when the house is clear of plants they can be given a smart appearance by painting them with Brunswick Black varnish paint.

For a water supply in the garden, underground pipes may be used to convey the water to taps or stand-pipes placed at convenient points. To avoid damage to the pipes by frost or cultivation they should be buried about 2 ft. deep, but if they are to be connected to a main supply the Local Authority should be consulted first so that any bye-laws may be complied with. Overhead irrigation by either galvanised or plastic pipes is a simpler job, and the latter may in fact be used underground with far less trouble than metal ones.

PIT, *see* Clamp.

PITCHER PLANT, *see* Nepenthes.

PITTOSPORUM *pit-os-***por***-um.* Evergreen shrubs or small trees grown principally for the beauty of their shining green foliage. All are a little too tender to be reliable outdoors except in the south and near the sea. The most popular species are *P. tenuifolium* with small leaves and black twigs and *P. tobira* with much larger leaves and fragrant cream flowers in spring and early summer. Both will reach 20 ft. but are usually much smaller.

Culture: Plant in March or April in well-drained soil and a warm, sunny, sheltered place. *P. tenuifolium* is often used as a plant for cut foliage and stems can be cut from it in moderation at almost any time of the year.

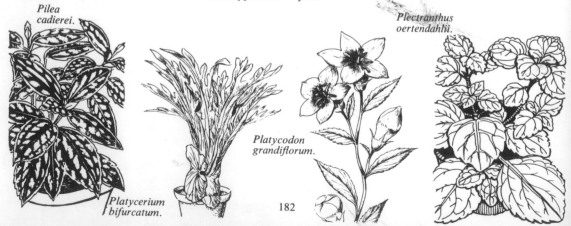

Pilea cadierei.

Platycerium bifurcatum.

Platycodon grandiflorum.

Plectranthus oertendahlii.

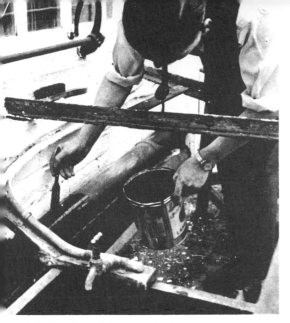

Painting pipes with a special paint to prevent rust.

Pittosporum tobira.

Propagation: By seed sown in a warm greenhouse or frame in March; by cuttings of firm young shoots in a propagating frame in July.

PLANTAIN LILY, *see* Hosta.

PLATYCERIUM *plat-ee-seer-ee-um* (Elk's-horn Fern; Stag's-horn Fern). Tender evergreen epiphytic ferns. Fronds divided, resembling a stag's horn. Most of the Stag's-horn Ferns require really warm treatment and given this they are among the most beautiful and interesting of all the ferns. Fortunately, however, one of the best of them, *P. bifurcatum*, does best in a cool greenhouse, where its fertile fronds, forked and divided as the common name suggests, make an outstanding feature.

Culture: Place plants on blocks of wood suspended from roof or sides of greenhouse; cover roots with a layer of sphagnum moss and fibrous peat and secure in position by means of copper wire. Top-dress annually with fresh peat and moss in February or March. Water freely April to September, moderately September to March. Unlike most ferns they should be given full light and allowed to almost dry out between waterings, which should then be very thorough. Shade from sun. Temperature: 45° to 55°, winter; 60° to 70°, March to October.

Propagation: The different species can be readily propagated by division except in the case of *P. grande*, which must be propagated by spores sown in sandy peat in temperature of 70° to 75°.

PLATYCODON *plat-ee-ko-don* (Balloon Flower). Hardy herbaceous perennials with blue or white flowers in summer. Suitable for sunny or partially shady borders. The species grown, *P. grandiflorum*, is about 2 ft. high.

Culture: Plant in spring in good, well-drained soil.

Propagation: By division of roots in spring.

PLECTRANTHUS *plek-tran-thus*. Closely related to the coleus, these plants need much the same treatment. They are grown chiefly for their spikes of bloom rather than their foliage. *P. chiradzulensis* (lavender blue) and *P. mahonii* (purple) are two of the best for the cool greenhouse, but a newer introduction, *P. oertendahlii*, is likely to oust them. This, with its loose spikes of mauve-pink bells, makes quite a good house plant and being of trailing habit it is ideal for hanging baskets or plant troughs.

Culture: Easy to grow in summer in the manner described for coleus, but needs a temperature of between 50° and 60° in winter.

Propagation: By stem cuttings in heat in spring or summer.

PLEIONE *ply-o-ne*. Small orchids which are nearly hardy and can be grown in almost unheated greenhouses. The flowers are white, pink or purple and are produced in spring. The most popular species are *P. pricei* and *P. formosana*.

Culture: Plant in pots or, better still, several plants together in a wide pan, February or March in a mixture of 3 parts loam, 2 parts peat and 1 part sand. Cover pseudo-bulbs to about half their depth. Grow without artificial heat in spring and summer and with only just sufficient to exclude frost in autumn and winter. Water freely March to September sparingly

Pleione formosana.

Plumbago capensis.

Removing branches
of plum affected with
Silver Leaf.

Mulching wall-
trained plum.

after this and almost withhold water for a month or
so in mid-winter.

Propagation: By division at potting time.

PLUM. This fruit succeeds best on fairly rich
soils well supplied with lime and not subject to waterlogging in winter. The best time for planting is in
early November, but the work can be continued at
any time until March, provided the weather is open.
Plums are even more surface-rooting than either
apples or pears, and so it is never wise to carry out
deep cultivation around established trees. They
should be mulched with rotted manure or compost
each February and also fed at about the same time
with a compound fruit fertiliser.

For planting in the open, the standard form is most
suitable, as it permits comparatively unrestricted
growth which plums like. Against walls or fences
plums should be trained as fans.

The pruning of plums grown in the open should be
as light as possible, and is best done as soon as the
crop has been gathered in late summer. More drastic
pruning is essential for wall-trained plums. Unwanted
side shoots can be cut back to within two dormant
buds of the main branches, but where possible young
laterals should be trained in at practically full length.

The most serious disease of the plum is silver leaf.
This is of fungal origin, but it cannot be controlled
by spraying as the sap becomes infected. The colour
of leaves attacked by silver leaf is very distinctive, a
metallic silver with no sign of corruption or mealy
covering on the outside. This is a feature which
distinguishes it from plum mildew, another rather
common but much less serious disease. The mildewy
leaves appear to be covered with a whitish-grey
powder. Mildew can be cured by spraying with lime
sulphur or Bordeaux mixture applied during the
summer months, but there is no cure for silver leaf,
and the only thing to do is to cut out all affected
branches, burn them, and paint the wounds with
Stockholm tar. By Government order such removal

184

of wood killed by silver leaf must be completed each year by July 15th.

Plums are increased by budding between June and August, on various stocks including the Common Mussel, the Common Plum, the St. Julien plum, the Myrobalan, the Pershore, and the Brompton stock. Pershore, Common Plum and Common Mussel are less vigorous than the others and so most suitable for garden trees.

PLUM MILDEW, *see* Plum.

PLUMBAGO *plum-***bay**-*go* (Leadwort; Cape Leadwort). Tender climbing plants with blue flowers in summer. The ten or so species include hardy, greenhouse and stove plants, all with terminal spikes of flowers which individually somewhat resemble those of the herbaceous phlox. For the cool greenhouse the best one is *P. capensis*, with pale blue flowers in summer, and although this is not a true climber it makes an excellent subject for training over a trellis or wire 'umbrella'.
Culture: Pot in spring in John Innes compost in large pots or tubs or plant in bed of good loamy soil in a greenhouse. Train shoots to stakes or wires in light part of house. Prune shoots moderately after flowering, cutting back to about a couple of buds from the old wood and keep on the dry side.
Propagation: By cuttings of young shoots, 3 in. to 6 in. long, inserted singly in 2 in. pots of sandy peat in a temperature of 60° to 65°, February to August.

PLUNGE BED. During the summer plants in pots need much less watering if they are buried up to the pot rim in a plunge bed in the open. This type of bed consists of a layer about 6 in. deep (or deeper for large pots) of some light, porous mixture in which the pots can be easily buried. Peat and sand, with or without the addition of soil, makes a suitable mixture It is usual to make the bed in a cold frame so that the plants can be covered with lights in bad weather, and if it can be made on a hard ash base less trouble will be caused by worms getting into the pots.

POET'S LAUREL, *see* Laurus.

POINSETTIA, *see* Euphorbia.

POLEMONIUM *pol-ee-***mone**-*ee-um* (Jacob's Ladder). Hardy perennials with divided, ferny foliage and spikes of flowers in early summer. The most popular kind is *P. caeruleum*, 1 ft., blue. There is also a white variety.
Culture: Plant in spring or autumn in ordinary soil and sunny or partially shady position.
Propagation: By seed sown in a greenhouse or frame in March; division at planting time.

POLIANTHES *pol-ee-***an**-*thes* (Tuberose). Half-hardy bulbous plant with fragrant white flowers in summer. *P. tuberosa plena* (the double form of the only species) has long been grown for the fragrant, pure white flowers used in buttonholes and bouquets.
Culture: Although, where sufficient heat is available, the tuberose may be had in bloom right through the year by planting the bulbs in succession, in a cool greenhouse these are best potted up in spring. 2 parts good soil and 1 part old cow manure, with enough sand to keep the mixture open, is a suitable compost and drainage should be good. 1 large bulb is sufficient for a 5 in. pot. After potting plunge the pots to the rim in a bottom heat of 65° to 70° and give very little water until growth begins. A lower temperature and more water is needed as the plants grow, and full exposure to light should be given. After flowering the bulbs should be discarded and propagation is impractical in this country.

POLLINATION. For a flower to produce seed it must be fertilised by suitable pollen coming into contact with its stigma. This process is known as pollination. Under glass it is sometimes necessary to pollinate by hand, notably in the case of peaches which flower very early. This may be done by transferring the pollen from one flower to another by means of a rabbit's tail or a camel hair brush. In many cases flowers may be pollinated by their own pollen or

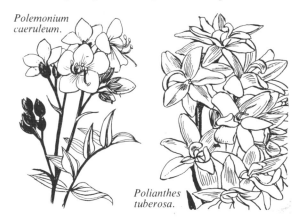

Polemonium caeruleum.

Polianthes tuberosa.

Pollinating peach flowers.

by that of other flowers on the same plant, in which case, the plant is said to be self-fertile. Sometimes, however, plants are self-sterile; that is, their flowers can only be fertilised by pollen from another plant of the same species.

POLYANTHUS, *see* Primula.

POLYGONATUM *pol-ig-on-***a**-*tum* (Solomon's Seal). Hardy herbaceous perennials with ornamental foliage and white flowers in May or June, suitable for partially-shaded beds, borders, or woodlands. The best species, *P. multiflorum*, grows 2 ft. to 3 ft. high.
Culture: Plant autumn or spring in ordinary soil. Do not disturb unless the plants become very overcrowded.
Propagation: By division of roots at planting time.

POLYGONUM *pol-***ig**-*on-um* (Knot-weed; Russian Vine). Hardy herbaceous perennials, and shrubby climbers. Large species suitable for sunny or shady moist borders or margins of ponds, where their mainly rather coarse growth may fill otherwise waste ground; climbing species for covering arbours, pergolas, or tree trunks; dwarf species for sunny borders or on rock gardens and dry walls. Flowers, white, cream, pink or crimson, mostly in late summer. Among the best species are *P. affine and P. vaccinifolium*, both prostrate plants with rose-pink flowers in late summer, suitable for rock gardens and dry walls; *P. campanulatum.* 3 ft., pink and *P. amplexicaule atropurpureum*, 3 ft. to 4 ft., red, the two least invasive of the herbaceous kinds, and *P. baldschuanicum*, the Russian Vine, white or pink, a vigorous climber which will grow to 30 ft. or 40 ft.
Culture: Plant autumn or spring in ordinary soil. *P. baldschuanicum* needs no regular pruning but can be cut back, if desired, in spring.
Propagation: Perennials by division of roots in October or March; *P. baldschuanicum* by cuttings of firm growth in a propagating frame in July or August.

POLYPODIUM *pol-ee-***pode**-*ee-um* (Polypody; Wall Fern). A big family of ferns many of which

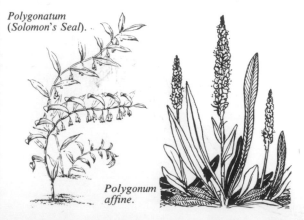

Polygonatum (Solomon's Seal).

Polygonum affine.

Polygonum campanulatum.

are tender but the most important for the garden are hardy. These include *P. vulgare*, a handsome fern with divided fronds up to 2 ft. long. There are a great many varieties, some with handsomely crested or plumed fronds.
Culture: Plant in April or September in good, loamy soil with the addition of peat or leaf-mould in shady positions as on north-facing banks or in fern borders.
Propagation: By division at planting time.

POLYPODY, *see* Polypodium.

POLYSTICHUM *pol-is-***tik**-*um* (Shield Fern). Ferns from many parts of the world some only suitable for greenhouse cultivation but the most important from the garden standpoint being fully hardy. The most popular are *P. aculeatum*, the Hard Shield Fern, and its variety *angulare*, often known simply as *P. angulare*, the Soft Shield Fern. They have much divided fronds and there are many garden forms often beautifully crested or even more finely divided.
Culture: Plant in April in good, loamy soil with the addition of peat or leaf-mould in a shady, sheltered place outdoors. Alternatively pot in March in a mixture of loam, peat and leaf-mould in equal parts with enough coarse sand to keep the mixture open. Grow in an unheated or very slightly heated greenhouse. Water freely spring and summer, sparingly in autumn and winter.
Propagation: By division at potting or planting time. One variety, known as *proliferum* makes little plantlets all along the fronds and if these are pegged down to the surface of peaty soil in summer they will make roots and can later be cut off and potted individually as soon as they have formed plantlets.

Removing surplus potato sprouts.   *Planting 'seed' potatoes.*   *Covering potatoes after planting.*

POLYTHENE. Plastics of this type have many uses in the garden. Apart from the usual equipment such as watering-cans, buckets, hose-pipes and so on which are made from them, one of the chief items of use to the gardener is polythene sheeting. In its transparent form this can provide protection from the weather for many plants, while under glass it can cut down heating costs, or increase humidity, if used as a lining near the glass, although a certain amount of trouble with condensation may occur when it is used in this way. Green polythene sheeting is useful for providing shade in summer.

POPPY, *see* Papaver.

PORTUGAL LAUREL, *see* Prunus.

PORTULACA *por-tu-***lak**-*a.* Half-hardy annuals with vividly coloured flowers in summer. The garden varieties of which there are both double-flowered and single-flowered types, are derived from *P. grandiflora*, a prostrate plant.
Culture: Sow on surface of sandy soil in a temperature of 60° to 65° in March. Transplant seedlings singly into 2 in. pots, gradually harden off, and plant 5 in. to 6 in. apart outdoors at end of May in ordinary well-drained soil in sunny rock gardens, raised beds, or borders.

POT MARIGOLD, *see* Calendula.

POTASH. One of the plant foods necessary for vegetable life. Potash is contained in animal manures, in vegetable refuse and in wood ashes. The chemical forms most commonly used are sulphate of potash, muriate of potash and kainit, and of these, sulphate of potash is the safest.

POTASSIUM CHLORIDE, *see* Muriate of Potash.

POTATO. This crop requires a good, rich, well-dug soil which can, with advantage, be dressed with animal manure in the autumn or winter preceding planting. In addition, a compound potato or vegetable fertiliser should be forked in at about 4 oz. per sq. yd. prior to planting.
Potatoes are grown from tubers known as 'seed'. It is an advantage if these are sprouted before planting. This is done by standing the potatoes, eye ends uppermost, in trays in a light but frost-proof place.
Plant in very sheltered places in late February or early March, in ordinary places late March for early varieties, April for maincrop and late varieties. Plant tubers 12 in. to 15 in. apart in rows 2½ ft. to 3 ft. apart, covering them 2 in. to 3 in. of soil. When shoots appear draw soil over them as protection from frost and continue this earthing-up till the potatoes are growing in ridges. Lift early varieties in June or July as soon as tubers are large enough for use. Lift maincrop varieties in August or September when the skin of the tubers adheres firmly to them. Spray maincrop and late varieties in early July and August with Bordeaux mixture against potato blight disease.
Store potatoes for winter use in sacks in a dark, frost-proof shed or in clamps made by heaping the potatoes up, covering them with a thick layer of straw and this with a good layer of beaten soil.

POTATO BLIGHT, *see* Potato.

POTATO VINE, *see* Solanum.

POTENTILLA *po-ten-***till**-*a* (Cinquefoil). Hardy herbaceous perennials, dwarf rock plants and some

Potting.
Above: *Crocking the pot.*
Left: *First potting.*
Below: *The final potting of a chrysanthemum.*

Pricking out streptocarpus seedlings.

shrubs. All are summer flowering, and many are brightly coloured, yellow and red being common colours. Among the best herbaceous kinds are *P. atrosanguinea*, 12 in. to 15 in., scarlet; *P. fragiformis*, 9 in., yellow; *P. nepalensis*, 12 in., rose-red or cerise, and *P. tonguei*, prostrate, yellow and red. The shrubby varieties, of which there are a number, are all derived from *P. fruticosa*, 3 ft. to 4 ft., yellow or white.

Culture of Herbaceous Species: Plant autumn or spring in ordinary soil and sunny, open positions. Lift, divide and replant border kinds every 3 or 4 years. Plant dwarf kinds on sunny ledges of rock gardens or on banks in porous soil.

Culture of Shrubby Species: Plant November to March in ordinary soil and sunny positions. No regular pruning is required but dead or dying growth can be cut out each spring.

Propagation: Herbaceous species by division of roots in spring; shrubby species by cuttings of firm young shoots in July or August in sandy soil in a propagating frame.

POTTING. The process of planting in pots. One of the first essentials in all potting is that the pots themselves should be clean and well provided with drainage material. The latter usually consists of old broken pots, known by the gardener as 'crocks'. One large piece of crock is placed, convex side uppermost, over the hole in the bottom of the pot, and in large pots smaller pieces are arranged around and over it. Some plants, such as tomatoes and chrysanthemums, appreciate firm potting, while others, notably ferns, succeed better with light potting—i.e., the soil is not pressed into the pot very hard. All the firming that is necessary for small plants can usually be done by hand, but with larger plants which require firm potting it is necessary to use a potting stick to press the soil in. This can be made from a length of old broom-handle rounded at one end so that it does not injure the roots.

First, a little soil is placed over the crocks in the bottom of a pot, then the plant is placed in position in the centre of the pot, and more soil is worked around it. This soil is either pressed in with the thumbs for small plants or rammed down with potting stick for larger plants. When the pot is nearly full of soil and well firmed, it should be given a sharp rap on the wooden potting bench to settle the plant in and shake the soil level on top.

Never fill a pot to the rim, but leave some space for water. When potting tomatoes, chrysanthemums, and other quick-growing plants, it is advisable to leave considerably more space so that top-dressings of rich compost may be given at intervals during the growing season. Similar remarks apply to stem-rooting lilies, which are potted low down in rather deep receptacles and are then top-dressed repeatedly as the stems lengthen.

One important point is never to overpot a plant.

It might seem reasonable to suppose that, as plants succeed perfectly well in an unrestricted root-run outdoors or even planted out in the greenhouse, it would be satisfactory to place them in the biggest pots available, and leave them to fill the soil with roots as and when they are able. In fact, soil in a pot is confined and conditions are artificial. When reasonably filled with roots, a circulation of moisture is maintained, but if a plant is placed in a pot many sizes too big for it, the soil will soon become sour and unhealthy. This is the reason why small plants must be potted in small pots and shifted on from time to time to larger sizes until they reach those in which they are to flower or fruit.

The potting of epiphytic orchids differs from that of other plants. These are grown principally in sphagnum moss and osmunda fibre or peat and this compost must be worked little by little between the roots with the aid of a pointed stick. It is impossible to make it firm in the sense in which that term is applied to soil.

POTTING SHED. In most gardens there is little need for a potting shed as jobs such as potting or pricking out are best done in the greenhouse, with a consequent saving of labour and less risk of chilling the plants. A conveniently placed shed is, however, useful for the storage of various materials used in greenhouse work, and if the actual work is to be done in it the shed should be properly designed. A suitably clean floor space for the mixing of composts, ample firm bench room and good lighting, preferably from the north, are a few of the essentials. Ample shelf and cupboard room are also advisable, as without this the potting shed is likely to turn into what it so often is—little more than a 'dump'.

POTTING SOIL. Years ago gardeners supposed that different plants needed vastly different mixtures of soil, leaf-mould, sand, and other materials. It has been shown that in fact most plants will grow perfectly well in standard mixtures, with minor modifications. The most successful standard mixtures are the John Innes composts, which see.

PRAYER PLANT, see Maranta.

PRICKING OUT. The process of transplanting seedlings from the pot, box or bed in which they were raised, thus giving them more space in which to develop. This task should be undertaken as soon as the seedlings are large enough to handle, usually when they have made their first pair of true leaves.

Care must be taken to transplant these tiny seedlings without injury. A sharpened label is a useful tool for loosening the roots. Fairly deep trays or pans are best, well supplied with drainage holes covered by broken crocks and rough rubble. John Innes seed compost is satisfactory for almost all plants. Make the compost fairly firm with the fingers and see that

it is just moist. Lift each seedling with a little soil attached to its roots, drop it into a hole made with a dibber of suitable size, making the soil firm around its roots. Water freely from a can fitted with a fine rose.

Pricking out into frames or the open ground is carried out in much the same way, protection from sun being given for the first few days.

PRICKLY HEATH, see Pernettya.

PRICKLY PEAR, see Opuntia.

PRICKLY POPPY, see Meconopsis.

PRIMROSE, see Primula.

PRIMULA prim-*u-la* (Auricula; Oxlip; Cowslip; Primrose; Polyanthus). Tender and hardy perennials. The primula family is an enormous one. Rock garden, bog, and other hardy species are numbered by the hundred, and there are in addition many varieties of polyanthus (*P. polyantha*), primrose (*P. vulgaris*) and auricula (*P. auricula*) and greenhouse species such as *P. obconica*, *P. sinensis*, and *P. malacoides*. *P. obconica*, with umbels of large flowers carried on 15 in. stems, is particularly valuable for its almost perpetual flowering, and *P. malacoides*, a more dainty type, is useful for spring flowering. Both of them are available in a wide range of shades, mostly pinks, mauves and reds, and for a yellow there is *P. kewensis*, a small-flowered hybrid which flowers in spring. *P. sinensis*, one of the most showy of all, is not grown as often as it might be, possibly because it is a bit touchy. A few of the best of the rock garden kinds are *P. denticulata*, the Drumstick Primrose, 1 ft., lavender, violet or white; *P. capitata*, 9 in. to 12 in., purple; *P. edgeworthii*, 3 in. to 4 in., lilac; *P. marginata*, 4 in. to 6 in., pale blue; *P. rosea*, 6 in., rose; and *P. viali*, 1 ft., purple.

Good bog-garden kinds are *P. bulleyana*, 2 ft., orange; *P. florindae*, 3 ft., yellow; *P. helodoxa*, 2 ft., yellow; *P. japonica*, 2 ft., crimson or white; *P. pulverulenta*, similar to last but with white mealy foliage; and *P. sikkimensis*, 3 ft., yellow.

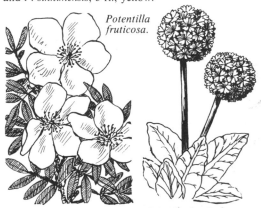

Potentilla fruticosa.

Primula denticulata.

Pricking out Primula malacoides.

Potting Primula obconica.

Culture of Greenhouse Primulas: *P. obconica*: Sow the seed thinly, from February to May, in John Innes seed compost in a temperature of about 60°. Cover with glass and paper and never let the compost become dry. As soon as the seedlings are ½ in. high prick them out singly into 3 in. pots of John Innes No. 1 potting compost, taking care not to bury the tiny crowns. With this and other primulas potting should be done quite lightly as too firm a compost hinders root growth. When the small pots are well filled with roots, pot the plants up into 5 in. pots, using John Innes No. 2 compost, and as soon as they are established plunge them to the pot rim in a cold frame, where they should be kept well watered and lightly shaded from hot sun. In September house the plants in a temperature of 55° and keep them evenly moist.

P. malacoides needs very much the same treatment as *P. obconica*, but the seeds should not be sown until early July and in winter the plants will succeed in a rather lower temperature. Feeding is more important with this plant and in winter plenty of air should be given.

P. kewensis, being almost hardy, this hybrid makes an excellent little plant for the greenhouse, with only just sufficient heat to keep frost out. It should be grown in the same way as the others from a sowing made in April and 3½ in. pots are usually large enough for it.

P. sinensis should be sown at the same time as *P. obconica* and grown on in the same way. Its main failing is a weakness at the collar and staking is often necessary to prevent a floppy appearance. Care must be taken not to bury the collar too deeply in an effort to avoid this weakness.

Culture of Polyanthus and Primrose: Sow in March in a cool greenhouse or frame, prick out seedlings into boxes, and harden off for planting out in May or early June in a nursery bed of good soil in a partially shaded place. Plants can be transferred to their flowering quarters during September or October. Water during dry weather. Plants need not be disturbed so long as they continue to grow and flower freely, but if desired can be lifted, divided and replanted after flowering.

Culture of Auricula: Pot florist varieties, February or March in 3 in. pots in John Innes compost. Place in a frame and water freely when making growth; during

Primula malacoides.

Primula pulverulenta.

Polyanthus hybrid.

Watering greenhouse primulas.

winter cut down supplies considerably. When in flower give plants weak, liquid feed. Annual re-potting is not essential; plants which are grown on a second year should, however, have a top dressing of rich soil in March. Plant alpine varieties in autumn or spring in well-drained beds or borders or in the rock garden.

Culture of Rock Garden Primulas: Plant autumn or spring in light, well-drained peaty loam, with which has been incorporated plenty of sand and stone chippings. Water freely during dry weather in 'summer. Species with downy foliage should have the protection during winter of a pane of glass held on notched sticks.

Culture of Bog Primulas: Plant by the margins of ponds or streams where plants will be sure of an ample supply of moisture at the roots. Ideal soil consists of a peaty loam, and planting may be carried out in either autumn or spring. Once established, they should not be disturbed.

Propagation: All species can be raised from seeds. The hardy kinds are usually best sown in pans of sandy soil in a cold frame in March or April. Division of the roots is another simple means of increasing stock and is usually done immediately after flowering.

PRINCE OF WALES' FEATHER, *see* Celosia.

PRINCE'S FEATHER, *see* Amaranthus.

PRIVET, *see* Ligustrum.

PRUNING. The act of removing any unwanted or superfluous growth. Pruning is an important item in the cultivation of almost all kinds of fruit, and is also frequently applied to ornamental trees and shrubs. General rules to be borne in mind for all pruning are that cuts should be clean and just above a bud, joint, or another shoot or branch from which new growth can be made; that the harder a plant is

Pruning buddleia.

pruned, the more strongly it is likely to grow; and that as a general rule winter is the best time for severe pruning of deciduous plants, while spring is the best time for severe pruning of evergreens. Light pruning or pinching can be done at practically any time of the year in either case. Shrubs that flower in spring or early summer are usually pruned after flowering, whereas shrubs that bloom after mid-summer are usually pruned in February or March.

PRUNUS pru-*nus* (Plum; Cherry; Apricot; Peach; Cherry Laurel; Portugal Laurel; Bird Cherry; Almond). A very large family of trees and shrubs, including some most useful fruits and also a number of highly decorative species and varieties. At one time the genus was split up considerably, the name 'Prunus' being reserved for the true plums, the cherries being known as 'Cerasus', the cherry laurel as 'Laurocerasus', the almonds as 'Amygdalus', the peaches and nectarines as 'Persica', and the apricots as 'Armeniaca'. Occasionally these names are still used, and it is convenient to split the genus into groups of this type when considering cultivation. All members of the Prunus family are hardy and, while most are deciduous, there are important evergreen species. Here the kinds grown for their edible fruits are separately described under their popular names.

Culture of Ornamental Plums: Such species as *P. cerasifera pissardii* and *P. blireana* are decorative small trees flowering in early spring. They can be grown in any ordinary garden soil and reasonably open positions, and should be planted between

November and March. Regular pruning is not necessary, but trees can be kept to a good shape by cutting out weak and unwanted growth in autumn. Propagate by seeds sown in a frame in March, or selected kinds by budding on to seedlings or plum stocks.

Culture of Ornamental Cherries: These include some of the most beautiful spring-flowering trees. Many lovely varieties have been introduced from Japan and have been developed from *P. serrulata*, a tree up to 30 ft. in height, flowering in April or May. There are double and single-flowered varieties in rose, pink, white, and even pale yellow. Habit may be erect, spreading or weeping. In addition there is our native gean (*P. avium*), which has itself produced some good garden varieties. *P. subhirtella autumnalis* is a beautiful small-flowered cherry which blooms in autumn.

Ornamental cherries will succeed in any ordinary garden soil, preferably containing some lime or chalk. Plant from November to March. Regular pruning is not necessary but badly placed branches can be removed in autumn. The species can be raised from seeds sown in a frame in March, but the garden varieties must be propagated by budding in the summer on to seedling cherries or cherry stocks.

Culture of Portugal and Cherry Laurel: These popular evergreen shrubs or small trees can be grown in practically any soil or situation. The cherry laurel, *P. laurocerasus*, is one of the best of all town shrubs, growing in places in which few other plants would exist. The Portugal Laurel, *P. lusitanica*, can reach a considerable height but, like the Cherry Laurel, stands pruning well. Both are hungry shrubs and it is not easy to cultivate other plants successfully close to them. Plant from September to May. Any hard pruning necessary to keep them within bounds should be done in April. Propagation by cuttings of ripened growth in a sheltered border or unheated frame in September.

Culture of Ornamental Almond and Peach: In general the same as that of cherries, but ornamental peaches appreciate a fairly rich but well-drained soil and a warm, sheltered position. There are double flowered varieties of the peach which are very beautiful.

PSEUDOSASA, *see* Bambusa.

PTERIS pet-*ris*. Tender ferns grown as pot plants in cool greenhouses or in rooms. The most popular kind is *P. cretica*, with simply divided fronds up to a foot in length. *P. serrulata* has even larger fronds and has a pretty crested variety, and the largest of all is *P. tremula*.
Culture: Pot in March in a mixture of equal parts peat and loam with ½ part sharp sand. Water freely in spring and summer, moderately in autumn and winter. Maintain a winter minimum temperature of 45° with natural rise in spring and summer. Shade in summer.
Propagation: By division at potting time.

PULMONARIA pul-mon-**air**-ee-a (Lungwort; Blue Cowslip). Low-growing hardy herbaceous perennials with blue, purple or red flowers in early spring. Some, such as *P. officinalis* have handsomely mottled foliage. One of the most attractive is *P. angustifolia azurea*.
Culture: Plant autumn or spring in ordinary soil in partially shaded rock gardens or borders. Lift and re-plant in fresh soil every 4 years or 5 years.
Propagation: By division of roots October or March.

PURPLE CONE-FLOWER, *see* Echinacea.

PURPLE LOOSESTRIFE, *see* Lythrum.

PURPLE MEXICAN ASTER, *see* Cosmea.

PURPLE ROCK-CRESS, *see* Aubrieta.

PYRACANTHA pi-ra-**kan**-tha (Firethorn). Evergreen hardy or slightly tender ornamental shrubs with white flowers and yellow, orange, or scarlet berries. Suitable for sunny, sheltered shrubberies, or trained against walls. Among the best kinds are *P. atalantoides*, deep red berries; *P. coccinea lalandii*, orange-scarlet berries; and *P. crenulata flava*, yellow berries.
Culture: Plant September to October and April to May in ordinary loamy soil. Prune wall-trained plants

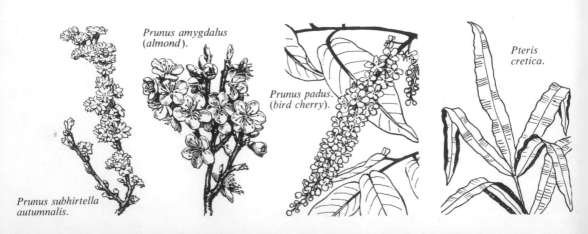

Prunus amygdalus (almond).

Prunus padus (bird cherry).

Pteris cretica.

Prunus subhirtella autumnalis.

Pyrethrum hybrid.

Ramonda pyrenaica.

into shape in early summer, but do not remove shoots carrying flowers or young berries.

Propagation: By seeds sown in sandy soil in a greenhouse or frame during March; cuttings of nearly ripened young growth in sandy soil in a frame during August or September.

PYRETHRUM *pi-re-thrum* (Coloured Marguerite; Painted Daisy). Hardy perennials with white, pink or red single or double daisy flowers in May and June. Botanically the pyrethrums have long been classified as chrysanthemums, their correct name being *C. coccineum*, but in gardens the old name of pyrethrum is always used.

Culture: Plant in March, April or July in good, well-drained loamy soil and open, sunny positions. Where drainage is suspect plant on the summit of low ridges so that water does not collect around the crowns of the plants. Lift and divide every second or third year.

Propagation: By division at planting time.

PYRUS pie-*rus* (Pear). Hardy flowering and fruiting trees. For cultivation of fruit garden varieties,

see Pear. There are also some ornamental kinds such as *P. salicifolia*, a tree up to 30 ft. with weeping habit, grey leaves and white flowers in spring.

Culture: Plant October to March in ordinary soil and open position. Remove overcrowded, misplaced or overgrown branches in winter.

Propagation: By seed sown in a frame or outdoors in March. Fruiting pears either by budding or grafting on to suitable stocks.

QUEEN-OF-THE-PRAIRIE, *see* Filipendula.

QUICK, *see* Crataegus.

RADISH. Sow seed thinly in drills $\frac{1}{2}$ in. deep and about 5 in. or 6 in. apart in good, rich soil or as a catch-crop in celery trenches. Sowings should be made every fortnight from March to mid-August and winter radishes, such as Black Spanish, can be sown in a heated frame or greenhouse in early autumn. All radishes need to grow fast if they are to be crisp and mild-flavoured. They should be watered freely in dry weather. If their leaves are punctured by flea beetles dust with DDT, aldrin, lindane or derris.

RAGWORT, *see* Senecio.

RAMONDA *ram-on-da* (Rosette Mullein). Hardy herbaceous perennials with violet or lavender-blue flowers in spring. Suitable for fissures of shady rock gardens or in chinks of dry walls. The most popular species, *R. myconi*, is 6 in. high. It is often called *R. pyrenaica*.

Culture: Plant March or April in a mixture of 2 parts sandy peat and 1 part loam. The plants are safer in the vertical or slanting position secured in a wall than in the horizontal position inevitable when planted on level ground. Water frequently in dry

Pulmonaria
angustifolia.

Pyracantha
coccinea lalandii.

193

weather. Should not be disturbed oftener than is absolutely necessary.

Propagation: By seed sown on surface of sandy peat in a shady frame or greenhouse in March; by careful division in March; by leaf cuttings in early summer, with the leaf stalks pressed into sand and peat in a cool greenhouse or frame.

RANUNCULUS *ran-un-ku-lus* (Crowfoot; Fair Maids of France; Fair Maids of Kent; Buttercup). Hardy herbaceous and tuberous-rooted perennials. Showiest of the genus are the tuberous-rooted French and Turban varieties derived from *R. asiaticus*, 1 ft. to 1½ ft. They have double or semi-double flowers in a wide range of colours and are excellent for cutting in spring and early summer. Some of the herbaceous species, such as *R. gramineus*, 9 in., yellow, are best suited for rock garden planting. Others, such as *R. aconitifolius flore-pleno*, 2 ft. to 3 ft., double white flowers in early summer and popularly known as Fair Maids of France or Fair Maids of Kent should be grown in moist, shady borders or by the waterside.

Culture of Tuberous-Rooted Species: In the south and on light, open soils plant October or November. On heavy soils plant late February or March. Deeply dug beds well enriched with manure or compost and in an open, sunny position are most suitable. Place tubers claws downwards 4 in. to 6 in. apart and cover

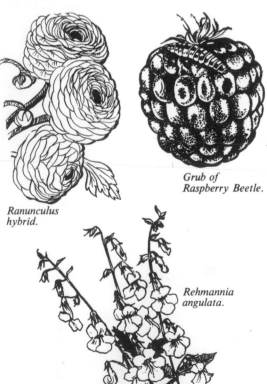

Ranunculus hybrid.

Grub of Raspberry Beetle.

Rehmannia angulata.

to a depth of 2 in. to 3 in. Water freely during dry weather. When foliage ripens in July lift tubers, dry, and store in sand in a cool place until planting time.

Culture of Herbaceous Species: Plant autumn or spring, preferably in partial shade in good, loamy, rather moist soil. Do not disturb until overcrowding makes lifting essential.

Propagation: All species by seeds sown as soon as ripe in boxes or pans of sandy soil. Germinate in a cold frame or a cool greenhouse. Transfer to outdoor nursery bed when large enough to handle. Herbaceous species also increased by division in autumn or spring.

RASPBERRY. Plant canes preferably certified free of virus disease, from October to March in deep, rich soil and open, sunny position. Space canes 2 ft. apart in the row and 5 ft. between rows for training to wires strained between posts. The topmost wire should be between 5 ft. and 6 ft. from the ground. Cut canes back to within 6 in. of the ground the first year; succeeding years cut out all old canes immediately after fruiting, and reduce the number of young canes at each root or stool to 5 or 6 of the strongest. Remove tips of canes in November or December, bringing the level à few inches above the topmost wire. Apply decayed manure or compost annually in March or April. Water freely if weather is dry during bearing period. Avoid deep digging which will injure surface roots.

Propagation: By division of roots in autumn.

RASPBERRY BEETLE. A most destructive beetle which appears from May to July and attacks raspberries, loganberries and blackberries, depositing its eggs on the blossoms. The resulting small, creamy-white grubs enter the young fruits on which they feed. The most effective remedy is to spray or dust with derris 10 days after the blossom has fallen and again 10 days later usually in late May and early June in the south and midlands and a little later further north.

RASPBERRY CANE BLIGHT. A fungus disease which attacks raspberries and the allied blackberries and loganberries. The leaves wither and the canes become brittle and may snap off at the base. Spraying with Bordeaux mixture in the early stages will check its progress. Affected canes should be cut out and burnt as soon as they are noted.

RED-BUD, *see* Cercis.

RED CAPE LILY, *see* Haemanthus.

RED HOT CAT TAIL, *see* Acalypha.

RED-HOT POKER, *see* Kniphofia.

RED SPIDER. The common name for minute plant pests belonging to the mite family. Red spider

Tipping back raspberry canes. Above right: *Cutting out old raspberry canes.*

mites attack a great variety of plants, including vines, fruit trees, violets, cucumbers, melons and carnations. They are usually worse in a hot, dry atmosphere, and in consequence, frequent syringing with clear water is one of the most effective methods of combating the pest in the greenhouse or frame.

Red spider is so small that it can only just be detected with the naked eye. The mites congregate on the undersides of the leaves, usually in the angles of the veins. Leaves develop a mottled yellow appearance. Under glass, fumigation with azobenzene is effective. Outdoors, spraying with derris or chlorbenside is recommended and on fruit trees the pest can be further controlled by winter washing with DNC or thiocyanate. Sulphur sprays used against apple scab and other fungal diseases also help to keep red spider down.

REDVALERIAN, *see* Centranthus.

REDWOOD, *see* Sequoia.

REED MACE, *see* Aquatic, Typha.

REHMANNIA *ray-***man***-ee-a.* The rehmannias are mostly showy, half-hardy perennials from 1 ft. to 3 ft. high, with flowers rather like those of the foxglove. They all grow well in the cool greenhouse. *R. angulata,* with red flowers orange-spotted on the lower lip, is one of the most showy species although its flowers are not quite so large as those of *R. elata*— these are up to 4 in. long, purple, with a yellow, red-spotted throat.
Culture: Pot in March in John Innes compost one plant in each 6 in. or 7 in. pot. Water fairly freely April to September, rather sparingly in winter. Temperature: October to March, 45° to 50°; natural rise in summer.

Raspberry Cane Blight.

Propagation: By seeds sown in a temperature of 60° in spring.

RESEDA *res-***e***-da* (Mignonette). A perennial, but usually grown as an annual. Suitable for sunny beds, borders or rock gardens, and much prized for the fragrance of its flowers in summer. The garden varieties are derived from *R. odorata,* 1 ft. high.
Culture Outdoors: Sow seeds ⅛ in. deep in ordinary soil containing lime in March or April. Thin seedlings when 1 in. high to 6 in. or 8 in. apart. Water freely in dry weather. In a warm, dry position, plants will often survive the winter outdoors.
Culture Under Glass: This is one of the finest, fragrant plants for the greenhouse, but to have it at its best, a little heat is needed so that the plants can be raised in autumn and grown on through the winter to flower in spring. It does best in a very rich and rather heavy soil with lime and this should be made very firm.

The seed should be sown in August in the pots in which the plants are to flower, usually 6 in. ones, and as soon as the seedlings are large enough to handle they should be thinned to an inch apart. Until October the pots may stand in the cold frame, but before there is any danger of frost they should be moved to a light position in the greenhouse, in a temperature not above 50°. Very little water is needed during the winter but copious supplies should be given when the plants are coming into bloom. Staking is necessary to keep the plants erect.

For summer and autumn flowering in the cold greenhouse, seed should be sown in spring, after which the plants should be thinned out and grown on under as cool conditions as possible.

RETARDING. In the same way that many plants can be forced into early growth many can also be retarded; that is, their flowering period is delayed until after the normal season. Perhaps the best known examples of this are the retarded crowns of Lily of the Valley, which may be brought into bloom at almost any time, but other plants which may be similarly treated are *Azalea mollis*, spiraeas and certain lilies. Retarding is usually effected by chilling the plants, and for the amateur it is hardly practical. With certain plants the production of bloom can be delayed by regulating the amount of light the plant receives, and this is not usually difficult to arrange.

REVERSION. A virus disease of blackcurrants which results in greatly reduced cropping. One of the symptoms of the disease is that the leaves at the ends of the branches tend to lose some of their lobes and become crowded or bunched together, a condition most clearly seen in July. Reversion is spread by greenfly and big bud mites. There is no cure and affected bushes should be grubbed up and burnt.

RHODOCHITON *ro-do-***ki***-ton.* The only member of its genus, *R. volubile*, also known as *R. sanguineum*, makes a very attractive climber for the cool greenhouse. The dark red flowers, each set off by a large, showy, bell-like calyx of bright pink, are produced freely during the summer on a plant which, like the clematis, climbs partly by means of its twisting leaf-stalks.

Culture: The plant flowers freely from seed sown the same year and, in fact, it is best treated as an annual. The seed should be sown early in the year in a temperature of at least 60° and the seedlings should then be potted on gradually into 6 in. pots. Any rich, light soil, over good drainage, suits it and plenty of water is needed in summer.

RHODODENDRON *ro-do-***den***-dron* (Rose Bay; Azalea). Hardy and half-hardy evergreen and deciduous shrubs. In gardens a distinction is made between the evergreen rhododendrons and the mainly deciduous azaleas, but this is not recognised by botanists, who class the 2 groups under the one heading 'Rhododendron', thus making a large and important genus of flowering shrubs. In addition to multitudinous species with a natural distribution throughout America, Europe and Asia, breeders have raised great numbers of hybrids. The species themselves are extremely variable in character, ranging from small bushes only a few inches in height with flowers to match, to trees 30 ft. to 40 ft. in height with immense trusses of showy blooms. There is material here for the rock gardens and the arboretum, with something for every intervening stage in garden planning. The hybrids have an even greater range in colour. Most are extremely showy shrubs with fine trusses of bell-shaped or funnel-shaped blooms, mostly in late spring or early summer.

While most of the evergreen rhododendrons are hardy, there are some species and hybrids which either require the protection of a greenhouse or must be planted in very sheltered places. *R. simsii*, better known to most gardeners as *Azalea indica*, requires greenhouse protection in winter, though high temperatures are not necessary.

The deciduous azaleas grown in gardens are mostly hybrids, classed as Ghent, Mollis, Sinensis, *Rustica flore pleno*, etc., according to the particular group to which they belong. These are hardy, and from the garden stand-point are chiefly distinguished from the evergreen rhododendrons by the fact that they lose their leaves in the autumn and that shades of orange, salmon and yellow are more common in their flowers.

Culture: Practically all dislike lime or chalk. They succeed in peaty soils but any ordinary garden soil that is well-drained and free from lime is capable of growing rhododendrons. Heavy clay soils can be made suitable by digging in leaf-mould or peat and sharp sand, while leaf-mould and peat will also improve light, sandy or gravelly soils. Pot-grown rhododendrons and azaleas should be cultivated in a compost of lime-free loam mixed with plenty of peat, leaf-mould and sand.

Rhododendrons and azaleas can be planted at any time between October and March. They will grow in full sun or partial shade but some of the species are better in shade. They are excellent shrubs to plant in thin woodlands, and some species and hybrids that

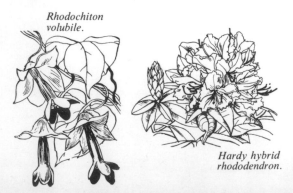

Rhodochiton volubile.

Hardy hybrid rhododendron.

Reseda odorata.

Azalea indica.

Azalea mollis hybrid.

are not quite hardy when fully in the open survive the winter uninjured when growing in the shelter of trees. Pruning is not necessary, but the faded flower trusses should be removed to relieve the plant of the strain of producing seeds.

Azalea indica, and also its numerous varieties, all popular as early-flowering greenhouse pot plants, are liable to be badly attacked by red spider if grown in too hot and dry an atmosphere. While in the greenhouse they should be syringed frequently with clear water, and from April to October they are better out of the greenhouse, first of all in a deep frame to harden off, and then, from June until the end of September, outdoors with their pots plunged to their rims in peat. They can be re-potted when necessary in a very peaty compost in October. In winter frost protection is all that is essential, but a rather higher temperature (55° to 65°) will give earlier flowers.

Propagation: The true species can be raised from seed, which must be sown on the surface of a fine compost of peat and sand with a little loam in March. The seeds require no covering or at most, a sprinkling of silver sand, as they are dust-like. Several years must elapse before the seedlings flower. Hybrids and selected varieties cannot be raised true to type from seed, and are propagated by layering in late winter or spring, cuttings in summer in sand and peat in a propagating frame, in the greenhouse, by mist propagation, or by grafting in spring usually in a slightly-heated greenhouse. The stock most commonly used is *R. ponticum.*

RHODOHYPOXIS *rode-o-hi-***poks***-is.* The only species grown, *R. baurii,* is a small rock plant with narrow leaves and carmine, pink or white flowers on 4 in. stems in spring.

Culture: Plant in March or April in gritty, well-drained soils containing a fairly liberal amount of peat or leaf-mould. A sunny position on a ledge in the rock garden or on top of a double-faced dry wall with a core of soil is a suitable position.

Propagation: By division at planting time.

Firming in rhododendron after planting.

Mulching rhododendron with peat to prevent drying out.

197

Left: *Cutting off flower stem on rhubarb*.   Right: *Ring culture of tomatoes; filling the bottomless pots.*

RHOEO ro-*ee-o*.   Although grown primarily for the decorative effect of its stiff, almost upright leaves, about a foot long and rich purple underneath, *R. discolor* is also interesting on account of the boat-like growths in which the small white or blue flowers are crowded together. There is only the one species, a native of Central America.

Culture: It is easily grown in rather high temperatures, 55° to 60° in winter and up to 75° in summer, though it will survive with less warmth. Water freely in spring and summer but only very moderately in winter. Re-pot when necessary in March. It needs a rich soil such as John Innes No. 2.

Propagation: By cuttings in warmth at practically any time, or careful division of the roots when re-potting.

RHOICISSUS ro-*ee*-**sis**-*us*.   The rhoicissus belong to the vine family. There are about 8 species, all woody climbers from Africa, but few of these are of horticultural interest although *R. rhomboidea* is sometimes grown as a greenhouse climber and is also

sold now as a house plant.

Culture: It succeeds in a peaty, sandy soil in a temperature above 50°. Indoors it likes cool shade in summer and plenty of heat in winter. Frequent feeding is required in summer, when the pots are full of roots, and pruning can be carried out at any time to keep the plant in shape.

Propagation: By cuttings struck in heat in spring or summer.

RHUBARB   Plant single roots with crowns 2 in. below surface 3 ft. apart in autumn or early spring in rich, well-cultivated soil in sunny, open positions. Top-dress with manure each February, forking it into surface of soil. Lift, divide and re-plant every 4 years. No stalks should be gathered the first year. Remove flower stems directly they appear.

Forcing: Cover crowns with pots or tubs and place fresh manure mixed with tree leaves over these in January or February, or lift strong roots and place them close together in deep boxes underneath staging in warm greenhouse, or in sheds or cellars. Keep

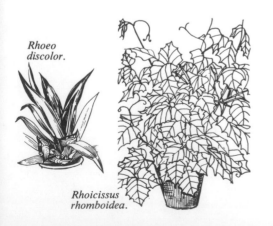

Rhoeo discolor.

Rhoicissus rhomboidea.

Rhus cotinus.

Ribes sanguineum.

Planting out the young tomatoes.   *Method of staking.*   *Feeding ring culture tomatoes.*

moist and dark. Temperature: 55° to 75°. Forcing season, November to February. Roots 2 years to 5 years old best for forcing. Roots force more readily if exposed on surface to frost for a few days before being brought inside.
Propagation: By seeds sown in ordinary soil outdoors in March or April; by division of roots with crowns or buds attached November to February.

RHUS *rus* (Sumach; Stag's Horn Sumach). Hardy deciduous shrubs or small trees with ornamental flowers and foliage. Suitable for sunny shrubberies. *R. typhina*, the Stags-horn Sumach, is 15 ft. high with large fern-like leaves which colour well in autumn, and erect red-purple inflorescences in late summer. The shrubs often known as *R. cotinus* and *R. cotinoides* are really species of Cotinus.
Culture: Plant October to March in ordinary soil. No regular pruning required.
Propagation: By cuttings of firm young shoots inserted in ordinary soil in a cold frame or under handlight October to November; cuttings of roots 2 in. to 3 in. long, planted 3 in. deep in sandy soil October or November; rooted suckers dug up in November.

RIBES *rye-bees* (Flowering Currant). Hardy ornamental shrubs with showy, pink or carmine flowers in spring. The best species is *R. sanguineum*, 6 ft. to 10 ft. It has several good varieties.
Culture: Plant October to March in ordinary soil in sunny or partially shady position. Prune directly after flowering cutting out branches that have carried flowers but retaining all strong, non-flowering stems.
Propagation: By cuttings, 6 in. to 8 in. long, of firm, young stems inserted in ordinary soil outdoors in October.

RICINUS riss-*in-us* (Castor Oil Plant). A tropical tree usually treated in gardens as a half-hardy annual. Flowers insignificant. Leaves hand-shaped, large, green or purplish. The only species is *R. communis*.
Culture: Sow seeds, previously steeped for a few hours in tepid water, ½ in. deep in sandy soil in temperature of 65° to 70° in March, transplanting seedlings when three leaves form, singly into 2 in. pots and keeping in similar temperature until well rooted, then transferring to 5 in. or 6 in. pots, after which remove to cool greenhouse or dwelling-room or harden off and plant outdoors in early June in sunny place. Water moderately.

RIDGING. The practice of throwing soil on vacant land in autumn into steep ridges so that as large a surface as possible is exposed to the beneficial effects of the winter weather.

RINGING. A method of checking excessive vigour in fruit trees and so encouraging fruitfulness. Ringing should be done in May by cutting away a ring of bark not more than ¼ in. wide around the main trunk or each of the main branches of the tree. This has the effect of checking the flow of food materials from the leaves back to the roots, and in consequence the roots are temporarily starved. In time the ring heals over and growth proceeds normally once more. The effect of ringing is exactly the same as that of root pruning. It can be applied to apples and pears, but should not be used on stone fruits (e.g., cherries, plums, etc.), as it tends to encourage gumming.

RING CULTURE. In recent years the growing of certain plants, chiefly tomatoes, in bottomless containers has come into vogue. Its chief advantages are that the amount of soil needed is relatively small and that there is less risk of soil infections. The general principles of the system are that the feeding roots are largely limited to a suitable compost placed in the containers, while the water supply is mainly obtained by the lower roots from a moist bed of some sterile material such as sand, ashes or peat on which the containers stand. The chief drawback is that unless this bed is kept constantly moist failure can very easily occur.

ROBINIA ro-**bin**-ee-a (False Acacia; Locust Tree; Rose Acacia). Hardy ornamental shrubs and trees with white or rose flowers in early summer. The most popular species is *R. pseudoacacia*, growing 70 ft. to 80 ft. high, with elegant, light green pinnate leaves and trails of white flowers. This is the False Acacia or Locust Tree and it grows very well in towns. *R. hispida*, the Rose Acacia, is much smaller, rarely exceeding 10 ft. with deep rose flowers. It needs a sheltered, sunny position, and because of the brittleness of its branches is often trained against a wall or trellis for support.
Culture: Plant October to March in ordinary soil and sunny position. Pruning is not essential but overgrown branches can be cut back in February.
Propagation: By seed sown in a frame or greenhouse in March; by suckers removed with some roots in autumn.

ROCHEA roke-ee-a. The rocheas are all succulent plants with leathery leaves and showy clusters of tubular flowers in red, pink, white or yellow. They make good plants for flowering in summer in the cool greenhouse, and *R. coccinea*, the best-known species, is also grown for house decoration.
Culture: Plenty of water and liberal feeding are needed in summer, but in winter the plants should be kept on the dry side. Flowering takes place about a year from propagation and large plants can be grown by carrying them on from year to year. Shading is not needed if the plants are kept adequately moist.
Propagation: *R. coccinea* may be raised from seed sown in heat in spring, but the more usual method of propagating the rocheas is by cuttings of the un-

flowered shoots about 4 in. long taken in spring or autumn. These root readily if inserted singly in 3 in. pots of sandy soil stood near the glass in a greenhouse with a minimum night temperature of 45°. Little water is needed until they have rooted, when the plants should be pinched out and potted on into 5 in. pots, using any good soil with thorough drainage.

ROCK CRESS, see Arabis.

ROCK FOIL, see Saxifraga.

ROCK FORGET-ME-NOT, see Omphalodes.

ROCK JASMINE, see Androsace.

ROCK ROSE, see Cistus and Helianthemum.

RODGERS' BRONZE-LEAF, see Rodgersia.

RODGERSIA roj-er-see-a (Rodgers' Bronze-Leaf). Hardy herbaceous perennials with ornamental foliage and pink or white flowers in early summer. Grand plants for margins of ponds, streams, etc., but keep above the floodline. The most popular is *R. pinnata*, 3 ft. to 4 ft., pink. *R. tabularis* is not quite so tall, has larger leaves and white flowers. The leaves of *R. aesculifolia* resemble those of a horse chestnut much enlarged.
Culture: Plant March or April in good loamy soil in partially-shaded border. Water freely in dry weather. Protect in severe weather with a covering of bracken or straw litter.
Propagation: By division, March or April.

ROMNEYA rom-nee-ah (Californian Tree Poppy). Slightly tender perennials with large white, poppy-like flowers in summer. Suitable for well-drained border at base of south wall or in sheltered places. The two species grown, *R. coulteri* and *R. trichocalyx*, are very much alike. There is also a hybrid between them. All grow 5 ft. to 7 ft. high.
Culture: Plant March or April from pots. Protect in severe weather with a covering of bracken or straw

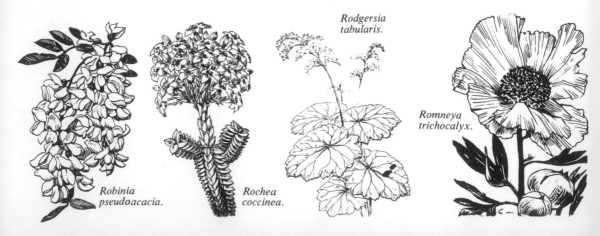

Rodgersia
tabularis.

Robinia
pseudoacacia.

Rochea
coccinea.

Romneya
trichocalyx.

Planting a rose.　　　　　　　　　　*Pruning newly-planted rose.*

litter. Prune all growths back to an inch or so of ground level each spring.

Propagation: By seed sown in sandy soil in March in a temperature of 55°; root cuttings in sandy compost during February in a temperature of 55°, place cuttings singly in small pots so that there need be no subsequent root breakage.

ROOT FLY, *see* Cabbage Root Fly.

ROOT PRUNING. This consists in the severance of strong roots, with the object of checking over-abundant growth and promoting fruitfulness in fruit trees. The reduction in the flow of sap has the effect of causing fruit buds to be formed instead of leaf buds. November is the best month for the work. With small trees, dig a trench all round, 3 ft. away from the trunk, and undercut beneath the soil ball to find any thick roots. These should be shortened, worked into a horizontal position then covered over and thoroughly firmed. With older trees the trench should be 4 ft. or 5 ft. from the trunk and should be carried only half-way round it. No undercutting should be done; merely sever any gross roots found, and repeat the operation on the other half of the tree in the following autumn.

ROSA ro-*sah* (Rose). Hardy-flowering shrubs of which a large number of types are in cultivation. Amongst these the most generally useful for bedding are the Hybrid Teas which make small to medium size bushes with large flowers borne more or less continuously from June to September. Floribundas, are similar in habit but with smaller or less shapely flowers in larger clusters. Polyantha Pompons, usually neat bushes with clusters of small double flowers and Hybrid Musks which make large bushes

flowering summer and autumn. Climbers include the climbing sports of the Hybrid Teas best suited for planting on house walls, and the Wichuriana multi-floras and Ramblers ideal for pillars, arches, pergolas and fences. Good types to form hedges include the Sweet Briars, the Hybrid Musks and the Hybrid Rugosas all of which are very vigorous. There are many other types, including the Bourbon, Moss, Cabbage, China, Austrian Briars, and Noisettes and innumerable varieties in these various types.

Culture: All roses like a deep rich, well-cultivated soil which has had a generous dressing of manure and bonemeal to provide lasting nourishment. Plant November to March. Before so doing, trim broken or bruised roots with a sharp knife. The union of rose and stock, which in bush roses is where the main stems join the main root, should be covered to a depth of 1 in. Stake standards immediately after planting. During summer water in dry weather and feed with chemical fertilisers or liquid manure. After first flowering cut shoots of bush varieties fairly hard back to encourage secondary growth. In autumn fork bonemeal into the surface soil of established beds at the rate of 4 oz. to the sq. yd. In spring mulch with rotted manure or compost.

Pruning: Hybrid Teas: After planting cut strong shoots back to 2 or 3 eyes each. Weak shoots remove entirely. In subsequent years cut out weak or dead shoots and shorten the rest 6 in. to 12 in. in length according to habit of growth. The weaker growing varieties require hardest pruning. Treat standards in identical manner.

Floribundas: First season after planting cut hard back as for Hybrid Teas. In subsequent years cut strongest growth back to 1 ft. to 2 ft. and weaker shoots to 3 or 4 buds.

Polyantha Pompons: First year after planting,

Feeding rose after planting.   *Taking rose cuttings.*   *Pruning an established rose.*

prune back to 6 in. to 8 in. In later years thin out old wood and shorten strong growing growths a little.

Hybrid Musks: Much the same as for Floribundas but allow them to make larger bushes.

Ramblers: First year after planting cut back to within 1 ft. of the ground. Subsequently prune after flowering, cutting out as much as possible of the growth which has borne flowers and training in strong new shoots to take its place.

Climbing Sports: First season after planting cut out weak shoots and remove tips of strong stems. Subsequently prune back side growths to 2 or 3 buds and cut out old and useless wood.

Propagation: Species by seeds sown in sandy soil in a cold frame or greenhouse in March or April. Hips should be buried in sand during the preceding winter and be left outdoors exposed to frost. Transplant seedlings when 1 year old. Another method is by cuttings taken from ripened shoots, 6 in. to 8 in. long, inserted in sandy soil in a cold frame or in a sheltered position out of doors or in an unheated frame in October. The most popular means of propagating the garden varieties is by budding in July or August on to various stocks such as canina, laxa or rugosa (*see* Budding).

ROSE, *see* Rosa.

ROSE ACACIA, *see* Robinia.

ROSE BAY, *see* Nerium and Rhododendron.

ROSE BLACK SPOT. A troublesome fungus disease, easily recognised by the large more or less circular black spots which develop on the foliage. Infected leaves soon drop, and in bad cases the trees may be entirely defoliated. All infected leaves must

be gathered and burnt as soon as they are noted, including any which have fallen. During winter the leafless stems and the surface soil of the beds should be sprayed with Bordeaux mixture. A useful preventive is to spray periodically during the summer with captan, thiram or colloidal copper.

ROSE BOX, *see* Cotoneaster.

ROSE CAMPION, *see* Lychnis.

ROSE MALLOW, *see* Hibiscus.

ROSEMARY, *see* Rosmarinus.

ROSE MILDEW. A common disease affecting roses. It is easily recognised by the typical greyish-white outgrowth on leaves and stems. In a bad attack, plants look as if they have been dusted with flour. Protective measures consist in spraying the plants at regular intervals of about 10 days throughout June and early July with colloidal sulphur or colloidal copper white oil emulsion. The same measure should at once be adopted if it does make an appearance. Another excellent preventive fungicide is karathane.

ROSE OF SHARON, *see* Hypericum.

ROSE RUST. This is a fungus disease which can prove exceedingly troublesome. It shows first in early spring in the form of orange spots on the undersides of leaves. In August these spots become blackish. Affected leaves should be picked off and burned and the plants sprayed at once with a good fungicide such as Bordeaux mixture or colloidal copper. Preventive spraying should be carried out in early summer of the following year.

ROSETTE MULLEIN, *see* Ramonda.

ROSMARINUS *roz-mar-ee-nus* (Rosemary). Hardy evergreen shrub. Leaves highly fragrant. Grey-blue flowers in May. Suitable for dryish sunny border or shrubbery. The only species, *R. officinalis*, is 6 ft. to 7 ft. tall but there is also a prostrate variety which is rather more tender.
Culture: Plant October to April in ordinary well-drained soil. Water freely in summer. No regular pruning required but the fragrant shoots can be cut for drying in summer.
Propagation: By seeds sown in sandy soil in a frame or greenhouse in March; by cuttings of firm young shoots in sandy soil in a propagating frame July to September.

ROTATION. The practice of following one crop with another according to some predetermined plan. Rotational cropping is of considerable importance in the vegetable garden as certain crops tend to exhaust the ground in a similar manner or to suffer from the same diseases, and it is consequently advisable to avoid growing them one after the other on the same plot of ground. Cabbages, brussels sprouts, broccoli, cauliflowers and kales form such a group, while peas and beans form another. A common method of rotational cropping is to divide the ground into 3 approximately equal sections, and to grow potatoes, root crops, and celery on one, peas and beans, onions, leeks and lettuces on another, and cabbages, brussels sprouts, cauliflowers and other green crops on the third. Then the next year the groups are shifted round one plot, potatoes, etc., going to plot 2, peas and beans, etc., going to plot 3 and cabbages to plot 1. A similar change is made the third year, and the fourth year the crops are back to their starting quarters again.

ROWAN, *see* Sorbus.

ROYAL FERN, *see* Osmunda.

RUDBECKIA *rud-bek-ee-a* (Cone-flower; Black-eyed Susan). Hardy herbaceous perennials and annuals with showy yellow, bronze or chestnut-red flowers in summer. The annual rudbeckias are derived from *R. hirta*, 2 ft., and other species. Best of the perennial kinds are *R. speciosa*, 3 ft., yellow and black; *R. nitida* Herbstonne, 6 ft. to 7 ft., yellow and green; and *R. laciniata* Golden Glow, 7 ft., to 8 ft., double yellow flowers.
Culture of Annual Species: Sow in March or April in ordinary soil and open sunny positions where desired to flower, thinning the seedlings to 12 in. apart.
Culture of Perennial Species: Plant autumn or spring in ordinary soil in sunny, well-drained borders. Lift, divide, and re-plant every 2 or 3 years.
Propagation: By seeds sown in ordinary soil and sunny position March or April, transplanting seedlings into flowering positions following autumn; by division of roots at planting time.

RUE, *see* Ruta.

RUELLIA *rew-ell-ee-a.* The ruellias are mostly stove-house plants, and given a sufficiently warm, moist atmosphere, they make fine, free-flowering subjects. The flowers are usually trumpet-shaped, and the rose-pink ones of *R. macrantha*, each nearly 2½ in. across, make this plant one of the finest warm house shrubs, up to 4 ft., or so high. *R. portellae* is a much smaller thing with pink flowers about an inch across and a trailing habit which makes it a good subject for pans or hanging baskets. Other good pot plants are *R. formosa*, scarlet; *R. herbstii*, pink; and *R. speciosa*, scarlet.
Culture: Pot in March in John Innes compost. Water freely March to October; moderately in winter. Temperature: March to October, 60° to 70°; November to February, 55° to 60°. Syringe frequently in summer and shade from all direct sunshine.
Propagation: Cuttings of all the ruellias root easily in a close frame in spring and the plants grow well in any light soil. The young plants should be pinched once or twice to produce a bushy habit.

RUNNER BEANS. These are more tender than French beans and even in the south of England it is

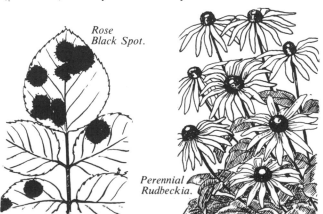

Rose Black Spot.

Perennial Rudbeckia.

Ruellia portellae.

seldom safe to sow outdoors before the end of April. Mid-May is more generally a suitable time, and for a late crop another sowing can be made during the last fortnight in June. Early crops can be had by sowing under cloches or in pots or boxes in a greenhouse or frame the seedlings being hardened off for planting out in late May or early June.

Runner beans like a fairly rich soil with plenty of moisture in summer. Open a trench in February or March at least 18 in. wide and 1 ft. deep and work some well-rotted manure or compost into the bottom. Return the soil, adding a little more manure or compost and a sprinkling of a compound fertiliser. Sow the seeds singly in a double row 12 in. between the two rows of seeds and 9 in. to 12 in. between the seeds in each row. Cover with 2 in. of soil. If more than 1 double row is required the successive pairs should be at least 6 ft. apart. Place long bean poles along the rows, one for each plant and lash to a cross bar near the top for additional stability as a row of full grown runner beans offers considerable resistance to wind. Water freely in dry weather and spray beans with clear water when in flower to assist setting. Pinch out the tip of each plant when it reaches the top of the bean pole. Gather beans regularly as soon as they reach useable size as to let them age on the plants would check cropping.

A new variety, known as Hammond's Dwarf, grows only 18 in. high and needs no staking. Plants should be spaced 1 ft. apart in rows 2 ft. apart. It is also possible to grow ordinary runner beans without stakes by frequently pinching out the tops of all young shoots or 'runners'. When grown in this way plants should be spaced 3 ft. each way.

RUSCUS rus-*kus* (Butcher's Broom). Hardy evergreen shrub. Male and female flowers borne on separate plants. Berries on female plants, round, red, lasting well into winter. Suitable for shady or sunny shrubberies, borders or woods. The species commonly grown, *R. aculeatus*, is 3 ft. high.
Culture: Plant autumn or spring in ordinary soil. Prune April if desired, but regular pruning is not essential.
Propagation: By division of roots in October.

RUSH LILY, *see* Sisyrinchium.

RUSSELIA rus-**ell**-*ee-a*. Some of the russelias are very showy plants, but they need plenty of warmth and moisture practically all the year round. Although actually evergreen shrubs the leaves are often little more than scales. The flowers, something like those of the penstemon, are scarlet and are often carried on slender, drooping shoots which make several of the species good subjects for hanging baskets. *R. juncea*, the Coral Plant, is particularly good for this purpose, and with adequate warmth it can be had in bloom almost continuously, although for winter flowering the hybrid *R. lemoinei*, with similar flowers, is better.
Culture: All the species grow well in light, rich soil in full sun. Pot in March. Water freely April to September but only moderately in autumn and winter. Temperatures: April to September, 60° to 70°; October to March, 55° to 60°. Syringe freely except when in flower.
Propagation: By cuttings which root at almost any time; an even simpler method is to peg the tips of the drooping shoots into damp soil, where they will soon root.

RUSSIAN SAGE, *see* Perovskia.

RUSSIAN VINE, *see* Polygonum.

RUST. Many plants suffer from one or other of the various rust diseases; the commonest victims under glass are the chrysanthemum and perpetual carnation, and outdoors the rose, hollyhock and antirrhinium. The symptoms are usually reddish-brown spots or pustules on the leaves and stems, followed by shrivelling of the affected parts. The source of the trouble is a group of fungus parasites known as rusts, some of which may attack only one particular species, while others may attack more than one. Most of the rusts met with in the garden can be controlled at an early stage by the use of copper sprays such as Burgundy or Bordeaux mixture, thiram or zineb, but where possible it is best to get rid of the affected plants and make a fresh start elsewhere in the garden.

RUTA roo-*ta* (Rue). Hardy evergreen shrub. Leaves finely divided, bluish-green, ornamental and also used for medicinal purposes. The only commonly-grown species, *R. graveolens*, is 2 ft. to 3 ft. tall.
Culture: Plant March in ordinary, well-drained soil in sunny border. Prune the plants closely in April.
Propagation: By seeds sown in light soil outdoors in April; cuttings in shady border in summer.

SAGE, *see* Salvia.

SAGITTARIA, *see* Aquatic.

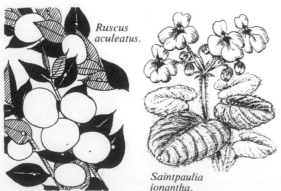

Ruscus aculeatus.

Saintpaulia ionantha.

Sowing early runner beans under glass.

Watering newly-planted runner beans.

ST. BERNARD'S LILY, *see* Anthericum.

ST. DABEOC'S HEATH, *see* Daboëcia.

ST. JOHN'S WORT, *see* Hypericum.

SAINTPAULIA *saint-***paw**-*lee-a* (African Violet).
Tender perennial of dwarf habit with violet, lilac,
pink or white flowers almost throughout the year.
Although there are about half-a-dozen species of
saintpaulia the only one commonly grown is the
well-known African Violet, *S. ionantha*, which is not
a violet but a very attractive little plant related to the
gloxinia, with violet-blue, inch-wide flowers rising
from a cluster of velvety leaves. There are also many
named varieties in different shades, and mixed strains
of seed are available. Although often sold as a house
plant, particularly in America, the saintpaulia is
much more at home in the warm humid conditions
of a greenhouse.

Ruta graveolens.

Culture: Pot February to May in 3 in. pots for small
and 4½ in. for large plants, using John Innes compost
with some extra peat. Pots to be well-drained. Temperatures: October to April, 55° to 65°; natural
increase in summer.

Careful watering, without splashing the foliage, is
necessary at all times and ample shade and humidity
should be provided in summer. Rather drier conditions, with less water and no shade, are needed in
winter.

Propagation: Seed may be sown in spring for
autumn flowering or in August for summer flowering
the following year, but in the latter case a temperature
of at least 50° is necessary to carry the plants safely
through the winter. The seeds should be sown thinly

Rooted leaf cuttings of saintpaulia.

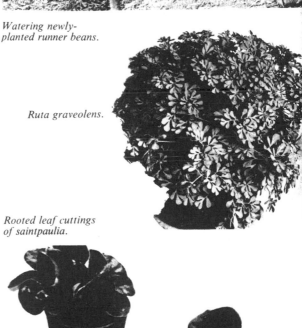

on the surface of the John Innes seed compost in about 70°, and as soon as the seedlings are large enough to handle they should be pricked out into boxes of John Innes No. 1 potting compost and finally transferred to 3½ in. pots of the same compost.

Leaf-stalk cuttings are best taken about mid-summer, when healthy leaves should be cut off with their stalks and inserted upright in a peaty- sandy mixture, with about an inch of the stalk buried. In a propagating frame at about 65° the cuttings should produce tiny plantlets in about a month, and these can be taken off and potted singly in the same way as seedlings.

SALIX say-*liks* (Willow).   Hardy deciduous trees, many of which are too quick growing and large for average gardens. The Weeping Willow, however, is a very beautiful and distinctive tree much planted and thriving in town as well as country gardens. The kind usually grown is the Golden Weeping Willow, *S. alba vitellina pendula*, with yellow stems and bright-green leaves. It is not so large as the true Weeping Willow, *S. babylonica*. Other willows worth planting are *S. daphnoides*, with purplish-violet stems; *S. vitellina britzensis*, with red stems; *S. repens argentea*, a prostrate shrub with silvery leaves, and *S. matsudana tortuosa*, a tree of 30 ft. or 40 ft. with light green leaves and curiously twisted branches.
Culture: Plant November to March in ordinary soil in open or partially-shaded places and by the side of pools and streams. Prune coloured bark varieties hard back each spring to encourage strong summer growth which colours most brilliantly the following winter.
Propagation: By cuttings of young stems taken in autumn and inserted in ordinary soil outdoors.

SALPIGLOSSIS sal-pi-**glos**-*sis*.   The salpiglossis family includes annual, biennial and perennial plants, mostly with large flowers something like those of alstroemeria. *S. sinuata*, a half-hardy annual about 18 in. high, is particularly variable in colour and is often grown as a summer bedding plant besides

making a very effective pot plant.
Culture Outdoors: Sow seeds in John Innes seed compost in a temperature of 60° to 65° February or March. Prick off into boxes when three leaves have formed. Keep in a temperature of 55° to 60° till May, then place in a cold frame to harden and plant out in early June in good soil in sunny beds or borders. Water freely in dry weather.
Culture Under Glass: As above seed should be sown in February or March, after which the seedlings should be transferred singly to small pots and finally to 5 in. pots in John Innes potting compost. For early summer flowering a sowing may also be made in September, as long as the young plants can be wintered out of the reach of frost. Stake plants early before they commence to flop and pinch out tips of shoots occasionally to induce a shorter, more branching habit.

SALSIFY sal-*sif-ee*.   A vegetable grown for its parsnip-like roots. Sow seed in April in soil prepared as for parsnips in rows 12 in. to 15 in. apart. Thin seedlings to 8 in. Lift roots in early November, cut off tips and store in sand or dry soil in a shed.

SALVIA sal-*vee-a* (Sage; Clary).   Half-hardy and hardy herbaceous perennials and evergreen shrubs with red or blue flowers in summer. The scarlet sage, *S. splendens* is usually treated as a half-hardy annual. It is a splendid summer bedding plant, 18 in. to 24 in. high with vivid scarlet flowers all summer. The common sage, used as a herb, is *S. officinalis*. It is a bushy plant 1 ft. to 2 ft. high with aromatic leaves. *S. patens* is a herbaceous species with tuberous roots and gentian blue flowers in summer. Many other species are commonly grown in gardens.
Culture of Scarlet Salvia: Sow seed in January or February in a temperature of 60° to 65°. Pot seedlings singly in John Innes potting compost and harden off for planting outdoors in June, in good, well-worked soil in sunny beds or borders.
Culture of Hardy Species: Plant autumn or spring in ordinary soil in sunny borders. Cut down stems in

Salix babylonica.

Salpiglossis hybrid.

Salsify.

Salvia splendens.

Left: *Bedfordshire sand—a good sharp sand for potting composts.*   Right: *Sanguinaria canadensis plena.*

October. Lift, divide and re-plant every third year. Roots of *S. patens* should be lifted in October or November and stored in a frost-proof place until April.

Culture of Shrubby Species: Grow in large pots in a frost-proof greenhouse or in sunny, sheltered borders outdoors with straw or sacking protection in winter. In spring cut back stems injured by winter frost.

Culture of Common Sage: Plant October to April in ordinary soil and sunny position. Cut and dry leaves in July.

Propagation: Hardy kinds by division in spring or autumn. Shrubby kinds by cuttings of firm, young growth in propagating frame in summer. Common Sage by cuttings in an unheated frame in autumn.

SANCHEZIA *san-kees-ee-a.*   The sanchezias are warm greenhouse plants grown for both foliage and flower, and on the Continent they are used to some extent as house plants. *S. parvibracteata* and *S. nobilis* are the two most commonly grown, and of these the latter is the more handsome, with bright yellow flowers, red bracts and broad, glossy leaves heavily veined with yellow. *S. parvibracteata* is, however, very similar; the main difference lies in the stem, which on *S. nobilis* is square and 'winged', while that of *S. parvibracteata* is round. Both plants are of a rather shrubby character and grow up to 3 ft. or so, although smaller plants are usually used for house decoration.

Culture: A fairly rich, peaty soil, suits them and in this they make rapid growth if given a humid atmosphere and light shade. A winter temperature of about 60° is needed to keep them at their best.

Propagation: By cuttings rooted when available in a warm, close frame.

SAND.   Sand is used in potting composts to assist drainage, but some sands are a good deal better than others for this purpose. Many soft builder's sands are very nearly useless and the often recommended silver sand is usually too fine. A good sand should be noticeably sharp and hard, with particles ranging up to $\frac{1}{8}$ in. in diameter, and it should be free from dust, lime and vegetable matter. Where suitable sands cannot be easily obtained sieved coke ash and fine coke breeze offer good substitutes provided they have been thoroughly weathered.

SANDWORT, *see* Arenaria.

SANGUINARIA *san-gwin-air-ee-a* (Blood-root). Hardy perennial, fleshy-rooted trailing herb with white flowers in spring. The only species, *S. canadensis*, is a prostrate plant. It has a double-flowered variety.

Culture: Plant dormant roots in autumn, or green plants immediately after flowering in spring, in sandy loam or peat in sunny borders or rock gardens. Water freely in dry weather. Top-dress annually with peat in February or March. Should be interfered with as little as possible.

Propagation: By seeds sown $\frac{1}{16}$ in. deep in equal parts leaf-mould and sand in a frame or greenhouse in spring; division of roots in late spring.

SANSEVIERIA *san-sev-eer-ee-a* (Bow String Hemp).   These plants are grown for the decorative effect of the leaves, which in most of those cultivated, are thick, upright and often brightly variegated. *S. trifasciata* has long been grown as a warm greenhouse plant, but nowadays the form known as *S. t. laurentii* is more popular and it is commonly seen as a house plant. On this variety the leaves, up to 30 in.

Sansevieria trifasciata laurentii.   *Santolina chamaecyparissus.*   *Gooseberry Sawfly caterpillars.*

long, are heavily striped yellow along their length, and to preserve this variegation when propagating it is necessary to rely on division of clumps, as leaf cuttings revert to the less colourful type plant.

Culture: Indoors the plants are very easily managed in a warm room, where during winter they can do without water for weeks on end, although in summer they are big drinkers. Re-potting is seldom needed and, in fact, the plants will grow on happily until the roots burst the pot, but before this stage is reached it is best to pot the plants on into a sandy compost with a little leaf-mould or peat. Winter temperature: 55° to 60°; natural rise in spring and summer. Water freely in summer, very sparingly in winter, moderately at other times. Re-pot when necessary in March.

Propagation: By removing rooted offsets at potting time.

SANTOLINA *san-to-***lie**-*na* (Lavender Cotton). Hardy evergreen shrubby plants with small, fragrant,

grey or green leaves and yellow flowers in summer. The species commonly grown *S. chamaecyparissus* is 2 ft. high.

Culture: Plant autumn or spring in ordinary sandy soil in sunny borders or as edging to shrubberies. Trim off flowers as soon as they fade and cut back plants at the same time if overgrown.

Propagation: By cuttings of shoots 2 in. to 3 in. long, pulled off with a small 'heel' of older stem and inserted in sandy soil in a cold frame, or in sheltered position outdoors September or October.

SAPONARIA *sap-on-***air**-*ee-a* (Soap-wort). Hardy annuals and perennials with pink or carmine flowers in summer. Suitable for sunny borders, beds or rock gardens. The annual varieties are all derived from *S. vaccaria*, 2 ft. to 2½ ft. high. The most popular perennial species is *S. ocymoides*, a trailing plant. *S. officinalis*, Bouncing Bet, is a rather coarse plant 2 ft. high. It has a showy double-flowered variety.

Culture of Annual Species: Sow seeds in ordinary soil ⅛ in. deep in March or April for summer flowering; September for spring flowering. Thin seedlings when 1 in. high to about 6 in. to 9 in. apart.

Culture of Perennial Species: Plant autumn or spring in ordinary soil. Lift and divide *S. officinalis* every 2 or 3 years.

Propagation: Perennials by division of roots in spring.

SATIN FLOWER, *see* Lunaria; Sisyrinchium.

SAUROMATUM *saw-ro-***ma**-*tum* (Monarch of the East). Half hardy perennial with tuberous roots and

Sauromatum guttaium.

Double-flowered soapwort.

Saxifraga burseriana (*Kabschia or Cushion type*).

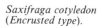

Saxifraga cotyledon
(*Encrusted type*).

arum-like flower spathes. The species grown, *S. guttatum*, is 1 ft. to 2 ft. high.

Culture: Purchase tubers in autumn, place them in a dry saucer in a warm room, and in a few weeks the flower spathe will appear. No soil or water is needed. After flowering plant the tuber in a moist place outdoors or in a pot, to make its leaf growth. Lift in August, keep in a cool place, and again place in a saucer indoors. Repeat the operation year by year.

SAVIN, *see* Juniperus.

SAVOY. This very hard, wrinkled-leaf type of cabbage is grown in exactly the same way as autumn or winter cabbage. There are numerous varieties differing in size and season of growth such as Early Drumhead, Late Drumhead, Early Medium, Late and Extra Late Ormskirk and Omega.

SAWFLY. The larvae of several species of sawfly do a great deal of damage to plants. Some, known as slugworms, strip the surface off leaves. Others, the leaf-rolling sawflies, curl up the leaves they attack in a very distinctive manner. The larvae of another, the apple sawfly, eat into apples. Those of the gooseberry sawfly devour the leaves of gooseberries soon leaving nothing but skeletons. In a general way treatment consists in spraying with insecticides such as DDT, BHC, or nicotine with a view to killing the larvae when they commence to feed but for apple sawfly it is necessary to time the spray application fairly accurately. Two sprays are advised, one about 10 days after blossoms fall, the other in early June.

SAXIFRAGA *saks-ee-***fra**-*ga* (Saxifrage; Rockfoil). Hardy perennial rock and border plants. This is one of the most important genera for the rock garden as it abounds in first-rate species and garden-raised varieties, many of which flower very early in the year. From the cultural point of view it is necessary to divide the genus into a number of subsections, as saxifrages differ considerably in their requirements. The principal sections are Cushion Saxifrages or Kabschias which make dense hummocks or mats of growth studded in early spring, with small flowers on short stalks; Encrusted Saxifrages or Silver Saxifrages which make handsome rosettes of silvery leaves and have sprays of flowers anything from 6 in. to 2 ft. in height, flowering mainly in late spring and early summer; Mossy Saxifrages, with mounds or mats of soft green leaves and flowers on 6 in. to 9 in. stems in mid-spring; London Pride, with rosettes of green leaves and 6 in. to 12 in. sprays of flower in late spring or summer; Oppositifolia with carpets of growth and practically stemless flowers in spring; and various miscellaneous species.

Culture Outdoors: Encrusted saxifrages prefer sunny positions in rock gardens, but will grow in northern aspects. Sand and limestone chippings should be mixed freely with the soil before planting in spring.

For mossy saxifrages a cool rather shady place is best, and the soil should be well supplied with humus. As an edging to borders and shady beds these are ideal plants. Their soft masses of growth often die off during the summer if planted in hot, dry places. Such plants should be lifted after flowering, divided, and re-planted after the soil has been improved by the addition of leaf-mould or peat. All saxifrages of this type delight in plenty of moisture and are unhappy in sun-baked places. They can be planted in March or immediately after flowering.

Cushion saxifrages delight in a very well-drained compost containing plenty of sand, stone chippings and either leaf-mould or peat. They should be given an open but not unduly exposed position. Planting can be done in spring immediately after flowering.

Saxifrages belonging to the Oppositifolia group require a rather cool position in deep, peaty soil with plenty of moisture during the summer and a little shade throughout the hottest part of the day. Stagnation in winter must be avoided.

The London Prides and also *S. granulata* and its varieties will succeed in any ordinary garden soil and sunny or slightly shaded position.

Culture Under Glass: Many of the saxifrages make good subjects for the alpine house or even for the cold greenhouse and very few need any artificial heat. Most will thrive in a gritty, well-drained compost such as John Innes plus half its bulk of stone chippings in well-drained pots or pans and, except when in bloom, are best in an unheated frame. But one species demands very different treatment to most of the others. This is *S. stolonifera* (better known as *S. sarmentosa*) an old-fashioned plant usually called Mother of Thousands on account of the tiny plantlets carried on the slender trailing runners. The flowers, white with yellow and red spots, are produced in summer, but the plant is grown chiefly for its foliage effect indoors, as well as in hanging baskets and at the front of stagings. Although tender it is very nearly hardy and it grows easily in any ordinary soil, in either sun or shade. The variety *tricolor* with the leaves heavily blotched with cream and red shades, are more difficult and requires a winter temperature of at least 50°. Both sorts need plenty of water in spring and summer, and little in winter.

Propagation: Almost all saxifrages can be increased by careful division at planting time, but there are just a few species that only make a single crown, and must be raised from seed. All the true species can be raised from seed sown thinly in March or April, covered with the lightest of scatterings of silver sand and germinated in an unheated frame or greenhouse. *S. stolonifera* is readily increased by the tiny plantlets it produces on its trailing stems.

SAXIFRAGE, *see* Saxifraga.

SCAB. Numerous disorders of vegetables and fruits pass under the general name 'scab' but they are not necessarily related in any way. Apple and pear scab are diseases caused by fungi which produce black or brown blotches on the foliage and fruit, often causing the latter to split and become malformed. These are controlled by spraying with lime sulphur wash or captan in the spring, before the blossom opens, and several times after blossom fall continuing into summer. Potato scab may merely consist of skin eruptions, usually brown and flaky, which are most likely to occur in soils containing a lot of lime or chalk. Surrounding planting sets with peat or leaf-mould will help to combat this disease.

SCABIOSA *skay-bi-o-sa* (Scabious; Pincushion Flower). Hardy biennial and perennial herbs with variously-coloured flowers useful for cutting. Some treated as annuals. The varieties commonly grown in this way, sometimes called Sweet Scabious because of the sweet perfume, are derived from *S. atropurpurea*, 1½ ft. to 3 ft. Colours include pink, crimson, maroon, blue and white. The most popular perennial species is *S. caucasica*, 2 ft. to 3 ft., blue, mauve or white flowers July to October. *S. graminifolia* is a smaller plant, 1 ft. high, blue flowers in summer.

Culture of Sweet Scabious: Sow seeds $\frac{1}{16}$ in. deep in light, sandy soil in a temperature of 60° to 65° in February or March, prick off seedlings into boxes and harden off for planting out in late May in ordinary soil in sunny beds or borders.

Culture of Perennial Species: Plant in spring in ordinary, preferably limy, soil, sunny, well-drained borders for *S. caucasica;* sunny rock gardens for *S. graminifolia.*

Propagation: By division of roots in March or April.

SCABIOUS, *see* Scabiosa.

SCALDING. The scalding of grapes, usually indicated by sunken, withered patches towards the top of the berry, is often due to faulty ventilation. It occurs where the sun is allowed to reach the berries before the condensation formed during the night has had time to dry off them, and the remedy lies in increasing ventilation at night and in the early morning. The scalding of fruits and leaves may also occur on other plants, but here again it can usually be prevented by providing plenty of ventilation when the plants are moist.

SCALE INSECT. Belonging to the same family as the mealy bugs, and related to the aphides, the

Schizanthus hybrid.

Scabiosa caucasica.

many kinds of scale insects settle down when adult in one place to suck the plant sap, covering themselves with a horny covering or 'scale', brown or greyish, so that they look like a miniature limpet. The fluted scale, which is scheduled as a noxious insect, is occasionally introduced from abroad. It is orange-brown, downy, and its posterior is raised up on a mass of white, fluted wax.

Scale insects on a small scale can be dealt with by hand, pushing the insects off the plant with a piece of wood or damp cloth dipped in insecticide. Suitable insecticides are nicotine or white oil emulsion. Spraying should be repeated to ensure that no young are hatched from eggs which have escaped treatment. On fruit trees scale insects can usually be killed by spraying with a tar-oil wash in the winter, but on soft-stemmed or greenhouse plants this remedy cannot be used, and they must be removed by sponging with a petroleum emulsion or nicotine insecticide or fumigation with nicotine.

The sweet excretions of scale insects dripping on to leaves below may become attacked by a fungus called sooty mould, which is harmless but disfiguring.

SCARBOROUGH LILY, *see* Vallota.

SCHIZANTHUS *ski-***zan**-*thus* (Butterfly or Fringe Flower). Half-hardy annual with variously-coloured flowers in spring or summer. This Poor Man's Orchid is one of the best plants for the cool greenhouse or even for the cold one in summer. Although there are several different species the hybrid forms such as *S. x wisetonensis*, Dwarf Bouquet and the Pansy-Flowered are chiefly grown, and these make magnificent plants from 1 ft. to 2 ft. high with large flowers in a wide range of colours.

Culture: For spring-flowering, seed should be sown in John Innes seed compost in August and September and germinated in a cold greenhouse or frame. When the seedlings are an inch or so high they should be potted up singly into 3 in. pots of John Innes No. 1 potting compost and wintered in a cool greenhouse, with only just enough heat to keep frost away. Plenty of light and air, but little water, are their main requirements at this time, but in spring plenty of water should be given, together with an occasional dose of liquid fertiliser. Before the plants have filled the small pots with roots they should be transferred to 7 in. pots of John Innes No. 2 potting compost and grown on, again as cool as possible. One stopping, when the plants are a few inches high, is usually sufficient to produce bushy plants.

For summer flowering seed should be sown about early April in a temperature of 55° to 60° and the plants eventually flowered in 5 in. pots. Being annuals the plants should be discarded after flowering.

SCHIZOPHRAGMA *ski-zo-***frag**-*ma* (Climbing Hydrangea). Hardy deciduous self-clinging, climb-

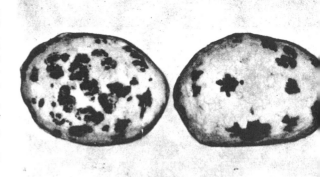

Potato Scab.

Grapes affected by Scalding.

Scale Insect on apple.

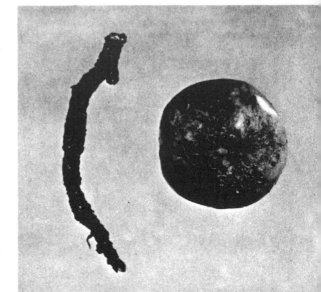

Schizophragma hydrangeoides.

Scilla hispanica.

ing flowering shrub with white flowers in early summer. The species most commonly grown, *S. hydrangeoides*, will reach a height of 30 ft.

Culture: Plant October to March in ordinary soil against sunny wall. No regular pruning required but overgrown or badly-placed growths can be removed in April.

Propagation: By cuttings inserted in sand in a propagating frame, temperature 55°, in early summer.

SCHIZOSTYLIS *ski-zos-til-is* (Caffre Lily; Crimson Flag). Hardy perennial with red or pink flowers in autumn. The only species, *S. coccinea*, is 18 in. high.

Outdoor Culture: Plant March to April in good, loamy soil in warm, sunny border. Protect in severe weather with covering of bracken or dry litter. Water freely in dry weather in summer.

Propagation: By division in March or April.

SCHLUMBERGERA, *see* Zygocactus.

SCILLA sil-*lah* (Squill; Bluebell). Hardy bulbous plants mostly with blue but sometimes pink or white flowers in spring. Suitable for sunny or shady beds or borders, in grass or on rock gardens. The common Bluebell is *S. nonscripta*. A better garden flower is the Spanish Bluebell, *S. hispanica*. It has larger flowers and stouter flower stems. Much smaller is the Siberian Squill, *S. sibirica*, 3 in. to 4 in., bright blue flowers. *S. peruviana* has a broad head of purple or white flowers on a stout 1 ft. stem.

Culture: Plant August to November in good, loamy soil, small bulbs 2 in. deep and 2 in. apart, large bulbs 4 in. deep and 3 in. to 4 in. apart; *S. peruviana*, 4 in. to 6 in. deep in sheltered spot. Lift and re-plant only when plants are overcrowded.

Propagation: By offsets from old bulbs removed when lifting and planted like full-sized bulbs.

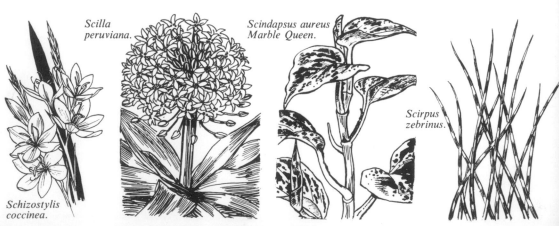

Scilla peruviana.

Scindapsus aureus Marble Queen.

Scirpus zebrinus.

Schizostylis coccinea.

Scolopendrium vulgare.

Seakale.

SCINDAPSUS *skin-**dap**-sus.* Tropical plants climbing by means of aerial roots, and until recently regarded as only suitable for the hot house. Several sorts are now sold however as house plants. Among these is *S. aureus*, with large, somewhat heart-shaped leaves, spotted and lined with gold. Its variety Marble Queen, with rather smaller and more silvery leaves, is a much slower-growing variety.
Culture: *S. aureus* and its varieties make excellent indoor climbers or trailers and are at their best where they can climb over a piece of bark. With really warm conditions and an evenly moist soil they grow quite rapidly, but if kept too much in the shade they tend to lose the markings on the leaves and should therefore be grown in a fairly good light, although not hot sun.
Propagation: Cuttings about 6 in. long root readily in sandy, peaty soil in about 70° and if these are inserted singly in 3½ in. pots they soon make effective little plants without re-potting.

SCION. That part of a grafted or budded plant which provides the top growth.

SCIRPUS **sker**-*pus.* The bulrush family includes a number of plants native to this country, and of these *S. riparius*, *S. cernuus* and *S. setaceus* are some of the smallest, growing to no more than 6 in. high. *S. cernuus*, with 3 in. long spikes carried on drooping stems, makes a quite good pot plant.
Culture: Grow in a cold greenhouse in a wet, peaty soil. Water freely in spring and summer, moderately at other times. Re-pot in March.
Propagation: By division at potting time.

SCORPION GRASS, *see* Myosotis.

SCOTCH THISTLE, *see* Onopordon.

SCREWPINE, *see* Pandanus.

SCOLOPENDRIUM *skol-o-**pen**-dre-um* (Hart's-Tongue Fern). Hardy ferns with undivided fronds. The most familiar is *S. vulgare* the British Hart's-Tongue fern to be found growing wild in many woods and on shady banks, hedgerows, etc. There are numerous garden varieties some with crested or very wavy fronds.
Culture: Plant in March or April in good, loamy soil with some peat or leaf-mould on shady banks, in ferneries or shady rock gardens, in thin woodland, near streams, etc.
Propagation: By division at planting time.

SCRIM. A light cotton material used for shading. Attached to a light wooden frame it provides an excellent method of shading delicate seedlings when general shading of the greenhouse is undesirable.

SEA BUCKTHORN, *see* Hippophae.

SEA HOLLY, *see* Eryngium.

SEAKALE. Grown for its young shoots which must be blanched in complete darkness. It can be raised from seed sown in April outdoors but a better method is to grow it from root cuttings 6 in. to 8 in. long planted right way up in March in well dug and manured soil. Drop the cuttings into dibber holes

SEA

sufficiently deep to allow tops of cuttings to be ½ in. beneath surface. Space them 1 ft. apart in rows 18 in. apart. Keep clear during summer and lift plants in November. Trim off side roots, tie up in bundles and lay in sand in a sheltered place to provide cuttings for re-planting the following spring. Lay crowns also in sand and pot them a few at a time, bringing into a warm greenhouse or shed to force into growth. Keep in complete darkness throughout this forcing.

SEA PINK, *see* Armeria.

SEAWEED. The common vegetation of the sea which often has high manurial value. The best sea-weeds for this purpose are the Bladder Wrack. or Fucus and the Oar Weed, Kelp or Laminaria, both of which are common all round the coasts of the British Isles. Seaweed can be used wet as gathered, or may be spread out thinly in the sun to dry, after which it can be stacked and kept for an indefinite period. Good samples of seaweed contain nitrogen, potash, and phosphates, and have much the same manurial value as stable manure.

SEDUM see-*dum* (Stonecrop). Hardy perennial, biennial, and annual rock and border plants, and tender greenhouse plants. This is a large genus containing many useful species and varieties. Stonecrops have succulent leaves, and in consequence are able to grow in dry, sun-baked places. The smaller varieties

such as *S. dasyphyllum, S. lydium, S. spathulifolium* and *S. spurium* are suitable for growing in the crevices between paving slabs, in the rock gardens and dry walls, the larger species such as *S. spectabile* and *S. maximum* for the herbaceous border. *S. sieboldii* is not quite hardy, and is usually cultivated as a greenhouse pot plant.

Culture of Hardy Species: All thrive in sunny positions, and the majority prefer rather poor, well-drained soil but one exception is *S. pulchellum*, which succeeds best in rather moist soil. The larger sedums, such as *S. spectabile* and *S. maximum*, appreciate a richer soil. The hardy perennial kinds can be planted in spring or early autumn. Seed of the hardy annual *S. coeruleum* should be sown outdoors in March or early April where the plants are to grow. *S. pilosum*, a biennial, is raised from seed sown in May.

Culture of Greenhouse Species: These all enjoy well lit, airy conditions in a greenhouse with a minimum winter temperature of 40° to 45°. A few of the special-ised species need higher temperatures. They can be grown successfully in John Innes potting compost with a little extra sand.

Propagation: The perennial sedums can all be increased by careful division at planting or potting time. Greenhouse species increase easily from stem cuttings.

SEED BOXES. Almost any clean, shallow box of reasonable size will do for seed sowing provided it has slits or holes for drainage, but there are certain advantages in using what is known as the standard seed-tray. This is 9 in. by 14 in. and from 2 in. to 3 in. deep. Being all of one size these can be easily arranged on the staging or stored away and it is fairly easy to estimate the amount of compost needed for them. To economise on the seed compost those 2 in. deep may be used, but as the seed-boxes are normally also used for pricking out the 2½ in. deep ones are usually the most practical. Seed trays steeped in copper naphthanate solution before being used in the first place will last for years.

SEEDLINGS. The tiny plants resulting from the germination of seed are known as seedlings, and at a later stage, when they have been pricked out at a certain distance apart, as transplanted seedlings. In these early stages great care is needed to keep the plants healthy, particularly immediately after germin-ation when they may be exceedingly small as in gloxinias and begonias. Damping off disease, caused by a soil-borne fungus, is a common trouble which causes the plants to decay at the base and eventually collapse, but the use of partially sterilised soil in the seed compost will help to overcome this. Other requirements are moisture, shade from hot sun, air and an appropriate temperature, and there must also be sufficient light to prevent the plants from becoming drawn.

Selaginella kraussiana.

Sedum spectabile.

Sempervivum tectorum.

Senecio cineraria.

Covering crocks with roughage.　　　　　　*Crocking seed box for drainage.*

Pricking out into other boxes or pots should be done as soon as the seedlings are large enough to handle, preferably when they are little more than ¼ in. high in many cases, and certainly before they become overcrowded. Apart from damping off. the most common causes of failure are probably dryness and very late pricking out.

SELAGINELLA *sel-aj-in-ell-a.*　The selaginellas, closely related to the ferns, do not flower and are grown as foliage plants. The family is an enormous one comprising more than 700 species, mostly tender and including erect, carpeting and trailing ones, but very few of these are grown to any extent. Probably the most popular is the trailing. green-leaved *S. kraussiana*, which is frequently grown both under stagings and as an edging for them, but the variegated forms *S. k. aurea* and *S. k. variegata* are more attractive, particularly as pot plants. Other fairly popular species are *S. caulescens, S. argentea* and *S. cuspidata.*
Culture: Damp conditions, both at the root and in the air, should be provided at all times, but there must be adequate warmth and the temperature should not be allowed to drop beneath 45° in winter. The plants should be shaded in summer. Re-pot when necessary in spring in an open, peaty compost with a little sand.
Propagation: Cuttings of these plants root readily at any time in about 70°, but the best time is in spring, when the cuttings may be rooted and left in the same pots to develop into plants. Three cuttings should

be put in a 3½ in. pot, or pans can be used for the selaginellas, being shallow-rooted, prefer these to pots.

SEMPERVIVUM *sem-per-vie-vum* (House Leek). Hardy, succulent perennials grown for their ornamental rosettes of leaves. All occasionally produce flowers in summer on stiff stems. Hardy species suitable for edgings to borders, crevices or ledges of rock gardens, dry walls, etc., in open sunny positions.
Culture: Plant September to April in ordinary, well-drained soil containing a little lime. The common house leek (*S. tectorum*) is adapted for growing on sunny roofs if planted in a mixture of cow dung and clay in March or April.
Propagation: By division in spring.

SENECIO *sen-ee-see-o* (Ragwort; Dusty Miller). Hardy or slightly tender perennial herbs and hardy-flowering shrubs. *S. cineraria*, the Dusty Miller, is used in summer bedding schemes for its grey leaves. *S. laxifolius* is an evergreen shrub, 3 ft. to 4 ft. high with grey leaves and yellow flowers in summer (*see* Cineraria for *Senecio cruentus*).
Culture of Hardy Herbaceous Species: Plant October to April in ordinary soil and sunny or partially-shady places. Suitable for margins of pools or streams, wild gardens, etc.
Culture of Dusty Miller: Plant in May or June in ordinary soil and sunny or partially shady position. Lift in autumn and overwinter in a frame or raise new plants annually from cuttings.
Culture of Shrubby Species: Plant October to March

Shading the greenhouse.

Grape Shanking.

in ordinary soil and sunny position. No regular pruning required.

Propagation: Hardy herbaceous kinds by division autumn or spring. Dusty Miller by cuttings in a frame or greenhouse spring or autumn; shrubby species by cuttings in a propagating frame July or August.

SENSITIVE PLANT, *see* Mi nosa.

SEQUOIA *se-*kwoy*-a* (Redwood; Big Tree; Wellingtonia). The only species, *S. gigantea*, is an evergreen, cone-bearing tree of the largest size. It will reach 100 ft. or more but is narrowly conical in habit so is suitable for planting as an isolated specimen in large gardens. It is a very handsome tree.
Culture: Plant October to April in good, rich, loamy, rather moist soil. No pruning is desirable.
Propagation: By seed sown in a greenhouse or frame in March.

SETCREASEA *set-*krees*-ee-a.* There are only slight botanical differences between this plant and *Zebrina pendula*, and both need the same treatment, described under the latter. *S. purpurea* has narrow, mauve leaves, and *S. striata*, green leaves pencilled with white.

SHADE. Some plants are damaged by excessive exposure to the direct rays of the sun. Filmy ferns are a notable example and must be grown in a comparatively feeble light. With many plants shade is desirable at some particular stage in their development, either to prevent excessive loss of moisture by evaporation, e.g., unrooted cuttings, or to encourage germination of seeds. The degree of shade required will vary according to the nature of the plant and the particular purpose for which the shade is needed. Permanent shading of a greenhouse is frequently achieved by spraying a special greenish wash upon the glass. Powder for this can be purchased from any horticultural sundriesman. Alternatively, ordinary limewash can be employed. If a little skimmed milk is added it will adhere to the glass more effectively. Temporary shading can be effected with the aid of lath or canvas blinds, paper, or with scrim or butter muslin. Shading should always be removed as soon as its useful purpose has been served as excessive shade will encourage weak growth.

SHALLOT. A deeply dug and well-drained soil is essential for shallots, but manure should not be used just before planting. The ideal is a sunny plot that has been well manured for a previous crop. Bulbs are planted 8 in. apart in rows 1 ft. apart in

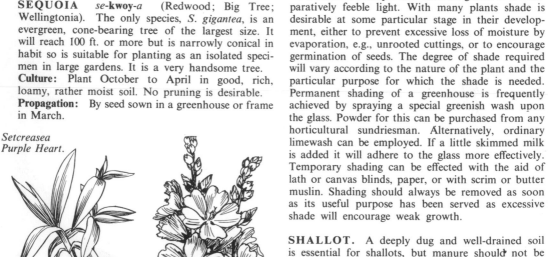

Setcreasea Purple Heart.

Sidalcea hybrid.

216

Shortia uniflora grandiflora.

Sieving loam for potting compost.

February or early March. Frequent hoeing is practically the only after-care required. In June remove a little soil around the base of the bulbs to assist ripening. As soon as the foliage dies down the bulbs should be lifted, dried and stored in an airy, cool, but frost-proof place. Propagation can be effected by division of the bulb clusters (cloves) and also by seed sown thinly in drills 8 in. apart in March.

SHANKING. This is a common trouble with grapes, on which it appears as a pronounced darkening of the footstalk of the berry, followed by shrivelling of the fruit. Sometimes only a few of the berries are affected, but in severe cases much of the fruit may be lost. It is not caused by a disease but by faulty cultivation of the vine and very often by unsuitable root conditions, in which case drainage and fertilisers may need investigation. Mild attacks are sometimes brought on by bad ventilation causing extremes of heat and cold, and by faulty pruning. Shanked berries should be removed as soon as they are seen as they are of no use and only restrict the flow of air round healthy fruits.

SHASTA DAISY, *see* Chrysanthemum.

SHIELD FERN, *see* Polystichum.

SHINGLE. A coarse, rounded gravel obtained mainly from the sea-shore and used for the surfacing of stagings in the greenhouse. Apart from providing an attractive finish it is fairly inimical to insect pests and helps to produce a moist atmosphere if it is regularly moistened.

SHINGLE PLANT, *see* Monstera.

SHORTIA shor-*te-a.* Dwarf, hardy perennial herbs with pale pink flowers in spring. Suitable for partially shady rock garden or margin of rhododendron beds. The species usually grown are *S. galacifolia* and *S. uniflora.* Both are 4 in. to 6 in. high.
Culture: Plant in April in a mixture of sandy peat and leaf-mould in a well-drained position. Water freely in dry weather.
Propagation: By division of roots in April.

SHRIMP PLANT, *see* Beloperone.

SIBERIAN WALLFLOWER, *see* Erysimum.

SIDALCEA sid-al-*see-a.* Hardy perennial herbs with pink or rose flowers in summer. The varieties grown are all derived from *S. malvaeflora* and range in height from 2 ft. to 5 ft.
Culture: Plant October to April in ordinary soil in sunny borders. Stake taller kinds in May. Lift, divide and re-plant every 3 or 4 years.
Propagation: By seeds sown $\frac{1}{8}$ in. deep in light soil in April; division of roots October to April.

SIEVES. Also known as riddles, these are essential in greenhouse work for bringing soils to a suitably divided condition, but there is no need to have too big an array of them. For general purposes one with a $\frac{1}{2}$ in. mesh is adequate, although a $\frac{1}{4}$ in. one is useful when surfacing seed composts for very small seeds. For larger quantities of soil, or to produce soils of a coarser texture, a 'screen' consisting of a large wooden frame and an appropriate wire mesh makes the work of sieving quicker and easier. This is leant up at a suitable angle and the soil is thrown through it. Very fine sieves are seldom useful as the practice of reducing soils for composts to a very fine stage is a bad one.

SILENE *si-lee-nee* (Catchfly). Hardy annuals and herbaceous perennials with pink or white flowers in summer. The perennial species commonly grown are *S. alpestris*, 6 in., white; and *S. schafta*, 1 ft., rose-pink, a tumbling mass of growth. The annual varieties are derived from *S. pendula*, a slender sprawling plant.

Silene schafta.

Culture of Annual Species: Sow seeds in March or April where required to grow and flower in ordinary light soil in sunny beds or borders in April, thinning out seedlings to 6 in. apart.
Culture of Perennial Species: Plant March or April in sandy loam in crevices or ledges of rock gardens.
Propagation: By careful division in spring.

SILK BARK OAK, *see* Grevillea.

SILK OAK, *see* Grevillea.

SILVER LEAF, *see* Plum.

SINNINGIA, *see* Gloxinia.

SISYRINCHIUM *sis-ee-rink-ee-um* (Satinflower; Rush Lily; Blue-eyed Grass). Hardy perennials with blue or yellow flowers in spring or summer. Suitable for sunny rock gardens or borders. The most popular species are *S. bermudiana*, and *S. angustifolium*, both 18 in., blue. *S. douglasii*, 12 in., amethyst; and *S. striatum*, 3 ft., yellow.
Culture: Plant October or May in ordinary soil; *S. grandiflorum* in a mixture of loam, peat and sharp sand in a place where it is unlikely to be overrun by stronger plants.
Propagation: By division in March.

SKEWERWOOD, *see* Cornus.

SKIMMIA skim-*ee-a*. Hardy evergreen ornamental shrubs with fragrant white flowers. Male and female flowers on the most familiar species, *S. japonica*, 3 ft. to 5 ft. are on separate plants. Scarlet berries are produced in autumn on female bushes if a male bush grows nearby for pollination. There are also hermaphrodite species such as *S. reevesiana*, 2 ft., and *S. foremannii*, 3 ft. to 5 ft. in which both male and female flowers are produced on the same plant.
Culture: Plant September to April in good loamy soil in partially shaded or open, sheltered borders. No pruning required.
Propagation: By seeds sown when ripe in sandy loam and peat in cold frame; by cuttings of firm shoots inserted in a propagating frame in summer.

SKUNK CABBAGE, *see* Lysichitum.

SLEEPY DISEASE. This is a tomato plant trouble which results in severe wilting and yellowing of the plant. It is usually caused by the fungus *Verticillium albo-atrum*, which attacks the roots and base of the plant and eventually poisons the sap. Although its effects are very similar to those produced by root-rot it can be identified by the fact that in sleepy disease the wilting normally affects the lower leaves first, whereas with root-rot the wilting usually starts at the top of the plant. Another difference is that unlike root-rot, sleepy disease is most apparent in cool air and soil conditions. Internal discolouration of the stem, which with root-rot seldom affects more than the lower few inches, may with sleepy disease extend to the top of the plant.
  Control consists in keeping the greenhouse shaded and as warm as possible, and plants frequently damped overhead rather than watered at the roots. If the house can be kept at a temperature of at least 77° for a fortnight a complete cure may sometimes be effected. Dead plants should be removed immediately and if new ones are to take their place the soil should be watered with Cheshunt Compound before planting.

SLIPPER FLOWER, *see* Calceolaria.

SLIPPER ORCHID, *see* Cypripedium.

SLUG. A number of different species of slug do a great deal of damage to plants. They are particularly destructive to seedlings, which they devour greedily. They can usually be pin-pointed as the source of the trouble by the presence of the slimy trail that they leave, but actual pin-pointing as a method of control is about as out of date as the hat-pins with which it used to be carried out. Slugs can be trapped by placing scooped-out halves of orange on the soil, while two effective methods of poisoning are either to

Sisyrinchium striatum.

Skimmia japonica.

Sleepy Disease.

Putting down slug bait.

Smithiantha hybrid.

mix 4 oz. of Paris Green with 7 lb. of bran, or 1 oz. of finely-powdered metaldehyde with 3 lb. of bran, and place small heaps of this here and there where the slugs can easily get at it. Paris Green is poisonous to human beings and domestic animals. Wet soils are always the most liable to infestation and where the pest persists improved drainage and the use of less humus may improve matters.

SMILAX, *see* Asparagus.

SMITHIANTHA *smith-ee-***an***-tha.* Tender tuber-ous-rooted perennials with ornamental foliage and spikes or red, orange or yellow flowers from July to December. Formerly known as gesnera. Most of the garden varieties are hybrids.

Culture: Pot in March placing tubers 1 in. deep singly in 5 in. pots in John Innes potting compost. Water moderately from time growth begins until plants are 3 in. or 4 in. high, then freely. After flowering gradually withhold water till foliage dies

Removing snails from lupins. *Pricking out seedlings into soil blocks.*

down, then keep dry till potting time. Apply weak liquid feed once or twice a week when flower buds are showing. When foliage has died down, place the pots on their sides under stage till potting time. Temperatures: March to August, 60° to 70°; September to October, 60°; November to February, 50° to 55°.
Propagation: By seeds sown on surface of well-drained pots of sandy peat in a temperature of 75°, March or April; cuttings of young shoots inserted in pots of sandy peat in a temperature of 75° in spring; fully matured leaves pegged on surface of pots in sandy peat in a temperature of 75°.

SMOKES. Many of the modern insecticides and fungicides are sold in the form of small containers which when ignited give off clouds of vapour carrying fine chemicals into all parts of the greenhouse. These devices are known simply as 'smokes' and where they can be used safely they probably provide the best method of dealing with pests under glass, but as certain plants are damaged by some insecticides the makers' instructions should be carefully followed. The more old-fashioned, but still very effective, method of burning nicotine shreds in a special lamp may also be described as a form of 'smoking'. Still, dull weather provides the best conditions for using smokes and the house should be sealed as far as possible to prevent the escape of the fumes. The greenhouse should be kept locked while the operation is in progress.

SMOKE-TREE, *see* Catinas.

SNAILS. These damage plants in much the same manner as slugs and can be trapped or poisoned in the same way. They shelter under stones or on walls particularly under cover of ivy and other dense growth.

SNAKE-ROOT, *see* Cimicifuga.

SNAPDRAGON, *see* Antirrhinum.

SNEEZE-WEED, *see* Helenium.

SNEEZE-WORT, *see* Helenium.

SNOW IN SUMMER, *see* Cerastium.

SNOWBALL TREE, *see* Viburnum.

SNOWBERRY, *see* Symphoricarpos.

SNOWDROP, *see* Galanthus.

SNOWFLAKE, *see* Leucojum.

SNOWY MESPILUS, *see* Amelanchier.

SOAP-WORT, *see* Saponaria.

SODA NITRATE, *see* Nitrate of soda.

SOIL BLOCKS. Some growers nowadays prefer soil-blocks to pots for the growing of young plants which are to be eventually planted out. These blocks are prepared on the spot by compressing the potting compost in special machines, often quite simple affairs, and the seedlings may be either raised direct in them or transplanted to them later on. By using

Collecting solanum berries.

Soldanella alpina alba.

soil-blocks much of the work and expense attached to the use of pots is eliminated and the plants themselves benefit by having a free circulation of air and warmth round their roots, but more care is needed to grow plants successfully in them. The compost must be of the right texture and moisture so that the blocks do not collapse, and very careful attention must be paid to watering as many of the roots are eventually fully exposed to the air. Provided these considerations are borne in mind excellent plants can be grown.

SOILLESS CULTIVATION.
Experiments in growing normally earth-grown plants without the use of soil have frequently been made, but only in recent years has the system become at all practical, and even now its use in this country is mainly limited to a few enthusiasts and to experimental work. Some crops however, are already being produced on a commercial scale by soilless cultivation and it is much used for growing food in desert areas.

Two methods are at present in use; one involves the use of nutrient solutions only and in the other the plants are grown in an inert material such as sand, gravel or clinker and fed with the appropriate solutions. In the former method the plants are more or less suspended above the solution with their roots reaching down to it, but this has not proved too satisfactory, owing to the difficulty of getting adequate aeration of the solution. The second method has proved more practical and is not beyond the powers of the experimentally-minded amateur. A much simpler aspect of soilless cultivation is of course, to be found in the soilless potting composts which are now being tried and which, with the recommended feeding, supply all the plants' requirements.

SOLANUM *sol-ay-num* (Winter Cherry; Christmas Cherry; Potato Vine). Tender berry-bearing plant (*S. capsicastrum*) and two slightly tender climbers, *S. crispum* and *S. jasminoides*, with purplish or white flowers, somewhat resembling those of a potato and produced freely from June to October.

Culture of Berry-Bearing Species: Although *S. capsicastrum* may be grown from cuttings it is more often raised from seed sown in gentle heat in February or March. As soon as the seedlings are about an inch high they should be potted into 3 in. pots of John Innes No. 1 potting compost to which Epsom Salts have been added at the rate of $\frac{3}{4}$ oz. per bushel. This addition is to prevent magnesium deficiency from which solanums soon suffer. Stopping of the plants is carried out, when they are about 4 in. high, when they should be pinched hard back to induce a bushy habit. The plants are then soon ready for potting into 4 in. or 5 in. pots of John Innes No. 2 potting compost plus 2 oz. of Epsom Salts to each bushel.

In June the plants should be plunged in an open cold-frame, where as soon as the flowers are open, they should be frequently sprayed with water to encourage a good set of berries. Both over and under watering must be avoided at this time. In the latter half of September the plants should be housed in a cool, dry atmosphere (45° to 50° is ample) and watered thoroughly only when they really need it.

Culture of Climbing Species: Plant October to April in ordinary, well-drained soil and sunny, sheltered place against wall, fence or trellis. Protect base of plant with bracken or straw in winter. In cold districts, where *S. jasminoides* cannot be grown successfully outside, it makes an excellent subject for the cool greenhouse if planted in light, rich soil with plenty of humus, and pruned by shortening the shoots back by about a third in February.

Propagation: Berry-bearing species by seeds sown in a temperature of 65° in February. Climbing species by cuttings of firm young shoots rooted in a warm propagating frame in May or June.

SOLDANELLA *sol-dan-***ell**-*a* (Blue Moonwort). Hardy perennial herbs with blue flowers in spring. Suitable for open rock gardens. The species commonly grown are *S. alpina*, 4 in. high and *S. montana*, 6 in.

Culture: Plant March or April in a mixture of peat, loam, sharp sand and some chippings. Top-dress annually in spring with similar gritty compost.

Propagation: By seeds sown in well-drained pans filled with a mixture of sandy loam, peat and sand lightly covered with fine soil and placed in a shady frame March or April; division of plants in March or April.

SOLIDAGO *sol-id-***ay**-*go* (Golden Rod). Hardy herbaceous perennials with yellow flowers in summer or early autumn. Suitable for sunny or shady borders, banks or margins of water. The species commonly grown is *S. canadensis*, and there are numerous varieties of this ranging from 2 ft. to 6 ft. in height, and colour from very pale to deep yellow. The plant commonly known in gardens as *S. missouriensis* is in fact *Solidaster luteus*, but its culture is the same as for Solidago. It has pale yellow flowers and grows 3 ft. high.

Culture: Plant October to April in ordinary soil. Lift, divide and re-plant every 3 or 4 years.

Propagation: By division of roots October to April.

SOLIDASTER, *see* Solidago.

SOLOMON'S SEAL, *see* Polygonatum.

SOOT. This is valuable in the garden for two distinct purposes. Fresh soot is a pesticide, and if forked into the soil, either alone or mixed with an equal quantity of lime, it will kill or drive out slugs, snails and other soil pests. But fresh soot must not be brought directly into contact with plants, as it will cause scorching of leaves and roots. Soot that has been allowed to weather outdoors for 2 or 3 months is a valuable nitrogenous fertiliser. It will improve the colour and size of leaves, and in consequence is particularly valuable for lettuces and crops of the cabbage type. It can be applied at any time of the year. Simply dust the soil fairly heavily with the soot and then fork or hoe it in.

SOOTY MOULD. A dark, almost black fungus which develops on the 'honeydew' excreted by certain pests, particularly scale and mealy bug. Although harmless in itself it hinders the natural processes of the plant and should be tackled at the source by getting rid of the pests. The actual mould has to be cleaned off by hand which can be done most easily with a soft cloth and soapy water.

SORBUS **sor**-*bus* (Mountain Ash; White Beam; Rowan). Hardy deciduous trees with white flowers in early summer followed by berries which are usually red but in some species pink or white. The best known are *S. aucuparia*, the Rowan or Mountain Ash, with fern-like leaves and *S. aria*, the White Beam, with undivided leaves which are white beneath. Both will grow to 50 ft. *S. hupehensis* resembles the Mountain Ash in leaf but has white instead of red berries.

Culture: Plant November to March in ordinary soil and open situations. All kinds, and particularly the White Beam, thrive on chalky soil. No regular pruning is necessary but trees can be thinned or reduced in size in winter.

Propagation: By seed sown in March.

SOUTH SEA LAUREL, *see* Codiaeum.

SOUTH SEA MYRTLE, *see* Leptospermum.

SOUTHERNWOOD, *see* Artemisia.

SOWBREAD, *see* Cyclamen.

SOWING. Under glass seed is normally sown in seed-boxes, pots or seed-pans, which should be clean and well-drained. These should be filled with a suitable seed compost such as John Innes, which should be pressed evenly and firmly all through and finally smoothed and levelled off with a wooden 'presser', a flat piece of wood fitted for convenience with some sort of handle. A very fine surface is not advisable, and even for minute seeds a compost put through a ¼ in. sieve will not be too coarse. The seed should then be spread thinly and as evenly as possible. For very fine seeds no covering of compost is needed but the seeds should be lightly pressed in, taking care that they do not adhere to the wooden presser. Slightly larger seeds will be deep enough if they are little

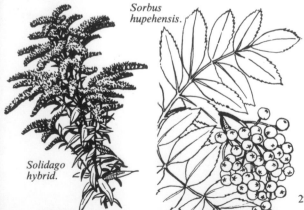

Sorbus hupehensis.

Solidago hybrid.

Sowing seed: 1) Crocking the seed box.   *(2) Filling with compost.*   *(3) Firming in the compost.*

4) Levelling off with a wooden presser.   *(5) Sowing the seed.*

(6) Covering with fine compost.   *(7) Watering with a fine rose.*   *(8) Covering with newspaper.*

more than hidden by the covering and still larger ones may be about $\frac{1}{4}$ in. deep. Few seeds need to be any deeper than this.

After sowing, the receptacles should be soaked from underneath in clean water until it seeps through to the surface, when they should be allowed to drain before being covered with glass and paper and placed in the appropriate temperature. These coverings must be removed at the first signs of germination, when the seedlings should be fully exposed to light but not hot sun. At no time must the seed be allowed to become dry—the commonest cause of poor germination.

Outdoors seed may be sown broadcast, i.e., scattered evenly all over the ground in which it is to grow, or in drills drawn out with a stick or the corner of a hoe or rake. Broadcast seeds may be covered by raking them. Seeds sown in drills are covered by drawing the displaced soil back into these. In general, seed outdoors needs to be sown just a little more

223

deeply than under glass. Drills will vary in depth from ¼ in. for the very smallest seed to 3 in. for very big seeds.

SPANISH BAYONET, *see* Yucca.

SPANISH BROOM, *see* Spartium.

SPANISH DAGGER, *see* Yucca.

SPARMANNIA *spar-***man**-*ee-a*. *S. africana* belongs to a small family of African trees or shrubs with clusters of white flowers and it makes an excellent plant for the cool greenhouse or well-lit room. In good conditions it will bloom, especially in early summer, but the plant is worth growing for its large, soft, downy leaves.
Culture: Cuttings of the young shoots root readily in a warm frame in spring and they should be potted on gradually until eventually they may go into 12 in. pots, in which the plants will grow up to about 4 ft. high. A compost of equal parts of soil and peat suits them. During the summer the plants are best stood outside and given plenty of water, but when housed in September they should be kept on the dry side. Pruning, by cutting the flowered shoots hard back, is done in February. Re-potting is best done in March, when as much of the old soil as possible should be removed so that reasonably small pots may be used.

SPARTIUM **spar**-*te-um* (Spanish Broom). *S. junceum* is a hardy deciduous shrub with sweetly-scented yellow flowers in summer. It will grow 10 ft. or 12 ft. high. Suitable for sunny, open borders or dry banks.
Culture: Plant October to March in ordinary soil, allowing ample head room for unrestricted development. Plant can be lightly pruned in spring.
Propagation: By seeds sown ½ in. deep in fine soil in sunny position outdoors, or in a frame in spring.

SPATHIPHYLLUM *spath-ee-***fil**-*um*. A family of almost stemless, evergreen plants grown chiefly for their large leaves and for the prominent leaf-like

spathe which encloses the fleshy spike of small flowers. *S. cannifolium*, with a rigid spathe, green on the outside and whitish within, and *S. floribundum* and *S. wallisii*, with an all-white spathe are three of those mainly grown.
Culture: All need high temperatures, with plenty of moisture at the root and in the air, and succeed best in practically all humus, i.e., peat with just a little sand and loam and also a little charcoal. Re-pot where necessary in March.
Propagation: By division at potting time.

SPAWN. The mycelium of a fungus is referred to as spawn. From the gardener's standpoint spawn is usually applied specifically to the mycelium of the mushroom. It provides the usual method of propagating the cultivated mushroom, and the spawn can either be purchased in the form of bricks or as a special sterilised culture in cartons.

SPEARMINT, *see* Mentha.

SPEEDWELL, *see* Veronica.

SPENT HOPS, *see* Hops.

SPHAGNUM. This 'Bog Moss', characterised by its long stems and spreading, bushy growth, is commonly found in this country as well as elsewhere, and it is widely used in horticulture. In the greenhouse it is particularly useful as an ingredient of composts for orchids and certain other plants, and it also makes excellent material for lining hanging baskets, a purpose for which its great moisture-holding capacity makes it ideal. It is also used for the wrapping of plants and cuttings which are to be sent away and for the wrapping of the wire frames used in wreath making and other floral work.

SPIDER FLOWER, *see* Cleome.

SPIDER PLANT, *see* Chlorophytum.

SPIDERWORT, *see* Tradescantia.

SPINACH. Two types of spinach are commonly grown, the Summer Spinach or Round Seeded and the Winter Spinach or Prickly Seeded. Both are cultivated solely for their leaves which are gathered a few at a time as they reach sufficient size. Sowings should be made about once a fortnight from mid-March to mid-July of round-seeded spinach and a further sowing in mid-August of prickly-seeded spinach. Sow in well dug and manured ground in sun or partial shade, in drills 1 in. deep and 1 ft. apart. Keep well watered in dry weather, as if allowed to get dry, spinach soon runs to seed and becomes useless. Thin to 3 in. and gather leaves as soon as of usable size.

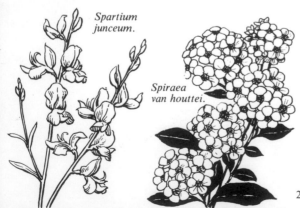

Spartium junceum.

Spiraea van houttei.

Spathiphyllum wallisii.

SPINACH BEET. A form of beetroot grown for its leaves which are gathered like spinach. Sow in early April, and again in early August, in good soil and an open situation in drills 1 in. deep and 18 in. apart. Thin to 9 in. Gather leaves a few at a time from each plant as they become of usable size.

SPINDLE-TREE, *see* Euonymus.

SPIRAEA *spi-***ree***-ah* (Meadowsweet; Bridal Wreath). Hardy deciduous-flowering shrubs and herbaceous perennials. Herbaceous species suitable for moist, partially shaded, or sunny borders, margins of streams, etc., but almost all the herbaceous plants, commonly known as spiraea in gardens, in fact belong to different genera. *S. aruncus* is now *Aruncus sylvester*, *S. lobata* is *Filipendula rubra* and *S. palmata* is *Filipendula palmata*. The florist spiraeas are now Astilbe. The common Meadowsweet with creamy-white sprays of flowers on 4 ft. stems in summer remains *S. alba*.

There are many fine shrubby spiraeas suitable for sunny borders and shrubberies. Amongst the best are *S. arguta*, the Bridal Wreath, white, April, 6 ft.; *S. thunbergii*, similar but a little earlier; *S. japonica*, Anthony Waterer, carmine, July, 4 ft.; and *S. van houttei*, white, May, 8 ft.

Culture of Hardy Herbaceous Species: Plant autumn or spring in rich soil. Top-dress annually in April with decayed manure or compost. Water copiously in dry weather. Lift, divide and re-plant every 3 or 4 years.

Culture of Deciduous Shrubs: Plant October to March in ordinary soil. Prune straggly shoots of spring-flowering kinds moderately close directly after flowering. Summer-flowering kinds can be cut back in March or April.

Propagation: Herbaceous kinds by division of the roots October to March; shrubby kinds by cuttings of firm young shoots inserted in sandy soil in a propagating frame in summer.

Sparmannia africana.

SPIRE LILY, *see* Galtonia.

SPLEENWORT, *see* Asplenium.

SPOTTED LAUREL, *see* Aucuba.

SPRUCE, *see* Picea.

SPUR. The narrow horn-shaped projections found at the base of some flowers, such as aquilegias, delphiniums, and violets. These spurs are usually filled with nectar to attract insects. The term spur is also applied to the close, often more or less twisted collections of fruit buds found on some fruit trees, notably mature apples and pears. The formation of these is encouraged by spur pruning, a process of cutting back side shoots severely to stimulate the production of basal fruit buds, which in turn give rise to the spur growths.

SPURGE, *see* Euphorbia.

SQUILL, *see* Scilla.

STACHYS stak-*is* (Betony; Woundwort; Lamb's Ears). Hardy herbaceous perennials for borders and rough places. *S. lanata* is known as Lamb's Ears

because its leaves are densely covered with silky, grey hairs. It is a creeping plant with 18 in. stems of purple flowers in summer. *S. officinalis*, the Betony, is better known in gardens as Betonica, the variety usually grown being *grandiflora* with spikes of purple flowers on 12 in. stems in June to July. Very different is *S. corsica*, a small creeping rock plant with pale pink flowers in summer.
Culture: Plant in spring or autumn in ordinary soil and open position. *S. corsica*, in well-drained gritty soil or sunny ledge in the rock garden.
Propagation: By division at planting time.

STAG'S-HORN FERN, *see* Platycerium.

STAG'S-HORN SUMACH, *see* Rhus.

STANDARD. Any tree, shrub or plant that is trained with a long, bare main stem or trunk and a head of branches or shoots on top. A half-standard has a shorter stem than that common in a standard of the particular plant in question. A weeping standard is a rose or other tree or shrub of naturally pendent habit is grown on a long, bare main stem so that its shoots may form a cascade of growth.

The large upper petal of flowers of the pea type are known as standards, and the term is also applied to the three erect inner segments of the flower of the flag, German Iris.

STAPELIA *stap-ee-le-a* (Carrion Flower; Toad Flower; Starfish Flower). Tender, succulent plants. Flowers disagreeably scented.
Culture: Pot March or April in well-drained pots in John Innes potting compost. Place in light, sunny greenhouse, but shade from scorching sun. Water moderately April to October; keep nearly dry remainder of year. Temperatures: October to March, 40° to 50°; natural rise in summer.
Propagation: By cuttings of stems exposed to air on shelf in the greenhouse for 2 or 3 days, then inserted singly in 2 in. pots half-filled with drainage, remainder with sand and brick rubble in spring.

STAR OF BETHLEHEM, *see* Ornithogalum.

STAR OF THE VELDT, *see* Dimorphotheca.

STARFISH FLOWER, *see* Stapelia.

STARTING. This term refers to the bringing into growth of plants which have had a dormant or resting period. Under natural conditions they would start into growth in their own time in any case, but in the artificial conditions of the greenhouse it is necessary to provide the necessary conditions to which they will respond. Thus dahlia tubers which have been stored for the winter are 'started' by placing them in a moist soil or peat and giving them increased warmth, when new shoots are soon produced. The time at which plants are started often decides the flowering period, as with hydrangeas which, started in batches from February onwards, will produce a long season of bloom. When starting plants, water and warmth should usually be applied only gradually, and in some cases, as with freesia corms, very little of either is needed to start with. Frequent syringing also helps, particularly with hard-wooded plants such as the fuchsia.

STEM ROT. A term often applied vaguely to several diseases which result in the decay of the stems of plants, although it is more specifically used for 'Stem Rot' of tomatoes, in which the base of the stem shrinks and cracks. This does not occur much these days and where it does it may be prevented from spreading by removing the affected plants and spraying the ground with Cheshunt Compound. Sterilisation or renewal of the soil is advisable before tomatoes are again planted, as the disease is soil-borne.

STEPHANOTIS *stef-an-o-tis* (Clustered Wax-flower; Chaplet Flower; Madagascar Jasmine). Tender evergreen twining shrubs with fragrant white flowers in May. Only one species however, is commonly grown. This is the beautiful *S. floribunda*,

Stachys lanata.

Stapelia variegata.

Stephanotis floribunda.

Stem Rot of tomatoes.

Simple apparatus for steam sterilisation.

with large clusters of fragrant, pure white flowers, somewhat trumpet-shaped, produced from the axils of the leaves.

Culture: Unfortunately it cannot be grown in a cool house, for it needs a winter temperature of at least 55°, but where sufficient heat is available it makes a superb climber, flowering from May to July. Although it may be grown in large pots, in which it may remain for years if properly fed, it is better planted out in good, rough loam with perfect drainage. Plenty of water is needed in summer but much less in winter. The only pruning required is the removal of weak shoots in spring. A careful watch must be kept for mealy bug and scale, for if not checked, these can become serious pests of this plant.

Propagation: By cuttings of shoots of previous year's growth inserted singly in 2 in. pots filled with a mixture of sand, peat and loam, in a propagating frame in a temperature of 65° to 75° in spring.

Sterilising soil with formaldehyde.

Covering with sacks to trap fumes.

STERILISATION. The process of rendering anything sterile. In gardens the term is usually applied to the partial sterilisation of soil for the purpose of destroying soil pests and also soil-borne diseases. Soil can be sterilised by baking in an oven or kiln, but this method suffers from the drawback that all organic matter in the soil may be charred, with a consequent deterioration in texture. Steam sterilisation does not suffer from this disadvantage. Apparatus of a compact and reasonably cheap nature is also now available for the electrical sterilisation of soil. Small quantities can be dealt with by placing the soil in a bucket, standing this in a copper of water, and keeping this at the boil for about an hour. The aim with

Sternbergia lutea.

Stokesia cyanea superba.

all heat sterilisation should be to maintain a soil temperature of at least 180° for 10 minutes. Soils intended for use in the John Innes potting composts should be sterilised before the other ingredients are added.

Chemical sterilisation provides a safe and easy method of dealing with many pests and diseases. The two chemicals most commonly used are cresylic acid and formaldehyde. The former can be purchased as a solution of 97% to 99% purity. This is prepared for use by diluting it with 39 times its own bulk of water. The soil is thoroughly soaked with this solution, 5 gal. being sufficient to treat about 1 sq. yd. of soil. The plot should then be turned over with a spade, after which sacks may be spread on the surface to trap the fumes. Formaldehyde is purchased as a 40% solution and is prepared for use by mixing it with 49 times its own bulk of water. Two galls. of this dilute solution is sufficient to treat about 1 bushel of soil. This solution should be poured as evenly as possible on the soil which must be immediately turned and covered with sacks to trap the fumes. There are also various proprietary chemicals for soil sterilisation which should be used according to manufacturers' instructions. In all cases of chemical sterilisation the soil should not be used for plants for some weeks— at least, not until it has completely lost the smell of the chemicals.

STERNBERGIA *stern-ber-gee-a* (Winter Daffodil; Yellow Star-flower; Flower of the Field). Bulbous plants with yellow crocus-like flowers in autumn.

The only species grown, *S. lutea*, is 6 in. high.
Culture: Plant bulbs in August 4in. to 6 in. deep in good, well-drained loamy soil in sunny, sheltered border. Lift and re-plant only when bulbs show signs of deterioration.
Propagation: By offsets removed and planted in August.

STOCK. A plant grown specially to provide the roots on which another plant can be grafted or budded. Thus dog roses (*Rosa canina*) are used as stocks for garden roses, crab or paradise apples are used as stocks for garden apples and so on.

STOCKS, *see* Matthiola.

STOKES' ASTER, *see* Stokesia.

STOKESIA *stoke-see-a* (Stokes' Aster). Hardy perennial herbs with blue flowers in late summer or autumn. Suitable for sunny, well-drained beds and borders. The only species, *S. laevis*, also known as *S. cyanea*, is 1 ft. tall.
Culture: Plant March or April in ordinary but porous soil in sunny, well-drained borders. Protect in winter in cold districts by covering with handlights. Plants may be lifted in September, placed in pots, and removed to greenhouse for flowering during autumn and winter; plant outdoors the following April.
Propagation: By division of roots in March or April.

STONE CRESS, *see* Aethionema.

Layering strawberry runners.

Netting strawberries against birds.

STONECROP, *see* Sedum.

STOOL. A term used to describe the root-stocks of plants that are capable of easy division or that throw up numbers of shoots direct from the roots. Familiar examples are the Michaelmas daisy, the raspberry, and the chrysanthemum; the term is most frequently used in connection with the last named.

STOPPING. The process of removing the growing tip of any plant, either with a view to checking its development or to encourage the formation of side growths. Fruiting laterals of grape vines and cucumbers are stopped a leaf or so beyond the fruit, while sub-laterals are also stopped to prevent excessive leaf formation. Stopping reaches its highest development in the cultivation of the chrysanthemum, in particular the exhibition types. It is also used to encourage varieties that would flower at different times, if left to grow naturally, to bloom at the same time and on the particular date at which they are to be exhibited. Some varieties are stopped once, some twice, and the actual dates for these stoppings vary according to the individual variety and also the district in which they are grown.

STOVE. A stove house was originally a greenhouse heated by a 'stove' of fermenting tan-bark or other vegetable matter. The term is now used, rather loosely to mean a greenhouse used for plants which need a high temperature all the year round, in which a night temperature of 55° to 60° in winter is normally

regarded as the minimum. As most of the plants grown in it are of tropical origin a very moist atmosphere is also essential. The stove may be a separate structure from the greenhouse, but on a small scale a portion of the latter may be divided off and converted to a stove by providing adequate heating. Plants needing such high temperatures are sometimes called stove plants, but it must be emphasised that many so regarded by the Victorians have been found to stand much lower temperatures and indeed many such plants are now grown as house plants. Many older books, therefore, tend to exaggerate the temperatures required by tropical plants.

STRAIN. A selection made from some particular variety of plant. Strain can be as important as variety. For example, in the case of strawberries, the variety Royal Sovereign has long been regarded as one of the best for general purposes, but it is essential to obtain a good strain of it. A poor strain may give disappointing results. Similarly, in the cultivation of onions, celery and many other vegetables, raisers make a point of selecting and re-selecting fresh strains from the best varieties in order to get the finest possible results.

STRAWBERRY. There are now many varieties in cultivation. Some, such as Royal Sovereign and Talisman, fruit in summer only, while others, such as St. Claude, Carnival and Red Rich, fruit in summer and early autumn for which reason they are known as perpetual fruiting strawberries.

STR

Culture: Best results are obtained on rather rich loam that has been deeply dug and enriched with well-rotted stable or farmyard manure. Plant in late summer or early autumn or in March. Spring-planted strawberries should not be cropped the same year. Best results are obtained from 2-year-old beds, and after the third year it is advisable to discard the old plants. The plants should be 15 in. apart in rows 2½ ft. apart. Clean straw should be spread around the plants and under the leaves each May to keep the fruit clean. At the same time it is advisable to cover the beds with fish net or some similar material to keep off birds. If there is any sign of mildew or other diseases, set light to the straw when all the fruit has been gathered. This will burn off the old foliage, but new leaves will soon appear, and these will be free from disease. Remove runners, unless required for propagation.
Propagation: By means of the plantlets formed on runners during the summer. Only the best plants should be used for propagation, and only from 4 to 6 runners from each should be pegged down. June and July are the best months for pegging down. By the end of August the runners should be well rooted, and they can then be severed from the parent plant. Some of the perpetual flowering strawberries do not make runners freely and must be increased by division at planting time. Alpine strawberries, which have small fruits produced over a long season, are raised from seed sown in a warm greenhouse in February or in a frame in March or April, the seedlings being planted out after a few weeks of hardening-off in a frame.

STRAWBERRY TREE, *see* Arbutus.

STREAK. This is a common trouble with sweet peas, and particularly with plants that are grown on the cordon system. The name aptly describes the appearance of the disease, which reveals itself as dark, depressed streaks and stripes on the stems and foliage. It appears to be mainly physiological in character, and it is certainly encouraged by poor drainage, a cold subsoil, excessive rainfall and over-feeding. There can be no doubt that the trench system of cultivation is responsible for much streak, as in heavy soil, water tends to collect in the bottom of the prepared trench, and in consequence roots of the sweet peas get into an unhealthy condition. No cure is known for streak, and affected plants should be removed and burned.

STRELITZIA *strel-**its**-ee-a* (Bird of Paradise Flower). The strelitzias, all natives of South Africa, are among the most striking plants for the warm greenhouse, where their large and colourful 'Bird of Paradise' flowers are sure to bring visitors to a stand-still in spring. *S. reginae*, with brilliant orange and purple flowers on stems up to 3 ft. high, is the one usually grown.
Culture: The plants should be potted up in spring or autumn in 7 in. pots of rich, peaty soil, with some small lumps of stone to keep it open, and during the summer they should be kept in full sun and given plenty of water. Less water is needed in winter, when the plants should be kept in a temperature not less than 50°. Better results are perhaps obtained by planting in a bed, but even in pots the plants flower profusely.
Propagation: Most easily effected by division of the rhizomes, but seeds (which set only after hand pollination) will germinate in a temperature of about 70°.

STREPTOCARPUS *strep-to-**kar**-pus* (Cape Prim-rose). Tender herbaceous perennials. There are a number of species of streptocarpus, some such as *S. dunnii* and *S. wendlandii*, being very handsome plants, but by far the most useful for greenhouse cultivation are the hybrids, of which seed is offered by every seedsman, usually in a range of colours including red, pink, purple, blue and white. The flowers are trumpet-shaped, and freely produced in clusters on stems usually about 18 in. high in the hybrids and are very decorative.
Culture: Seeds should be sown in January or February to give flowers in the autumn, or in July to give flowers early the following summer. The seed is small and should be germinated in a temperature of

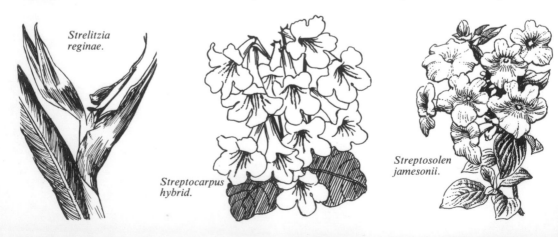

Strelitzia reginae.

Streptocarpus hybrid.

Streptosolen jamesonii.

65°. Seedlings are potted first into 3 in., later into 4 in., and finally into 5 in. or 6 in. pots for flowering, the ordinary John Innes potting compost being used throughout. Water should be given freely throughout this period and the plants fed with weak liquid manure as soon as the final pots are comfortably filled with roots. The plants should be shaded from May onwards and should be syringed frequently during this period to maintain a moist atmosphere. Throughout the summer a temperature of 60° to 70° should be maintained. After flowering, the plants can either be discarded or they may be overwintered, if kept rather dry in the greenhouse in a temperature of about 50° to 55°.

Propagation: Plants can also be grown from mature leaves removed in summer and the leaf stalk pressed on to the surface of a compost of sand and peat in a close frame with bottom heat. This method of propagation is often used for the species, or for specially selected forms.

STREPTOSOLEN *strep-toe-so-len.* Tender ever-green shrub with orange flowers in June. The only species cultivated, *S. jamesonii*, is a handsome climber with bright orange flowers in June and July. It makes a good pot plant in a 6 in. or 7 in. pot, or can be planted directly in the greenhouse.

Culture: Pot February to April in well-drained pots in John Innes potting compost or plant in a bed of good loamy soil. Place pots close to glass in light, sunny greenhouse. The plants will require plenty of water during spring and summer, but throughout the autumn and winter only sufficient water should be given to keep the soil just moist. No artificial heat should be needed during the summer months, but the winter temperature should not fall below 50°. Plants can be trained up bamboo canes or wires fixed to rafters of the greenhouse. Prune shoots fairly hard back after flowering. Apply weak liquid food occasionally during the summer.

Propagation: By cuttings inserted in light, sandy soil in a propagating frame, temperature 60° to 65°, spring or summer.

STROMANTHE, *see* Maranta.

SUCCULENT. The plants known as succulents possess fleshy leaves or stems, or both, which are specially adapted to store water and prevent the loss of moisture through transpiration. They are mostly natives of hot countries with a long, dry season and a shorter one of sun and heavy rain. During the latter period the plants make most of their growth and flower but also take up sufficient water to last them through the dry season, which is largely a resting period. The cacti, mostly characterised by spines, are perhaps the best known of the succulents, but there are many others from many plant families, including some of great beauty or curious form.

Removing rose suckers.

Streptocarpus propagation: (left) Rooted leaf cutting; (centre) Young plant potted up; (right) Mature leaf suitable for cutting.

SUCKER. The gardener uses this term to describe any shoot that grows directly from the roots. Suckers are not necessarily harmful; indeed in some cases they are definitely beneficial. For example, it is the young sucker roots from chrysanthemum stools that make the best cuttings, while suckers provide a ready means of propagating raspberries and many shrubs. When the sucker does become a danger is in the case of all grafted or budded plants, e.g. apples, pears, plums, roses, etc. As the suckers come from the rootstock and not from the scion grafted or budded on it they will resemble the rootstock in character, and not the cultivated variety of fruit or rose. If allowed to remain, these suckers will gradually take more and more nourishment from the trees or bushes on which they are growing and may in time entirely starve them out. Choice varieties of lilacs and rhododendrons are also grafted on to suitable stocks, and with these, too, sucker growths may be a source of danger. Whenever plants are known to be grafted or budded a careful watch should be maintained for suckers and if any are noted they must be removed at once. It is useless to cut the sucker off at ground level. It must be traced right back to its source, and then be removed cleanly without leaving any stub from which more and stronger shoots might be produced.

SULPHATE OF AMMONIA. A quick-acting nitrogenous fertiliser useful to encourage rapid growth. It is the principal source of nitrogen in compound fertilisers and may also be used alone as a top-dressing in spring or summer at $\frac{1}{2}$ oz. to 1 oz. per sq. yd., or as a liquid feed dissolved in water at $\frac{1}{4}$ oz. to $\frac{1}{2}$ oz. per gal. In excess, sulphate of ammonia can cause severe scorching, a characteristic made use of in lawn sand which is made by mixing 3 parts by weight sulphate of ammonia, 1 part sulphate of iron and 20 parts fine silver sand and applying to lawns in spring or summer at 4 oz. per sq. yd. The mixture lies on the flat leaves of dandelions, plantains and other weeds, so killing them, but only does superficial damage to the narrower, more erect leaves of grass, which soon recover and grow up the more strongly.

SULPHATE OF COPPER. A chemical known also as Bluestone. It is a powerful fungicide, with strong caustic properties. A wash prepared by dissolving 1 oz. of sulphate of copper in each gallon of water will destroy the winter spores of many fungal diseases, but on no account must it be used on plants that are still in leaf, as it would scorch their foliage badly. For spring and summer use, the acidity of sulphate of copper is neutralised by mixing it with lime or soda, thus producing the fungicides known as Bordeaux Mixture and Burgundy Mixture.

SULPHATE OF IRON. Used as a fertiliser for plants requiring extra iron, for which purpose it is most effectively applied as a foliage spray. A solution is prepared by dissolving 1 oz. to 2 oz. sulphate of iron in each gallon of water. Stronger solutions, up to 4 oz. per gallon, are also used as soil fungicides to treat fairy ring and various root rots, including that caused by the honey fungus (armillaria).

SULPHATE OF MAGNESIUM (Epsom Salts). Used to supply magnesium to plants which are deficient of this plant food, a condition indicated by yellowing of the foliage. For this purpose it may be applied to most plants at 1 oz. per sq. yd. or in solution at $\frac{1}{4}$ oz. per gal. either to the soil or as a foliage spray. For solanums, which are particularly prone to magnesium deficiency, $\frac{3}{4}$ oz. of Epsom salts should be

Magnesium deficiency in tomato.

incorporated into each bushel of the potting compost. Where tomatoes are affected Epsom salts may be dug into the soil before planting at the rate of 2 oz. to 4 oz. per sq. yd. or at a later stage it may be applied as a foliage spray, 1 lb. to 10 gal. of water plus a suitable spreader.

SULPHATE OF POTASH. A soluble chemical fertiliser which is rich in potash. It is a useful ingredient of compound fertilisers. and can also be used by itself to check excessive vigour due to an over-abundance of nitrogen and to improve fruitfulness and flavour. For this purpose solutions of $\frac{1}{4}$ oz. to $\frac{1}{2}$ oz. per gal. are employed and may be used every week or 10 days until the trouble is cured. As a dry fertiliser it may be used at rates up to 1 oz. per sq. yd. at practically any time of the year.

SULPHUR. This is a powerful fungicide available in various forms. Flowers of sulphur or the less unsightly green sulphur may be dusted on the foliage and stems of plants attacked by mildews and other fungal diseases, while liver of sulphur (potassium sulphide) is prepared as a spray by dissolving it in water, the usual strength being 1 oz. in 5 gal. Lime sulphur is a powerful fungicide principally used on fruit-trees. It can be purchased in concentrated form ready for mixing with water according to the manufacturers' instructions. Colloidal sulphur is also applied as a spray after dilution with water and can be used on most plants with safety. Dispersible sulphur

Lifting swedes.

Summer pruning
cordon apple.

Potash scorch.

is mixed with water and applied as a spray but as it does not actually dissolve in the water it must be constantly agitated or it will settle to the bottom of the spraying machine. If vapourised by heat ordinary yellow sulphur makes a very effective fumigant against mildew and red-spider mites, but it must not be allowed to ignite as burning sulphur is very injurious to plants as well as to pests and fungi. It may, however, be burnt to good effect in empty greenhouses.

SULPHUR, COLLOIDAL, *see* Colloidal Sulphur.

SUMACH, *see* Rhus.

SUMMER CHAFER, *see* Chafer Beetles.

SUMMER CYPRESS, *see* Kochia.

SUMMER PRUNING. Many fruit-trees, and in particular those that are grown in restricted forms, such as cordons, espaliers or fans, are pruned in summer as well as winter. The principal object of this is to prevent an excessive amount of growth and to concentrate sap upon the formation of fruiting buds. The work is usually spread over a period from early July until the middle of August, so that the trees do not suffer too severe a defoliation all at once. In general, summer pruning consists of the removal of two-thirds or more of each young side shoot to divert sap to the basal buds, but a specialised form of summer pruning, known as disbudding, is applied to Morello cherries, peaches, nectarines and vines.

Further particulars will be found under the fruits in question. A system of summer pruning is also applied to well-established wisterias. The laterals are shortened 5 or 6 leaves in July and are further cut back in winter.

SUMMER SNOWDROP, *see* Leucojum.

SUN DROPS, *see* Oenothera.

SUNFLOWER, *see* Helianthus.

SUN ROSE, *see* Helianthemum.

SUPERPHOSPHATE OF LIME. A quick-acting phosphatic fertiliser. Average dressings vary from 1 oz. to 3 oz. per sq. yd., according to the plants upon which it is used. As it is a very soluble fertiliser, it is most economical to apply it in the spring or early summer. It is the usual source of phosphates in compound fertilisers.

SWAMP CYPRUS, *see* Taxodium.

SWEDE. This root crop is grown in exactly the same way as turnip and is useful because of its hardiness and good storage qualities. Sowings are usually made in May and June in good soil in shallow drills 15 in. to 18 in. apart, seedlings being thinned to 6 in. or 8 in. As swedes are quite hardy they may be left in the ground in winter and be lifted as required, but it is convenient to lift part of the crop in early November and store in sand or dry soil in a shed for use when the weather makes outdoor lifting difficult.

SWEET BAY, *see* Laurus.

SWEET CORN. The partly ripened cobs are cooked and eaten as a vegetable. Sow seeds singly ⅛ in. deep in light soil in well-drained pots in temperature of 55° to 60° in April. Harden off and plant outdoors in June in good, well-manured soil and sunny situation, spacing plants 15 in. apart in rows 3 ft. apart but making short rows to produce blocks of plants rather than long single rows, as in blocks the female flowers which produce the cobs are more effectively fertilised by pollen from the flowers or 'tassels'. Alternatively, sow seeds 2 or 3 together at similar spacing outdoors in early May where plants are to mature, thinning seedlings to one at each station. Water freely in dry weather. Gather cobs when the seeds emit a milky juice if punctured with the finger nail or the point of a knife.

SWEET GUM, *see* Liquidambar.

SWEET PEA, *see* Lathyrus.

SWEET ROCKET, *see* Hesperis.

SWEET-SCENTED TOBACCO, *see* Nicotiana.

SWEET SULTAN, *see* Centaurea.

SWEET WILLIAM, *see* Dianthus.

SWISS CHEESE PLANT, *see* Monstera.

SWORD LILY, *see* Gladiolus.

SYCAMORE, *see* Acer.

SYMPHORICARPOS *sim-for-ee-*kar-*pos* (Snowberry; Coral Berry). Hardy deciduous shrubs with pink or white flowers, which are much sought after by bees. Berries white or purple in autumn. Suitable for sunny or shady shrubberies, copses, or woodlands. The species commonly grown are *S. albus*, white berries, 6 ft. to 8 ft. and *S. orbiculatus*, known as the Coral Berry because it has rose-purple berries, grows up to 7 ft.
Culture: Plant October to March in ordinary soil. Prune October to February, simply thinning out old or decayed wood.
Propagation: By cuttings of firm wood inserted in ordinary soil in shady position outdoors, October to February; suckers removed and planted October to February; seed sown in a greenhouse or frame in March.

SYNGONIUM *sin-go-ne-um* (Goosefoot Plant). Climbing shrubs from tropical America. Their main ornamental feature is the divided leaves, often shaped like an arrow-head, and although stove-house plants they are occasionally grown as foliage house plants. The two species most commonly grown are *S. vellozianum*, with green leaves, and *S. podophyllum*, with silvery markings.
Culture: Easily grown provided they are given ample warmth and a moist atmosphere, together with moderate watering and light shade. Pot in March in a compost 4 parts loam, 3 parts leaf-mould, 2 parts sharp sand and 1½ parts rotted manure. Train stems up pieces of cork bark and keep this moist.
Propagation: Syngoniums produce aerial roots, which if removed with a leafy length of stem provide a ready means of propagation.

SYRINGA *ser-*ing-*a* (Lilac). Hardy deciduous flowering shrubs or small trees with lilac, purple or white flowers in May or June. Suitable for sunny borders or shrubberies. Most of the lilacs grown in gardens are varieties of *S. vulgaris*, which will grow to 15 ft. There are both single and double flowered varieties of this. Attractive species include *S. chinensis*, 10 ft., lilac or purplish red; *S. josikaea*, 12 ft., lilac; *S. reflexa*, 12 ft., pink; and *S. villosa*, 10 ft., lilac-pink. Graceful hybrids between the last two species are known as Preston Hybrids or *S. prestoniae*.
Culture: Plant October to March in good, well-dug soil. Allow no suckers to grow from roots. No other regular pruning required but it helps to remove faded flower trusses and so prevent seed forming.
Propagation: By suckers removed and planted from October to February; layering shoots in spring; choice varieties by budding on common species in July, or by grafting on common species in March or April; species by seed sown in a greenhouse or frame in spring. It should be noted that suckers removed from grafted or budded lilacs will take after the rootstock which will probably be common lilac.

SYRINGE. The syringe is an essential item of equipment for greenhouse work. Among its uses are the spraying of insecticides, the syringing of plants and stagings to create a moist atmosphere, and the watering of tiny seedlings. There are two main types of syringe. One is the single-action type, which has to

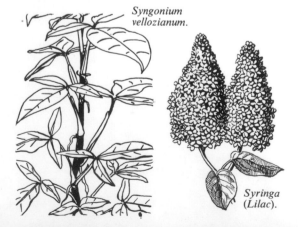

Syngonium vellozianum.

Syringa (Lilac).

Symphoricarpos (Snowberry).   *Syringa prestoniae hybrid.*   *Syringing.*

be refilled each time the solution is ejected, and the other is the double-action type, which is usually connected to a bucket of the solution by means of a light hose and which keeps up a continuous spray by means of a series of ball-valves. For large scale work the latter type effects a great economy in time and labour. On a good syringe the metal parts should be made of brass, and the single-action ones should be fitted with a drip-sleeve which serves to protect the barrel from knocks and the user from drips. The syringe should also have two or three different nozzles or roses so that the density of the spray can be varied from a mist to a coarse spray, and for use with insecticides there should also be a bend to which the nozzles are fitted. This enables the under-sides of leaves to be reached easily. After using the syringe with insecticides or other solutions it should be washed out thoroughly, and when not in use it should be stored out of the sun, which may otherwise have an injurious effect on the rubber or leather plunger.

TAGETES *tag-ee-tees* (African Marigold; French Marigold).   Half-hardy annuals with yellow or orange flowers sometimes marked with maroon, in summer. The African Marigolds are derived from *T. erecta*, a rather stiffly erect plant about 3 ft. high. The French Marigolds are derived from *T. patula*, a more branching plant about 18 in. tall. *T. signata* is a pretty species, 9 in. to 12 in. high with small orange flowers. Both African and French varieties are suitable for beds or border planting. The numerous dwarf kinds make good edgings.
Culture: Sow in March in light soil in temperature

Sweet Corn.

Tagetes (French Marigold).

of 60° to 65°. Prick off 3 in. apart each way in boxes and harden off gradually in preparation for planting in late May or early June in ordinary soil, in a sunny, open position. For good quality flowers of the African kinds for exhibition, allow only four shoots to form on each plant and restrict each to a single flower. Water freely in dry weather.

TAIL FLOWER, *see* Anthurium.

TAMARISK, *see* Tamarix.

TAMARIX tam-*a-riks* (Tamarisk). Hardy ever-green and deciduous shrubs with pink flowers in spring or summer and feathery foliage. Suitable for shrubberies and hedges, particularly in seaside gar-dens. The most showy species is *T. pentandra* which flowers in August. *T. tetrandra* flowers in May. Both will reach a height of 12 ft.
Culture: Plant October to March in ordinary or sandy soil. Prune *T. pentandra* hard back in March, *T. tetrandra* as soon as it has finished flowering in May or early June.
Propagation: By cuttings of shoots 4 in. to 6 in. long inserted in sandy soil outdoors or in a frame September to October.

TAR OIL. Principally used as a winter spray for fruit trees to destroy the eggs of aphides, apple sucker and some caterpillars. It also kills lichen and moss on the bark. Tar-oil must be used while trees are dor-mant in winter as it will damage shoots and opening buds.

TARRAGON, *see* Artemisia.

TAXODIUM taks-*o-de-um* (Swamp Cypress). Hardy deciduous cone-bearing trees. The only species commonly grown, *T. distichum*, makes a handsome conical tree 80 ft. to 100 ft. high with feathery foliage which colours well before it falls in autumn.
Culture: Plant November to April in good, rather moist, loamy soil and open situation. Though it will grow far removed from water its natural habitat is in

swamps and it can be planted where its roots will be constantly covered by a few inches of water.
Propagation: By seed sown in a greenhouse or frame in spring.

TAXUS taks-*us* (Yew). Hardy evergreen trees with ornamental foliage. By far the most popular species is the English Yew, *T. baccata*, and its variety *stricta*, the Irish Yew. Leaves poisonous to cattle. Common kinds suitable for sunny or shady shrubberies; variegated and Irish yews also as isolated specimens. English and Irish yews are also suitable for hedges.
Culture: Plant October to April in good, deep soil. Distance for planting for hedge-making, 12 in. for small, young stock; 18 in. to 3 ft. for larger, well-developed plants. Prune, trim or clip in April or September.
Propagation: By seeds sown 1 in. deep in light soil outdoors in March, or $\frac{1}{4}$ in. deep in pans or boxes of light soil, in a cold frame or greenhouse in March; by cuttings of firm young growths inserted in sandy soil in a propagating frame in July or August.

TEA PLANT, *see* Camellia.

TECOMA, *see* Campsis.

TEMPERATURE. The maintaining of an appro-priate temperature is one of the first essentials of greenhouse work, and although in practice consider-able latitude has to be allowed the aim should be to keep the temperature as near as possible to that required by the plants. This may be done by means of artificial heat, and by shading, damping down and correct use of the ventilators. As far as possible only those plants requiring a similar temperature should be grown in any one house.

TENDER. This term is usually applied to those plants which will not stand the winter in the open. Such plants normally need the protection of a heated glasshouse in winter, but in some cases, as with many alpine plants, protection from damp, rather than cold is the important factor.

TETRACHLORETHANE. This fumigant may be used to control greenhouse white-fly, but although harmless to tomatoes it is very injurious to chrysanthe-mums, cinerarias, pelargoniums and other plants. It has largely been replaced by more modern insecticides, but if used the makers' instructions should be very carefully followed.

THALICTRUM thal-*ik-trum* (Meadow Rue). Hardy herbaceous perennials, with finely divided green leaves and yellow or purplish flowers in sum-mer. Tall species adapted for sunny borders; sunny rock gardens for dwarf species. The most popular kinds include *T. aquilegifolium*, 3 ft., purple; *T.*

Tamarix tetrandra.

Thalictrum (Meadow Rue).

Thinning brassica seedlings.

Taxodium distichum.

Thinning peaches.

dipterocarpum, 5 ft., lilac and yellow; *T. glaucum*, 4 ft., yellow; and *T. minus*, 18 in., greenish-yellow.
Culture: Plant October to March in deep, well-dug soil with plenty of leaf-mould or other humus-forming material. Lift, divide and re-plant when really necessary.

Propagation: By division of roots in March or April.

THERMOMETER. For the measurement and consequent maintenance of correct temperature in the greenhouse a thermometer is absolutely essential. In this country those calibrated on the Fahrenheit scale, with freezing points of water 32°, and boiling point at 212°, are mostly used, and where temperatures are quoted they nearly always refer to this scale, but the Centigrade scale with freezing point of water at 0° and boiling at 100° is now coming into more general use in Britain. Thermometers are available in several forms, and probably the most useful of these is the type which registers minimum and maximum temperature by means of a small needle which remains in position when the mercury recedes. For soil sterilising a soil thermometer is very useful.

THERMOSTAT. A device for regulating temperatures by automatically cutting off the source of artificial heat as soon as a pre-set temperature is reached and turning it on again as soon as the temperature drops below this level. It is mostly used in conjunction with electrical heating, but thermostats can also be used to regulate automatic ventilating equipment.

THINNING. The term is used to denote the operation of removing superfluous seedlings in order that those remaining may have sufficient room to grow. It is an operation which should be undertaken just as soon as the young plants are large enough to handle, and it is best spread over a period of about a fortnight. There is then less root disturbance, and the possibility of further mortality after the first thinning can be allowed for. When thinning seedlings care should be taken not to disturb unduly, adjacent seedlings, and it may be necessary to firm these in after the surplus seedlings have been removed.

The thinning of fruit is done not only to relieve overladen trees of the tax of bearing over-heavy crops, but to increase the size and quality of the remaining specimens. First of all misshapen, awkwardly placed, or injured fruits are removed. The clusters are then reduced to 1, or at most 2 fruits apiece. The final thinning should leave each specimen ample room to develop to its fullest size. Final thinning should always be delayed until after the stoning or seed-forming period, as many fruits drop naturally at that time.

Thymus nitidus.

Thrips on carnation.

Tiarella cordifolia.

THORN, *see* Crataegus.

THREE QUARTER SPAN. Where a greenhouse is to be built on to a wall not high enough to take a lean-to structure a three-quarter span house will often solve the difficulty. In this type of greenhouse the rear part of the roof rises direct from the wall at a similar angle to that used in the normal span roof, but it extends upwards for only a short distance, usually about half of that attained by the side of a span-roof house. At this point it is joined by the front side which may be constructed in exactly the same way as that of the span-roof. The advantages of this type of house are that it gives more headroom than a lean-to and requires less heating than a full span.

THRIFT, *see* Armeria.

THRIPS. Small but very active pests which do much damage to a great variety of plants. The fully-grown thrip is only about ¼ in. in length, yellow to black in colour, and very narrow. It runs very rapidly when disturbed and so is extremely difficult to locate. Leaves and stems, and, in the case of peas, the flower buds as well, will develop silvery streaks and patches, and in time become dwarf or distorted. The most effective remedy is to spray with a DDT, BHC or nicotine insecticide. Under glass, fumigation with DDT or BHC may be carried out.

THUJA thu-*ya* (Arbor-vitae). Evergreen coniferous trees suitable for planting as isolated specimens and also for forming hedges and screens. The two best kinds are *T. plicata*, dark green, and *T. occidentalis*, lighter green. Both have numerous varieties including some with variegated leaves.
Culture: Plant October to April in ordinary soil and open positions. For hedgemaking space 2 ft. apart and trim annually in late summer. For screens plant 5 ft. to 10 ft. apart.
Propagation: By seed sown in a frame or greenhouse in March; selected varieties by cuttings in a frame in September.

THUNBERGIA *thun-***ber**-*gee-a*. Tender evergreen flowering shrubs and perennials, mostly of climbing habit. The most popular is *T. alata*, a species with numerous varieties varying in colour from white to orange, often with a deep purple, almost black zone in the middle. Where a good deal of heat is available the spectacular blue-flowered *T. grandiflora* can be grown.
Culture: Seed should be sown in March, in a temperature of at least 65°. Seedlings are potted individually in ordinary John Innes potting compost, first into 3 in. and later into 5 in. pots, or hanging baskets for flowering. Throughout, a temperature of at least 55° should be maintained and plants will appreciate

more than this. They should be watered freely throughout the spring and summer. If grown in pots the plants should be given canes or other suitable supports up which to twine. May also be planted outdoors in June against sunny walls, in window-boxes or vases. Water freely.

THYME, *see* Thymus.

THYMUS tie-*mus* (Thyme). Hardy aromatic shrubby perennials. Suitable for sunny, warm borders, or sunny rock gardens. Excellent plants for carpeting bare soil over spring bulbs. Among the best kinds are *T. serpyllum*, completely prostrate, pink, carmine or white; its variety *citriodorus*, the Lemon-scented Thyme; and *T. nitidus*, an 18 in. high bush, pink. The common thyme used as a herb is *T. vulgaris*, 8 in. to 12 in. high.
Culture: Plant October or March in ordinary soil and sunny, open position. Prune bushy kinds in spring to counteract straggling. Shoots of common thyme required for seasoning should be gathered as soon as blossoms appear in summer, tied in small bundles and hung head downwards in a cool, airy place to dry.
Propagation: By seeds sown ⅛ in. deep in sandy soil in April; by division in March or April, each portion being furnished with a few roots; gold and silver kinds by cuttings in a cold frame in summer.

TIARELLA *tie-ar-***ell-***a* (False Mitrewort; Foam Flower). Hardy perennial herb with small white flowers in summer. Suitable for cool shady beds or rock gardens. The species commonly grown, *T. cordifolia*, is 12 in. high.
Culture: Plant March or April in ordinary soil. Water well in dry weather.
Propagation: By division of roots in March or April.

TICKSEED, *see* Coreopsis.

TIFFANY. A fine, silky gauze, sometimes used in greenhouses to provide light shade.

TIGER FLOWER, *see* Tigridia.

TIGRIDIA *tie-***grid-***ee-a* (Tiger Flower). Nearly hardy bulbs suitable for unheated greenhouses or sunny, sheltered places outdoors. The showy, three-petalled flowers appear in summer and each lasts only one day, although each plant produces several flowers successively. The species commonly grown, *T. pavonia*, is 2 ft. high.
Outdoor Culture: Plant in April in sunny border and good, well-drained soil. Place bulbs 3 in. deep. Water freely in dry weather. Lift bulbs in October and store in cool, dry, airy, frost-proof place until following spring.
Pot Culture: Pot bulbs, several in 5 in. pot in March or April in John Innes potting compost. Place in a cold frame or under stage in a greenhouse until growth begins, then remove to greenhouse staging. Water moderately after growth begins; freely when well advanced. No shading is required. After flowering, gradually withhold water until foliage turns yellow, then keep quite dry until potting time the following spring.
Propagation: By offsets removed and treated as advised for old bulbs in April.

TOAD-FLAX, *see* Linaria.

TOAD FLOWER, *see* Stapelia.

TOBACCO PLANT, *see* Nicotiana.

TOLMIEA tol-*me-a*. The solitary species, *T. menziesii*, is actually a hardy perennial but it is occasionally grown as a pot plant. It bears some resemblance to heuchera, although its long spikes of green flowers are not so showy, but it is more often grown for the novelty of its peculiar method of self-propagation than for its decorative effect. It produces tiny plantlets at the base of the leaf-blade and these may easily be removed and potted up.
Culture: Tolmiea thrives in any reasonably good soil with plenty of humus and does best in light shade. Water freely in spring and summer, moderately in autumn and winter. No artificial heat is required.
Propagation: By removal of the plantlets as already described. This is best done in spring.

Thunbergia alata.

Tigridia pavonia.

Tolmiea menziesii.

239

TOMATO. May be grown under glass or outdoors in sheltered, sunny places. There are a great many varieties some of which, such as Sunrise, Harbinger, Essex Wonder and Earliest of All, are specially suitable for outdoor cultivation. Most tomatoes are restricted to a single stem but the so-called 'bush' varieties are allowed to grow naturally without removal of side shoots and they then produce quite low, freely-branched plants which need little or no support. They, too, are popular for outdoor cultivation. One of the most popular bush tomatoes is Amateur.

Cultivation Under Glass: Sow in January, February or March, in temperature of 60° to 65°. Prick off seedlings 2 in. apart as soon as possible into boxes filled with John Innes potting compost and pot individually in similar compost and 3 in. pots as soon as leaves touch in boxes. Pot on into 9 in. pots or boxes filled with John Innes No. 2 potting compost, or plant in good, loamy soil. Alternatively plant in beds of good, loamy soil, spacing the plants 18 in. apart in rows 3 ft. apart. Restrict each plant to a single stem by removing all side shoots as they appear. Tie this main stem to a cane or support by soft string secured to rafters of the greenhouse or to wire strained below the rafters. Pinch out the growing point of each plant when it reaches the glass. Water moderately at first, freely as plants become established and grow quickly. Feed once a week with fertiliser (liquid or dry) from the time first fruits are set. Maintain minimum temperature of 55° throughout, rising to 75° or more with sun heat.

Outdoor Cultivation: Sow in late March or early April as for indoor cultivation and treat seedlings in the same way, but remove to a frame in early May and harden off for planting outdoors at end of May or early June. Plant 18 in. apart in rows 2½ ft. apart in good, loamy soil and sunny, sheltered position. Restrict each plant to a single stem and tie this to a stout cane or stake. Pinch out the growing tip of each plant when four flower trusses have been produced. Pick fruits as soon as they commence to colour and complete ripening indoors. Water freely in dry weather. Spray plants in July, August and September with Bordeaux mixture to prevent attacks of potato blight disease.

Ring Culture: This may be practised under glass or outdoors. Treatment to final potting or planting as already described, but plants are then placed in special bottomless rings filled with John Innes No. 2 potting compost and standing on a 4 in. deep layer of gravel or old, sifted cinders. After the first few weeks water is applied freely to the gravel or cinders only and liquid feed is applied once a week to the soil in the rings. Plants are trained and stopped in the ordinary way. (*See* also Ring Culture).

TOP-DRESSING. To maintain soil fertility around established plants, fertilisers or other materials such as good soil, compost or humus, may be applied to the surface of the soil. This is known as top-dressing, or, where bulky materials are used, as mulching. In both cases the materials should only be applied when the soil is moist, as otherwise there is a tendency for artificial fertilisers to burn the roots and for the more bulky materials to prevent water from penetrating the soil. Where artificial fertilisers are used for pot-plants these should be applied carefully, without getting them on the foliage, and watered in straight away. Soil compost and humus are mostly used on those plants which form surface roots, such as chrysanthemums, tomatoes and stem-rooting lilies, but they may also be applied to plants which remain in pots for a very long time. In this case the old surface soil should be scraped away before applying the top-dressing.

TOPIARY *top*-ie-a-ree. The art of clipping evergreen shrubs into formal shapes and the semblance of animals, birds and other objects. Topiary specimens are especially useful in small formal or paved gardens for courtyards. Yew, because of its comparatively slow growth, has always been a favourite shrub for this purpose; box is also suitable, and bay-trees are frequently employed. Sometimes frames of wire or cane are used as an aid to obtain the shape required, but often the specimens are formed exclusively by repeated clipping and shaping.

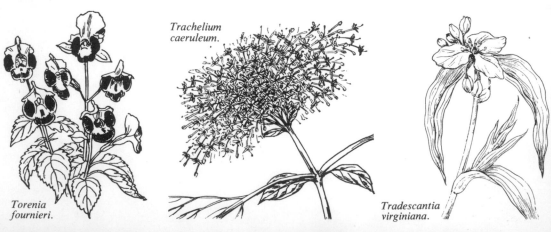

Torenia fournieri.

Trachelium caeruleum.

Tradescantia virginiana.

TORCH LILY, *see* Kniphofia.

TORCH THISTLE, *see* Cereus.

TORENIA *tor-ree-ne-a.* These are greenhouse annuals. The flowers are produced very freely in summer and are blue with yellow blotches in the popular variety, *T. fournieri.*
Culture: They are readily grown from seed sown in late February or early March, in a temperature of 60° to 65°. The seedlings are potted on into 3 in. and later into 5 in. or 6 in. pots, in John Innes No. 1 potting compost which may contain a little extra peat, and after early May should require no artificial heat. Alternatively they may be planted in hanging baskets for which they are well adapted because of their semi-pendant habit.

TOUCH-ME-NOT, *see* Impatiens.

TRACHELIUM *trak-eel-ee-um.* *T. caeruleum* is a very pretty plant usually grown in the greenhouse as an annual. The small blue flowers are produced in close heads on 18 in. stems during June and July.
Culture: Seed is sown in a temperature of 60° to 65° in February or early March. The seedlings are potted on first into 3 in. pots and later into 4 in. or 5 in. pots, in John Innes No. 1 potting compost, and when they reach their final pots, should be staked carefully with small canes or bushy twigs as the growth is rather fragile. The plants succeed best in a sunny greenhouse with plenty of ventilation and no artificial heat after about the beginning of May. They should be watered freely throughout. After flowering the plants are discarded.

TRADESCANTIA *trad-es-kan-tee-a* (Spider-wort; Wandering Jew). Hardy herbaceous and tender perennials. The most popular hardy kind, *T. virginiana,* has showy, three-petalled blue or purple flowers in summer and is suitable for partially shady or sunny beds or borders. Perhaps the most popular indoor plant of all is *T. fluminensis,* the Wandering Jew, usually sold in white, cream or pink-variegated forms. *T. blossfeldiana* and *T. purpurea* have bigger leaves. All are suitable for draping the edge of staging in a greenhouse. Tradescantias are often confused with *Zebrina pendula,* which has larger, more regularly marked leaves, and with Setcreasea, all species of which have similar angular trailing stems.
Culture of Hardy Species: Plant autumn or spring in ordinary soil. Lift, divide and replant every 3 or 4 years.
Culture of Greenhouse Species: Pot March or April in well-drained pots in John Innes potting compost and place in sunny or shady greenhouse. Water freely March to September, moderately at other times. Maintain as moist an atmosphere as possible in rooms, as in dry air the lower leaves tend to shrivel.

Feeding greenhouse tomatoes.

Removing side shoots from tomatoes.

Tradescantia fluminensis.

241

Temperatures: March to September, up to 75°; September to March, 50° to 60°. Variegated forms should be given a stronger feed than the green ones, as otherwise there is a tendency for them to lose their colour. If plain-leaved shoots appear on a variegated specimen they should be removed from the point of origin.

Propagation: Hardy species by division in spring; tender species by cuttings of the tips of the shoots, about 3 in. long, root readily at almost any time. Five cuttings placed around the edge of a 3½ in. pot will make a good specimen in a very short time.

TRANSVAAL DAISY, *see* Gerbera.

TRAVELLER'S JOY, *see* Clematis.

TREASURE FLOWER, *see* Gazania.

TREE MALLOW, *see* Hibiscus.

TREE PRIMROSE, *see* Oenothera.

TRENCHING. A method of digging ground deeply. First, a trench is opened at one end of the plot and the soil is wheeled to one side, or to the far end of the plot. This first trench should be 1 ft. deep and at least 3 ft. wide. Now a second trench is opened in the bottom of the first trench this also is 1 ft. deep but only half the width of the first trench. The soil is also removed to one side or to the further end of the plot. The subsoil in the bottom of the deep, narrow trench is broken up thoroughly with a fork. The step of soil left in the first wide trench is then turned over on top of the broken subsoil, thus exposing another strip of subsoil, which in turn is broken up with a fork. Now a new surface trench, half the width of the first wide trench and 1 ft. in depth, is opened and the soil is turned over on top of the step of soil in the first trench. The second spit of soil is turned over on to the pulverised subsoil and the newly exposed subsoil is broken up with a fork. The work proceeds in a similar manner until the whole plot is completed. It is convenient to divide wide plots in half, longitudinally, trenching down one strip and back up the other.

Trenching.

TRICKLE IRRIGATION. A method of watering which involves the use of perforated pipes connected to the water supply and laid along the surface of the soil. The perforations are spaced out at an even distance apart so that the whole surface of the soil is wetted. Alternatively the pipe is fitted with adjustable nozzles which allow the water to drop through on to the soil at an appropriate rate. It is mostly used for plants growing in the actual soil of the greenhouse.

TRILLIUM trill-*ee-um* (Wood Lily; Wake Robin). Hardy tuberous-rooted perennials with attractive, lily-like leaves and showy three-petalled flowers in early spring. Among the most popular species are *T. grandiflorum*, 12 in. to 18 in., white to rose; *T. erectum*, 12 in., deep purple; and *T. sessile*, 12 in., purple or green.

Culture: Plant in March in peaty soil in shady borders or in woodlands. Top-dress annually in March with a layer of decayed leaves. Lift and replant only when absolutely necessary.

Propagation: By division of roots at planting time.

TRITONIA, *see* Montbretia.

TROLLIUS trol-*lee-us* (Globe Flower). Hardy herbaceous perennials with yellow or orange globe-shaped flowers in May or June. Suitable for shady borders or margins of ponds. Most of the varieties grown are derived either from *T. europaeus*, 2 ft. high, or from *T. ledebouri*, 3 ft.

Culture: Plant October to April in deep, moist soil of a loamy nature. Water freely in dry weather. Lift, divide and re-plant every 3 or 4 years.

Propagation: By division of roots October to April.

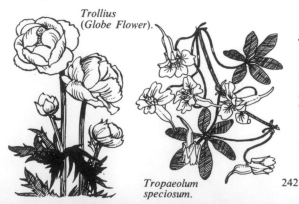

Trollius (Globe Flower).

Tropaeolum speciosum.

Trickle irrigation.

Trillium grandiflorum.

TROPAEOLUM *trop-ee-o-lum* (Nasturtium; Indian Cress; Flame Flower; Canary Creeper). Tender half-hardy or hardy perennials, dwarf or climbing in habit, several of which are commonly treated as annuals. Flowers horn-shaped, very showy, produced throughout the summer. The familiar annual nasturtiums are all derived from *T. majus*. There are both climbing and dwarf varieties. The Canary Creeper, *T. peregrinum*, is also an annual, a more slender climber with yellow flowers. Two of the finest hardy perennial kinds are *T. speciosum*, the Flame Flower, a climber with scarlet flowers, and *T. polyphyllum*, a trailing plant with yellow flowers.

Culture of Canary Creeper: Sow seeds ⅛ in. deep in light, sandy soil in temperature of 55° in March; harden off seedlings for planting outdoors in May; or sow ¼ in. deep outdoors in April where required to grow in ordinary soil against sunny or shady walls, fences, arbours, trellis, etc.; does well on a north aspect. Water freely in dry weather.

Culture of Nasturtium: Sow seed 1 in. deep in April where plants are required to grow in ordinary soil, climbing kinds against sunny or shady walls, fences, arbours, etc., dwarf kinds in sunny or shady borders or beds. Thin seedlings of climbers to 18 in., dwarf kinds to 6 in. or 9 in. apart.

Culture of Hardy Species: Plant *T. polyphyllum* August to November in well-drained soil on sunny bank or rock garden; *T. speciosum* October or March in good loamy soil against shaded wall or hedge facing north. Water freely in dry weather.

Propagation: Hardy species by seeds sown in light soil in a cold frame or greenhouse in April; division of roots at planting time.

TROUT LILY, *see* Erythronium.

TRUMPET CREEPER, *see* Campsis.

TUBER. A thickened, fleshy root or stem used by the plant as a food storage organ. There are many different types of tuber, ranging from the claw-like tubers of the turban ranunculus to the large, fleshy tubers of the dahlia. Tuberous means having the nature or qualities of a tuber.

TUBEROSE, *see* Polianthes.

TULIP, *see* Tulipa.

TULIPA tu-*lip-a* (Tulip). Hardy bulbous plants of which there are thousands of varieties, grouped by specialists into numerous classes. Most important of these are the Early Single, rather short and flowering in April; the Early Double, similar but with double flowers; the Mendels, taller and a little later flowering; and the May-flowering and Darwins, taller still and flowering in May. Parrot Tulips have curiously cockled or cut petals often splashed with several different colours. Culturally, all require identical treatment, including the many species, the smaller of which are suitable for rock gardens.

Any variety of tulip can also be grown in pots for greenhouse decoration in spring, but the most popular for this purpose are the early-flowering single and double varieties of the Mendel and the Triumph tulips which, with a little forcing, can be had in bloom during February and March. For earlier flowering the smaller Duc van Thol varieties are recommended.

Culture Out of Doors: Plant September to November, in sunny, well-drained beds or borders in moderately rich soil. Bulbs should be 4 in. deep and about 6 in. apart. Hoe surface soil as soon as growths show through. Bulbs in beds required for summer plants should be lifted directly after flowering and transferred to a reserve border until foliage is thoroughly ripened, when they may be lifted, dried, and stored in a cool place till planting time. All garden varieties are best lifted annually—when foliage dies down.

Culture in Pots: The bulbs should be potted or boxed in John Innes potting compost in August or September, and may be almost shoulder to shoulder. For at least 8 weeks after potting or boxing they should be placed outdoors in a cool but sheltered position, preferably under a covering of 3 in. to 4 in. of well-weathered ashes or sand. This is to enable them to make roots before they are hurried into growth, then successive batches can be brought into the greenhouse in a temperature which should not at first exceed 60°, but, once the flower buds are well formed, may rise for the last week or so to 70°. Water should be given freely at this stage. After flowering the bulbs can be stood outdoors again in a sheltered place and should be kept watered until the foliage turns yellow and dies down, the bulbs can then be moved from the soil and stored for replanting outdoors. They should not be used for forcing a second time.

Propagation: By natural increase of the bulbs separated when lifted.

TULIP TREE, *see* Liriodendron.

TURFING. Lawns can be made most rapidly by laying good turves on the surface of ground prepared by thorough cultivation and raking to a fine, crumbly surface. Turves should be cut from good, clean meadows. They may be in 1 ft. squares or in 3 ft. by 1 ft. rectangles and should be 2 in. thick. Autumn is the best season for turfing but it can be done at almost any time except during the summer. Lay turves in straight rows with joins between turves staggered in adjacent rows. Beat firmly on the surface of soil with back of spade or wooden turf beater. Brush sifted soil into crevices between turves. Water freely in dry weather until established. Roll moderately and cut as soon as grass commences to grow. For the first cutting set blades fairly high.

TURNIP. To be good, turnips must be grown quickly and without check in rich, well-worked soil. Sow successionally from March to July in shallow drills 12 in. to 15 in. apart and thin seedlings to 4 in. to 6 in. apart. Dust seedlings with DDT to kill turnip flea beetles. Feed occasionally with small top-dressings of a compound vegetable fertiliser. Keep well hoed. Pull for use as soon as of reasonable size. For winter use, turnips should be lifted in October and stored in sand or peat in a shed or cellar. Turnip tops for use as 'greens' in spring are produced by sowing a hardy variety in early September and leaving unthinned.

TURNIP FLEA BEETLE. A beetle about $\frac{1}{8}$ in. in length, dark in colour and able to jump a considerable distance when disturbed. It attacks seedlings of turnips, swedes, cabbages, etc., riddling them with holes and, if not checked, entirely destroying them. The beetle is most troublesome on light, sandy soil during dry weather, and one method of preventing an attack is to encourage seedlings to make really good vigorous growth by watering, hoeing, and the use of artificial fertilisers. Seedlings should also be dusted occasionally with DDT.

TURNIP GALL WEEVIL. A blackish weevil rarely exceeding $\frac{1}{8}$ in. in length. In summer it lays its eggs at the base of the stems of cabbages, turnips, etc., and in due course white, legless grubs appear and start to feed upon the roots, causing the formation of galls. If these are cut open, the maggots will be found within. The damage caused by this pest is often confused with that due to the club-root fungus. Good cultivation and the application of a quick-acting nitrogenous fertiliser such as Nitro-chalk prior to planting will help to reduce damage. Where gall weevil has been persistently troublesome plants should be dipped into DDT prior to planting.

TUTSAN, *see* Hypericum.

TYPHA tie-*fa* (Reed Mace). Hardy aquatic perennials, suitable for margins of shallow rivers or ponds.

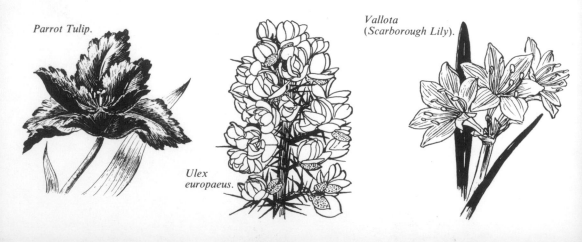

Parrot Tulip.

Ulex europaeus.

Vallota (Scarborough Lily).

Inflorescence brown and cigar-like, produced in summer. These plants are often wrongly referred to as Bulrushes. The common Reed Mace is *T. latifolia* but a better garden plant is *T. angustifolia*. Both are about 8 ft. high.

Culture: Plant April or May in ordinary soil in shallow water at the side of pools. Alternatively, plants may be potted in loamy soil and stood in water so that their crowns are 3 in. or 4 in. beneath the surface.

Propagation: By division at planting time.

U LEX you-*leks* (Furze; Gorse; Whin). Hardy evergreen shrubs. Suitable for sunny banks, rock gardens or woodlands. The species commonly grown, *U. europaeus*, is 4 ft. to 5 ft. high. The yellow flowers, double in variety, *flore pleno*, are produced mainly in spring.

Culture: Plant October to March in ordinary, well-drained soil and an open, sunny position. Pruning unnecessary, but overgrown plants can be cut back in May.

Hedge Culture: Plant 18 in. apart in single row. Trim in June after flowering.

Propagation: By seeds sown ¼ in. deep in light soil outdoors in April; double form by cuttings inserted in very sandy soil in a propagating frame during July or August.

UMBRELLA PLANT, *see* Cyperus.

URSINIA ur-**sin**-*ee-a*. Half-hardy annuals, with orange flowers throughout the summer. The garden varieties are mainly derived from *U. anethoides* which grows 12 in. to 18 in. tall.

Culture: Sow seeds February or March in light soil in temperature of 60° to 65°, and transplant seedlings 2 in. apart in shallow boxes; place in a cold frame in April, harden off, and plant outdoors in ordinary, well-drained soil in sunny beds or borders in May or June.

VALLOTA *val*-**lot**-*a* (Scarborough Lily). Greenhouse evergreen bulbous plants suitable for well-drained pots in light, sunny greenhouse or window. Though often called Scarborough Lily, *V. speciosa* is not a true lily; it has scarlet trumpet-shaped flowers, superficially rather like those of some lilies. The flowers are produced in late summer and early autumn, clustered on stout bare stems, and the leaves are strap-shaped.

Culture: Vallotas are very easily grown in a cool greenhouse and need no more than frost protection in winter. The best time for potting is in March and the ordinary John Innes potting compost can be used. Annual re-potting is not, as a rule, necessary as vallotas flower most freely when a little pot bound, but they should not be allowed to become starved and old plants may need quite big pots, up to 9 in. or 10 in.

Tulipa kaufmanniana (Waterlily tulip).

Ursinia anethoides.

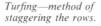

Turfing—method of staggering the rows.

in diameter. They have no complete resting season and should be watered moderately in autumn and winter, freely in spring and summer.

Propagation: They can be increased by division of the bulb clusters at potting time.

VARIEGATED. A term applied to any part of a flower which is irregularly blotched or marked, and to foliage which has white or yellow areas among the normal green. Many shrubs have variegated forms. For the most part they have originated as sports and have been perpetuated by propagating from grafts or cuttings. Most brilliant of all variegated plants are the tropical caladiums, coleus, dracaenas and crotons. Too great a degree of variegation may weaken a plant by depriving it of the means of manufacturing its food with the aid of chlorophyll in sunlight.

VARIEGATED LAUREL, *see* Aucuba.

VEGETABLE MARROW. Seeds should be grown singly in small pots in a temperature of 60° to 65° during April. It is also possible to sow outside where the plants are to grow, but this should not be attempted before the middle of May. Rich, loamy soil or old turves mixed with a little well-rotted manure make the best compost and this may either be built up into a heap, or a wide trench excavated and filled with the compost, leaving the surface a little below ground level so that water can be flooded round the growing plants during dry weather. Plant early in June and pinch the ends of the long trailing growths occasionally to encourage the formation of laterals. If these become too numerous thin them out to allow the strongest branches more room. There are also bush marrows which need no pinching or thinning. Water freely at all times and feed with weak liquid manure as soon as the first marrows commence to swell. Cut the marrows for use while still young and tender.

VELTHEIMIA *vel-***thy**-*me-a*. Tender bulbous-rooted plants which produce their tubular orange or reddish flowers in short spikes on the top of a bare stem, much in the manner of a small red-hot poker. The flowering time is in spring and the best species is *V. viridifolia*.

Culture: Veltheimias are quite easily grown in a cool greenhouse with a temperature between 45° and 55° in winter. Bulbs should be potted in August or September in 4 in. or 5 in. pots in John Innes No. 1 potting compost. They should be watered rather sparingly at first, more freely as growth appears, and then after flowering the water supply should be gradually decreased until, by June the soil is almost completely dry, in which conditions the plants can be allowed to rest until they are restarted in late summer.

Propagation: By dividing the fleshy roots at potting time.

VENIDIUM *ven-***id**-*ee-um*. Half-hardy annuals with large, showy daisy-flowers in summer. The species commonly grown, *V. fastuosum*, is 2 ft. to 3 ft. tall and has orange and maroon (or nearly black) flowers.

Culture: Sow in a greenhouse or frame in March, temperature 60° to 65°. Prick off seedlings into boxes or pot individually in John Innes potting compost and harden off for planting outdoors in late May or early June in well-drained, ordinary soil and a sunny position.

VENTILATION. The process of obtaining a circulation of fresh air in greenhouses and frames. Ventilation is one of the most important points in the management of greenhouses. All plants require fresh air, and ventilation must be supplied even during the winter, but fresh air must not be allied to cold draughts. These can be avoided by opening ventilators on the leeward side of the house. Even in houses where high temperatures are maintained, some ventilation is essential, as healthy growth cannot be maintained in a stagnant atmosphere.

VENUS'S NAVELWORT, *see* Omphalodes.

VERATRUM *ver-***at**-*rum* (False Hellebore). Hardy herbaceous perennials. Leaves large, much-ribbed. Flowers small in densely-packed spikes in summer.

Veltheimia viridifolia.

Venidium fastuosum.

Veratrum nigrum.

Verbascum thapsus (Great Mullein).

Adjusting ventilator.

Verbena hybrid.

Suitable for partially shady or sunny borders. Roots poisonous. The species most commonly grown are *V. album*, 6 ft., greenish-white; *V. nigrum*, 6 ft., dark maroon; and *V. viride*, 8 ft., green.

Culture: Plant October to April in good, well-drained soil. Protect from slugs with metaldehyde bait. Lift and re-plant only when really necessary.

Propagation: By seeds sown in peaty soil in a cool greenhouse during February or March; division of roots October or April. Seed frequently takes several months to germinate.

VERBASCUM *ver-bas-cum* (Mullein). Hardy biennial and perennial herbs with yellow, bronze or pink flowers in summer. Suitable for sunny borders and wild gardens. Among the best of the perennial kinds are *V. chaixii*, 3 ft., yellow and purple; *V. phoeniceum*, 3 ft., purple; *V. thapsiforme* (also known as *V. densiflorum*) 5 ft., yellow; and *V. nigrum*, 3 ft., yellow and purple. There are also many good garden varieties. *V. brousa*, best grown as a biennial, is 6 ft. high and covered in white woolly hairs.

Culture of Biennial Species: Sow seeds in light soil in sunny position outdoors in April or May, transplanting seedlings in ordinary soil where required to flower, or to a nursery bed for removal to flowering quarters in October, March or April.

Culture of Perennial Species: Plant in spring or early autumn in deep, light soil and allow to grow undisturbed.

Propagation: By seeds, as advised for biennial species; in the case of choice perennial varieties, by root cuttings in January or February in a frame or cool greenhouse.

VERBENA *ver-bee-na*. Half-hardy and hardy perennials with showy flowers of various colours throughout summer. Half-hardy kinds suitable for sunny beds and borders in summer or as greenhouse pot plants. Hardy kinds in sunny, sheltered beds and borders. The half-hardy verbenas are mainly derived from *V. teucrioides*, a trailing plant. There are many colours. *V. chamaedrifolia*, scarlet, is similar in habit and hardy; *V. rigida* (also known as *V. venosa*) 12 in., violet; and *V. bonariensis*, 5 ft., lilac.

Culture of Half-Hardy Kinds: Plant 12 in. apart in good, well-cultivated soil in May or early June. Peg down shoots until they meet, then pinch. Water freely during dry weather. Alternatively, pot February and March in John Innes potting compost and place in light, airy greenhouse. Pinch out points of shoots until 6 weeks before plants are required to flower. Water freely when in growth and feed when buds form. Plants may be wintered in a cold frame.

Culture of Hardy Kinds: Plant March or April in sunny position and light, moderately rich soil. In cold districts plants may be removed to a frame in autumn.

Propagation: Half-hardy kinds by seeds sown in January or February in sandy compost and germinated in temperature of 60° to 65°. Prick off seedlings and later pot up singly before hardening off. Cuttings may be rooted in a cold frame in August in boxes, or in February in temperature of 60° to 65° from stock wintered under glass. Hardy kinds by division at planting time.

VERMICULITE *ver-mik-u-lite*. In recent years this material has become fairly extensively used for

Veronica hybrid.

Viburnum carlcephalum.

the rooting of cuttings and the raising of seedlings. It is a form of mica which has been specially heat-treated to produce a flaky material, very light in weight and with a great capacity for retaining both moisture and air. Being sterile it makes an excellent medium for the purposes mentioned, but as it contains no food for plants it is essential to see that these are transferred from the vermiculite to a nourishing medium as soon as possible; or if delay is unavoidable they should be fed with a weak fertiliser until they can be moved. Before use the vermiculite should be soaked and allowed to drain after which little if any further watering should be needed.

VERNALISATION, *see* Forcing.

VERONICA *ver-on-ik-a* (Speedwell). Hardy herbaceous perennials with blue, pink or white flowers in summer. Medium and tall kinds suitable for sunny

borders; dwarf kinds for sunny rock gardens. Among the best species are *V. gentianoides*, 12 in., light blue; *V. incana*, 9 in., dark blue; *V. longifolia*, 2½ ft., blue-purple; *V. latifolia*, 3 ft., purple, pink or white: *V. spicata*, 12 in., blue, pink or white; and *V. teucrium dubia*, 4 in., blue. (For shrubs known as veronica see Hebe.)

Culture: Plant in spring or early autumn in ordinary soil. Lift, divide and re-plant when overgrown.

Propagation: By division of roots in autumn or spring.

VIBURNUM *vie-bur-num* (Guelder Rose; Laurustinus; Wayfaring Tree; Snowball Tree). Hardy deciduous and evergreen flowering shrubs, with white or pink flowers in winter, spring or summer. Among the best kinds are *V. carlesii*, 5 ft., white, April; *V. fragrans*, 10 ft., pale pink winter; *V. opulus sterile*, 12 ft., white, May; *V. tinus*, evergreen, 8 ft., white

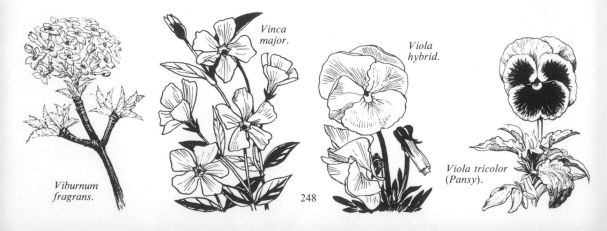

Viburnum fragrans.

Vinca major.

Viola hybrid.

Viola tricolor (Pansy).

Viburnum tinus.

Viburnum tomentosum plicatum.

tinged pink, late winter; *V. carlcephalum*, 5 ft., white, April; and the several forms of *V. tomentosum*, 9 ft., white, May.

Culture: Plant October to March in good, well-cultivated loam in open, sunny shrubberies and borders. No regular pruning required.

Propagation: By cuttings of half-ripened shoots inserted in sandy loam in a propagating frame July and August, or by layering shoots in winter or spring.

VICTOR'S LAUREL, *see* Laurus.

VINCA vin-*ka* (Periwinkle). Hardy evergreen trailing shrub with blue or white flowers in spring. Suitable for ground cover in sunny or shady positions. The two species commonly grown are *V. major*, to 2 ft. high, and *V. minor*, to 1½ ft. There are numerous varieties of each including double-flowered forms of *V. minor*.

Culture: Plant October to April in ordinary soil in shady borders, rock gardens, shrubberies, woodland gardens, and wild gardens.

Propagation: By division at planting time.

VINE, *see* Vitis and Grape Vines.

VIOLA vi-o-*la* (Violet; Pansy; Heart's-ease). Hardy perennials tufted or sprawling. The generic name embraces the sweet violet, *V. odorata;* the pansy, which in its many types and strains has been developed from *V. tricolor;* the garden and exhibition viola, or so-called tufted pansy, a race which was originally produced from *V. cornuta*, commonly called the horned pansy, also a considerable number of natural species

which are of value for cultivation in the rock garden.

Culture of Violet: Plant young plants 6 in. apart in rows 1 ft. apart in partially shaded position and deep, rich, well-worked soil. Keep hoed, watered and frequently syringed against red spider mite and greenfly throughout summer. Prevent development of runners by frequent pinching. At beginning of September make up bed in a frame with rubble drainage covered with layer of flaky manure or hops, then 9 in. of good loam, leaf-mould, and well-rotted manure or compost. Plant violets in frame just wide enough to let each plant stand free of its neighbours. Water thoroughly when needed; syringe in dry weather. Protect with thick mats when frosty, but otherwise allow all daylight possible. Pick all flowers so preventing production of seed. Alternatively, plants can be left to flower in the open, but a sheltered position should be chosen.

Culture of Viola and Pansy: Plant in April or May in good soil and sunny or shady position. Pick off faded flowers regularly then plants will go on flowering most of the summer.

Propagation: Pansies and violas may be raised from seeds sown in spring in sandy soil in a shaded frame or cool greenhouse. Prick out seedlings into boxes filled with John Innes seed compost while small, and plant out during May or early June in a nursery bed of good loam. Selected varieties of viola or pansy are best raised from cuttings from young shoots taken during summer or early autumn, inserted in a frame. Violets can be raised similarly from cuttings prepared from the runners. Violas and violets, and other tufted species, may also be increased by division in spring.

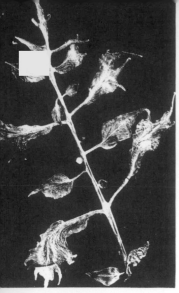
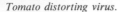

Tomato distorting virus. *Vitis henryana.* *Vriesia splendens marginata.*

VIOLET, *see* Viola.

VIRGINIA CREEPER, *see* Parthenocissus.

VIRGINIA STOCK, *see* Malcomia.

VIRGIN'S BOWER, *see* Clematis.

VIRUS. This omnibus term covers a great number of diseases attacking a great variety of plants. The virus-causing organisms are quite distinct from fungi or bacteria, being very much smaller, but no one knows exactly what a virus is. The symptoms of virus include yellowish mottling and streaking, blotching, distortion and stunting, and the diseases usually weaken plants and reduce their cropping powers. Viruses multiply rapidly in plant sap and are transmitted from one plant to another by sap-sucking insects, as well as on knives or fingers. No practical methods of cure are open to the amateur, although there are techniques of heat treatment and making micro-cuttings with which virus-free stocks of certain plants can be built up commercially. All the amateur can do is pull up and destroy affected plants, to spray susceptible plants with insecticides to prevent aphides and other sap-suckers transmitting disease, and avoid taking cuttings from infected plants, or otherwise propagating them vegetatively. Only in a few cases are viruses soil or seed-borne.

VISCARIA *vis-**kare**-ee-a.* Hardy annuals with slender growth to 15 in. high and variously coloured flowers in summer. Botanically these plants are classified as Lychnis, but in gardens the old name viscaria is always used.
Culture: Sow seed thinly in March, April or September in ordinary, well-drained soil and open, sunny position. Thin seedlings to 6 in. or 9 in. apart.

VITIS vie-*tis* (Vine). Hardy perennial climbing plants, grown for their ornamental foliage which often colours brilliantly before it falls in autumn. *V. coignetiae* needs some support such as a trellis or an old tree. Some kinds of vitis are sometimes incorrectly called Ampelopsis and the types, such as *V. henryana*, that cling by tendrils are correctly Parthenocissus, which see.
Culture: Plant October or March in ordinary soil and sunny or shady position. No regular pruning required except for excessive growth in November.
Propagation: By cuttings of firm growth in sandy soil in a frame in autumn.

VRIESIA vree-*see-a.* The vriesias are mostly herbaceous plants forming large rosettes of long, stiff leaves, often beautifully variegated, and producing eventually spikes of long, narrow flowers, sometimes surrounded by brightly coloured bracts. One of the most striking species is *V. regina*, with leaves 4 ft. long and white, fragrant flowers surrounded by pink bracts, but for the smaller greenhouse, *V. splendens* is more suitable. On this species the leaves, green on the upper side and cross-banded with reddish-brown beneath, grow to about 15 in. long and the flowers are yellow with bright red bracts.
Culture: All vriesias are warm-house plants, requiring a minimum temperature of about 50° in winter. They thrive in full sun, with frequent overhead sprayings and plenty of water at the root in summer, but in winter they should be kept drier. Coarse fibrous peat with some sphagnum and charcoal is the best compost for them and the pots should be half-filled with crocks. Re-pot when necessary in March.
Propagation: By seeds sown in a temperature of 70° to 75° in spring or by offsets taken in spring.

Wasp damage to pear.

Testing pots for water with a wooden hammer.

WAKE ROBIN, *see* Trillium.

WALL FERN, *see* Polypodium.

WALLFLOWERS, *see* Cheiranthus.

WALNUT, *see* Juglans.

WAND FLOWER, *see* Dierama.

WANDERING JEW, *see* Zebrina; Tradescantia.

WART DISEASE. The most serious disease of potatoes, readily recognised by wart-like outgrowths on the tubers. There is no known cure, but there are many varieties which are immune to it. Where this disease is at all prevalent these varieties should be grown exclusively. They are usually indicated in seed catalogues by the word 'immune' after the name of the potato. Wart disease is not to be confused with scab, which affects the skin of the potato only. Wart disease attacks flesh as well and can destroy the potato.

WASPS. These do much damage to ripening fruits. DDT or BHC dust can be placed in the entraces to any nests found and will soon be carried in by the wasps going through these narrow passages. Wasps can also be trapped in jam-jars containing a little beer or treacle, and with a lid in the form of an inverted paper cone with a small hole in the centre.

WATER FUCHSIA, *see* Impatiens.

WATER HAWTHORN, *see* Aquatic.

WATER HYACINTH, *see* Aquatic.

WATER LILY, *see* Nymphaea.

WATERING. This is one of the most important tasks in the cultivation of plants under glass, and is also frequently necessary with plants outside, if they are not well established, or the weather is very dry and hot.

One of the commonest causes of failure with indoor plants is the application of water too frequently and an inadequate quantity. It is absolutely essential that the soil in the seed box, pan, pot, or greenhouse border should be moistened right through every time it is watered. Watering by immersion is recommended in the case of seed-pans and particularly difficult plants; by this means the soil is thoroughly moistened and the foliage is kept dry.

Over-watering can be as damaging as underwatering for pot plants, as it drives out the air from the soil and drowns the roots. Good drainage and a porous potting compost will help to prevent these evils, but a generally safe rule, is to apply water only when soil begins to get dry, and then to give sufficient to soak the soil right through. Outdoors there is less danger of doing damage by overwatering. Most crops and ornamental plants benefit from some extra water in dry weather, and when in doubt, it is probably wise to err on the side of giving too much than too little.

WATERING CAN. This useful and often misused implement is among the first requirements of the greenhouse gardener. Several types are available in both polythene and metal, but for greenhouse work the one made on what is known as Haw's pattern, with a long spout which enables the back of beds or stagings to be easily reached, is the most useful. In

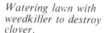
Watering lawn with weedkiller to destroy clover.

Using selective weedkiller.

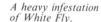
A heavy infestation of White Fly.

selecting a watering can careful consideration should be given to the size, as too small a can means a good deal of fetching and carrying and too large a can makes heavy work of watering, particularly on stagings. A can holding 1 gal. will be found a very useful size for watering ordinary pot plants. Other points of a good can are a strong handle, a well-braced spout and a projecting rim at the base which keeps the bottom clear of soil and dirt when the can is stood down. A suitable selection of roses, to vary the fineness of the spray, is also useful.

WATTLE, *see* Acacia.

WAX FLOWER, *see* Hoya.

WAYFARING TREE, *see* Viburnum.

WEEDKILLER. Chemicals of various kinds are used to kill weeds. Some, such as sodium chlorate, are universal in action and will kill any plants with which they come in contact. Others are selective, killing some kinds of plant but not others. Selective hormone weedkillers such as 2, 4-D and MCPA can be used on lawns to kill daisies, plantains, dandelions, buttercups, etc., without injury to the grass. Others, such as dalapon, will kill grass but do little or no harm to trees, shrubs and fruit bushes. In all cases weedkillers should be used strictly in accordance with manufacturers' instructions.

WEEVIL. Small plant-eating beetles of which there are a great many species. Amongst the most common are the apple blossom, bean and pea, clay coloured, and vine weevils. All these can be destroyed by occasional spraying or dusting with DDT or BHC.

WEIGELA *wy*-**jee**-*la* (Bush Honeysuckle). Hardy deciduous shrubs formerly known under the name Diervilla. The pink or crimson flowers are produced in early summer. The garden varieties of which there are several are derived from *W. florida* and will grow to 10 ft.
Culture: Plant from November to March in good soil and open, sunny positions. If desired to restrict growth, bushes may be pruned immediately after flowering, cutting out all growths which have already borne flowers.
Propagation: Cuttings of young shoots taken in June or July will root easily in a sandy soil in a propagation frame or cuttings of riper growth can be rooted in sandy soil outdoors in October.

WELLINGTONIA, *see* Sequoia.

WELSH POPPY, *see* Meconopsis.

WHIN, *see* Ulex.

WHITE BEAM, *see* Sorbus.

WHITE FLY. A small, white-winged insect which causes much havoc in greenhouses. It is extremely troublesome with tomatoes. The larvae feed on the juices of the plants, and their sticky, grey excrement blocks up the breathing pores of the leaves. During the summer it may also attack plants in the open.

Under glass, fumigation with DDT or BHC will control this pest, and outdoors, spraying with the same insecticides, but either treatment may need to be repeated several times at intervals of 10 to 16 days to make a clean sweep.

WIG TREE, *see* Cotinus.

WILLOW, *see* Salix.

WILT. Various unrelated diseases which cause sudden flagging of growth and eventual death of the plant pass under the general name 'wilt'. Several are soil borne and attack roots or stems at soil level. Tomato wilts are of this character and can only be kept in check by changing soil or by sterilising soil. (See also Sleepy Disease). Aster wilt is also soil carried, but some strains of aster are resistant to it. Spotted wilt attacks gloxinias, arums and other greenhouse plants, the earliest symptom being ring-shaped spots on the leaves. It is caused by virus and there is no remedy.

WIND FLOWER, *see* Anemone.

WINTER ACONITE, *see* Eranthis.

WINTER CHERRY, *see* Physalis; Solanum.

WINTER DAFFODIL, *see* Sternbergia.

WINTER MOTHS. These are pests of fruit-trees, principally attacking the apple. It is the larvae or caterpillars of the moths that do the damage, devouring the foliage and, in the case of bad attacks, sometimes completely stripping the trees when the fruit starts into growth. The wingless female moths appear from October onwards and crawl up the trunks to lay their eggs. Caterpillars usually commence to appear just before the buds burst in the spring, and continue until about the middle of June. When they are fully grown they let themselves down to the ground on silken threads and pupate. Effective methods of destroying this pest are by spraying with tar-oil wash, or DNC in January or February, or with DDT or BHC in March. Grease-bands placed round trees in September and kept sticky throughout the winter, will trap the ascending female moths.

WINTER SWEET, *see* Chimonanthus.

WIREWORM. The larvae of click beetles. The thin, worm-like grubs about 1 in. in length, with hard, shining yellow skins, are especially numerous in

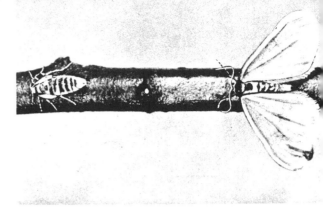

Male and wingless female winter moths with egg in the centre.

Winter Moth caterpillar on apple.

grassland. They eat the roots of plants and can do great damage to potatoes, carrots, etc. Wireworms can be destroyed by digging or raking into the soil aldrin, or they may be trapped by burying pieces of potatoes or carrots close to the attacked plants. If these traps are lifted daily, the wireworms will be found feeding thereon and can be destroyed.

WISTERIA *wis-***tare**-*ree-a* (Wistaria). Hardy deciduous climbing shrubs with trails of blue or white flowers in May. Suitable for south or south-west walls, sunny pergolas, or as standards in shrubbery or on lawns. The best kinds are *W. sinensis*, the species commonly planted, and *W. floribunda*, with longer flower trails.

Culture: Plant October to April in deep, rich, well-drained loam. Young plants do not require pruning,

Wisteria floribunda.

Woolly Aphis on apple.

but established specimens which have filled their allotted space may be pruned twice annually. In July side shoots are shortened to 5 or 6 leaves, and in winter they are cut back to 1 or 2 dormant buds.
Propagation: By layering young shoots during spring and summer.

WITCH HAZEL, *see* Hamamelis.

WOLFSBANE, *see* Aconitum.

WOOD ASH. The ash from burned wood or any other vegetable matter is a valuable potash fertiliser which can be used with safety for practically any crops or plants at any time of the year. In a dry state it contains anything up to 12% potash, but as this is readily lost if the ashes become wet they should always be stored under cover until required. Average rate of application is 6 oz. to 8 oz. per sq. yd.

WOODLICE. These pests do considerable damage to seedlings. As a rule they are most troublesome in greenhouses. They are nocturnal feeders, hiding in the crevices of wood and brickwork and under pots, slates, and similar places during the day. They can be trapped by laying unwashed flower pots, stuffed with chopped hay, near to their haunts. Traps should be examined every day so that any woodlice within may be destroyed. They may also be poisoned by scattering a mixture of ¼ lb. Paris green in 7 lb. of bran over the soil, or placing it in small heaps where the woodlice can get at it. The mixture is poisonous to human beings and domestic animals. Other remedies are to dust plants and soil with DDT or BHC.

WOOD LILY, *see* Trillium.

WOOD SORREL, *see* Oxalis.

WOOLLY APHIS. A species of aphis recognised by its white, wool-like patches on the bark of the apple trees it attacks. Also found on cotoneasters. The insects which shelter beneath this covering can be destroyed by brushing all affected patches with a stiff brush dipped in methylated spirits. Winter spraying with tar-oil or DNC wash will also kill many.

WORMS. On the whole these do far more good than harm, aerating soil and dragging leaves, etc., down into it. But in flower pots worms can be a nuisance as they may block up the drainage holes, and on lawns their 'casts' of soil may kill small patches of grass. The casts may be removed by sweeping, and worms can also be killed by dressing lawns with mowrah meal at 4 oz. per sq. yd. and watering in very thoroughly. The treatment is most effective in spring and autumn. Standing flower pots on a hard ash base or on tiles or slates prevents entry of worms to some extent, but where the worms are persistent the pots should be watered occasionally with ½ oz. of permanganate of potash dissolved in a gallon of water. This will bring the worms to the surface, when they can be removed.

WORMWOOD, *see* Artemisia.

WOUNDWORT, *see* Stachys.

YAM, *see* Dioscorea.

Zantedeschia aethiopica.

Yucca filamentosa.

YARROW, *see* Achillea.

YELLOW LOOSESTRIFE, *see* Lysimachia.

YELLOW PIMPERNEL, *see* Lysimachia.

YELLOW STAR-FLOWER, *see* Sternbergia.

YEW, *see* Taxus.

YUCCA yuk-*er* (Adam's Needle; Spanish Bayonet; Spanish Dagger). Hardy or slightly tender evergreen perennials, with stiff rosettes of sword-shaped leaves and creamy-white flowers in late summer. Suitable for sunny beds and for planting singly as specimens. Two of the hardiest kinds are *Y. filamentosa*, the Adam's Needle, and *Y. flaccida*. Particularly stiff, handsome rosettes are produced by *Y. gloriosa*, the Spanish Bayonet or Spanish Dagger.
Culture: Plant October to April in light, well-drained soil. Protect in severe winter weather with mats, or sacking, but remove the covering when danger is over.
Propagation: By offsets removed in March or April; seeds sown in a temperature of 60° to 65° in spring.

YULAN, *see* Magnolia.

ZANTEDESCHIA *zan-ted-***esh**-*ee-a* (Arum Lily). Tender perennials with white spathes in spring. Despite its common name the Arum Lily is not related in any way to the true lilies. In addition to the familiar white Arum Lily, *Z. aethiopica*, there are also several yellow-flowered species of which the best are *Z. pentlandii*, deep yellow, and *Z. elliottiana*, pale yellow.

Both are more tender and, therefore, require more protection and slightly higher temperature. Synonyms of this genus include Arum, Calla and Richardia.
Culture: This is a plant with fleshy roots which should be potted in August or early September in an ordinary John Innes compost which may contain a little extra peat. One good root may be accommodated in a 6 in. or 7 in. pot, or alternatively 2 or 3 roots can be placed in a larger pot. For a month after potting the plants are best kept in a frame but before any sharp autumn frosts they should be removed to a cool greenhouse with plenty of ventilation at first, though frost should at all times be excluded. Later the temperature can be increased gradually to obtain early flowers, which can be had from about January to May according to the amount of warmth supplied. At no time should the temperature exceed 70° and care should be taken that water does not drop from the roof glass on to the white spathes (flowers), as they open or they will be damaged.

After flowering the water supply can be reduced again, more ventilation given and by early June the plants can be stood outdoors in a sheltered place. Some growers prefer to stand the pots on their sides and keep the plants quite dry for a while. Others find it better to tap the plants out of the pots and plant them in trenches in the open, keeping them well watered in dry weather. Extra early flowers in December can be obtained by re-potting in July, bringing into the greenhouse in early September and maintaining a temperature of 60° during the autumn.
Propagation: By division at potting time.

ZEBRA GRASS, *see* Miscanthus.

Zinnia hybrid.

Zephyranthes candida.

pink; and *Z. grandiflora*, deeper pink. All are 9 in. to 12 in. in height.

Culture: Plant August to November in light, sandy loam in well-drained sunny beds, borders, or rock gardens, placing bulbs 3 in. to 4 in. deep and 4 in. apart. Protect in winter with a layer of dry litter or cinder ashes. Lift and re-plant only when bulbs show signs of deterioration.

Propagation: By offsets, planted and treated as advised for large bulbs August to November.

ZEPHYR FLOWER, *see* Zephyranthes.

ZINNIA zin-*ee-a.* Half-hardy annuals with showy flowers of various colours in late summer. The garden varieties of which there are many, vary in height from a few inches to 3 ft. Some have broad flat petals, some rolled or frilled petals.

Culture: Sow seeds in light soil, in temperature of 55° to 60° in April. Prick off seedlings in deep boxes or pot individually in small pots. Harden off for planting out, 8 in. to 12 in. apart, in early June in good loamy soil in sunny beds or borders. Sow also outdoors in early May where plants are to flower and thin seedlings to 8 in. Water liberally in dry weather.

ZYGOCACTUS *zi-go-***kak-***tus* (Christmas Cactus). A favourite greenhouse and room plant, the cerise-flowered Christmas Cactus is *Z. truncatus*. The pendulous growth makes it an attractive basket plant, though it grows perfectly well in a pot.

Culture: Provide a rich compost of 2 parts loam, 1 part leaf-mould, or peat, and 1 part coarse sand, with a good sprinkling of hoof and horn meal. For success, feed in summer and syringe overhead on hot days; the plant can be stood outside in a shady place. In autumn it should be brought into a greenhouse or room where a steady temperature of 50° to 60° is maintained. Watering should be continued in winter, but avoid waterlogging. Bud dropping is caused by dry, stuffy air, varying temperatures, draughts or erratic watering.

Propagation: By cuttings of 2 to 3 stem segments, the lowest of which is pushed into a mixture of soil and coarse sand in a warm greenhouse.

ZEBRINA *zeb-***rye-***na* (Wandering Jew). Often confused with the tradescantias, and like them called Wandering Jew, *Z. pendula* has slightly larger leaves, usually about 3 in. long and about 1½ in. wide, striped with silver and backed with purple.

Culture: Any good, light soil suits zebrina and it should be watered well in summer, but less in winter, when it needs protection from frost.

Propagation: Cuttings 3 in. long, prepared from the shoot tips root readily.

ZEPHYRANTHES *zef-ee-***ran-***thes* (Zephyr Flower; Flower of the West Wind). Hardy bulbous plants with flowers of various colours in summer. There are numerous species such as *Z. ajax*, pale yellow; *Z. citrina*, deeper yellow; *Z. candida*, white; *Z. rosea*,

Zebrina pendula.

Zygocactus truncatus.